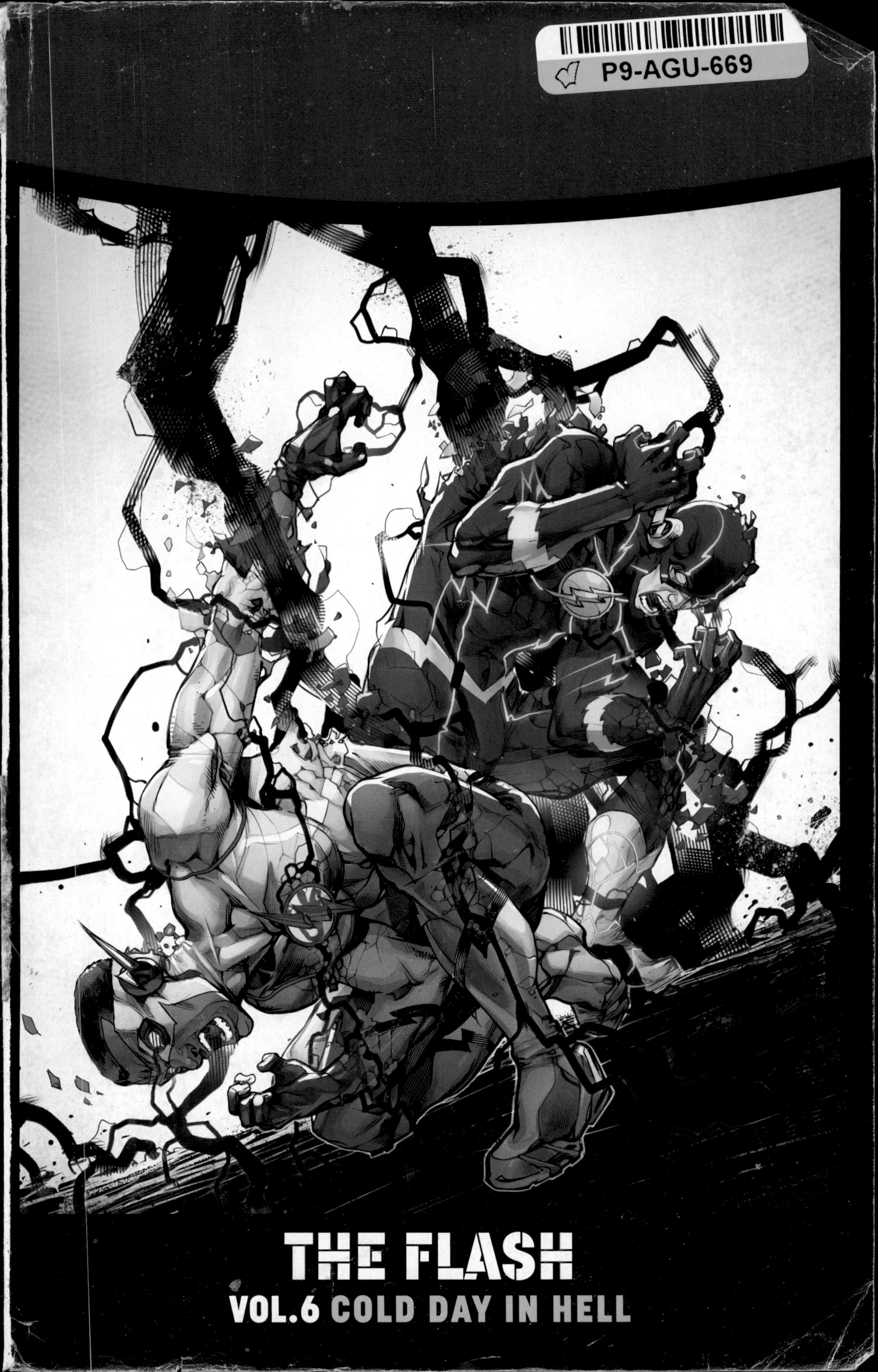

THE FLASH

VOL.6 COLD DAY IN HELL

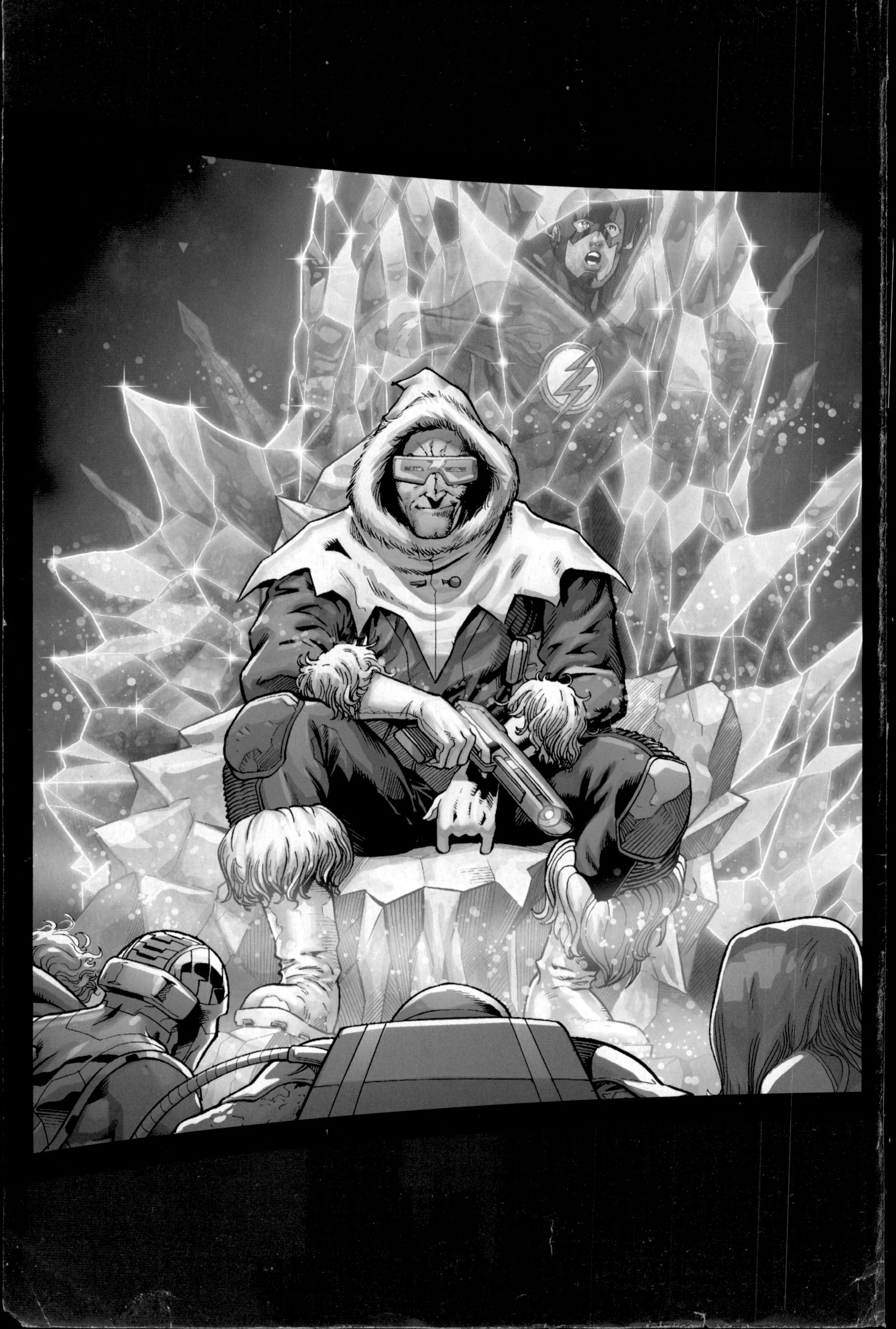

THE FLASH

VOL.6 COLD DAY IN HELL

JOSHUA WILLIAMSON

MICHAEL MORECI

writers

POP MHAN * CHRISTIAN DUCE * HOWARD PORTER
SCOTT KOLINS * SCOTT McDANIEL * MICK GRAY

artists

HI-FI

IVAN PLASCENCIA

colorists

STEVE WANDS

CARLOS M. MANGUAL * TRAVIS LANHAM

letterers

BARRY KITSON and HI-FI

collection cover artists

SUPERMAN created by **JERRY SIEGEL** and **JOE SHUSTER**

By special arrangement with the Jerry Siegel family

REBECCA TAYLOR Editor - Original Series ✳ **ANDREW MARINO** Assistant Editor - Original Series
JEB WOODARD Group Editor - Collected Editions ✳ **ROBIN WILDMAN** Editor - Collected Edition
STEVE COOK Design Director - Books ✳ **MONIQUE NARBONETA** Publication Design

BOB HARRAS Senior VP - Editor-in-Chief, DC Comics
PAT McCALLUM Executive Editor, DC Comics

DIANE NELSON President ✳ **DAN DiDIO** Publisher ✳ **JIM LEE** Publisher ✳ **GEOFF JOHNS** President & Chief Creative Officer
AMIT DESAI Executive VP - Business & Marketing Strategy, Direct to Consumer & Global Franchise Management
SAM ADES Senior VP & General Manager, Digital Services ✳ **BOBBIE CHASE** VP & Executive Editor, Young Reader & Talent Development
MARK CHIARELLO Senior VP - Art, Design & Collected Editions ✳ **JOHN CUNNINGHAM** Senior VP - Sales & Trade Marketing
ANNE DePIES Senior VP - Business Strategy, Finance & Administration ✳ **DON FALLETTI** VP - Manufacturing Operations
LAWRENCE GANEM VP - Editorial Administration & Talent Relations ✳ **ALISON GILL** Senior VP - Manufacturing & Operations
HANK KANALZ Senior VP - Editorial Strategy & Administration ✳ **JAY KOGAN** VP - Legal Affairs ✳ **JACK MAHAN** VP - Business Affairs
NICK J. NAPOLITANO VP - Manufacturing Administration ✳ **EDDIE SCANNELL** VP - Consumer Marketing
COURTNEY SIMMONS Senior VP - Publicity & Communications ✳ **JIM (SKI) SOKOLOWSKI** VP - Comic Book Specialty Sales & Trade Marketing
NANCY SPEARS VP - Mass, Book, Digital Sales & Trade Marketing ✳ **MICHELE R. WELLS** VP - Content Strategy

THE FLASH VOL. 6: COLD DAY IN HELL

DC Comics, 2900 West Alameda Ave., Burbank, CA 91505
Printed by LSC Communications, Kendallville, IN, USA. 5/11/18. First Printing.
ISBN: 978-1-4012-8078-9

Library of Congress Cataloging-in-Publication Data is available.

PEFC Certified

Printed on paper from
sustainably managed
forests, controlled
sources

PEFC/29-31-337   www.pefc.org

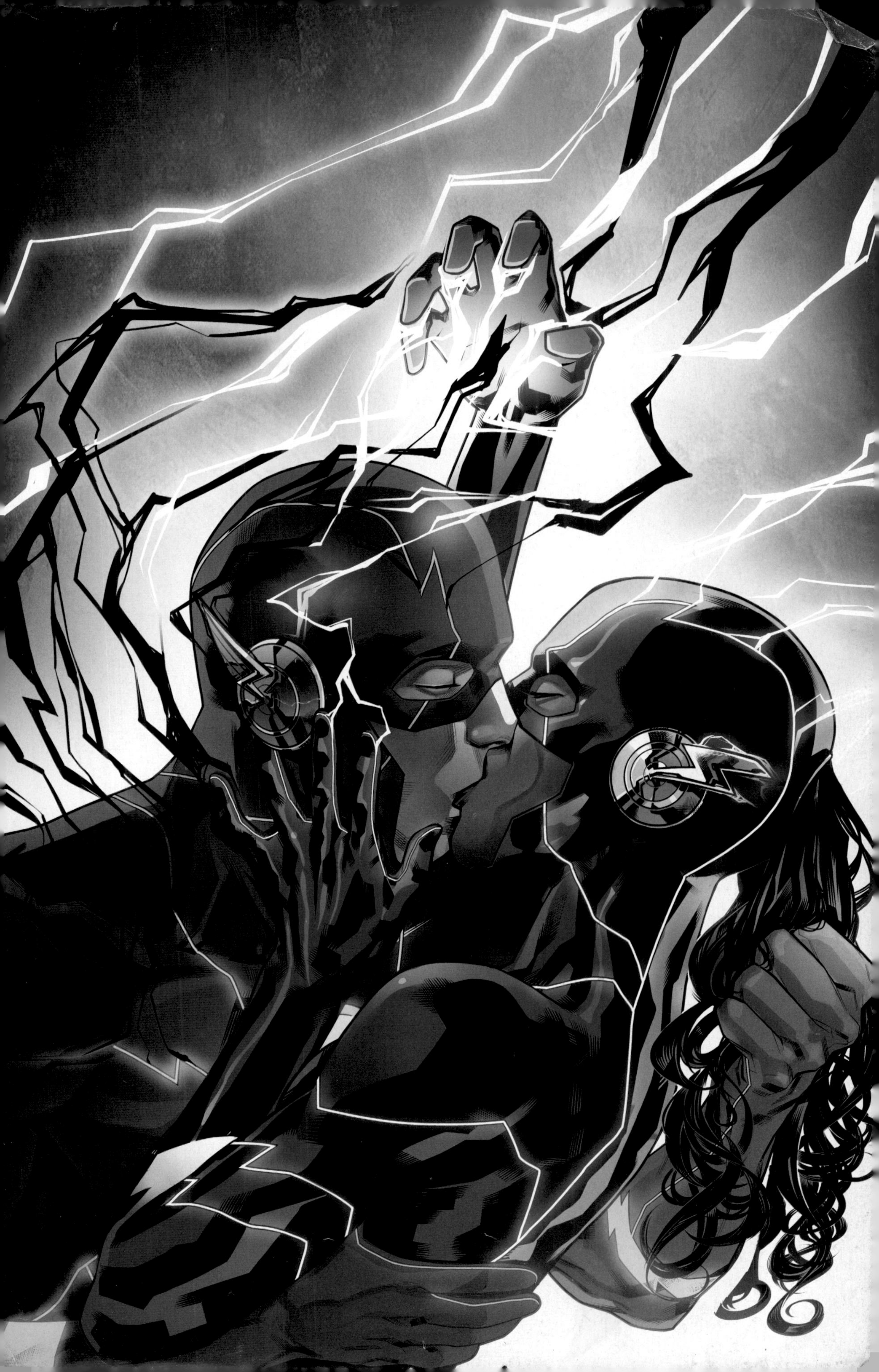

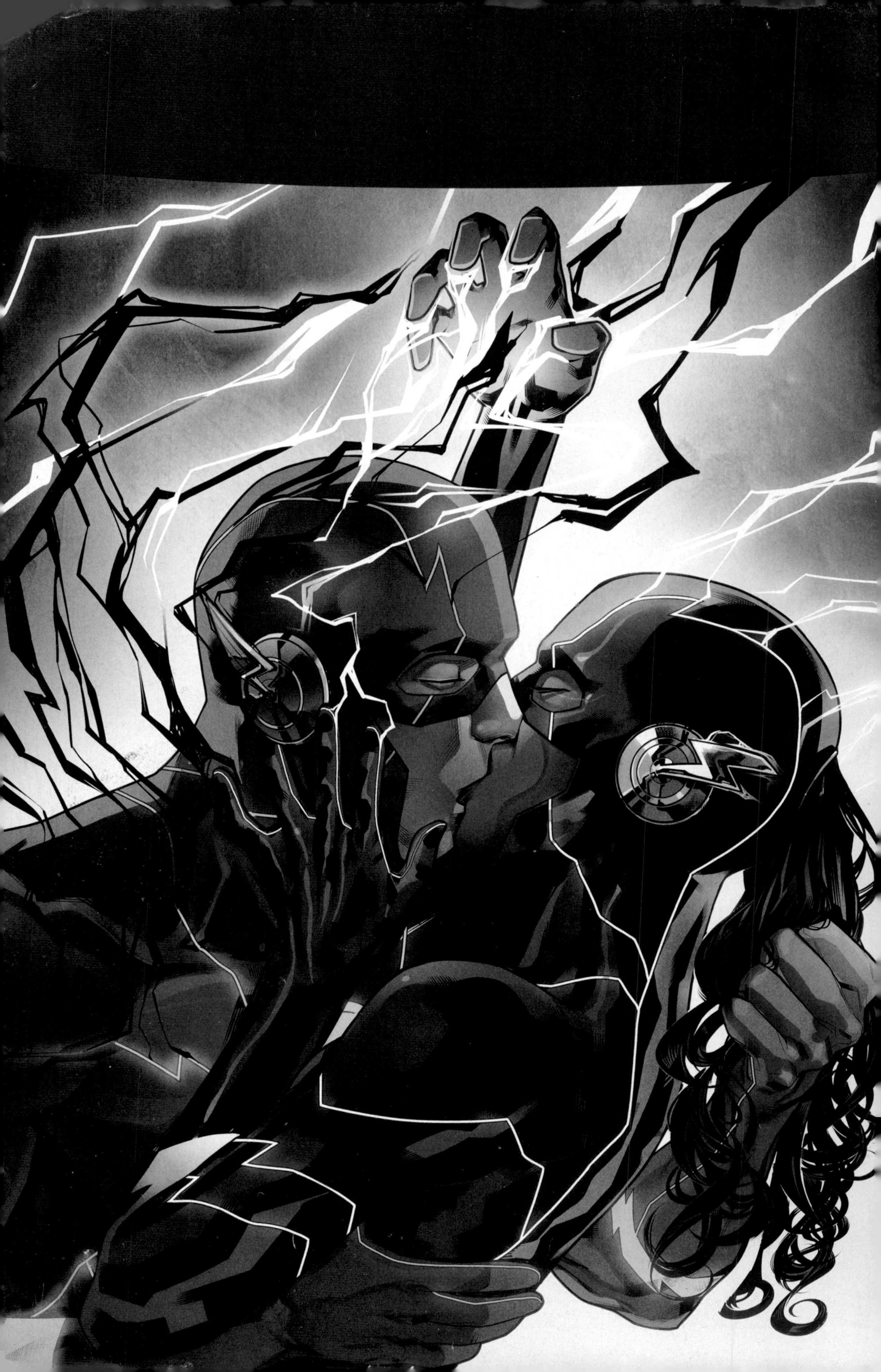

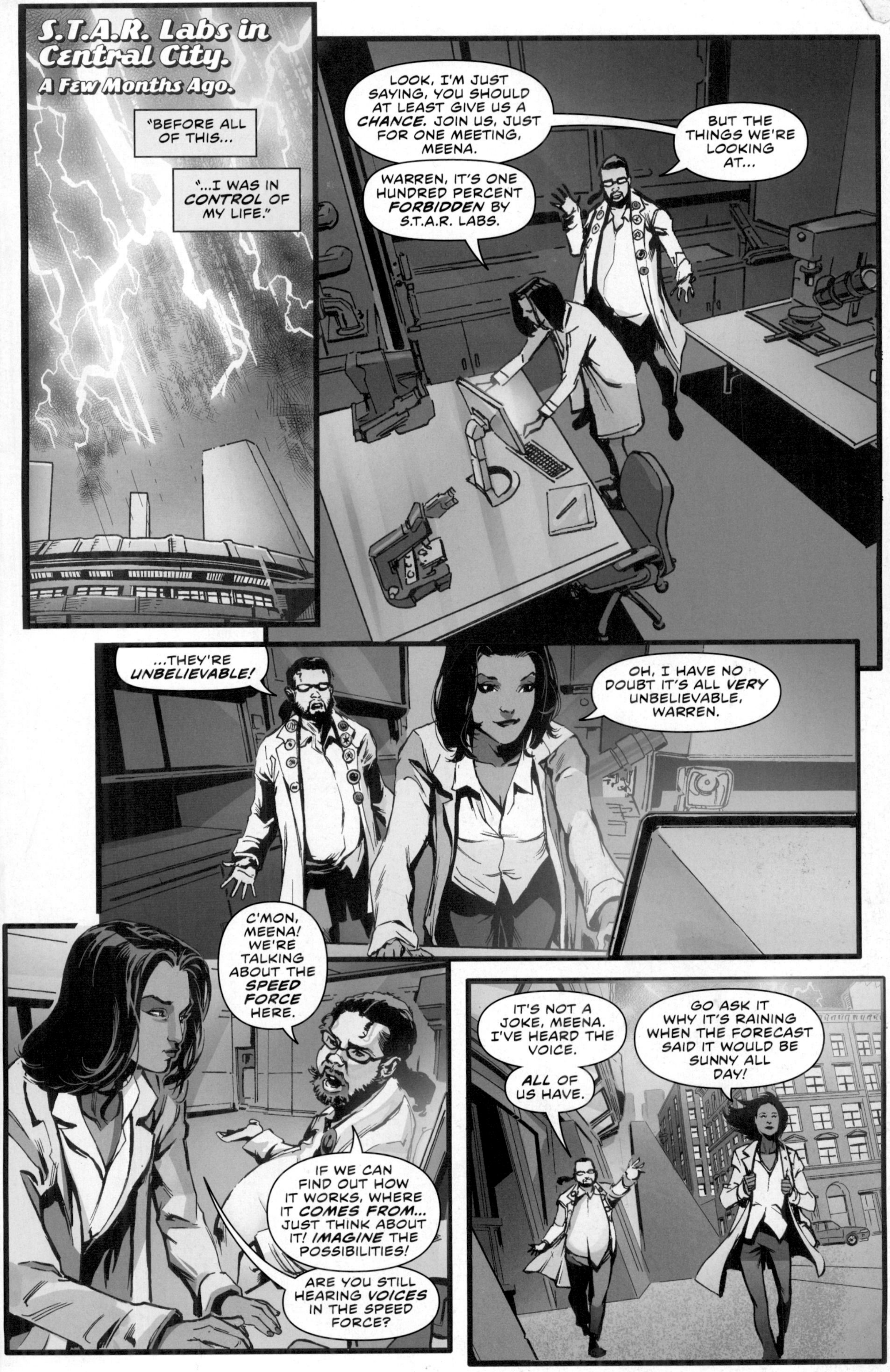
S.T.A.R. Labs in Central City.
A Few Months Ago.
"BEFORE ALL OF THIS...
"...I WAS IN CONTROL OF MY LIFE."
LOOK, I'M JUST SAYING, YOU SHOULD AT LEAST GIVE US A CHANCE. JOIN US, JUST FOR ONE MEETING, MEENA.
BUT THE THINGS WE'RE LOOKING AT...
WARREN, IT'S ONE HUNDRED PERCENT FORBIDDEN BY S.T.A.R. LABS.
...THEY'RE UNBELIEVABLE!
OH, I HAVE NO DOUBT IT'S ALL VERY UNBELIEVABLE, WARREN.
C'MON, MEENA! WE'RE TALKING ABOUT THE SPEED FORCE HERE.
IF WE CAN FIND OUT HOW IT WORKS, WHERE IT COMES FROM... JUST THINK ABOUT IT! IMAGINE THE POSSIBILITIES!
ARE YOU STILL HEARING VOICES IN THE SPEED FORCE?
IT'S NOT A JOKE, MEENA. I'VE HEARD THE VOICE.
ALL OF US HAVE.
GO ASK IT WHY IT'S RAINING WHEN THE FORECAST SAID IT WOULD BE SUNNY ALL DAY!

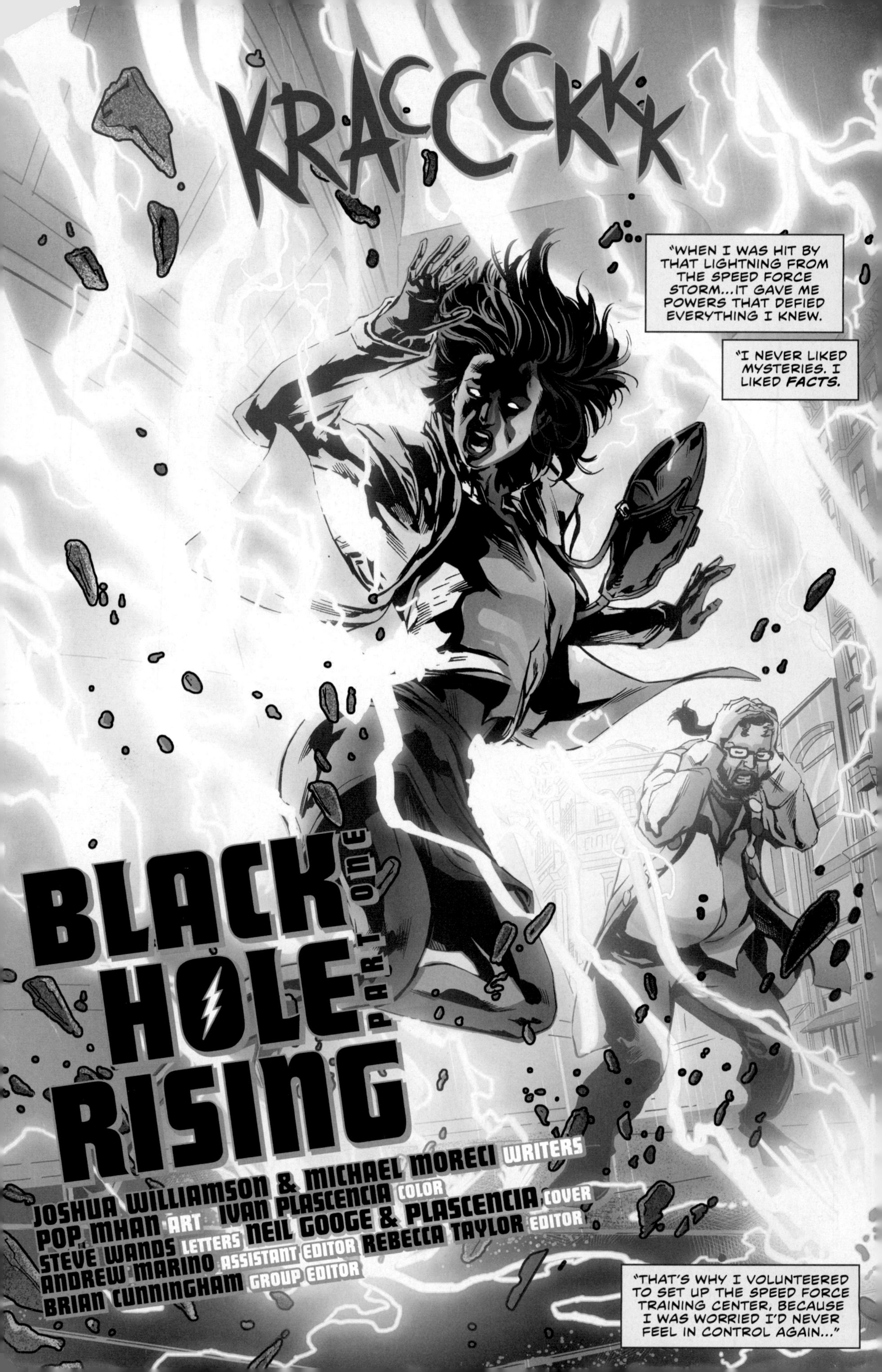

KRACCCKKK
"WHEN I WAS HIT BY THAT LIGHTNING FROM THE SPEED FORCE STORM...IT GAVE ME POWERS THAT DEFIED EVERYTHING I KNEW.
"I NEVER LIKED MYSTERIES. I LIKED *FACTS.*
BLACK HOLE RISING PART ONE
JOSHUA WILLIAMSON & MICHAEL MORECI WRITERS
POP MHAN ART IVAN PLASCENCIA COLOR
STEVE WANDS LETTERS NEIL GOOGE & PLASCENCIA COVER
ANDREW MARINO ASSISTANT EDITOR REBECCA TAYLOR EDITOR
BRIAN CUNNINGHAM GROUP EDITOR
"THAT'S WHY I VOLUNTEERED TO SET UP THE SPEED FORCE TRAINING CENTER, BECAUSE I WAS WORRIED I'D NEVER FEEL IN CONTROL AGAIN..."

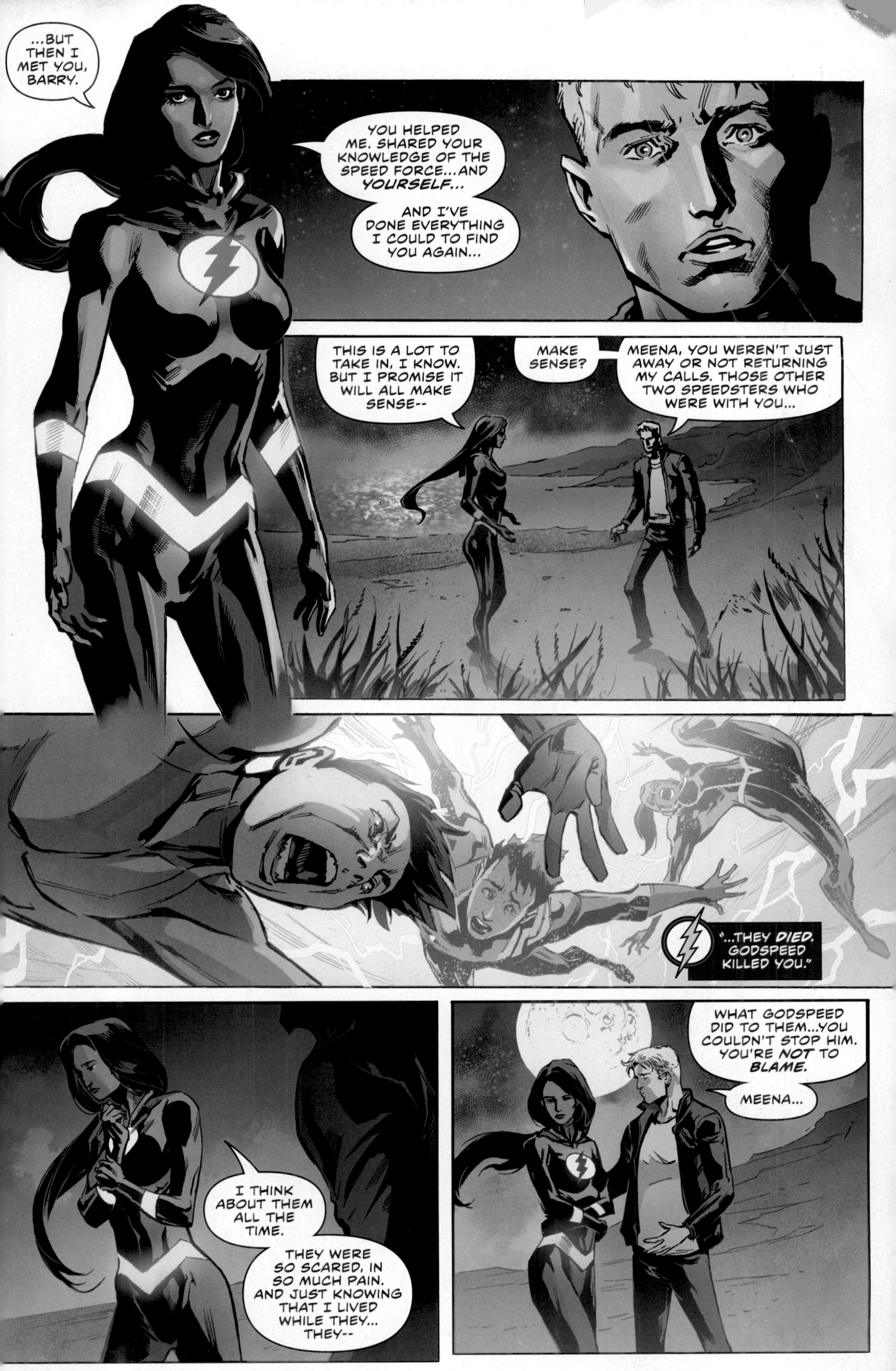
...BUT THEN I MET YOU, BARRY.
YOU HELPED ME. SHARED YOUR KNOWLEDGE OF THE SPEED FORCE...AND *YOURSELF*...
AND I'VE DONE EVERYTHING I COULD TO FIND YOU AGAIN...
THIS IS A LOT TO TAKE IN, I KNOW. BUT I PROMISE IT WILL ALL MAKE SENSE--
MAKE SENSE?
MEENA, YOU WEREN'T JUST AWAY OR NOT RETURNING MY CALLS. THOSE OTHER TWO SPEEDSTERS WHO WERE WITH YOU...
"...THEY *DIED*. GODSPEED KILLED YOU."
I THINK ABOUT THEM ALL THE TIME.
THEY WERE SO SCARED, IN SO MUCH PAIN. AND JUST KNOWING THAT I LIVED WHILE THEY... THEY--
WHAT GODSPEED DID TO THEM...YOU COULDN'T STOP HIM. YOU'RE *NOT* TO *BLAME*.
MEENA...

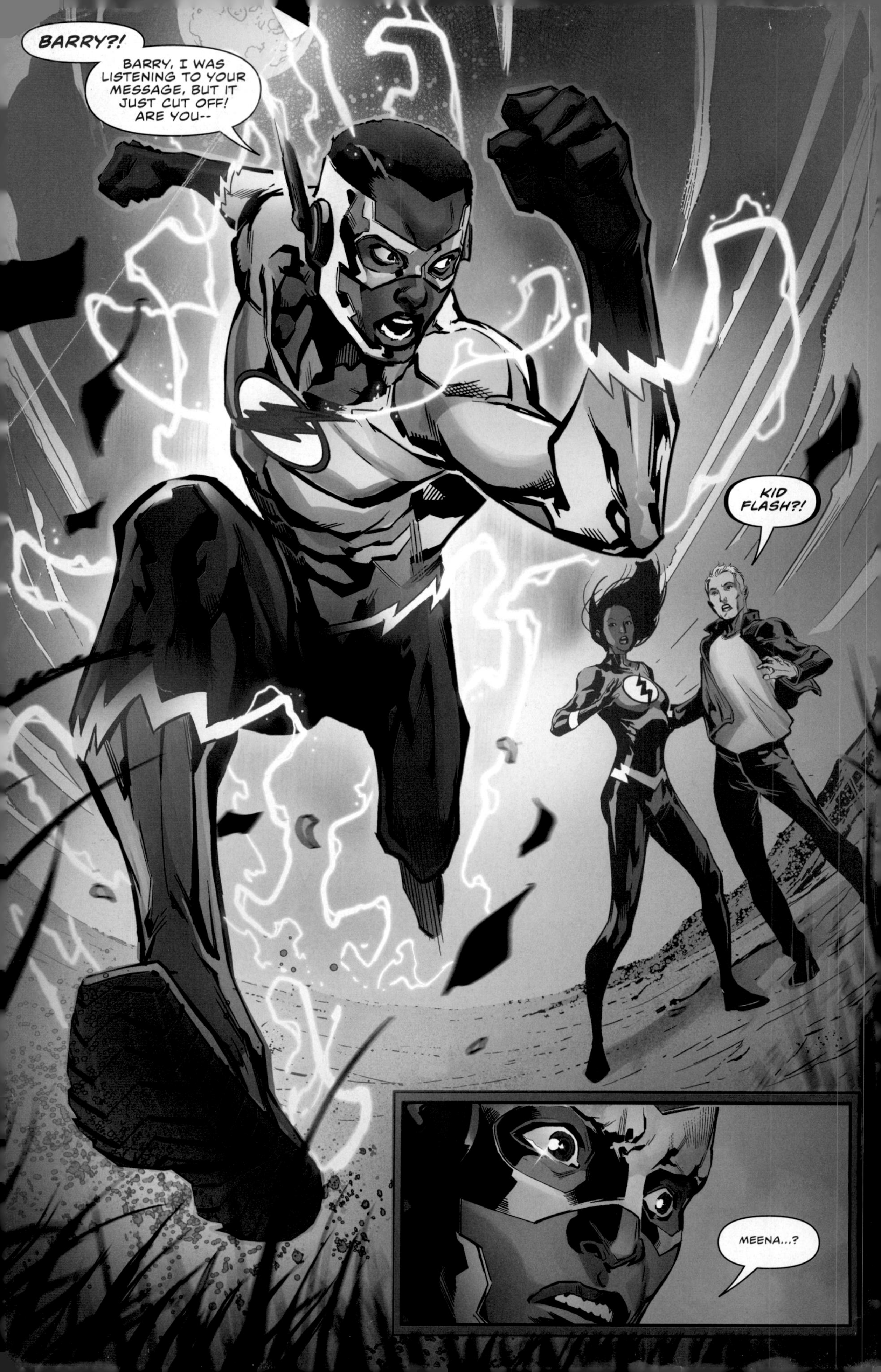
BARRY?!
BARRY, I WAS LISTENING TO YOUR MESSAGE, BUT IT JUST CUT OFF! ARE YOU--
KID FLASH?!
MEENA...?

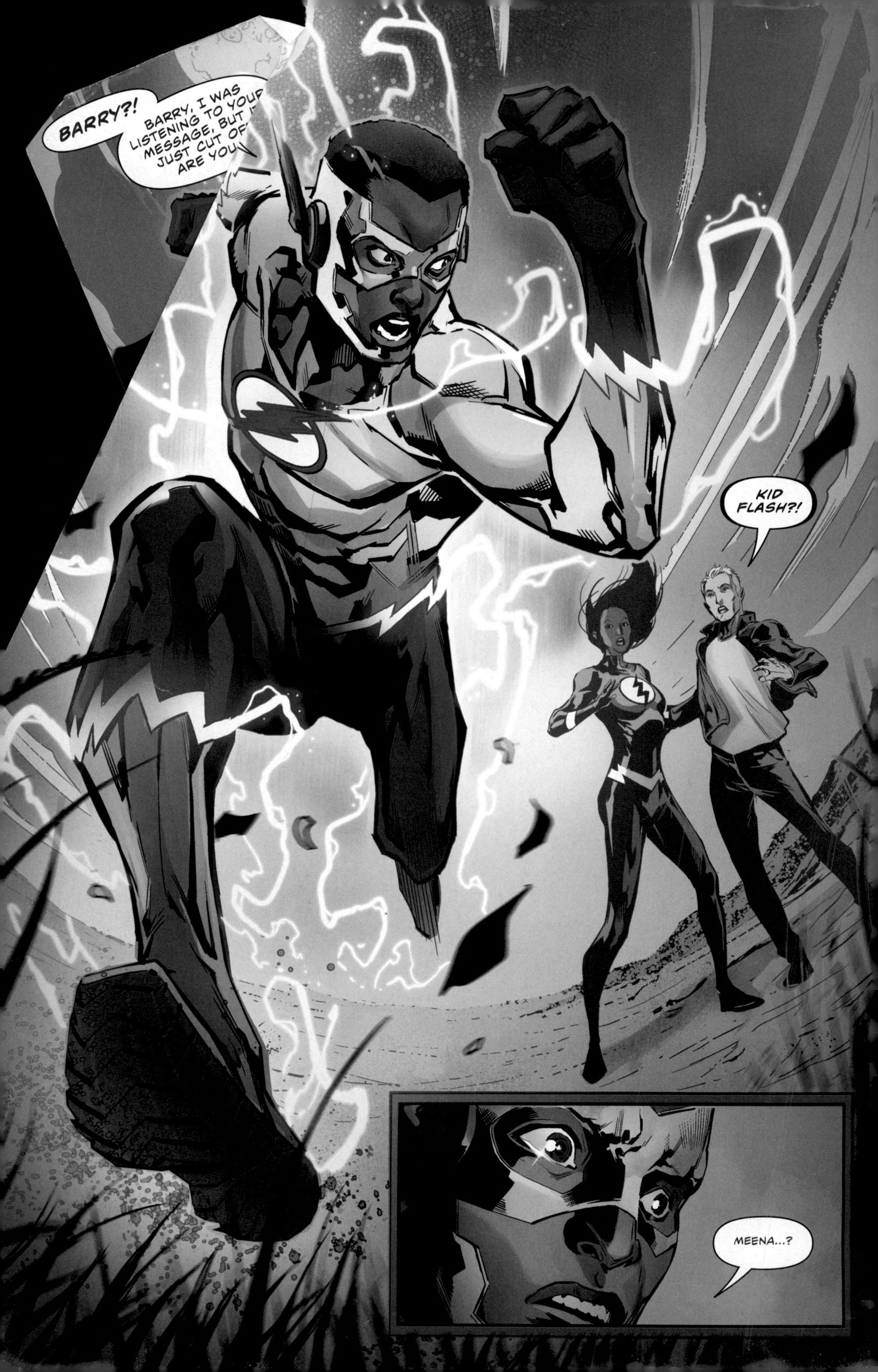
BARRY?!
BARRY, I WAS LISTENING TO YOUR MESSAGE, BUT I JUST CUT OF ARE YOU
KID FLASH?!
MEENA...?

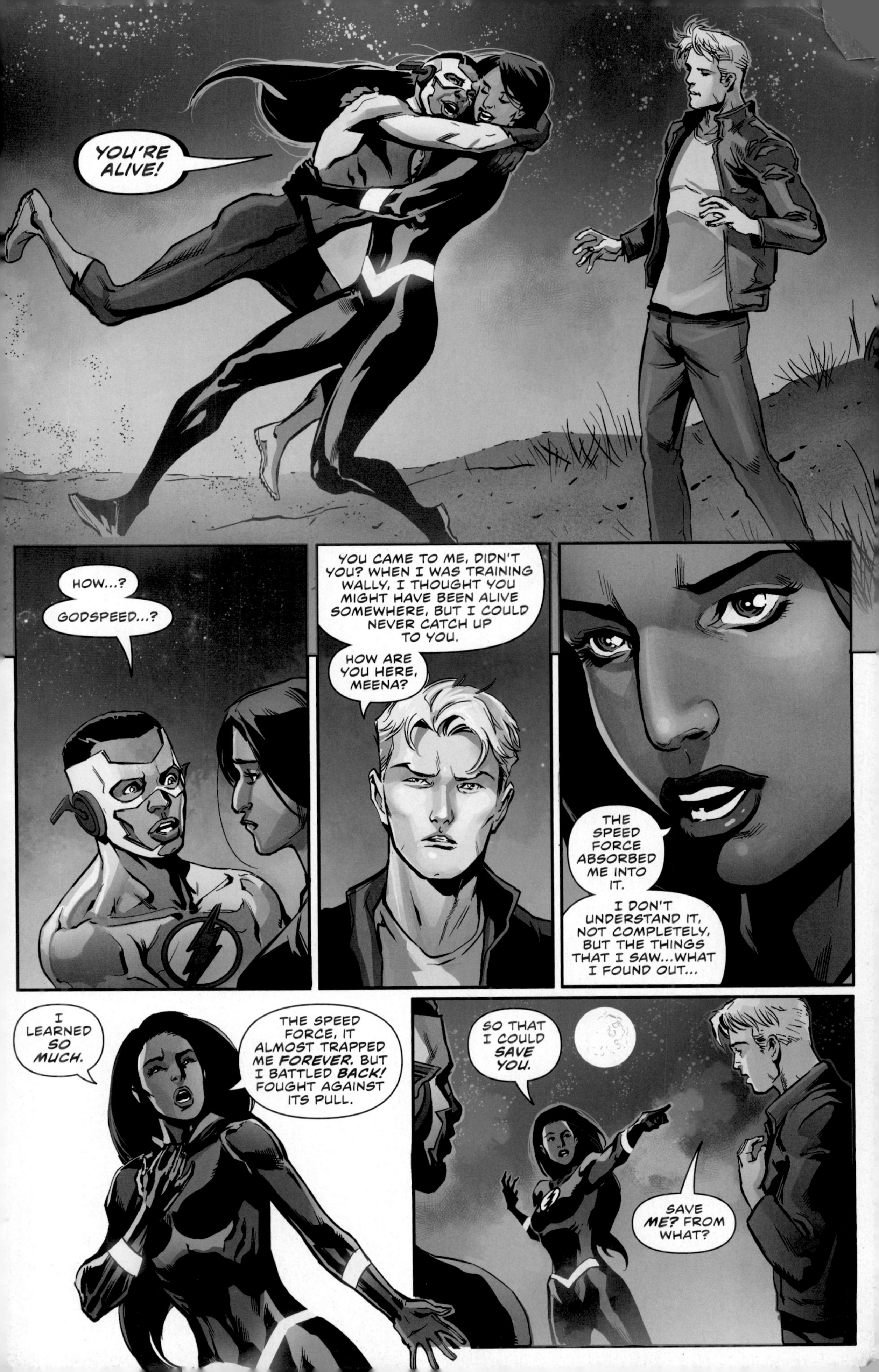
YOU'RE ALIVE!
HOW...?
GODSPEED...?
YOU CAME TO ME, DIDN'T YOU? WHEN I WAS TRAINING WALLY, I THOUGHT YOU MIGHT HAVE BEEN ALIVE SOMEWHERE, BUT I COULD NEVER CATCH UP TO YOU.
HOW ARE YOU HERE, MEENA?
THE SPEED FORCE ABSORBED ME INTO IT.
I DON'T UNDERSTAND IT, NOT COMPLETELY, BUT THE THINGS THAT I SAW...WHAT I FOUND OUT...
I LEARNED SO MUCH.
THE SPEED FORCE, IT ALMOST TRAPPED ME FOREVER. BUT I BATTLED BACK! FOUGHT AGAINST ITS PULL.
SO THAT I COULD SAVE YOU.
SAVE ME? FROM WHAT?

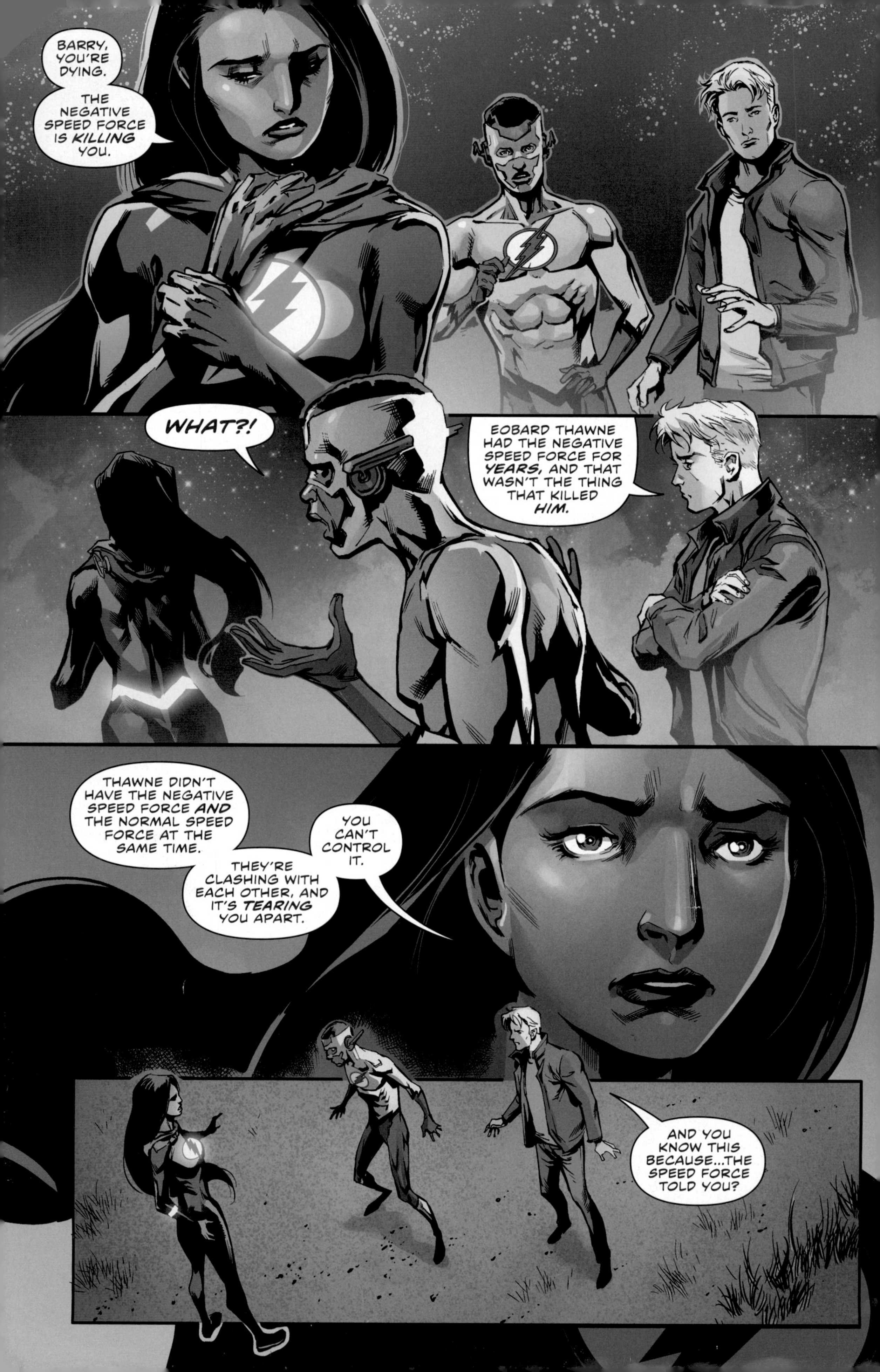
BARRY, YOU'RE DYING.
THE NEGATIVE SPEED FORCE IS *KILLING* YOU.
WHAT?!
EOBARD THAWNE HAD THE NEGATIVE SPEED FORCE FOR *YEARS,* AND THAT WASN'T THE THING THAT KILLED *HIM.*
THAWNE DIDN'T HAVE THE NEGATIVE SPEED FORCE *AND* THE NORMAL SPEED FORCE AT THE SAME TIME.
THEY'RE CLASHING WITH EACH OTHER, AND IT'S *TEARING* YOU APART.
YOU CAN'T CONTROL IT.
AND YOU KNOW THIS BECAUSE...THE SPEED FORCE TOLD YOU?

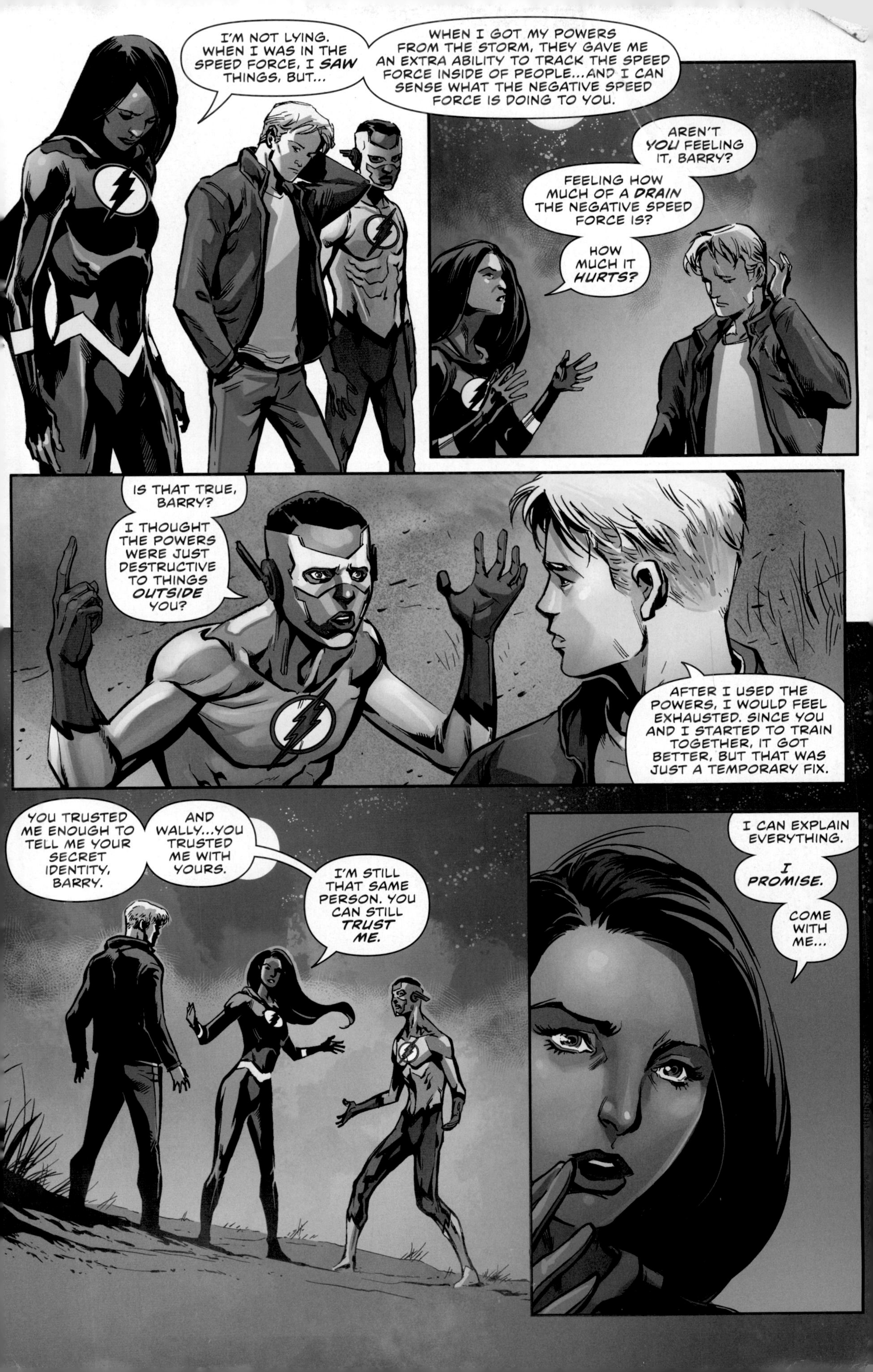

I'M NOT LYING. WHEN I WAS IN THE SPEED FORCE, I *SAW* THINGS, BUT...
WHEN I GOT MY POWERS FROM THE STORM, THEY GAVE ME AN EXTRA ABILITY TO TRACK THE SPEED FORCE INSIDE OF PEOPLE...AND I CAN SENSE WHAT THE NEGATIVE SPEED FORCE IS DOING TO YOU.
AREN'T *YOU* FEELING IT, BARRY?
FEELING HOW MUCH OF A *DRAIN* THE NEGATIVE SPEED FORCE IS?
HOW MUCH IT *HURTS?*
IS THAT TRUE, BARRY?
I THOUGHT THE POWERS WERE JUST DESTRUCTIVE TO THINGS *OUTSIDE* YOU?
AFTER I USED THE POWERS, I WOULD FEEL EXHAUSTED. SINCE YOU AND I STARTED TO TRAIN TOGETHER, IT GOT BETTER, BUT THAT WAS JUST A TEMPORARY FIX.
YOU TRUSTED ME ENOUGH TO TELL ME YOUR SECRET IDENTITY, BARRY.
AND WALLY...YOU TRUSTED ME WITH YOURS.
I'M STILL THAT SAME PERSON. YOU CAN STILL *TRUST ME.*
I CAN EXPLAIN EVERYTHING.
I PROMISE.
COME WITH ME...

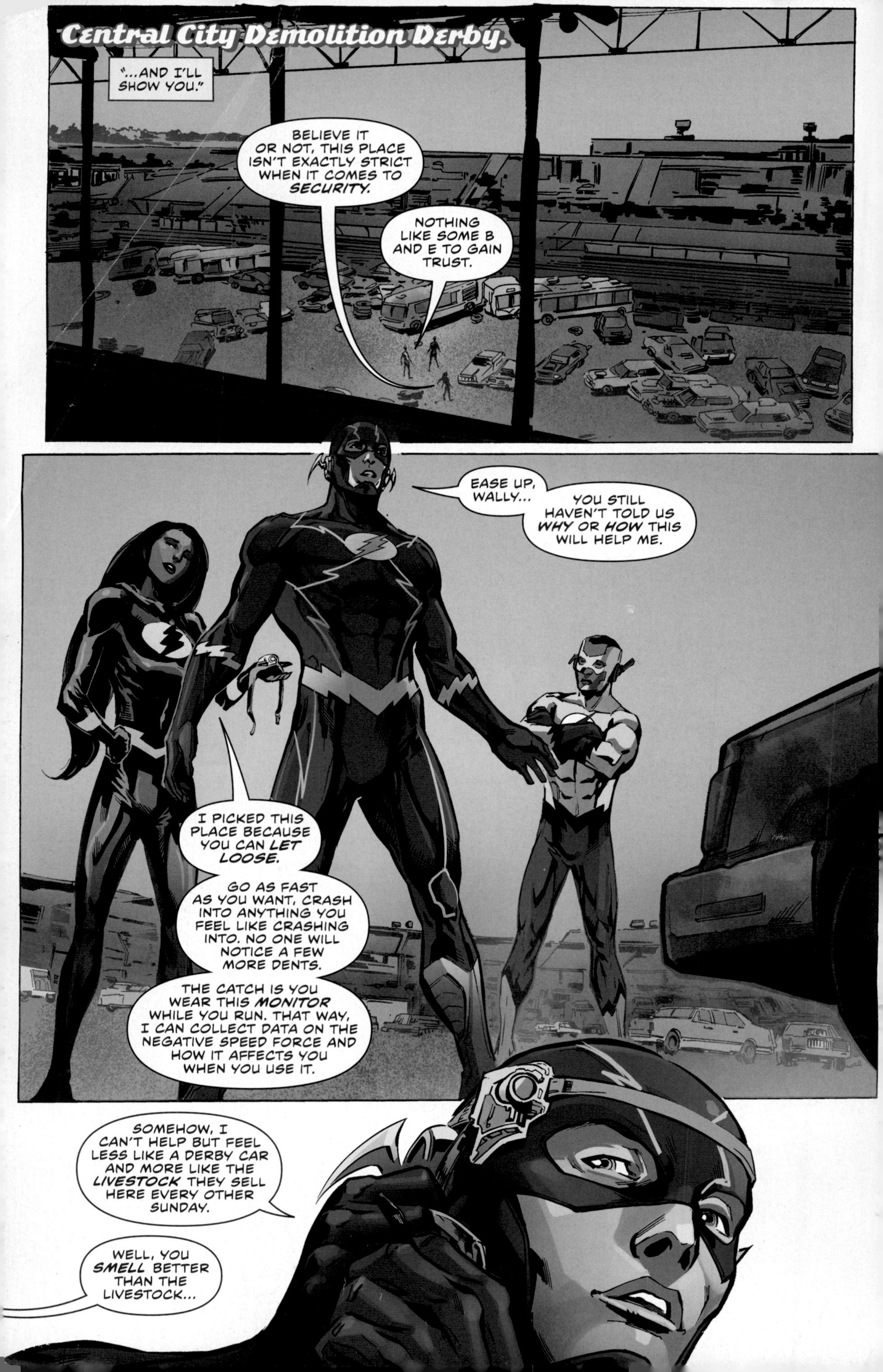

Central City Demolition Derby.
"...AND I'LL SHOW YOU."
BELIEVE IT OR NOT, THIS PLACE ISN'T EXACTLY STRICT WHEN IT COMES TO *SECURITY.*
NOTHING LIKE SOME B AND E TO GAIN TRUST.
EASE UP, WALLY...
YOU STILL HAVEN'T TOLD US *WHY* OR *HOW* THIS WILL HELP ME.
I PICKED THIS PLACE BECAUSE YOU CAN *LET LOOSE.*
GO AS FAST AS YOU WANT, CRASH INTO ANYTHING YOU FEEL LIKE CRASHING INTO. NO ONE WILL NOTICE A FEW MORE DENTS.
THE CATCH IS YOU WEAR THIS *MONITOR* WHILE YOU RUN. THAT WAY, I CAN COLLECT DATA ON THE NEGATIVE SPEED FORCE AND HOW IT AFFECTS YOU WHEN YOU USE IT.
SOMEHOW, I CAN'T HELP BUT FEEL LESS LIKE A DERBY CAR AND MORE LIKE THE *LIVESTOCK* THEY SELL HERE EVERY OTHER SUNDAY.
WELL, YOU *SMELL* BETTER THAN THE LIVESTOCK...

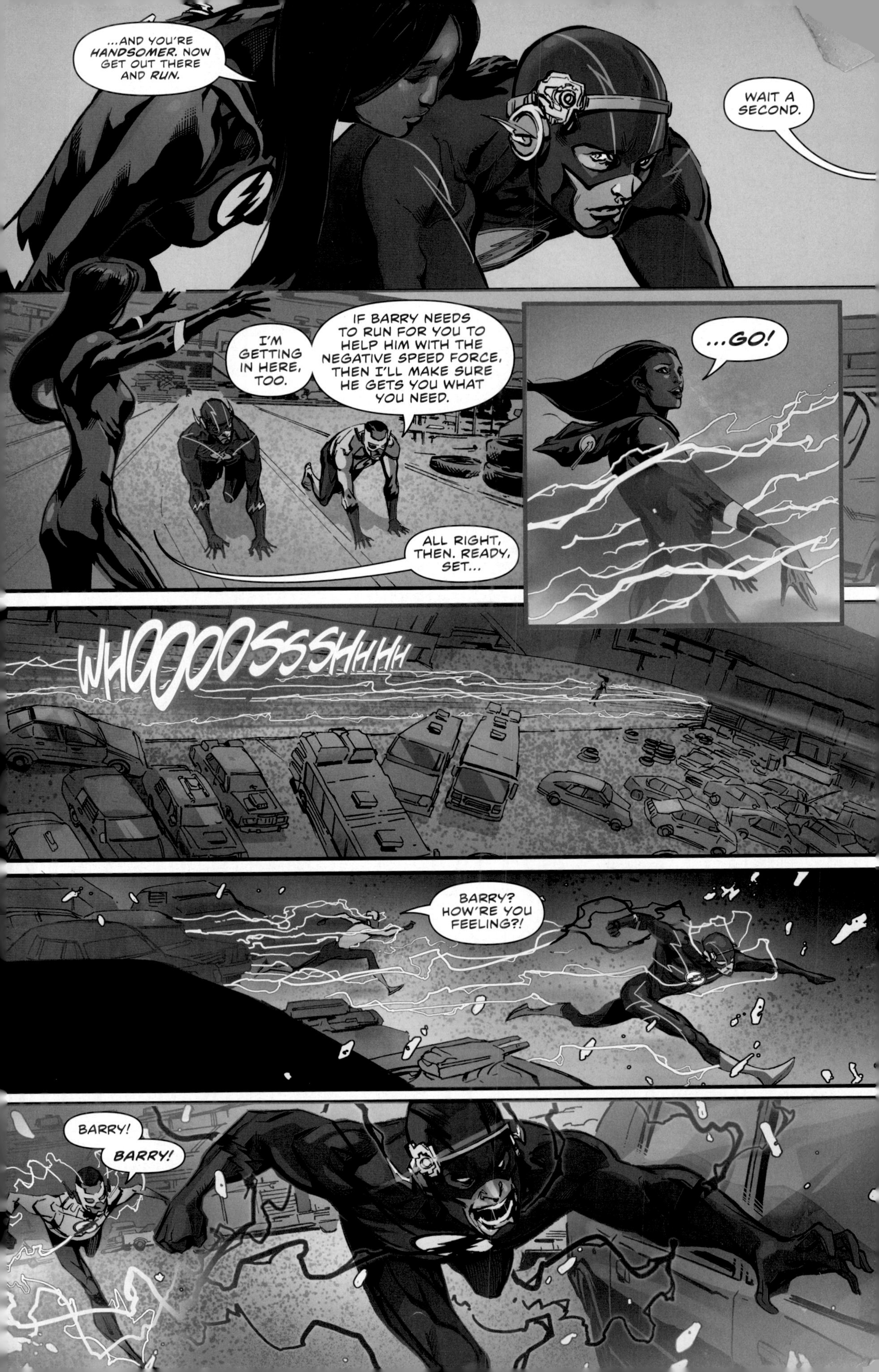

...AND YOU'RE HANDSOMER. NOW GET OUT THERE AND RUN.
WAIT A SECOND.
I'M GETTING IN HERE, TOO.
IF BARRY NEEDS TO RUN FOR YOU TO HELP HIM WITH THE NEGATIVE SPEED FORCE, THEN I'LL MAKE SURE HE GETS YOU WHAT YOU NEED.
ALL RIGHT, THEN. READY, SET...
...GO!
WHOOOOOSSSHHHH
BARRY? HOW'RE YOU FEELING?!
BARRY!
BARRY!

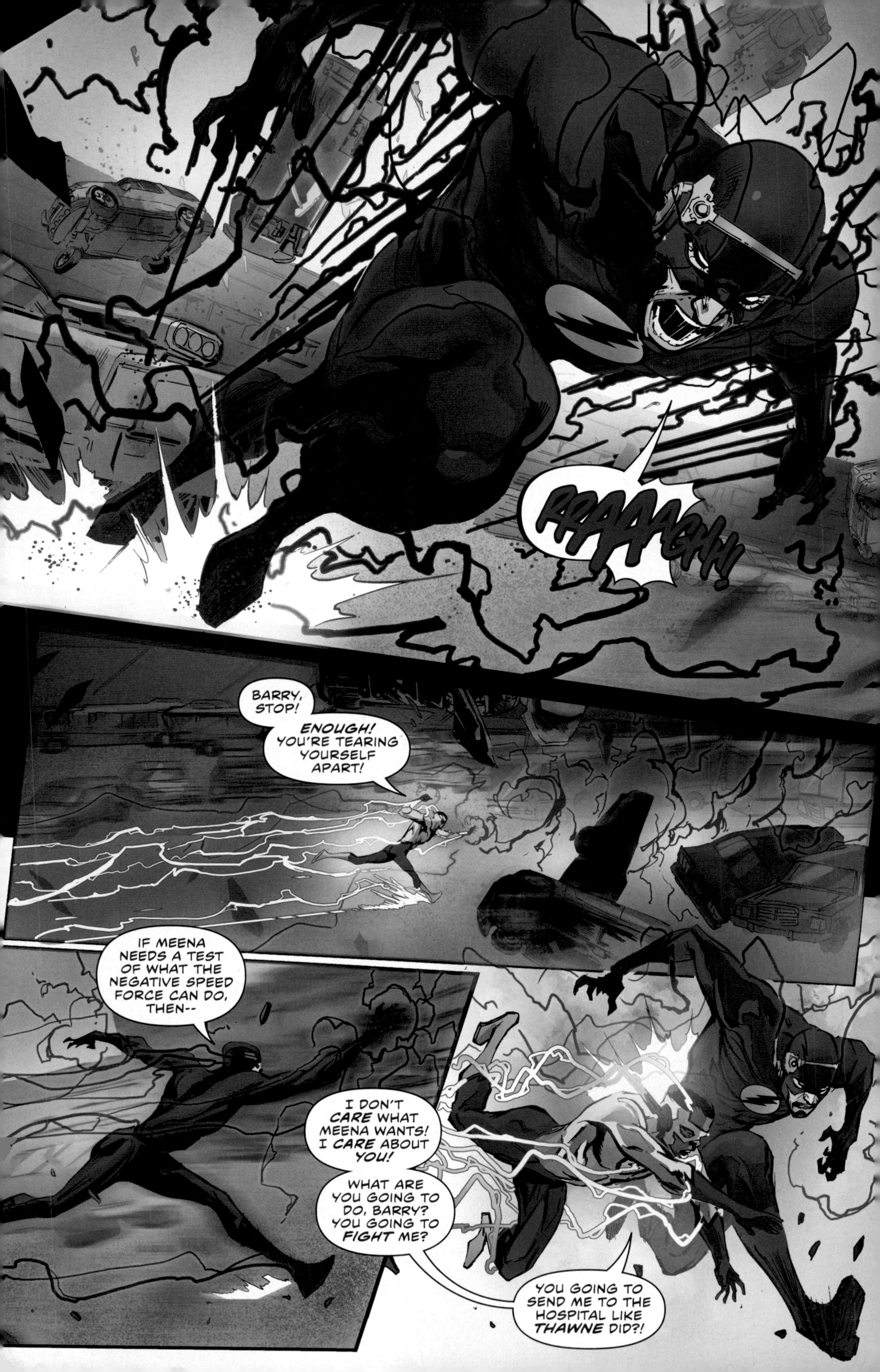
RRAAAAGHH!
BARRY, STOP!
ENOUGH! YOU'RE TEARING YOURSELF APART!
IF MEENA NEEDS A TEST OF WHAT THE NEGATIVE SPEED FORCE CAN DO, THEN--
I DON'T CARE WHAT MEENA WANTS! I CARE ABOUT YOU!
WHAT ARE YOU GOING TO DO, BARRY? YOU GOING TO FIGHT ME?
YOU GOING TO SEND ME TO THE HOSPITAL LIKE THAWNE DID?!

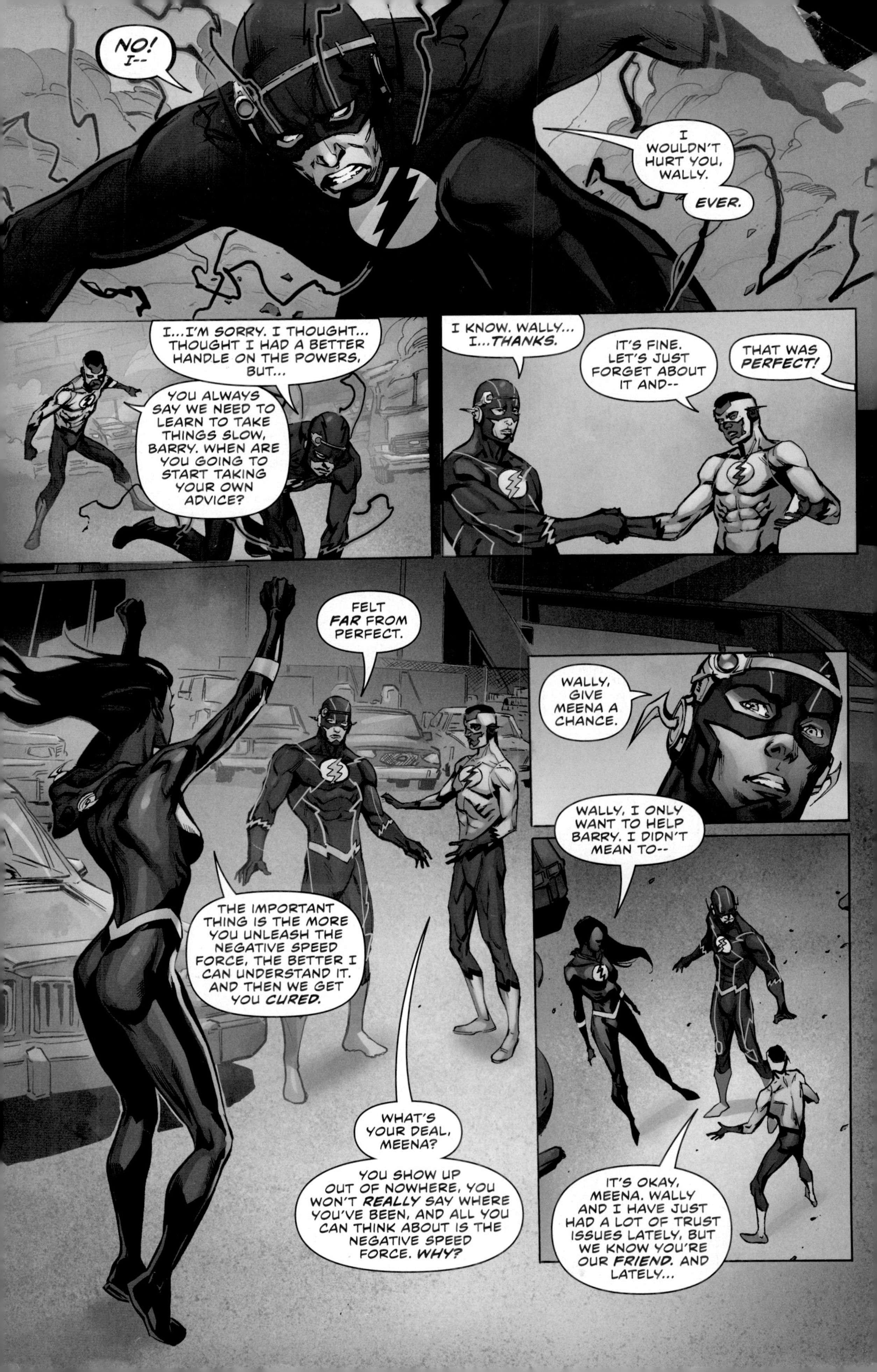
NO! I--
I WOULDN'T HURT YOU, WALLY.
EVER.
I...I'M SORRY. I THOUGHT... THOUGHT I HAD A BETTER HANDLE ON THE POWERS, BUT...
YOU ALWAYS SAY WE NEED TO LEARN TO TAKE THINGS SLOW, BARRY. WHEN ARE YOU GOING TO START TAKING YOUR OWN ADVICE?
I KNOW. WALLY... I...THANKS.
IT'S FINE. LET'S JUST FORGET ABOUT IT AND--
THAT WAS PERFECT!
FELT FAR FROM PERFECT.
THE IMPORTANT THING IS THE MORE YOU UNLEASH THE NEGATIVE SPEED FORCE, THE BETTER I CAN UNDERSTAND IT. AND THEN WE GET YOU CURED.
WHAT'S YOUR DEAL, MEENA?
YOU SHOW UP OUT OF NOWHERE, YOU WON'T REALLY SAY WHERE YOU'VE BEEN, AND ALL YOU CAN THINK ABOUT IS THE NEGATIVE SPEED FORCE. WHY?
WALLY, GIVE MEENA A CHANCE.
WALLY, I ONLY WANT TO HELP BARRY. I DIDN'T MEAN TO--
IT'S OKAY, MEENA. WALLY AND I HAVE JUST HAD A LOT OF TRUST ISSUES LATELY, BUT WE KNOW YOU'RE OUR FRIEND. AND LATELY...

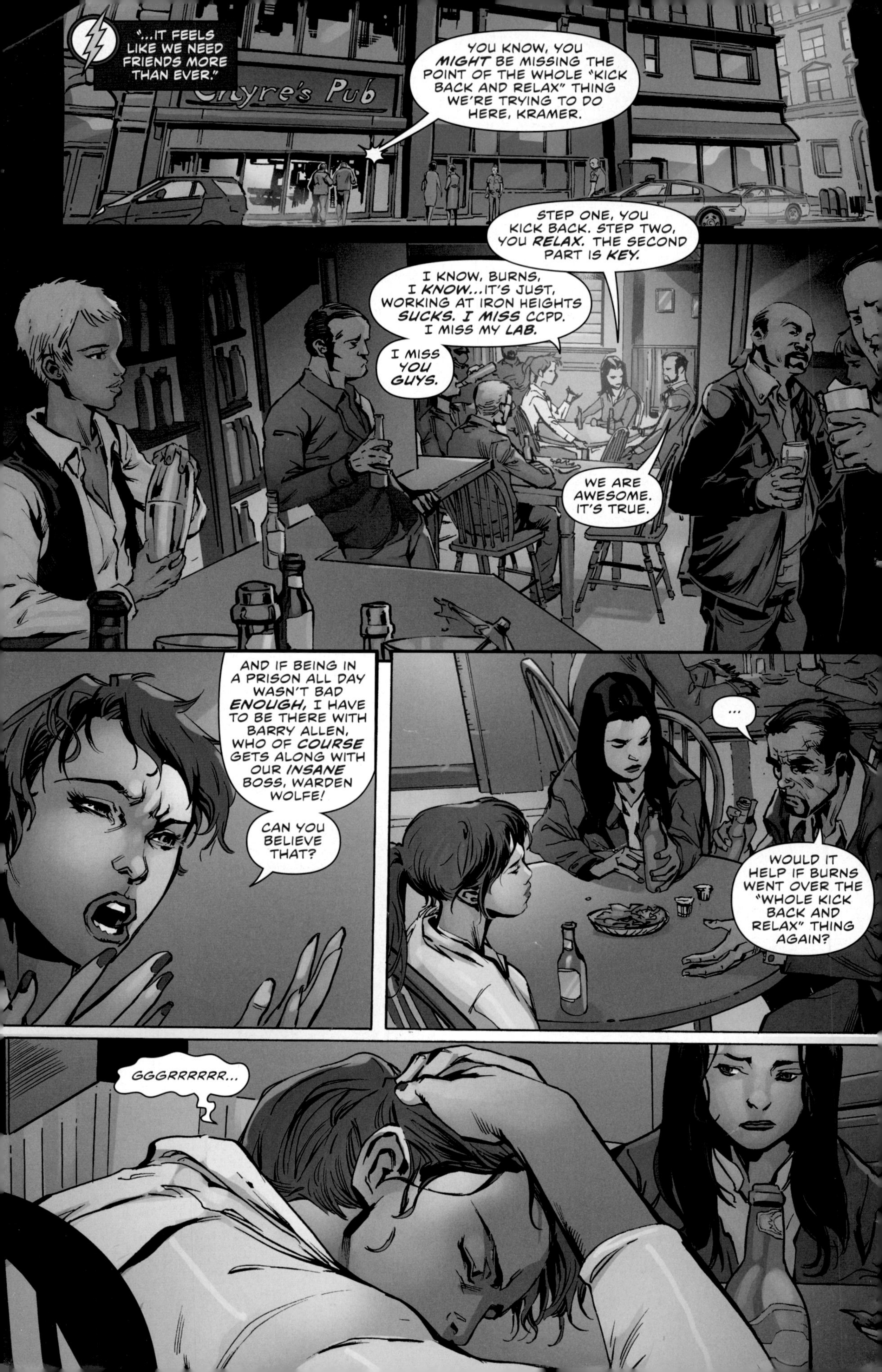
"...IT FEELS LIKE WE NEED FRIENDS MORE THAN EVER."
YOU KNOW, YOU MIGHT BE MISSING THE POINT OF THE WHOLE "KICK BACK AND RELAX" THING WE'RE TRYING TO DO HERE, KRAMER.
STEP ONE, YOU KICK BACK. STEP TWO, YOU RELAX. THE SECOND PART IS KEY.
I KNOW, BURNS, I KNOW...IT'S JUST, WORKING AT IRON HEIGHTS SUCKS. I MISS CCPD. I MISS MY LAB.
I MISS YOU GUYS.
WE ARE AWESOME. IT'S TRUE.
AND IF BEING IN A PRISON ALL DAY WASN'T BAD ENOUGH, I HAVE TO BE THERE WITH BARRY ALLEN, WHO OF COURSE GETS ALONG WITH OUR INSANE BOSS, WARDEN WOLFE!
CAN YOU BELIEVE THAT?
...
WOULD IT HELP IF BURNS WENT OVER THE "WHOLE KICK BACK AND RELAX" THING AGAIN?
GGGRRRRRR...

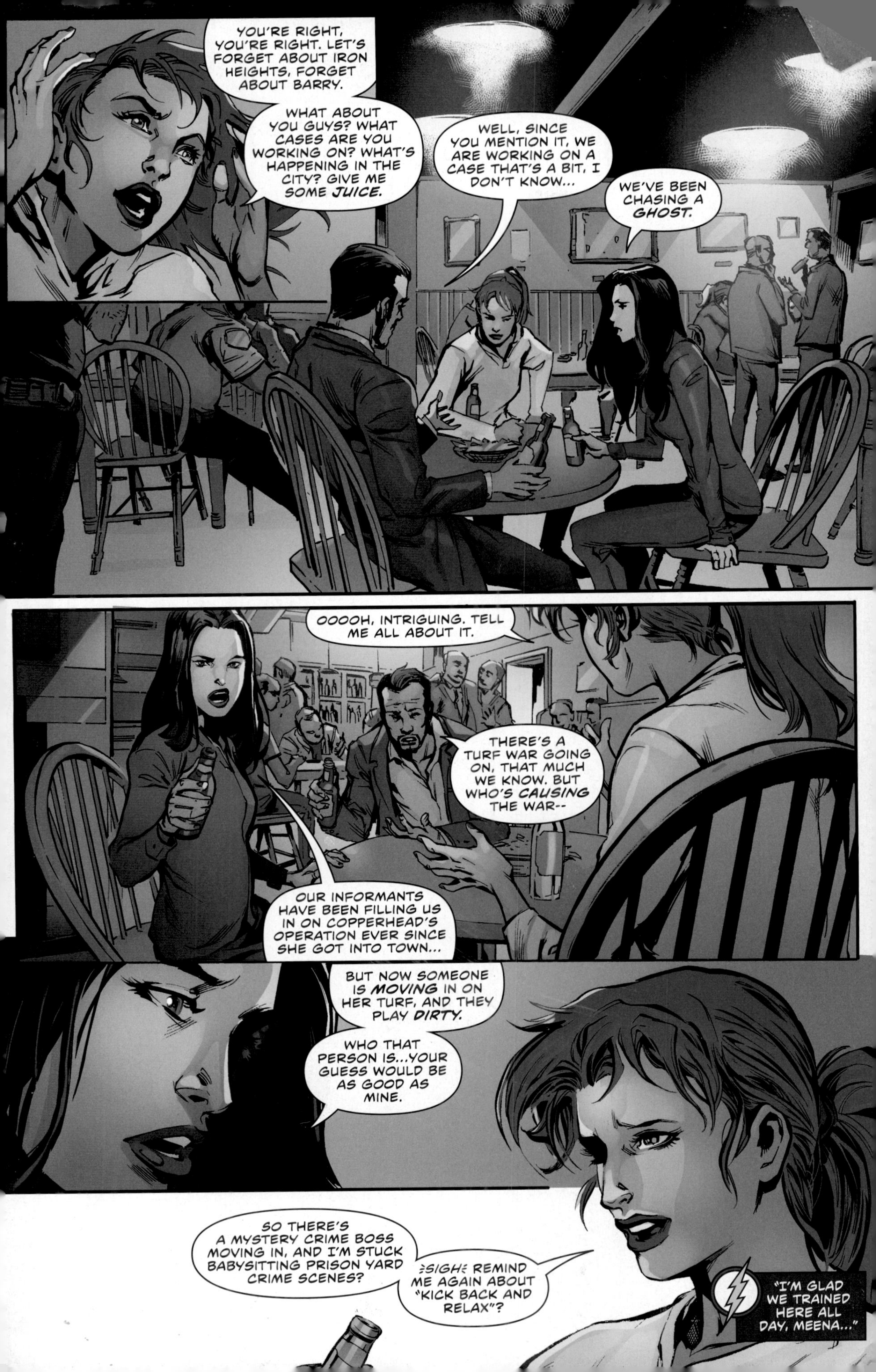

YOU'RE RIGHT, YOU'RE RIGHT. LET'S FORGET ABOUT IRON HEIGHTS, FORGET ABOUT BARRY.
WHAT ABOUT YOU GUYS? WHAT CASES ARE YOU WORKING ON? WHAT'S HAPPENING IN THE CITY? GIVE ME SOME JUICE.
WELL, SINCE YOU MENTION IT, WE ARE WORKING ON A CASE THAT'S A BIT, I DON'T KNOW...
WE'VE BEEN CHASING A GHOST.
OOOOH, INTRIGUING. TELL ME ALL ABOUT IT.
THERE'S A TURF WAR GOING ON, THAT MUCH WE KNOW. BUT WHO'S CAUSING THE WAR--
OUR INFORMANTS HAVE BEEN FILLING US IN ON COPPERHEAD'S OPERATION EVER SINCE SHE GOT INTO TOWN...
BUT NOW SOMEONE IS MOVING IN ON HER TURF, AND THEY PLAY DIRTY.
WHO THAT PERSON IS...YOUR GUESS WOULD BE AS GOOD AS MINE.
SO THERE'S A MYSTERY CRIME BOSS MOVING IN, AND I'M STUCK BABYSITTING PRISON YARD CRIME SCENES?
SIGH REMIND ME AGAIN ABOUT "KICK BACK AND RELAX"?
"I'M GLAD WE TRAINED HERE ALL DAY, MEENA..."

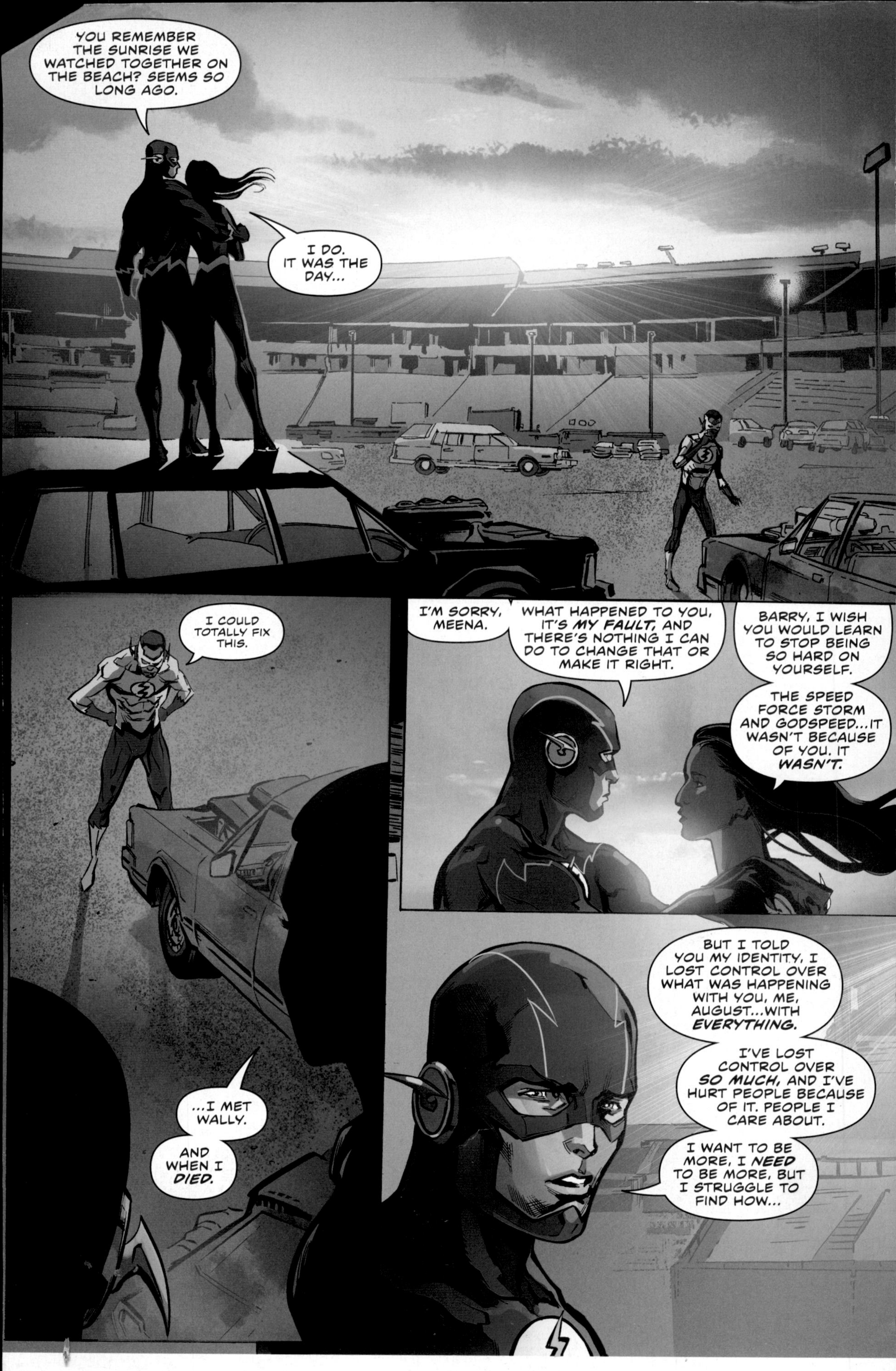
YOU REMEMBER THE SUNRISE WE WATCHED TOGETHER ON THE BEACH? SEEMS SO LONG AGO.
I DO. IT WAS THE DAY...
I COULD TOTALLY FIX THIS.
...I MET WALLY.
AND WHEN I DIED.
I'M SORRY, MEENA.
WHAT HAPPENED TO YOU, IT'S MY FAULT, AND THERE'S NOTHING I CAN DO TO CHANGE THAT OR MAKE IT RIGHT.
BARRY, I WISH YOU WOULD LEARN TO STOP BEING SO HARD ON YOURSELF.
THE SPEED FORCE STORM AND GODSPEED...IT WASN'T BECAUSE OF YOU. IT WASN'T.
BUT I TOLD YOU MY IDENTITY, I LOST CONTROL OVER WHAT WAS HAPPENING WITH YOU, ME, AUGUST...WITH EVERYTHING.
I'VE LOST CONTROL OVER SO MUCH, AND I'VE HURT PEOPLE BECAUSE OF IT. PEOPLE I CARE ABOUT.
I WANT TO BE MORE, I NEED TO BE MORE, BUT I STRUGGLE TO FIND HOW...

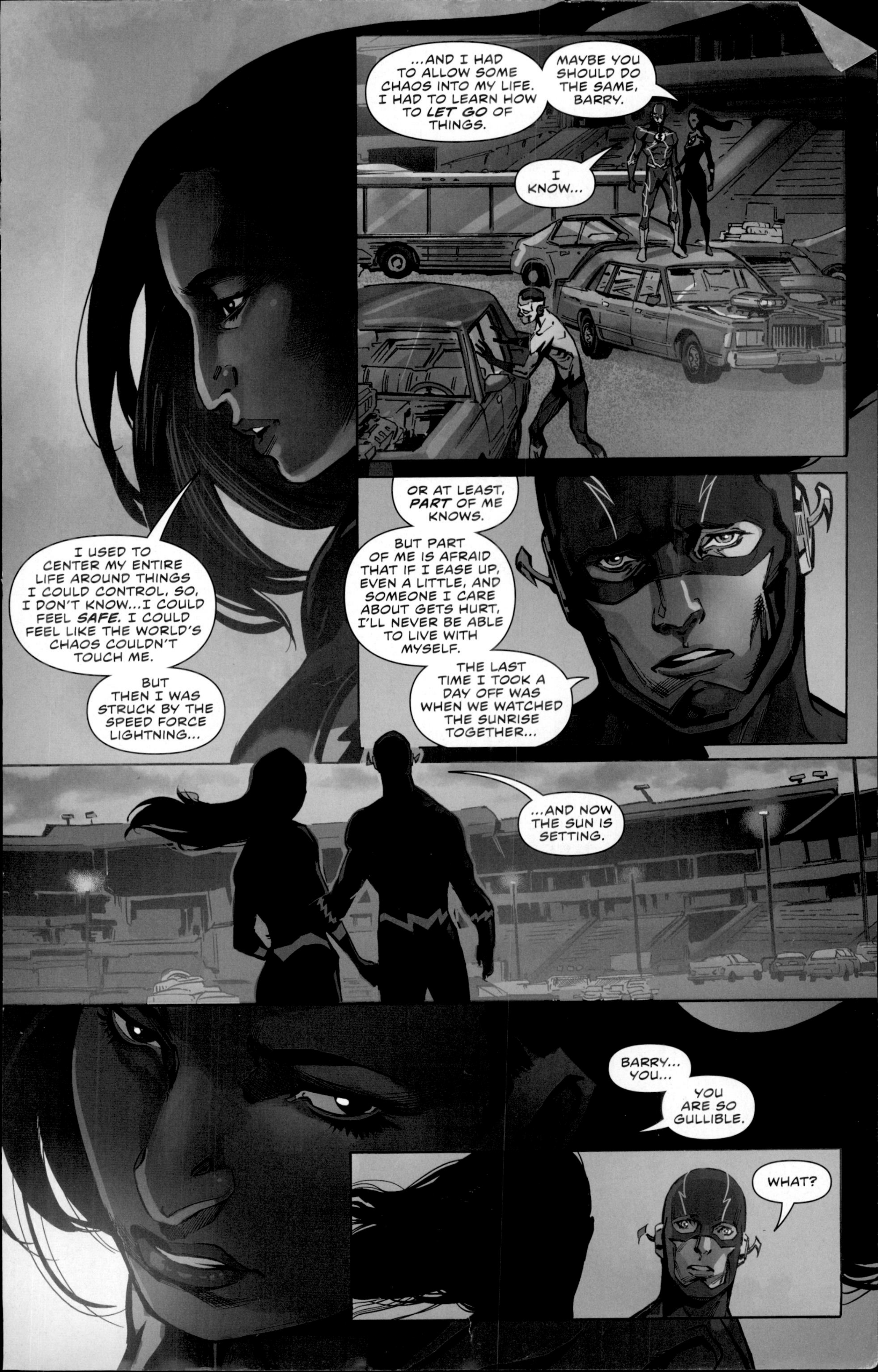
...AND I HAD TO ALLOW SOME CHAOS INTO MY LIFE. I HAD TO LEARN HOW TO LET GO OF THINGS.
MAYBE YOU SHOULD DO THE SAME, BARRY.
I KNOW...
I USED TO CENTER MY ENTIRE LIFE AROUND THINGS I COULD CONTROL, SO, I DON'T KNOW...I COULD FEEL SAFE. I COULD FEEL LIKE THE WORLD'S CHAOS COULDN'T TOUCH ME.
BUT THEN I WAS STRUCK BY THE SPEED FORCE LIGHTNING...
OR AT LEAST, PART OF ME KNOWS.
BUT PART OF ME IS AFRAID THAT IF I EASE UP, EVEN A LITTLE, AND SOMEONE I CARE ABOUT GETS HURT, I'LL NEVER BE ABLE TO LIVE WITH MYSELF.
THE LAST TIME I TOOK A DAY OFF WAS WHEN WE WATCHED THE SUNRISE TOGETHER...
...AND NOW THE SUN IS SETTING.
BARRY... YOU...
YOU ARE SO GULLIBLE.
WHAT?

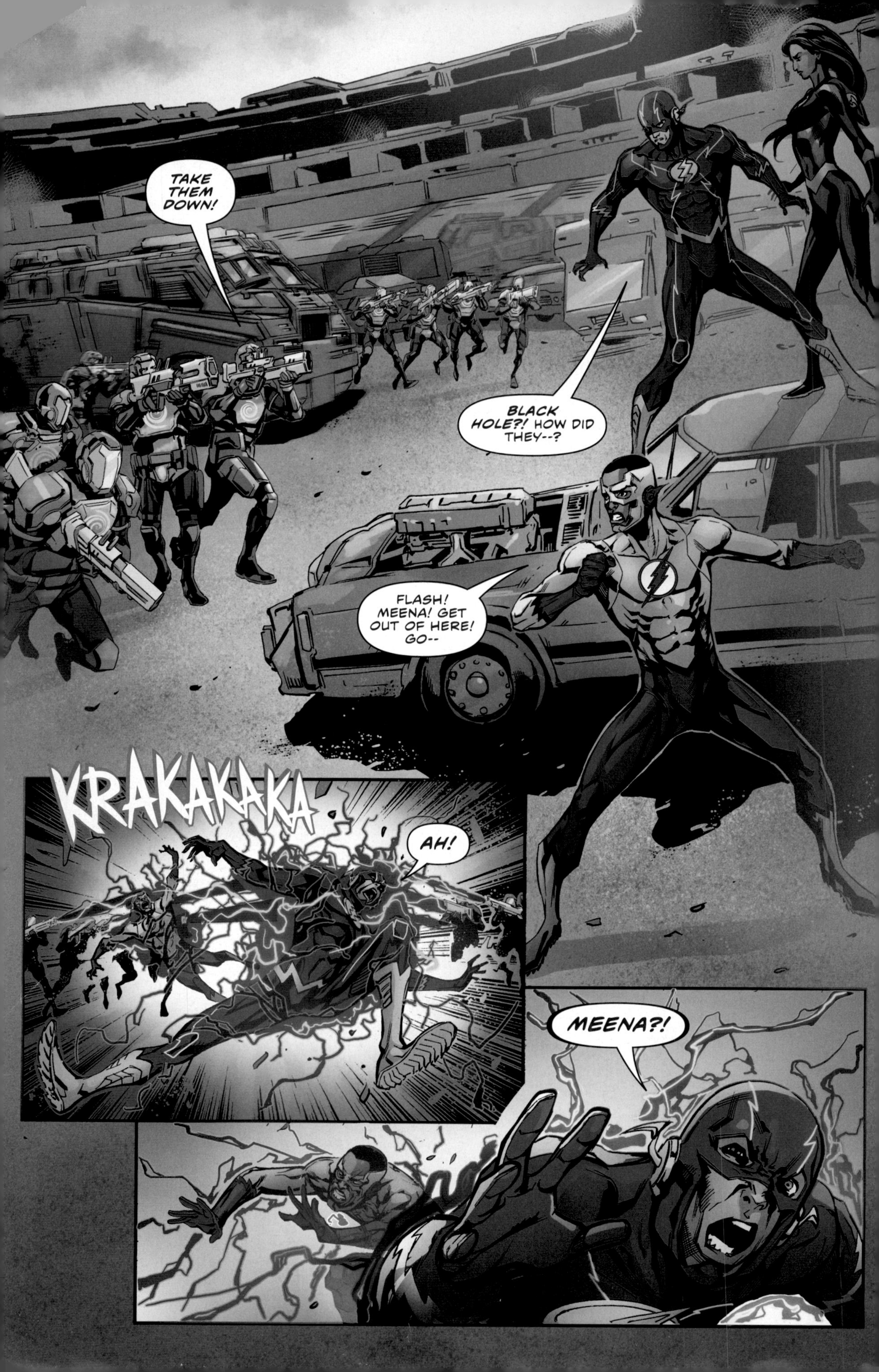
TAKE THEM DOWN!
BLACK HOLE?! HOW DID THEY--?
FLASH! MEENA! GET OUT OF HERE! GO--
KRAKAKAKA
AH!
MEENA?!

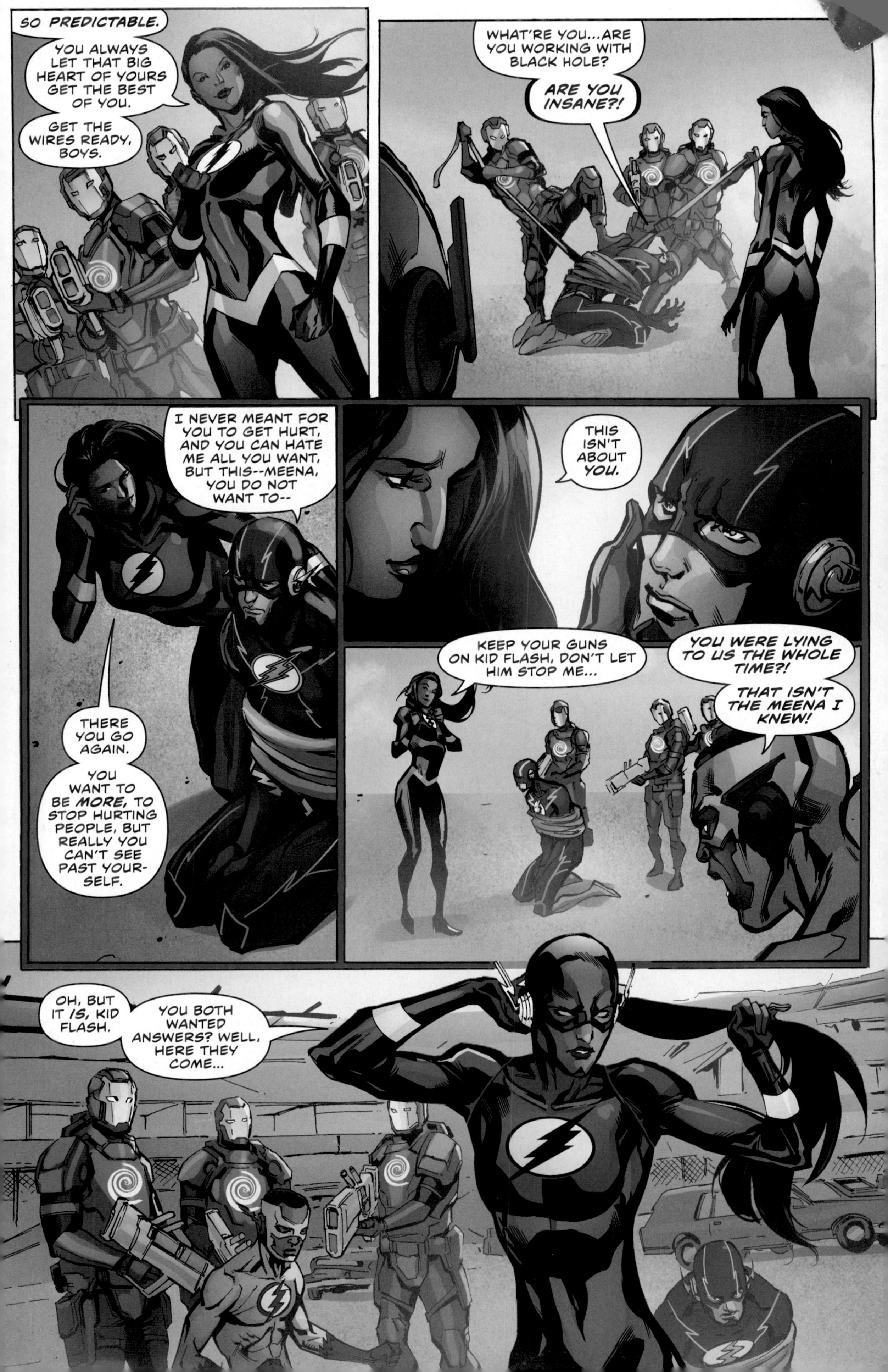
SO PREDICTABLE.
YOU ALWAYS LET THAT BIG HEART OF YOURS GET THE BEST OF YOU.
GET THE WIRES READY, BOYS.
WHAT'RE YOU...ARE YOU WORKING WITH BLACK HOLE?
ARE YOU INSANE?!
I NEVER MEANT FOR YOU TO GET HURT, AND YOU CAN HATE ME ALL YOU WANT, BUT THIS--MEENA, YOU DO NOT WANT TO--
THERE YOU GO AGAIN.
YOU WANT TO BE MORE, TO STOP HURTING PEOPLE, BUT REALLY YOU CAN'T SEE PAST YOUR-SELF.
THIS ISN'T ABOUT YOU.
KEEP YOUR GUNS ON KID FLASH, DON'T LET HIM STOP ME...
YOU WERE LYING TO US THE WHOLE TIME?!
THAT ISN'T THE MEENA I KNEW!
OH, BUT IT IS, KID FLASH.
YOU BOTH WANTED ANSWERS? WELL, HERE THEY COME...

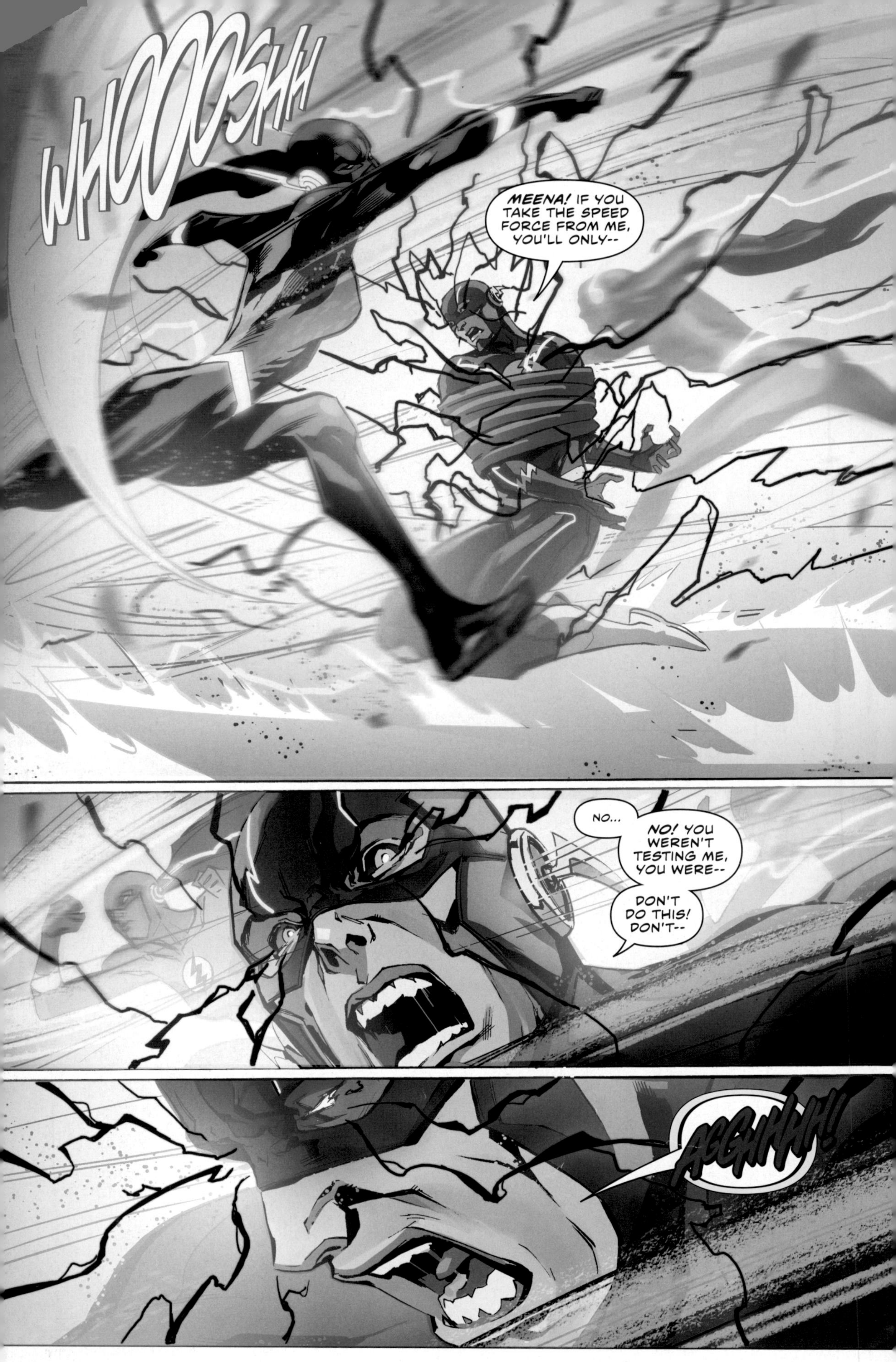
WHOOOOSHH
MEENA! IF YOU TAKE THE SPEED FORCE FROM ME, YOU'LL ONLY--
NO...
NO! YOU WEREN'T TESTING ME, YOU WERE--
DON'T DO THIS! DON'T--
AGGHHHH!

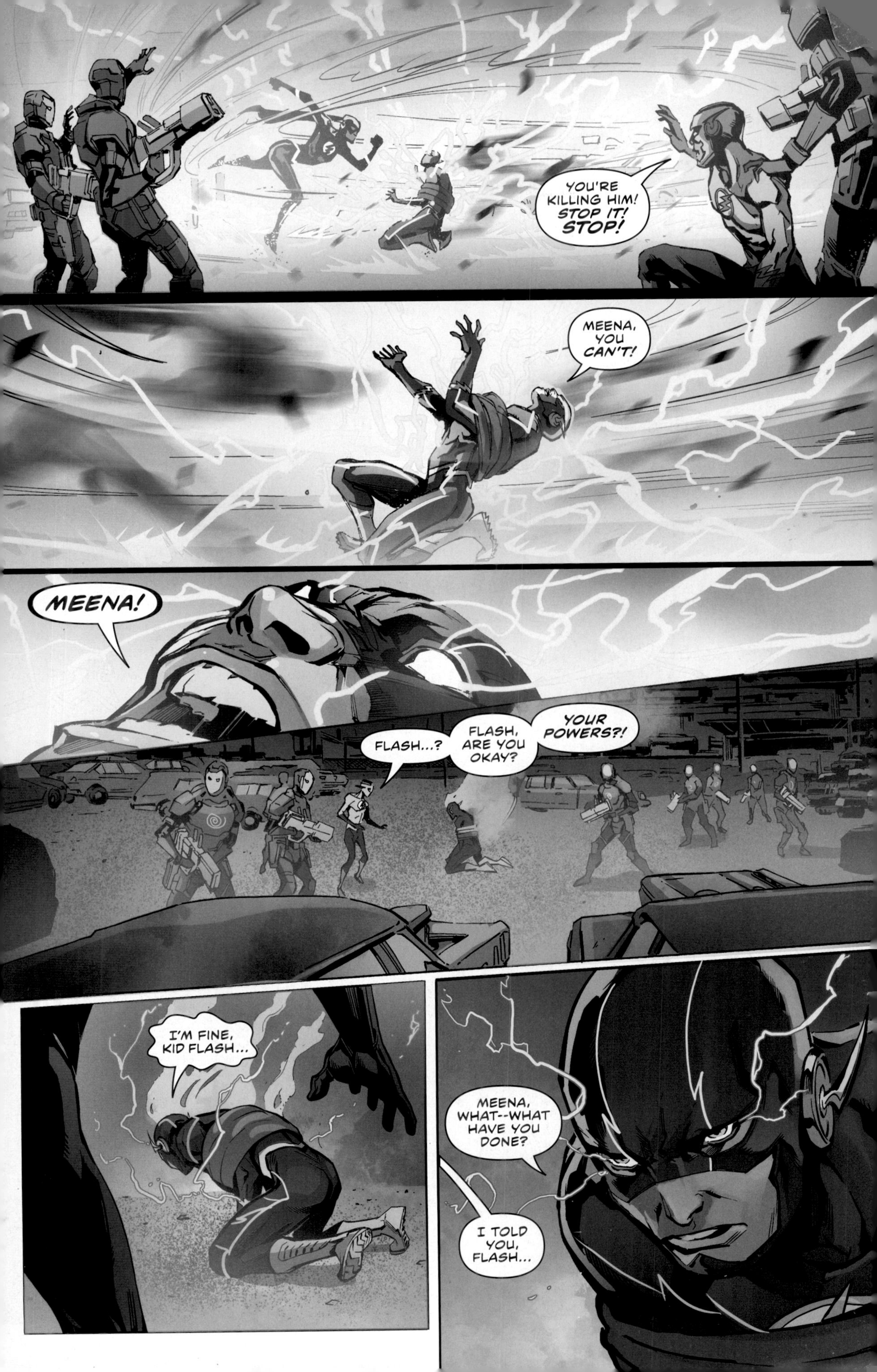
YOU'RE KILLING HIM! STOP IT! STOP!
MEENA, YOU CAN'T!
MEENA!
FLASH...?
FLASH, ARE YOU OKAY?
YOUR POWERS?!
I'M FINE, KID FLASH...
MEENA, WHAT--WHAT HAVE YOU DONE?
I TOLD YOU, FLASH...

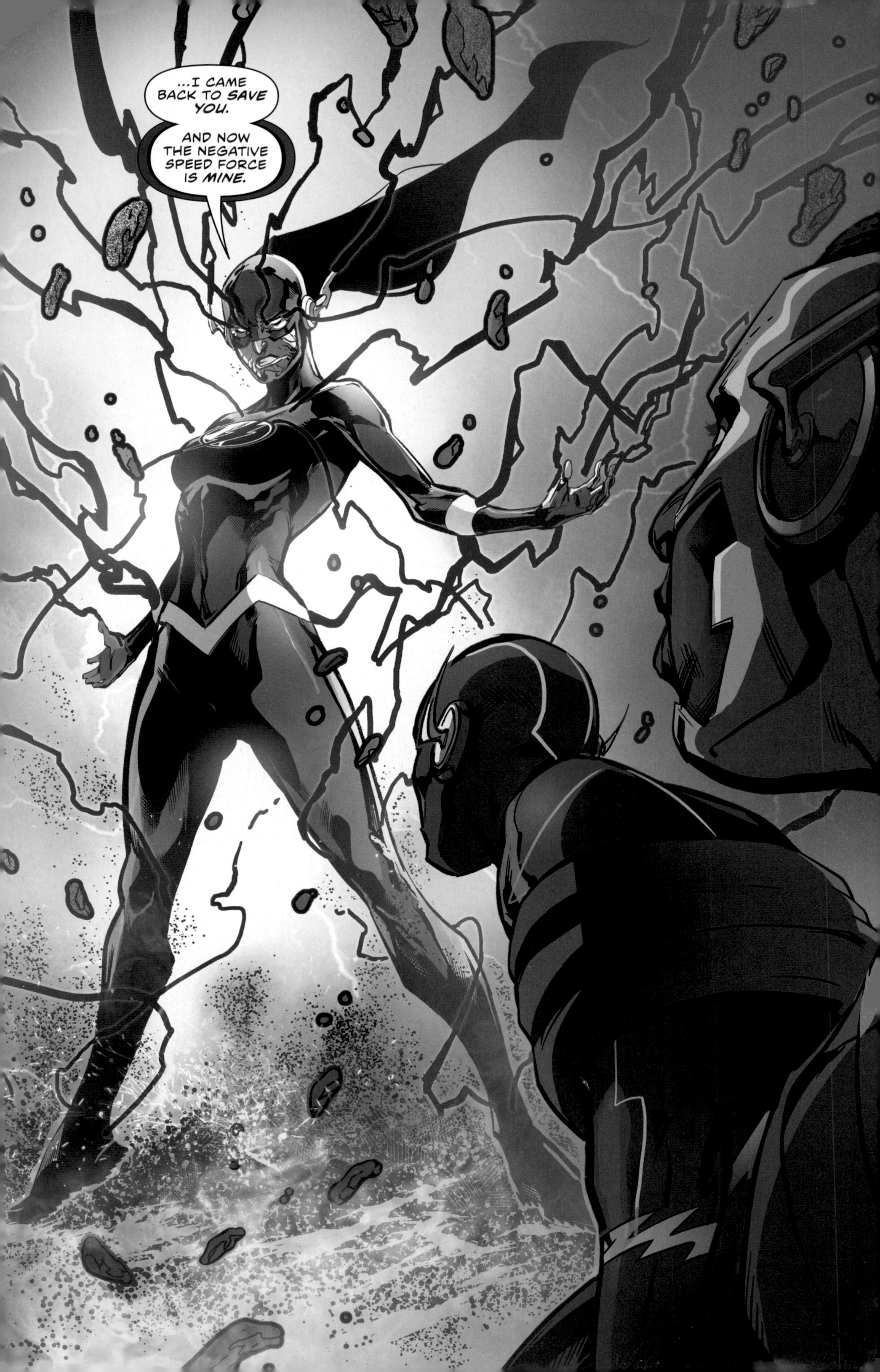
...I CAME BACK TO SAVE YOU.
AND NOW THE NEGATIVE SPEED FORCE IS MINE.

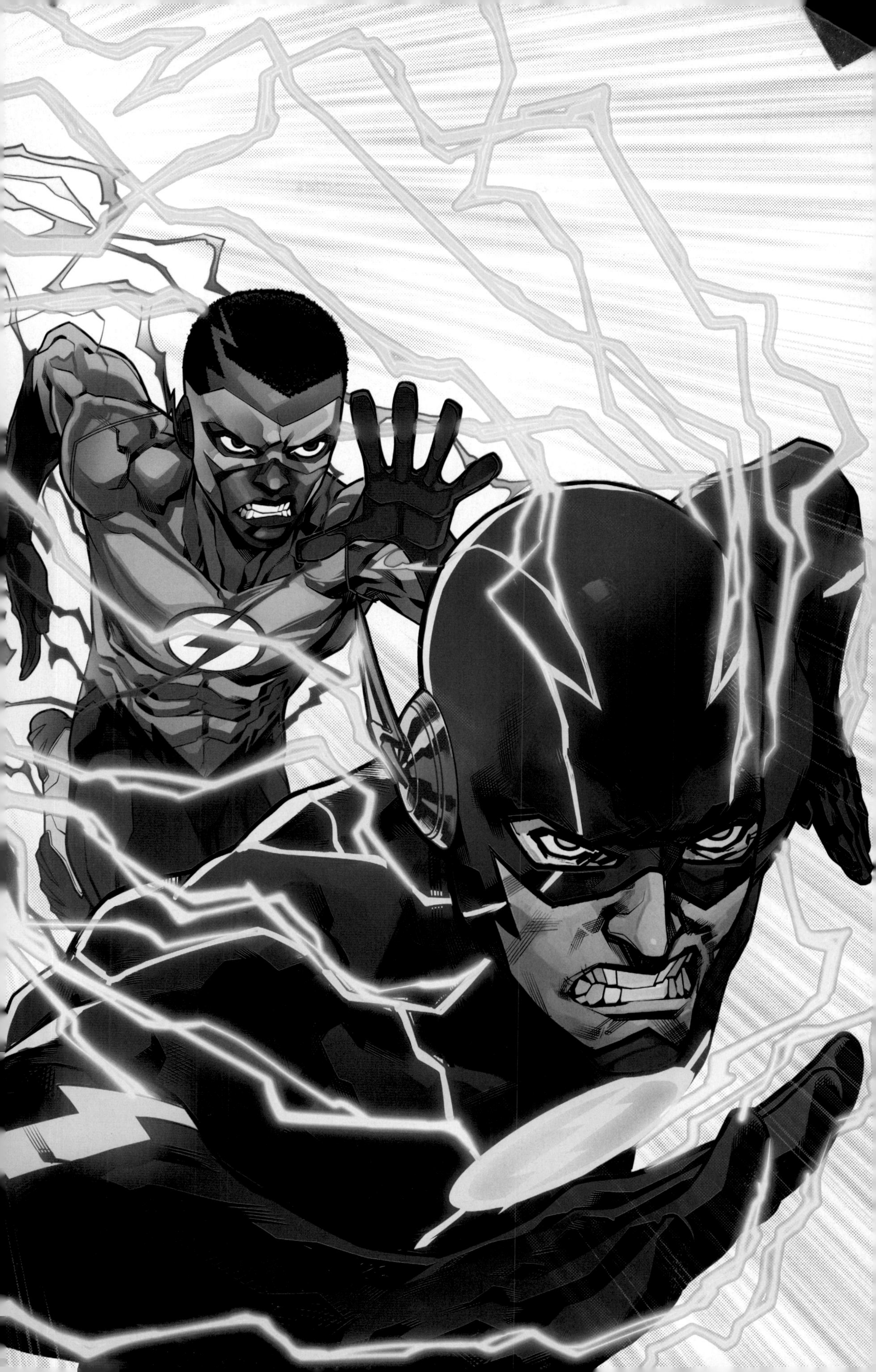

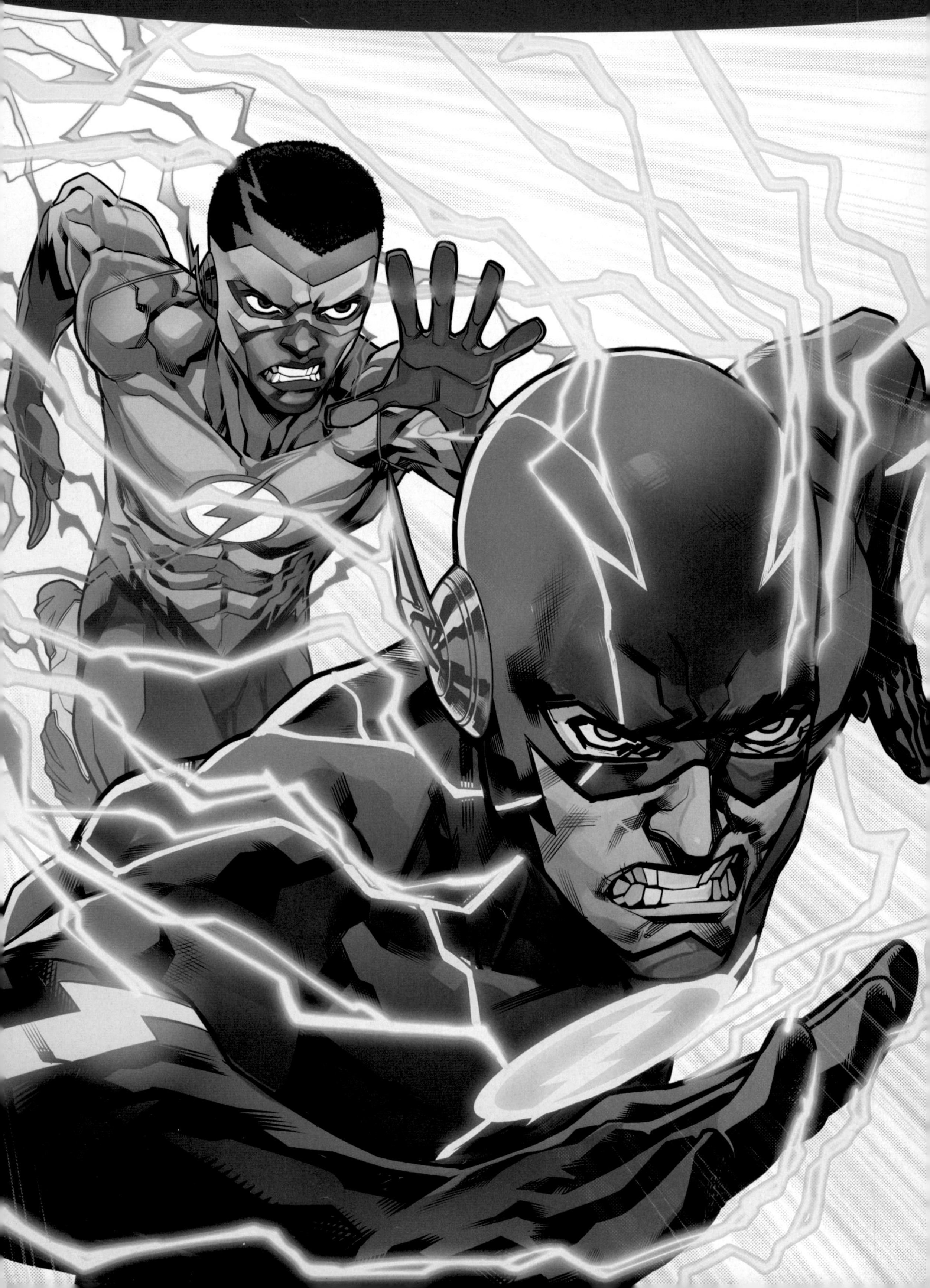

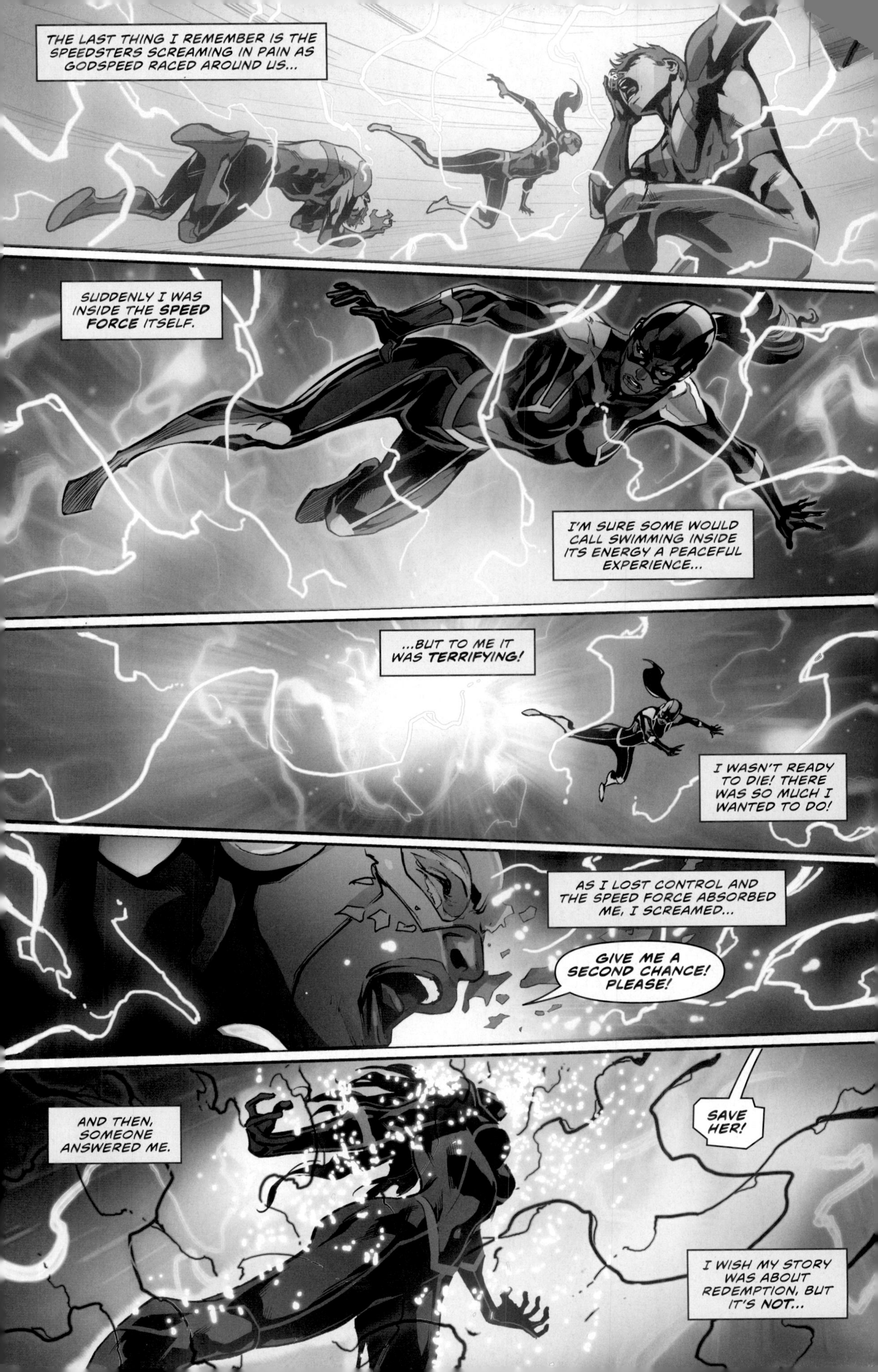
THE LAST THING I REMEMBER IS THE SPEEDSTERS SCREAMING IN PAIN AS GODSPEED RACED AROUND US...
SUDDENLY I WAS INSIDE THE SPEED FORCE ITSELF.
I'M SURE SOME WOULD CALL SWIMMING INSIDE ITS ENERGY A PEACEFUL EXPERIENCE...
...BUT TO ME IT WAS TERRIFYING!
I WASN'T READY TO DIE! THERE WAS SO MUCH I WANTED TO DO!
AS I LOST CONTROL AND THE SPEED FORCE ABSORBED ME, I SCREAMED...
GIVE ME A SECOND CHANCE! PLEASE!
AND THEN, SOMEONE ANSWERED ME.
SAVE HER!
I WISH MY STORY WAS ABOUT REDEMPTION, BUT IT'S NOT...

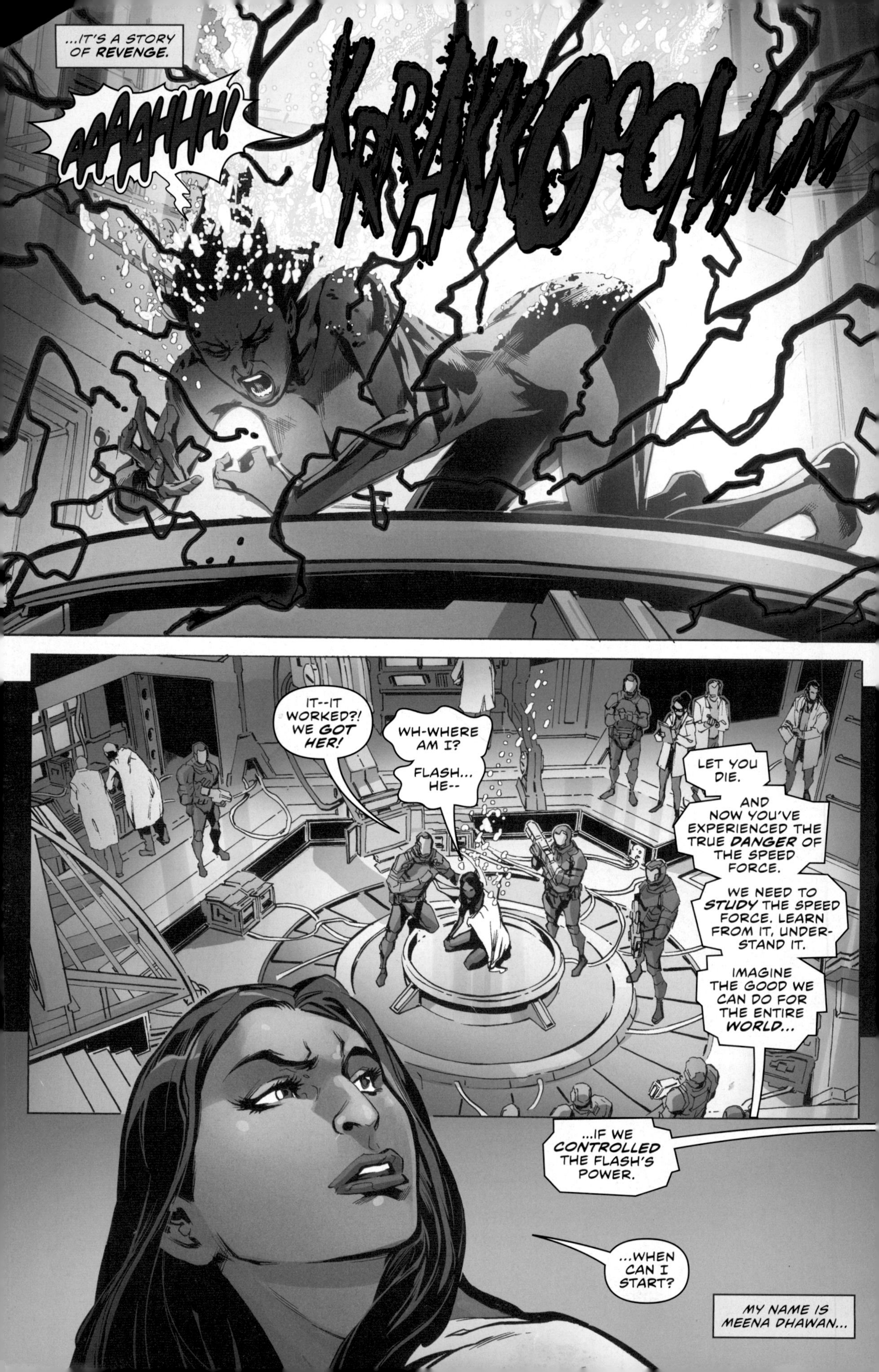
...IT'S A STORY OF REVENGE.
AAAAHHH!
KRAKKOOOM!!!
IT--IT WORKED?! WE GOT HER!
WH-WHERE AM I?
FLASH... HE--
LET YOU DIE.
AND NOW YOU'VE EXPERIENCED THE TRUE DANGER OF THE SPEED FORCE.
WE NEED TO STUDY THE SPEED FORCE. LEARN FROM IT, UNDERSTAND IT.
IMAGINE THE GOOD WE CAN DO FOR THE ENTIRE WORLD...
...IF WE CONTROLLED THE FLASH'S POWER.
...WHEN CAN I START?
MY NAME IS MEENA DHAWAN...

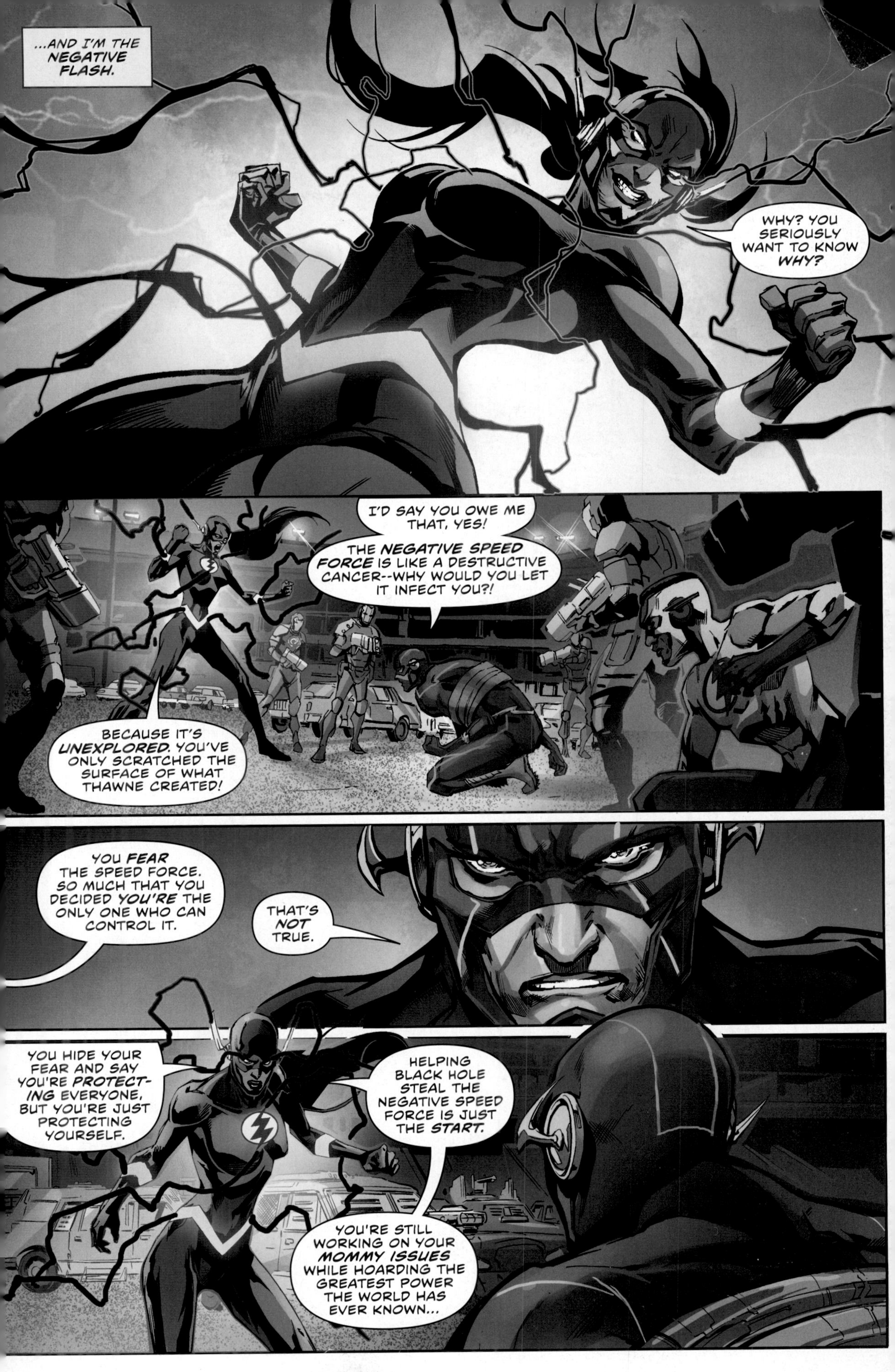
...AND I'M THE NEGATIVE FLASH.
WHY? YOU SERIOUSLY WANT TO KNOW WHY?
I'D SAY YOU OWE ME THAT, YES!
THE NEGATIVE SPEED FORCE IS LIKE A DESTRUCTIVE CANCER--WHY WOULD YOU LET IT INFECT YOU?!
BECAUSE IT'S UNEXPLORED. YOU'VE ONLY SCRATCHED THE SURFACE OF WHAT THAWNE CREATED!
YOU FEAR THE SPEED FORCE. SO MUCH THAT YOU DECIDED YOU'RE THE ONLY ONE WHO CAN CONTROL IT.
THAT'S NOT TRUE.
YOU HIDE YOUR FEAR AND SAY YOU'RE PROTECTING EVERYONE, BUT YOU'RE JUST PROTECTING YOURSELF.
HELPING BLACK HOLE STEAL THE NEGATIVE SPEED FORCE IS JUST THE START.
YOU'RE STILL WORKING ON YOUR MOMMY ISSUES WHILE HOARDING THE GREATEST POWER THE WORLD HAS EVER KNOWN...

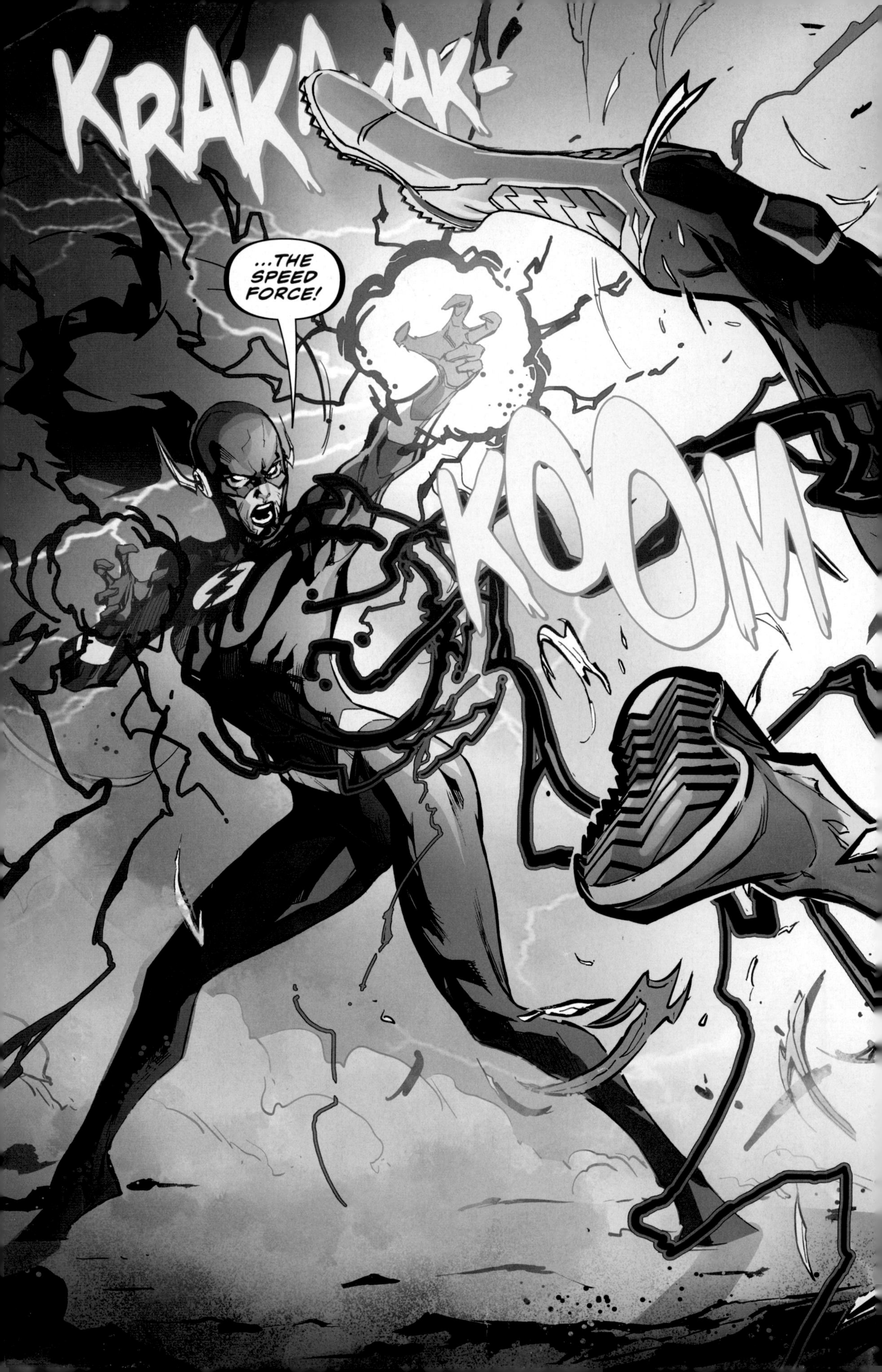
KRAK AK-
...THE SPEED FORCE!
KOOM

AAARRGGH!!
BLACK HOLE RISING
PART TWO
JOSHUA WILLIAMSON & MICHAEL MORECI WRITERS
POP MHAN ART IVAN PLASCENCIA COLOR
STEVE WANDS LETTERS NEIL GOOGE & IVAN PLASCENCIA COVER
ANDREW MARINO ASSISTANT EDITOR
REBECCA TAYLOR EDITOR BRIAN CUNNINGHAM GROUP EDITOR

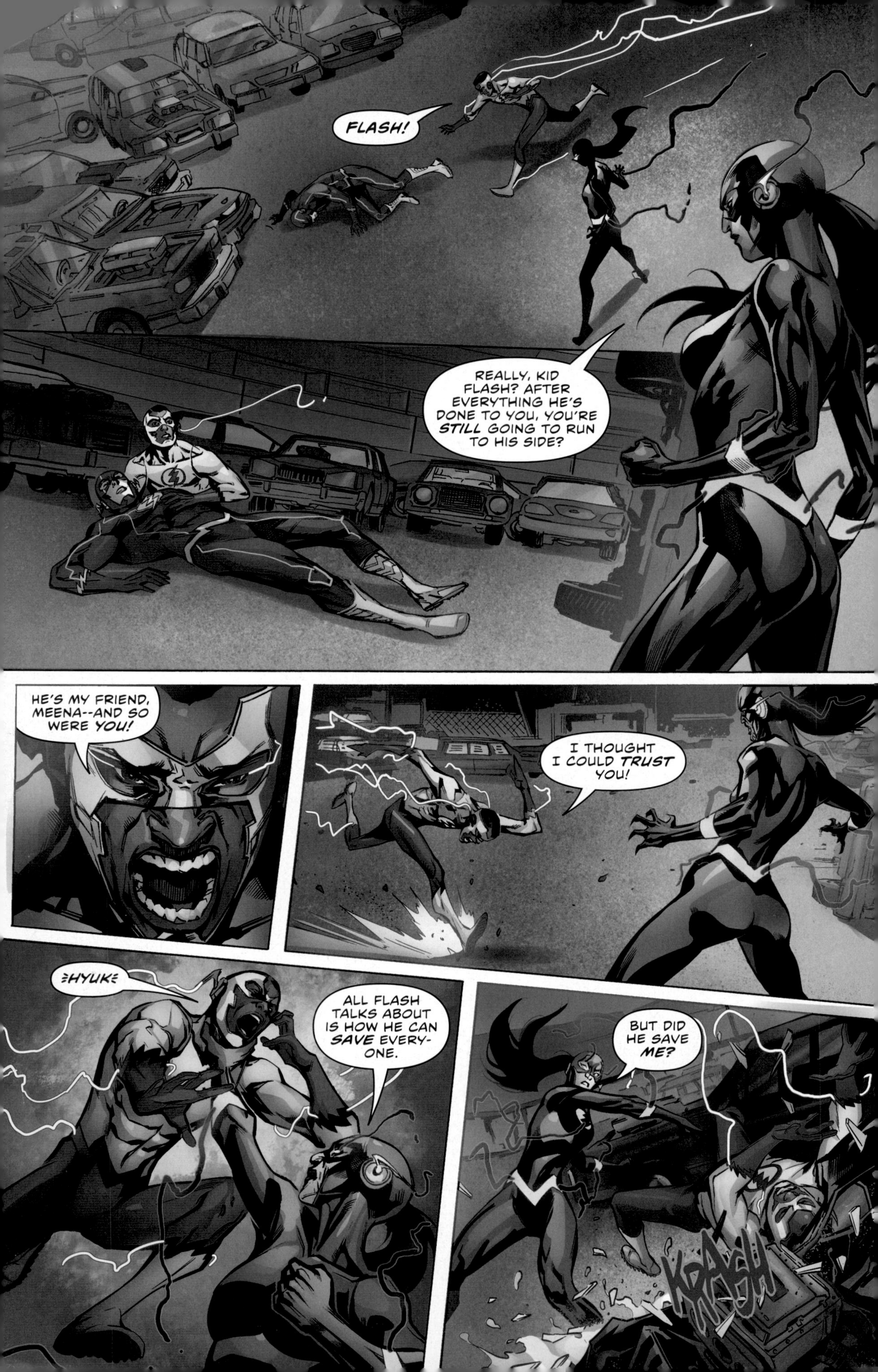
FLASH!
REALLY, KID FLASH? AFTER EVERYTHING HE'S DONE TO YOU, YOU'RE STILL GOING TO RUN TO HIS SIDE?
HE'S MY FRIEND, MEENA--AND SO WERE YOU!
I THOUGHT I COULD TRUST YOU!
HYUK
ALL FLASH TALKS ABOUT IS HOW HE CAN SAVE EVERY-ONE.
BUT DID HE SAVE ME?
KRASH

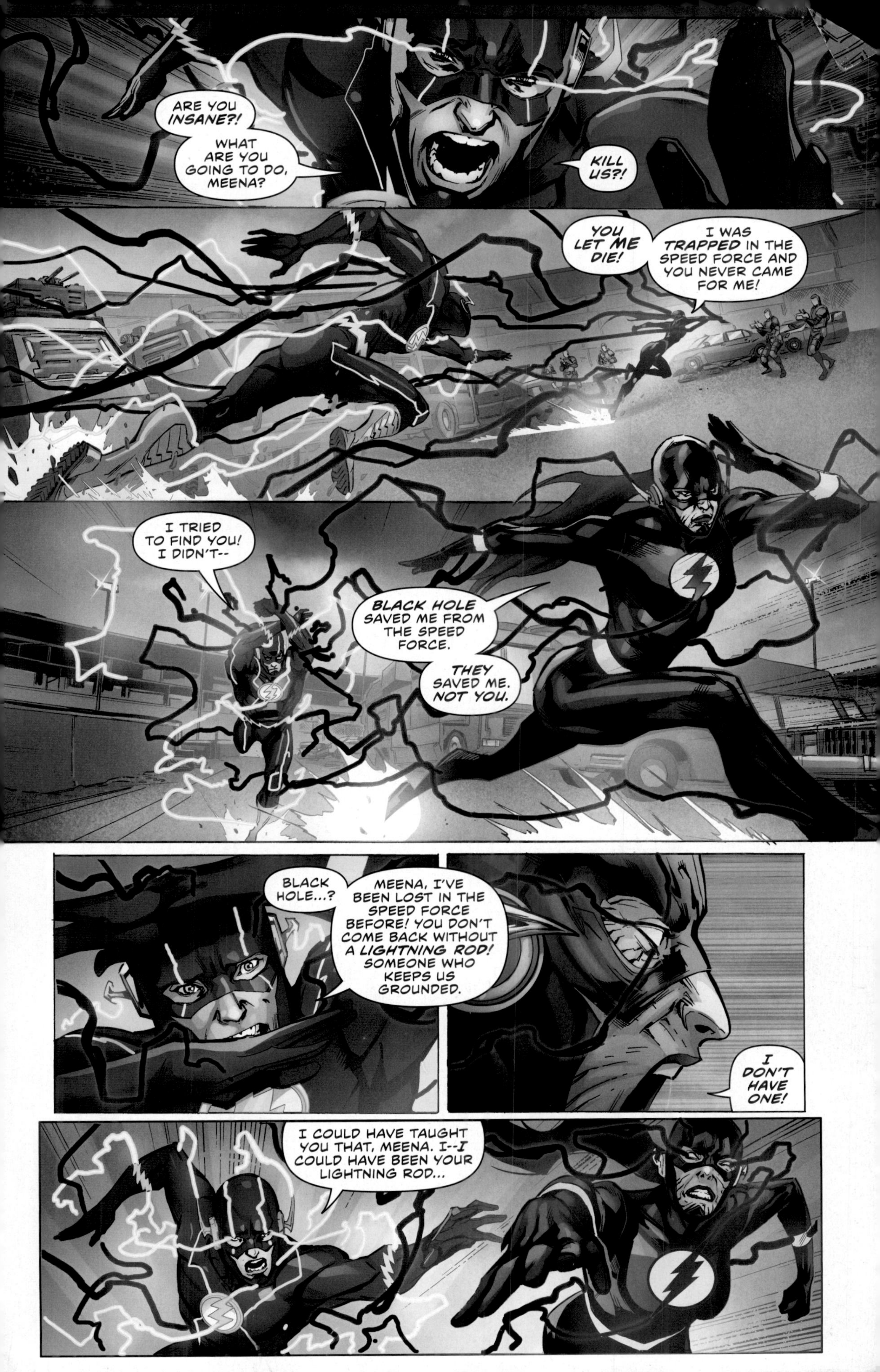
ARE YOU INSANE?!
WHAT ARE YOU GOING TO DO, MEENA?
KILL US?!
YOU LET ME DIE!
I WAS TRAPPED IN THE SPEED FORCE AND YOU NEVER CAME FOR ME!
I TRIED TO FIND YOU! I DIDN'T--
BLACK HOLE SAVED ME FROM THE SPEED FORCE.
THEY SAVED ME. NOT YOU.
BLACK HOLE...?
MEENA, I'VE BEEN LOST IN THE SPEED FORCE BEFORE! YOU DON'T COME BACK WITHOUT A LIGHTNING ROD! SOMEONE WHO KEEPS US GROUNDED.
I DON'T HAVE ONE!
I COULD HAVE TAUGHT YOU THAT, MEENA. I--I COULD HAVE BEEN YOUR LIGHTNING ROD...

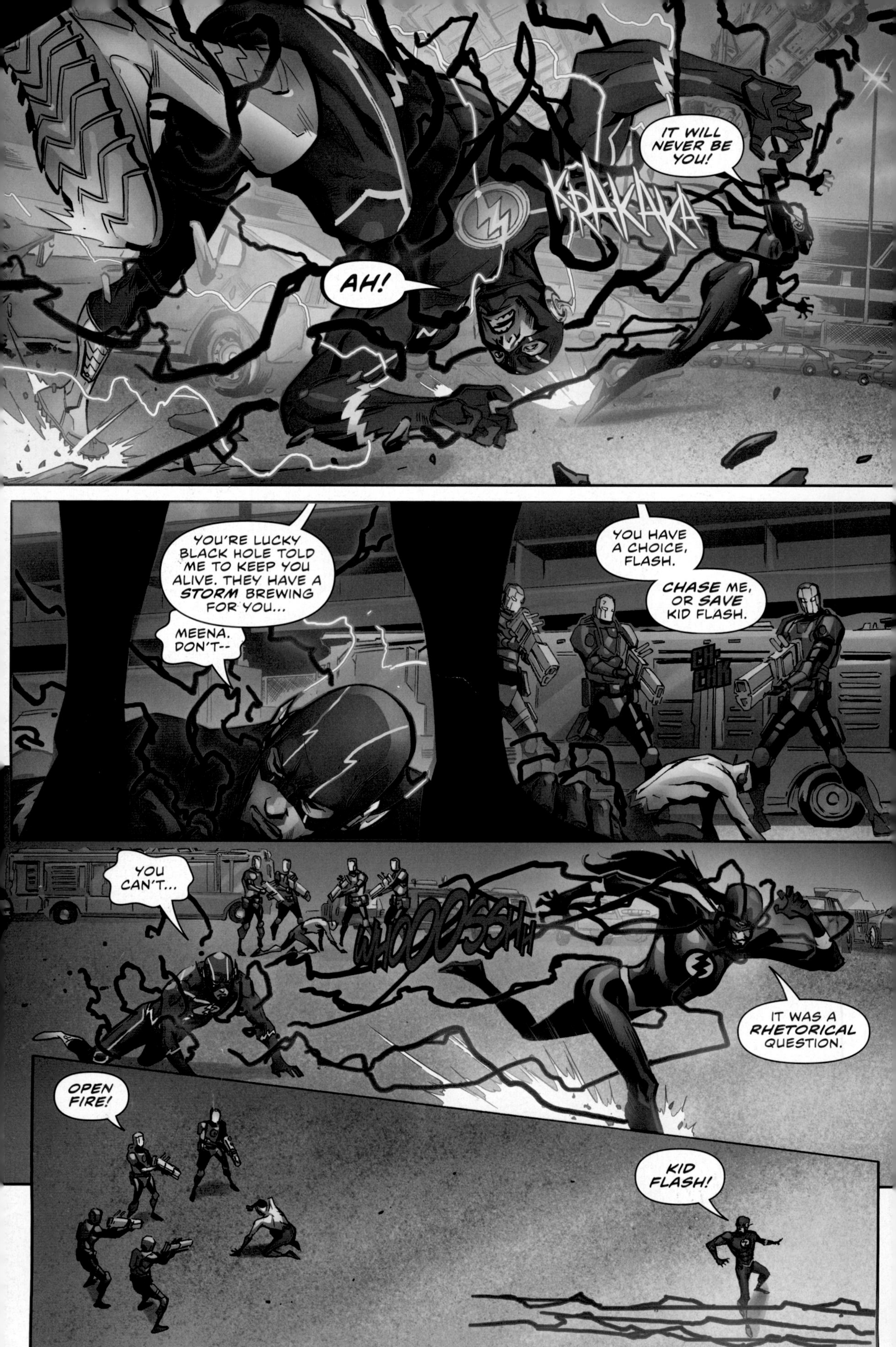
IT WILL NEVER BE YOU!
KRAKAKA
AH!
YOU'RE LUCKY BLACK HOLE TOLD ME TO KEEP YOU ALIVE. THEY HAVE A STORM BREWING FOR YOU...
MEENA. DON'T--
YOU HAVE A CHOICE, FLASH.
CHASE ME, OR SAVE KID FLASH.
YOU CAN'T...
WHOOOOSSHH
IT WAS A RHETORICAL QUESTION.
OPEN FIRE!
KID FLASH!

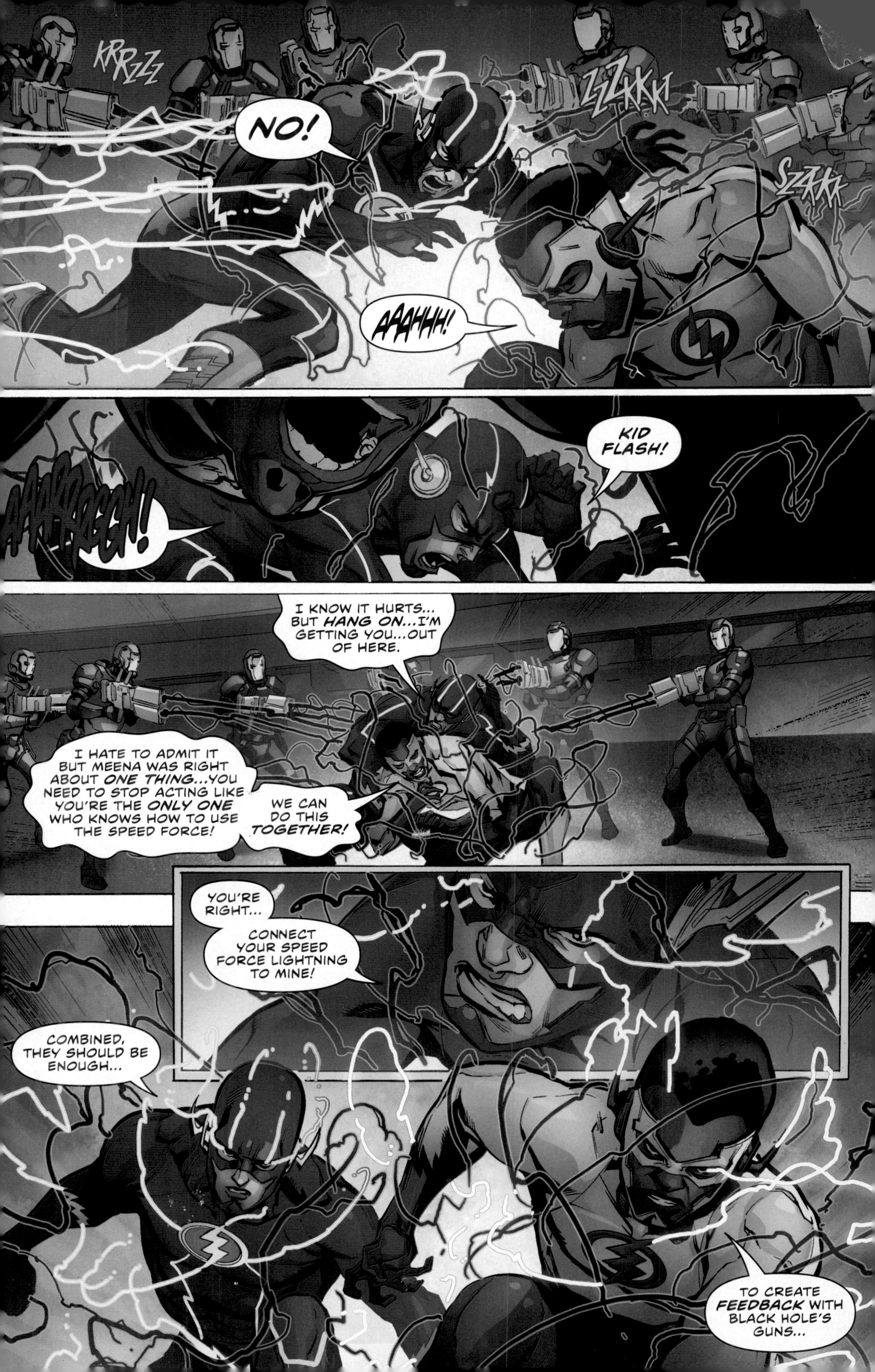
KRRZZZ
NO!
ZZZKKK!
SZZKKK
AAAHHH!
AAARRGGH!
KID FLASH!
I KNOW IT HURTS... BUT HANG ON...I'M GETTING YOU...OUT OF HERE.
I HATE TO ADMIT IT BUT MEENA WAS RIGHT ABOUT ONE THING...YOU NEED TO STOP ACTING LIKE YOU'RE THE ONLY ONE WHO KNOWS HOW TO USE THE SPEED FORCE!
WE CAN DO THIS TOGETHER!
YOU'RE RIGHT...
CONNECT YOUR SPEED FORCE LIGHTNING TO MINE!
COMBINED, THEY SHOULD BE ENOUGH...
TO CREATE FEEDBACK WITH BLACK HOLE'S GUNS...

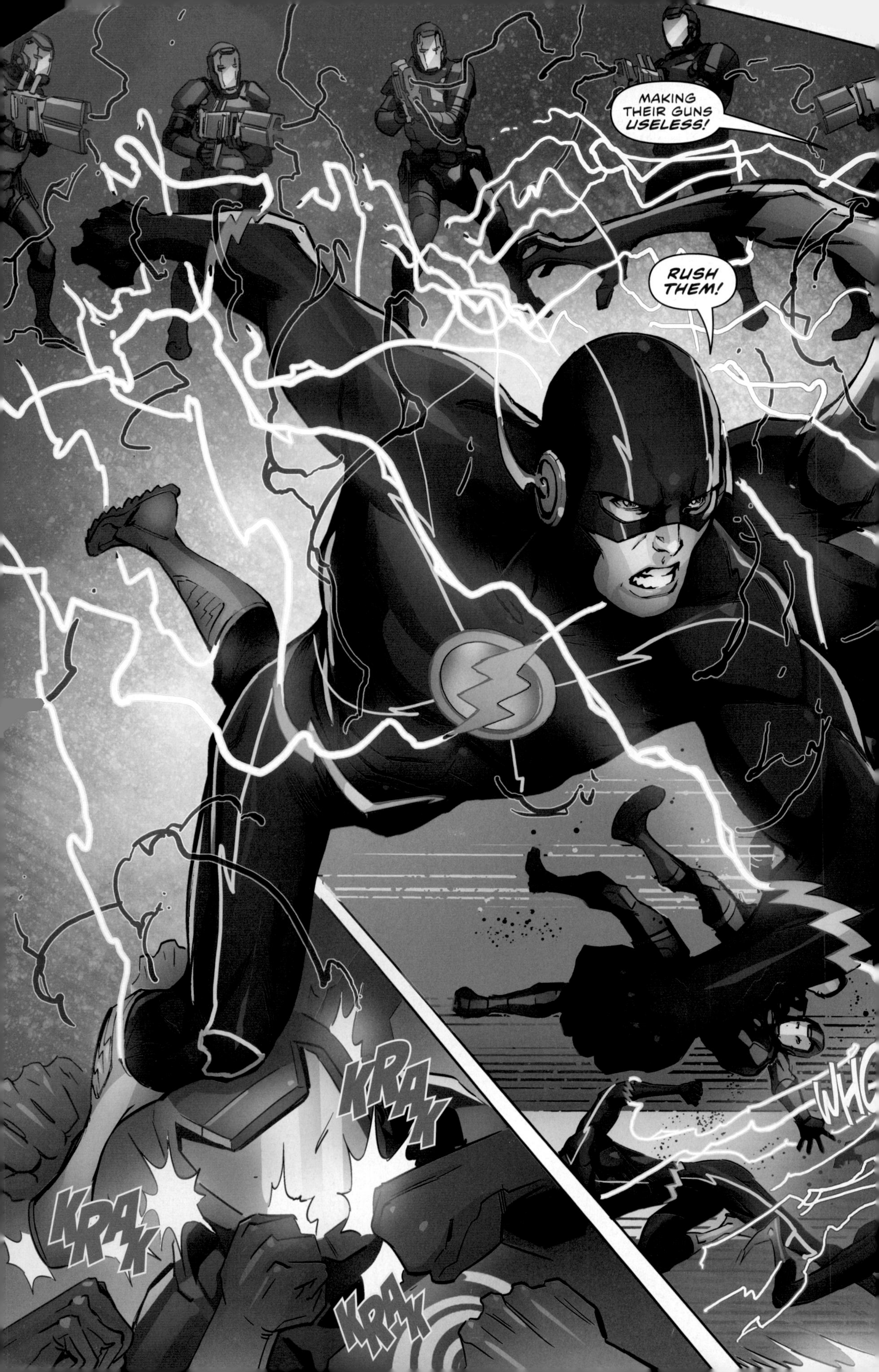
MAKING THEIR GUNS USELESS!
RUSH THEM!
KRAK
KRAK
KRAK

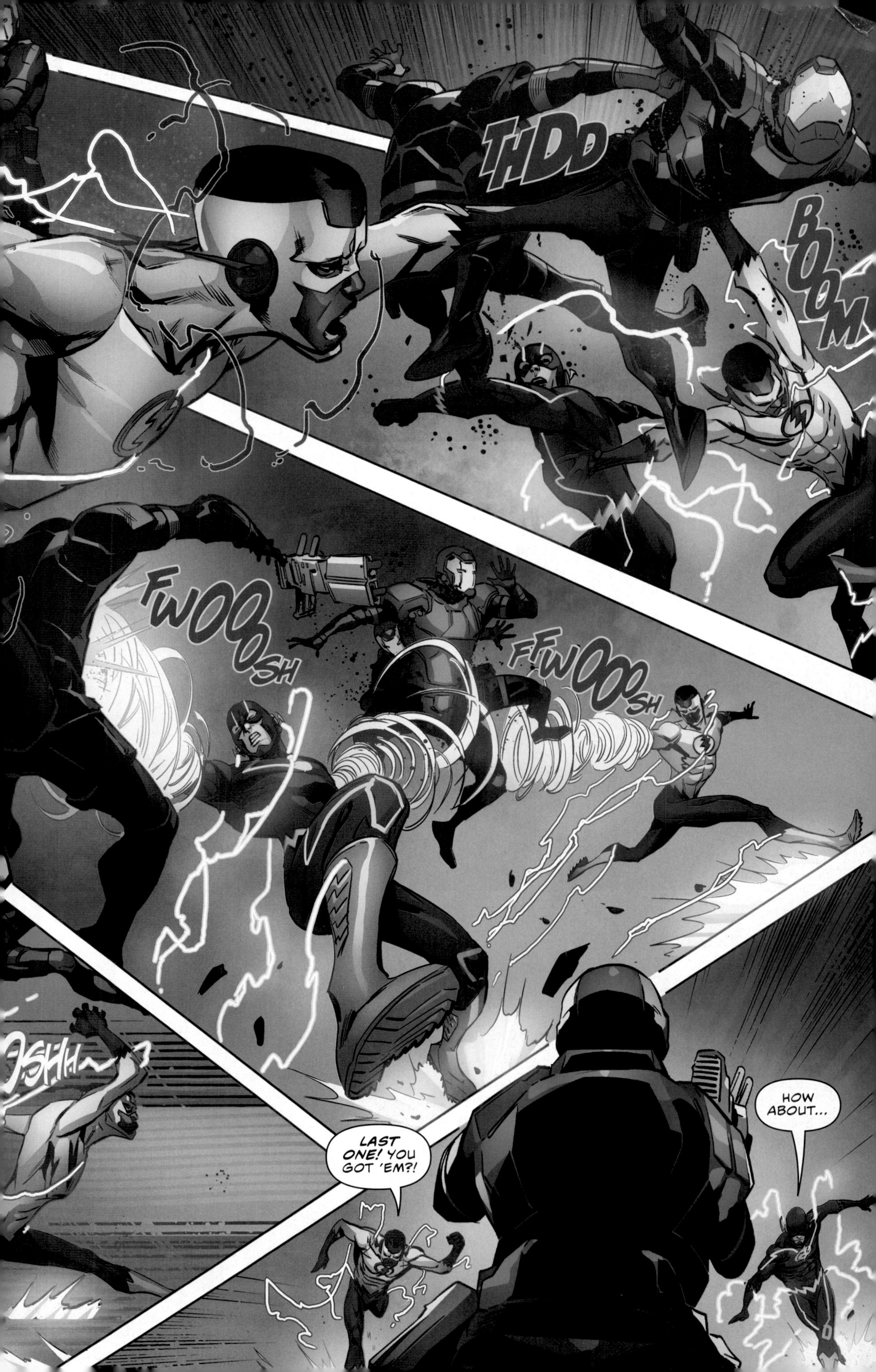
THDD
BOOOM
FWOOOOSH
FFWOOOOSH
OSHH
LAST ONE! YOU GOT 'EM?!
HOW ABOUT...

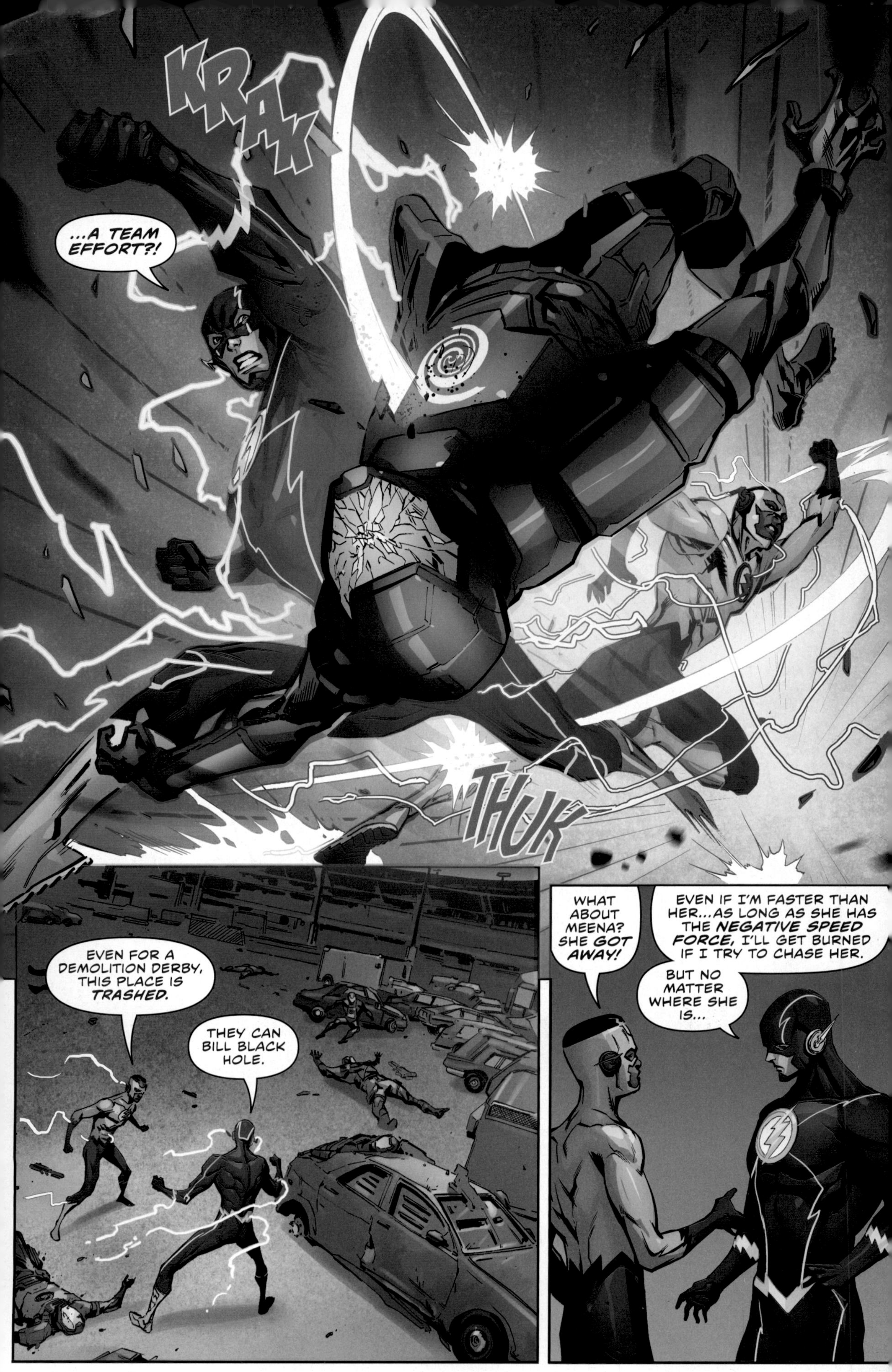
KRAK
...A TEAM EFFORT?!
THUK
EVEN FOR A DEMOLITION DERBY, THIS PLACE IS TRASHED.
THEY CAN BILL BLACK HOLE.
WHAT ABOUT MEENA? SHE GOT AWAY!
EVEN IF I'M FASTER THAN HER...AS LONG AS SHE HAS THE NEGATIVE SPEED FORCE, I'LL GET BURNED IF I TRY TO CHASE HER.
BUT NO MATTER WHERE SHE IS...

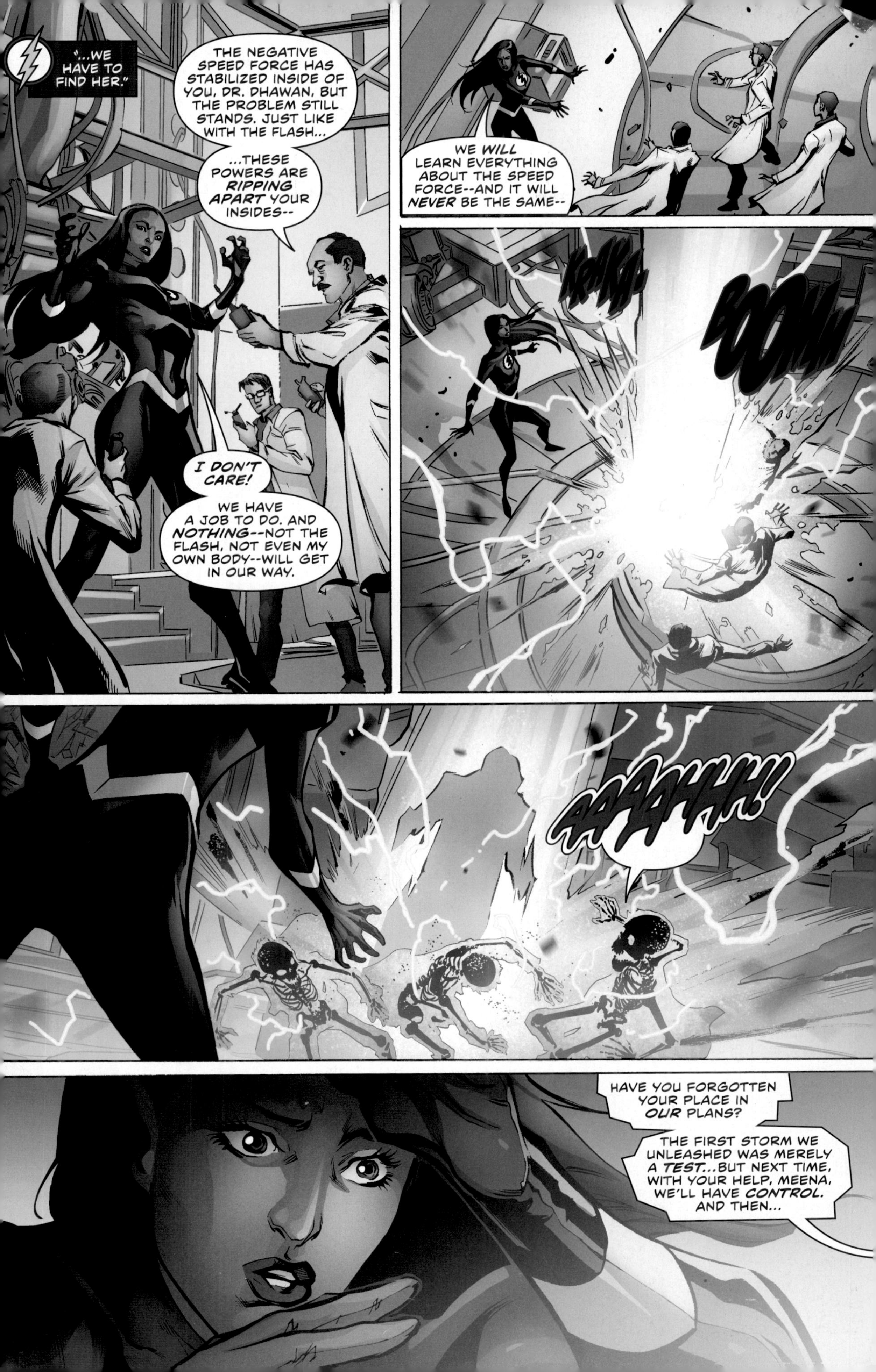
"...WE HAVE TO FIND HER."
THE NEGATIVE SPEED FORCE HAS STABILIZED INSIDE OF YOU, DR. DHAWAN, BUT THE PROBLEM STILL STANDS. JUST LIKE WITH THE FLASH...
...THESE POWERS ARE RIPPING APART YOUR INSIDES--
I DON'T CARE!
WE HAVE A JOB TO DO. AND NOTHING--NOT THE FLASH, NOT EVEN MY OWN BODY--WILL GET IN OUR WAY.
WE WILL LEARN EVERYTHING ABOUT THE SPEED FORCE--AND IT WILL NEVER BE THE SAME--
KRAKA
BOOM
AAAAHHH!
HAVE YOU FORGOTTEN YOUR PLACE IN OUR PLANS?
THE FIRST STORM WE UNLEASHED WAS MERELY A TEST...BUT NEXT TIME, WITH YOUR HELP, MEENA, WE'LL HAVE CONTROL. AND THEN...

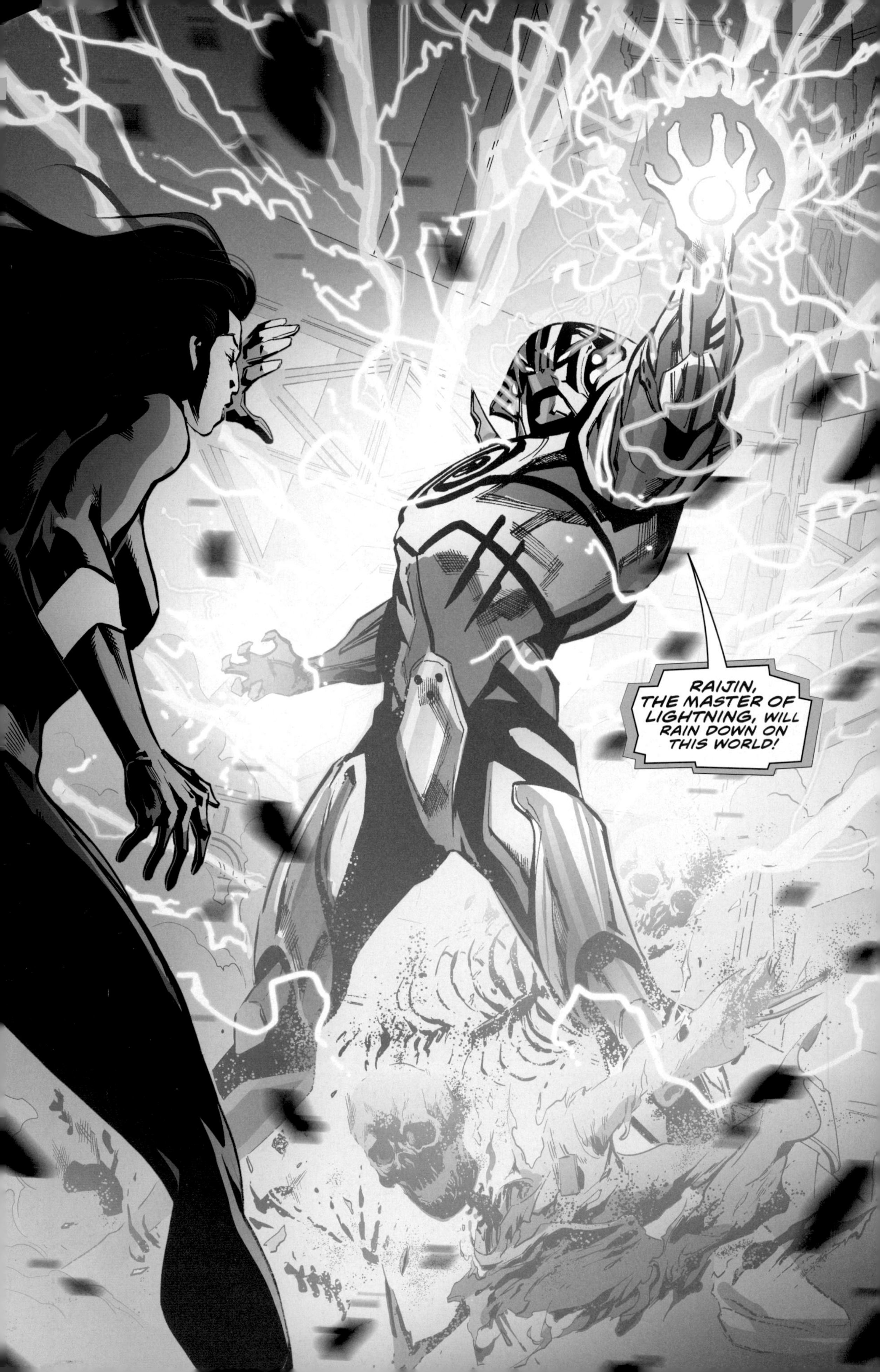
RAIJIN, THE MASTER OF LIGHTNING, WILL RAIN DOWN ON THIS WORLD!

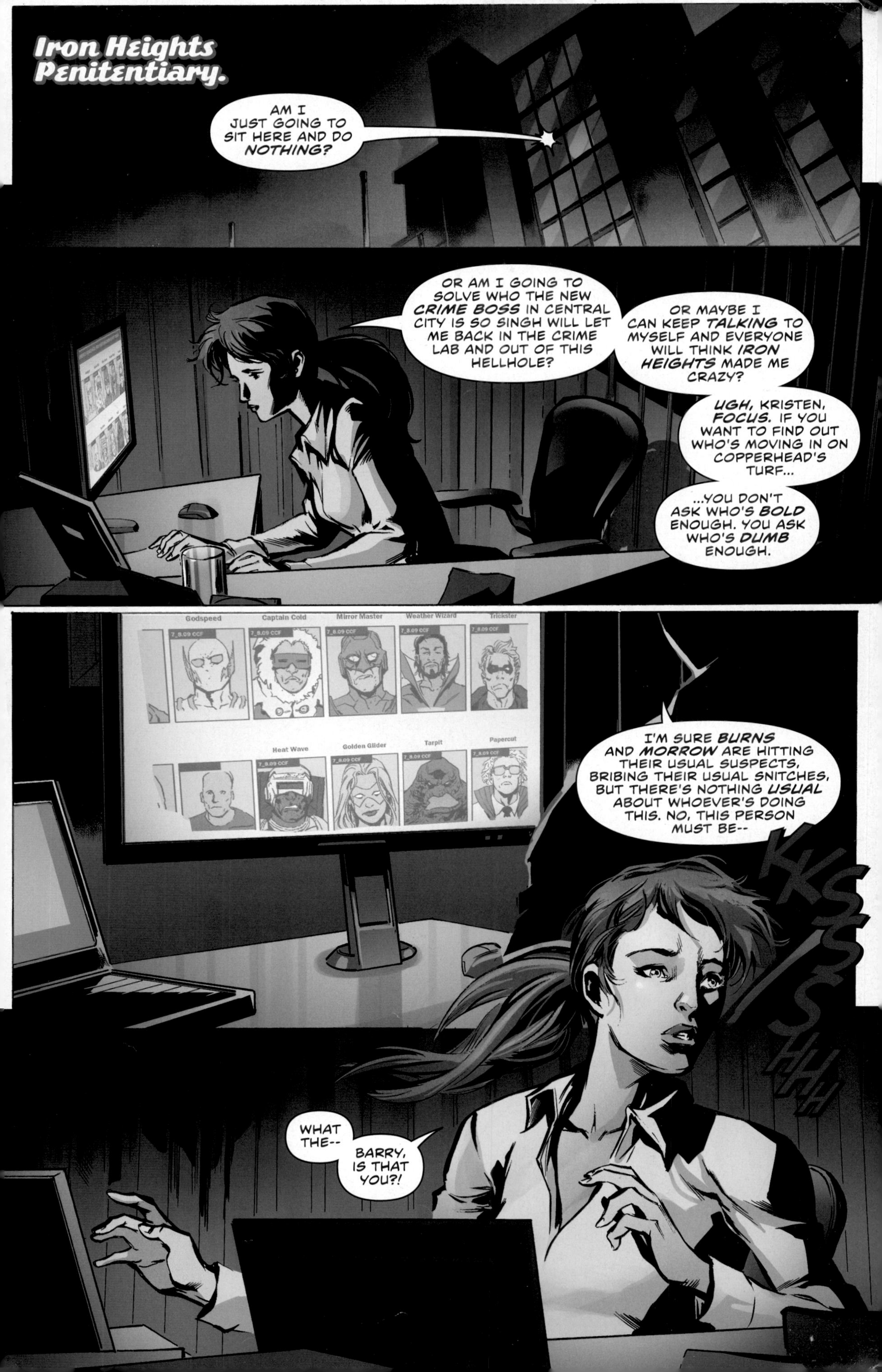
Iron Heights Penitentiary.
AM I JUST GOING TO SIT HERE AND DO NOTHING?
OR AM I GOING TO SOLVE WHO THE NEW CRIME BOSS IN CENTRAL CITY IS SO SINGH WILL LET ME BACK IN THE CRIME LAB AND OUT OF THIS HELLHOLE?
OR MAYBE I CAN KEEP TALKING TO MYSELF AND EVERYONE WILL THINK IRON HEIGHTS MADE ME CRAZY?
UGH, KRISTEN, FOCUS. IF YOU WANT TO FIND OUT WHO'S MOVING IN ON COPPERHEAD'S TURF...
...YOU DON'T ASK WHO'S BOLD ENOUGH. YOU ASK WHO'S DUMB ENOUGH.
Godspeed
Captain Cold
Mirror Master
Weather Wizard
Trickster
Heat Wave
Golden Glider
Tarpit
Papercut
I'M SURE BURNS AND MORROW ARE HITTING THEIR USUAL SUSPECTS, BRIBING THEIR USUAL SNITCHES, BUT THERE'S NOTHING USUAL ABOUT WHOEVER'S DOING THIS. NO, THIS PERSON MUST BE--
KKSSSHHH
WHAT THE--
BARRY, IS THAT YOU?!

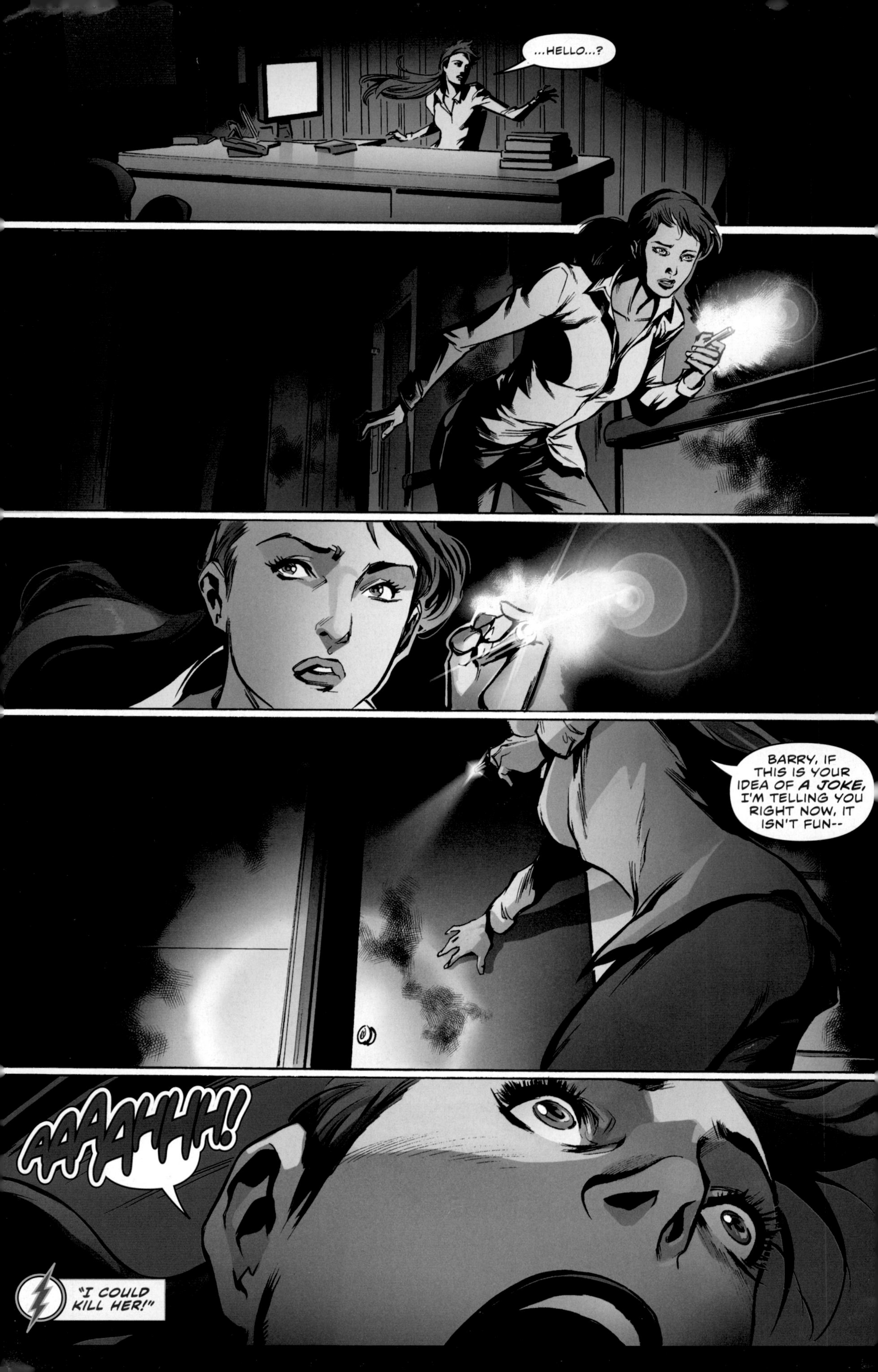
...HELLO...?
BARRY, IF THIS IS YOUR IDEA OF A JOKE, I'M TELLING YOU RIGHT NOW, IT ISN'T FUN--
AAAAHHH!
"I COULD KILL HER!"

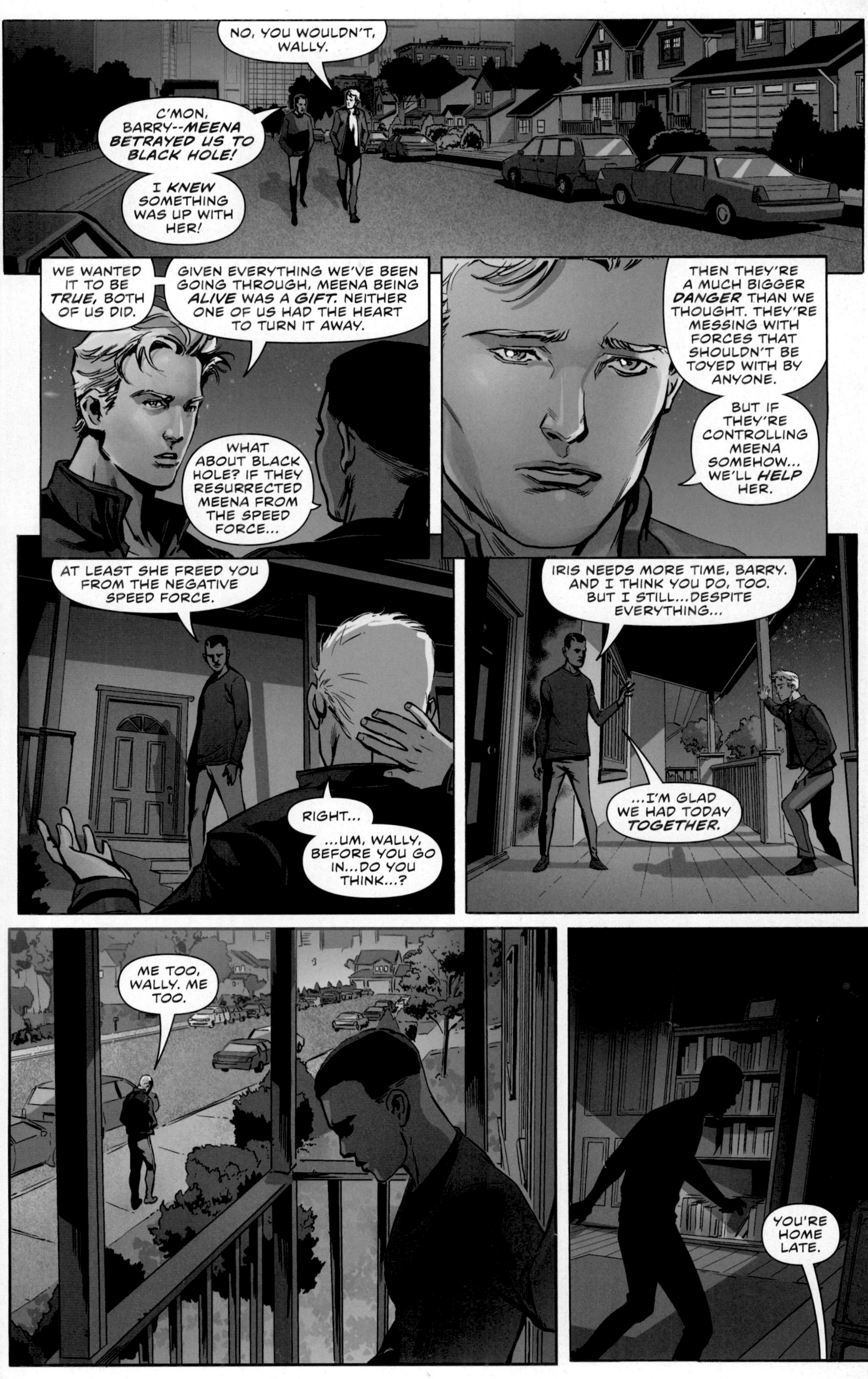
NO, YOU WOULDN'T, WALLY.
C'MON, BARRY--MEENA BETRAYED US TO BLACK HOLE!
I KNEW SOMETHING WAS UP WITH HER!
WE WANTED IT TO BE TRUE, BOTH OF US DID.
GIVEN EVERYTHING WE'VE BEEN GOING THROUGH, MEENA BEING ALIVE WAS A GIFT. NEITHER ONE OF US HAD THE HEART TO TURN IT AWAY.
WHAT ABOUT BLACK HOLE? IF THEY RESURRECTED MEENA FROM THE SPEED FORCE...
THEN THEY'RE A MUCH BIGGER DANGER THAN WE THOUGHT. THEY'RE MESSING WITH FORCES THAT SHOULDN'T BE TOYED WITH BY ANYONE.
BUT IF THEY'RE CONTROLLING MEENA SOMEHOW... WE'LL HELP HER.
AT LEAST SHE FREED YOU FROM THE NEGATIVE SPEED FORCE.
RIGHT...
...UM, WALLY, BEFORE YOU GO IN...DO YOU THINK...?
IRIS NEEDS MORE TIME, BARRY. AND I THINK YOU DO, TOO. BUT I STILL...DESPITE EVERYTHING...
...I'M GLAD WE HAD TODAY TOGETHER.
ME TOO, WALLY. ME TOO.
YOU'RE HOME LATE.

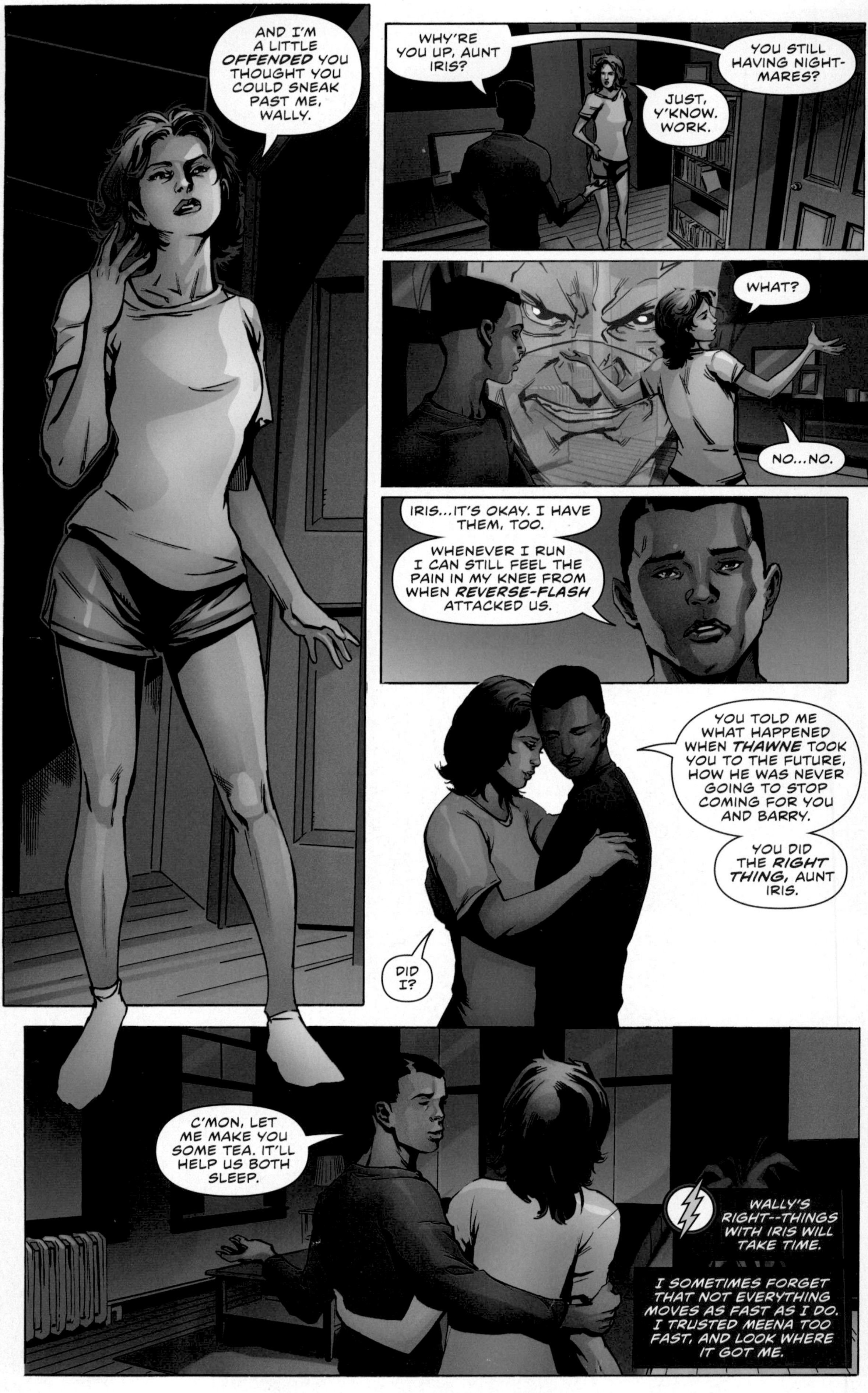
AND I'M A LITTLE OFFENDED YOU THOUGHT YOU COULD SNEAK PAST ME, WALLY.
WHY'RE YOU UP, AUNT IRIS?
YOU STILL HAVING NIGHT-MARES?
JUST, Y'KNOW. WORK.
WHAT?
NO...NO.
IRIS...IT'S OKAY. I HAVE THEM, TOO.
WHENEVER I RUN I CAN STILL FEEL THE PAIN IN MY KNEE FROM WHEN REVERSE-FLASH ATTACKED US.
YOU TOLD ME WHAT HAPPENED WHEN THAWNE TOOK YOU TO THE FUTURE, HOW HE WAS NEVER GOING TO STOP COMING FOR YOU AND BARRY.
YOU DID THE RIGHT THING, AUNT IRIS.
DID I?
C'MON, LET ME MAKE YOU SOME TEA. IT'LL HELP US BOTH SLEEP.
WALLY'S RIGHT--THINGS WITH IRIS WILL TAKE TIME.
I SOMETIMES FORGET THAT NOT EVERYTHING MOVES AS FAST AS I DO. I TRUSTED MEENA TOO FAST, AND LOOK WHERE IT GOT ME.

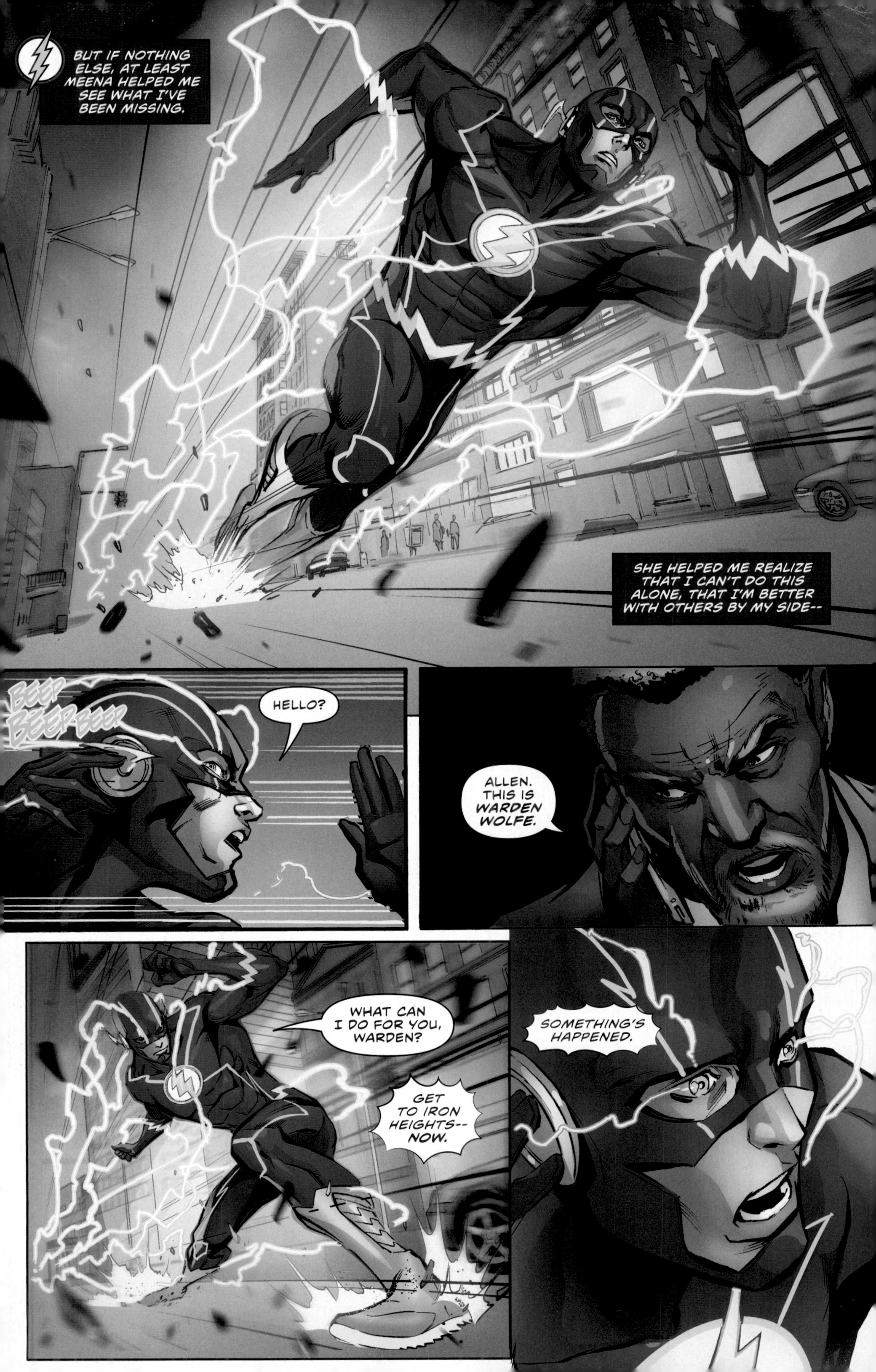
BUT IF NOTHING ELSE, AT LEAST MEENA HELPED ME SEE WHAT I'VE BEEN MISSING.
SHE HELPED ME REALIZE THAT I CAN'T DO THIS ALONE, THAT I'M BETTER WITH OTHERS BY MY SIDE--
BEEP BEEP BEEP
HELLO?
ALLEN. THIS IS WARDEN WOLFE.
WHAT CAN I DO FOR YOU, WARDEN?
GET TO IRON HEIGHTS-- NOW.
SOMETHING'S HAPPENED.

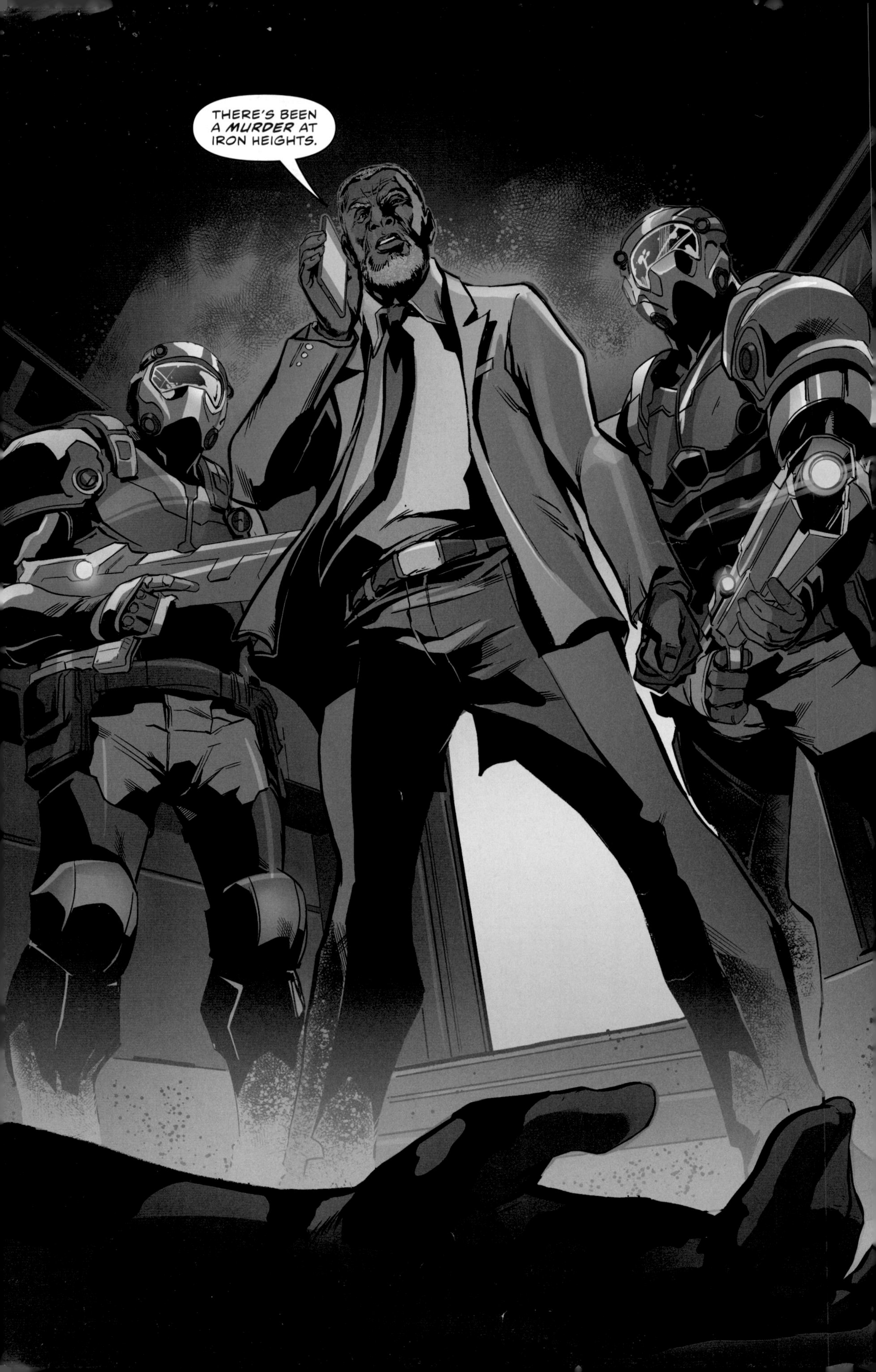
THERE'S BEEN A *MURDER* AT IRON HEIGHTS.

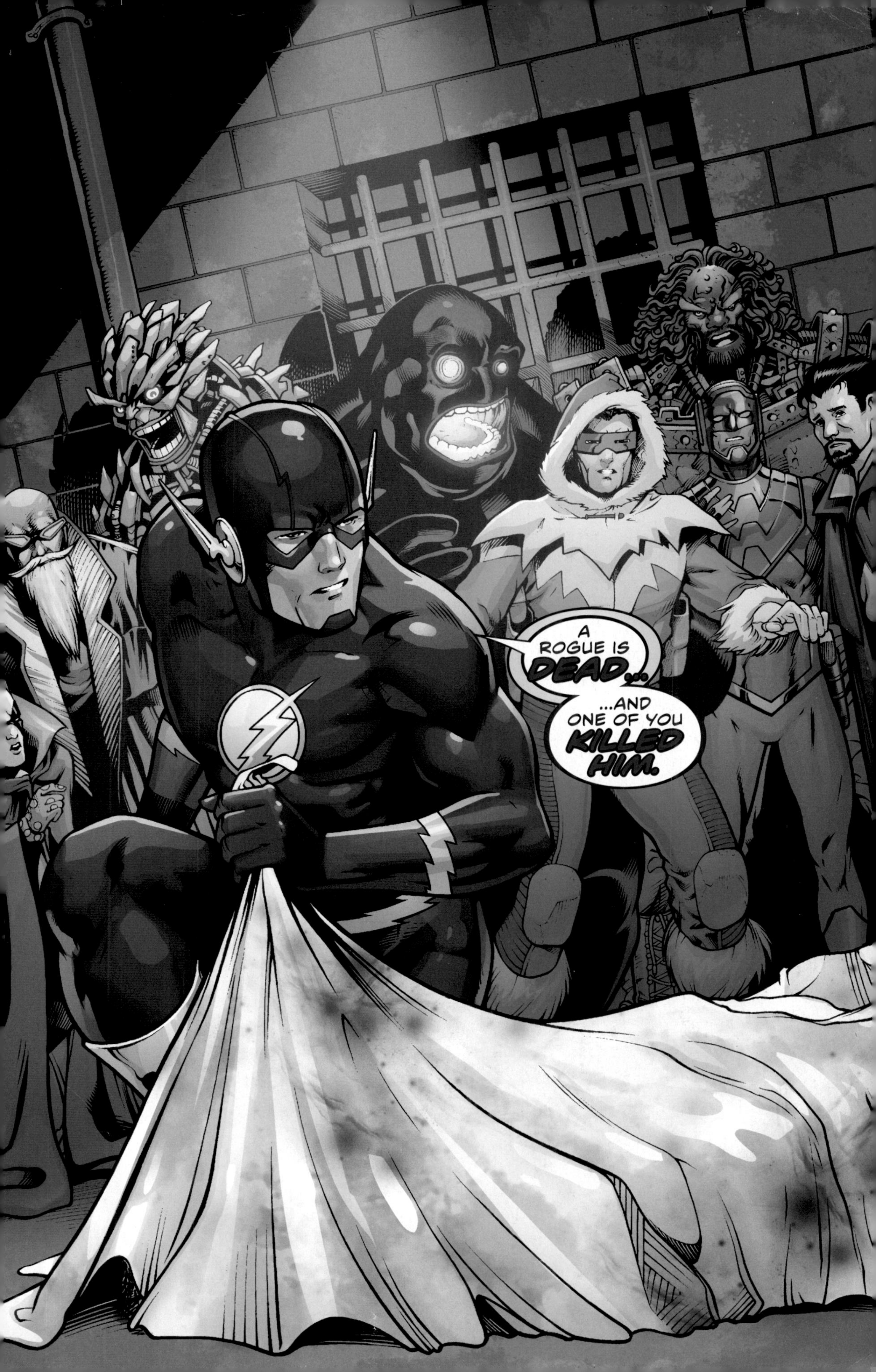
A ROGUE IS DEAD...
...AND ONE OF YOU KILLED HIM.

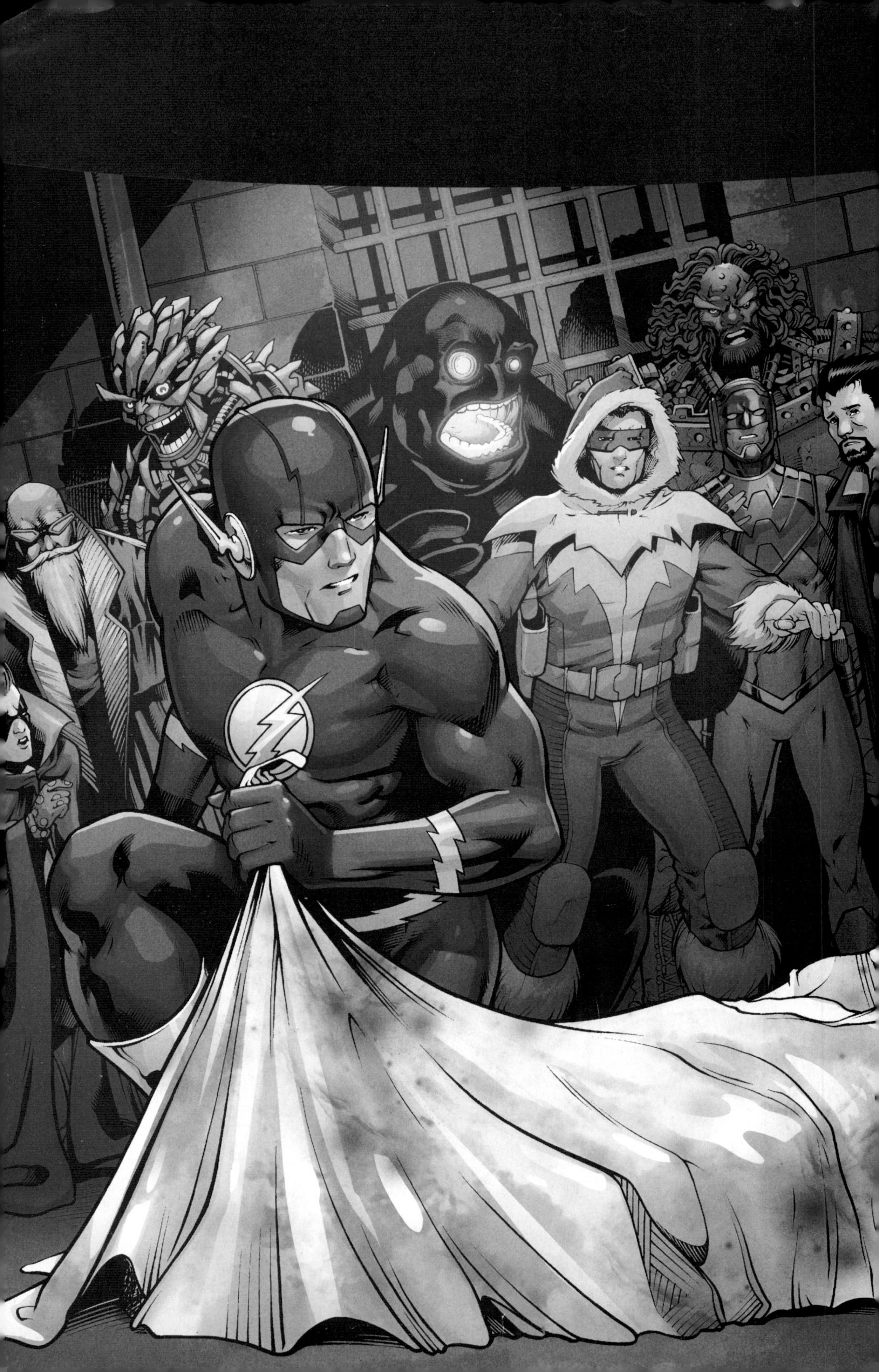

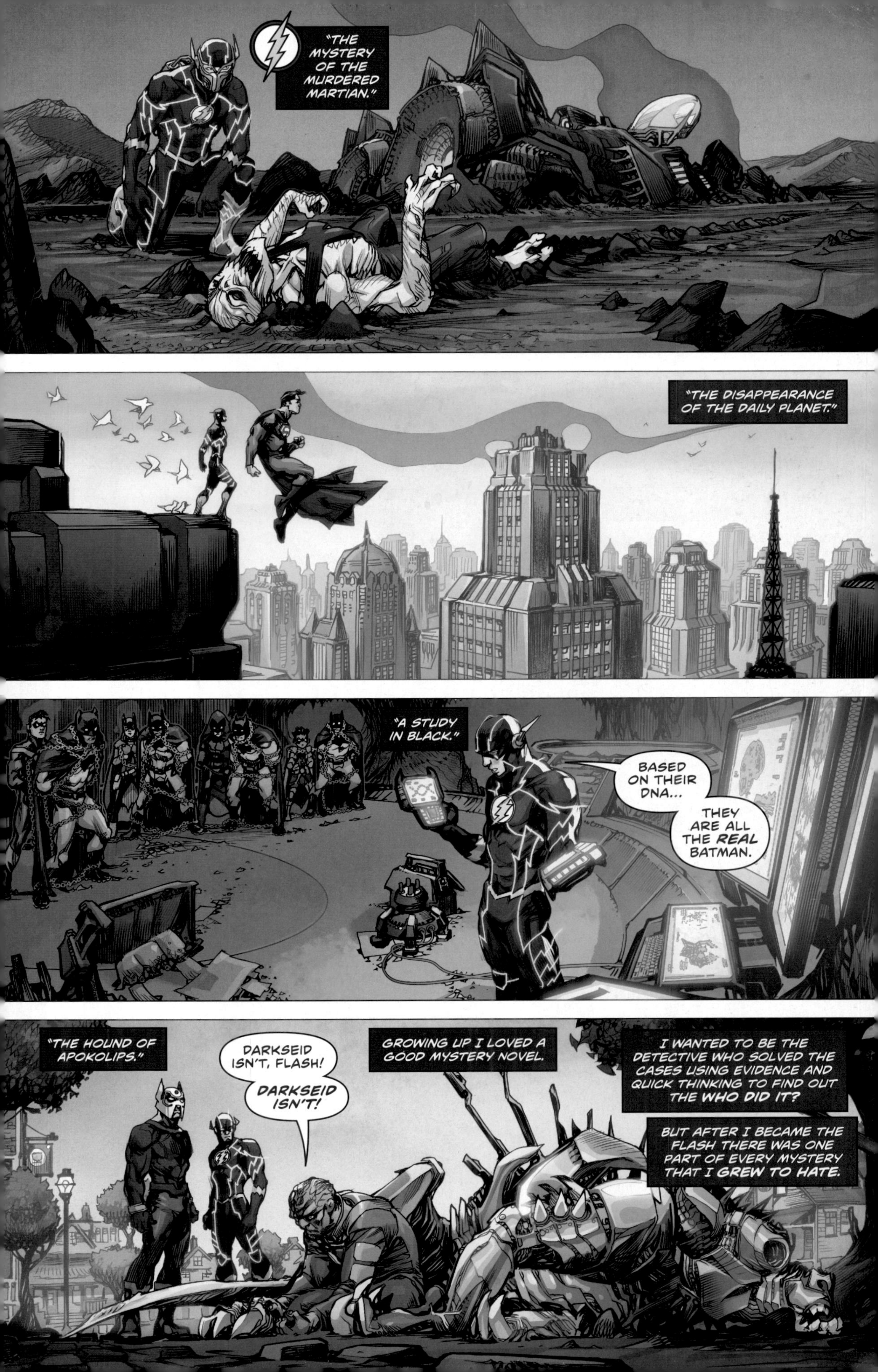
"THE MYSTERY OF THE MURDERED MARTIAN."
"THE DISAPPEARANCE OF THE DAILY PLANET."
"A STUDY IN BLACK."
BASED ON THEIR DNA...
THEY ARE ALL THE REAL BATMAN.
"THE HOUND OF APOKOLIPS."
DARKSEID ISN'T, FLASH!
DARKSEID ISN'T!
GROWING UP I LOVED A GOOD MYSTERY NOVEL.
I WANTED TO BE THE DETECTIVE WHO SOLVED THE CASES USING EVIDENCE AND QUICK THINKING TO FIND OUT THE WHO DID IT?
BUT AFTER I BECAME THE FLASH THERE WAS ONE PART OF EVERY MYSTERY THAT I GREW TO HATE.

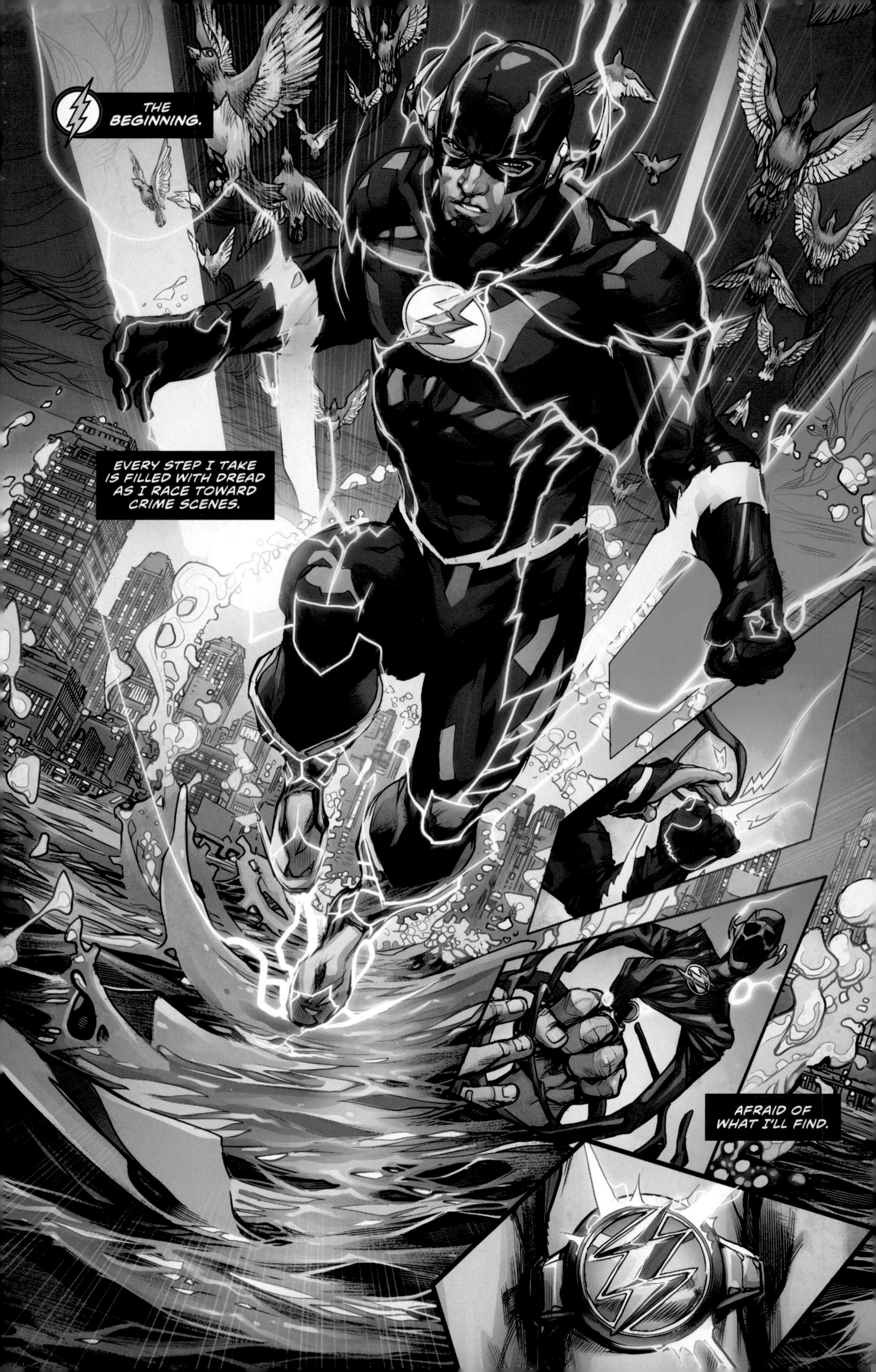
THE BEGINNING.
EVERY STEP I TAKE IS FILLED WITH DREAD AS I RACE TOWARD CRIME SCENES.
AFRAID OF WHAT I'LL FIND.

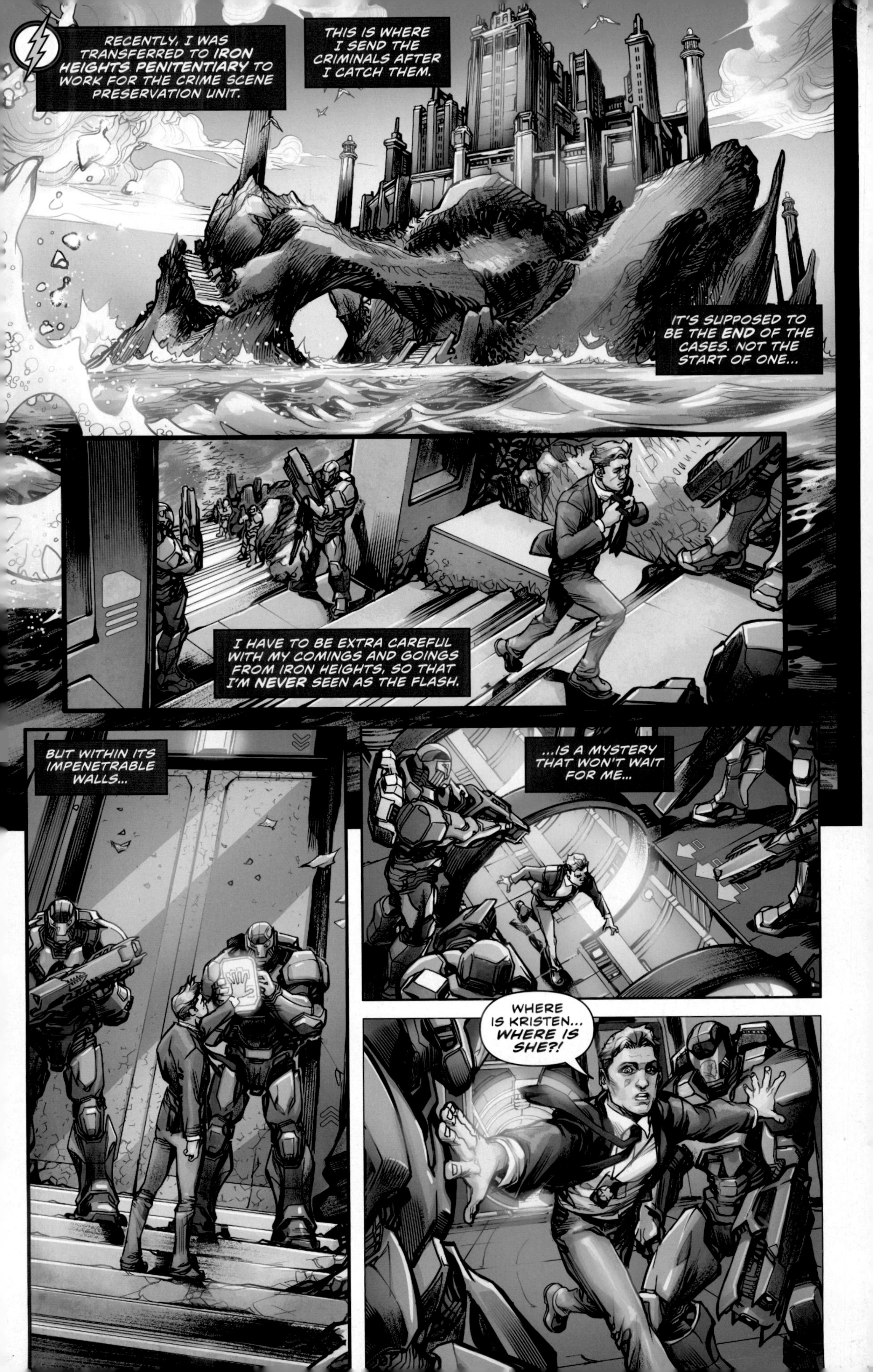
RECENTLY, I WAS TRANSFERRED TO IRON HEIGHTS PENITENTIARY TO WORK FOR THE CRIME SCENE PRESERVATION UNIT.
THIS IS WHERE I SEND THE CRIMINALS AFTER I CATCH THEM.
IT'S SUPPOSED TO BE THE END OF THE CASES. NOT THE START OF ONE...
I HAVE TO BE EXTRA CAREFUL WITH MY COMINGS AND GOINGS FROM IRON HEIGHTS, SO THAT I'M NEVER SEEN AS THE FLASH.
BUT WITHIN ITS IMPENETRABLE WALLS...
...IS A MYSTERY THAT WON'T WAIT FOR ME...
WHERE IS KRISTEN... WHERE IS SHE?!

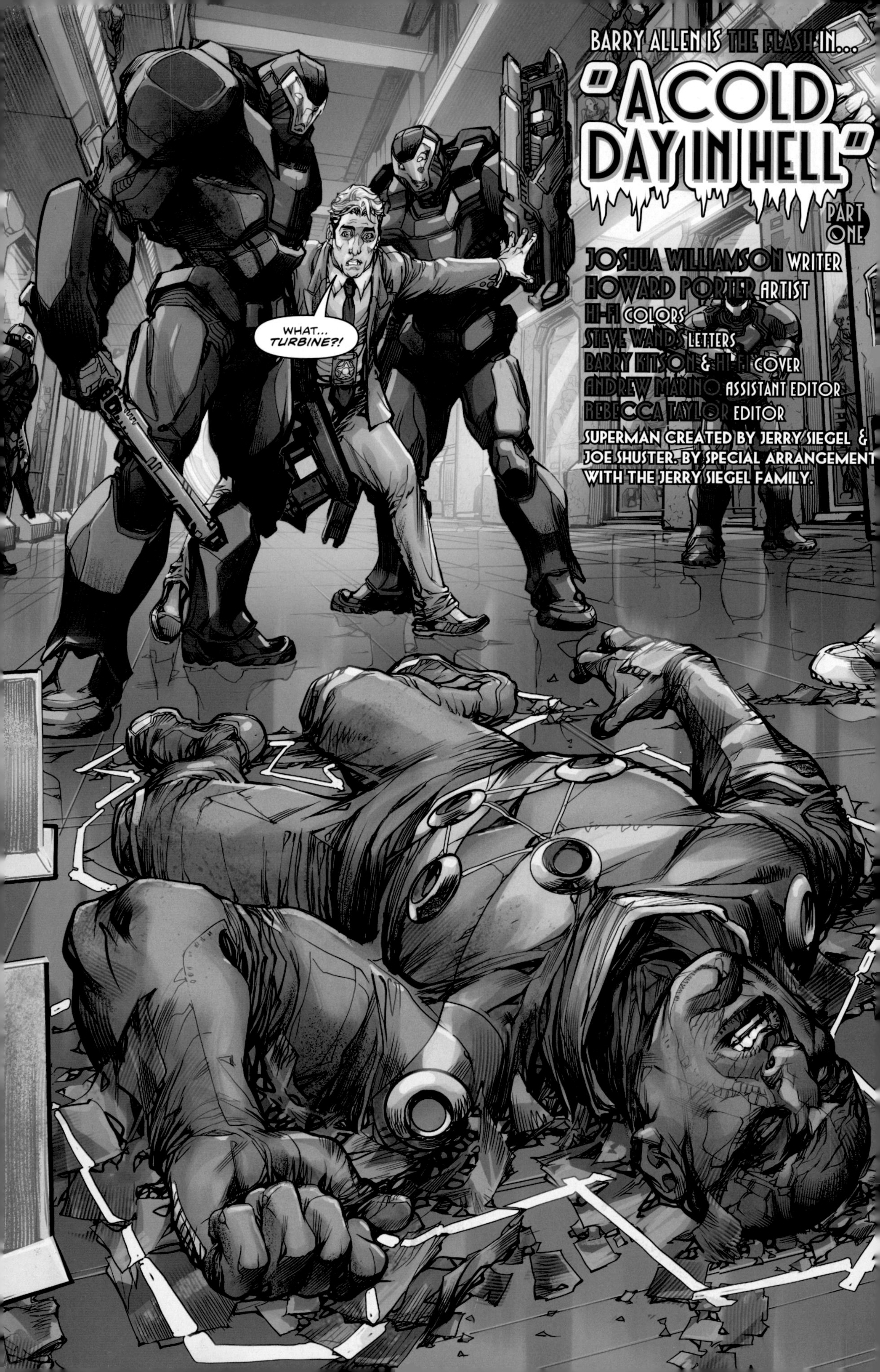
BARRY ALLEN IS THE FLASH IN...
"A COLD DAY IN HELL"
PART ONE
JOSHUA WILLIAMSON WRITER
HOWARD PORTER ARTIST
HI-FI COLORS
STEVE WANDS LETTERS
BARRY KITSON & HI-FI COVER
ANDREW MARINO ASSISTANT EDITOR
REBECCA TAYLOR EDITOR
SUPERMAN CREATED BY JERRY SIEGEL & JOE SHUSTER. BY SPECIAL ARRANGEMENT WITH THE JERRY SIEGEL FAMILY.
WHAT... TURBINE?!

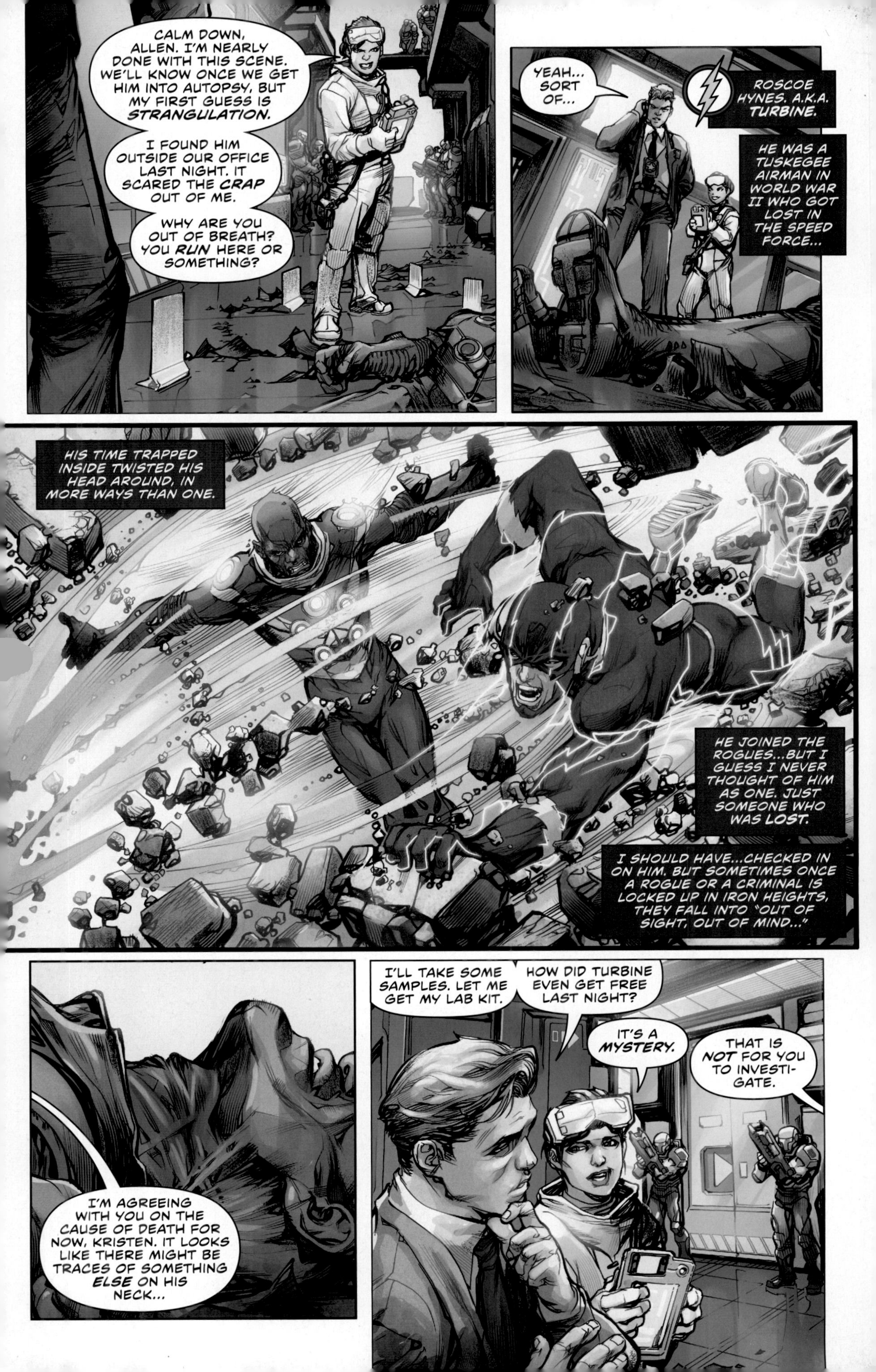
CALM DOWN, ALLEN. I'M NEARLY DONE WITH THIS SCENE. WE'LL KNOW ONCE WE GET HIM INTO AUTOPSY, BUT MY FIRST GUESS IS STRANGULATION.
I FOUND HIM OUTSIDE OUR OFFICE LAST NIGHT. IT SCARED THE CRAP OUT OF ME.
WHY ARE YOU OUT OF BREATH? YOU RUN HERE OR SOMETHING?
YEAH... SORT OF...
ROSCOE HYNES. A.K.A. TURBINE.
HE WAS A TUSKEGEE AIRMAN IN WORLD WAR II WHO GOT LOST IN THE SPEED FORCE...
HIS TIME TRAPPED INSIDE TWISTED HIS HEAD AROUND, IN MORE WAYS THAN ONE.
HE JOINED THE ROGUES...BUT I GUESS I NEVER THOUGHT OF HIM AS ONE. JUST SOMEONE WHO WAS LOST.
I SHOULD HAVE...CHECKED IN ON HIM. BUT SOMETIMES ONCE A ROGUE OR A CRIMINAL IS LOCKED UP IN IRON HEIGHTS, THEY FALL INTO "OUT OF SIGHT, OUT OF MIND..."
I'M AGREEING WITH YOU ON THE CAUSE OF DEATH FOR NOW, KRISTEN. IT LOOKS LIKE THERE MIGHT BE TRACES OF SOMETHING ELSE ON HIS NECK...
I'LL TAKE SOME SAMPLES. LET ME GET MY LAB KIT.
HOW DID TURBINE EVEN GET FREE LAST NIGHT?
IT'S A MYSTERY.
THAT IS NOT FOR YOU TO INVESTI-GATE.

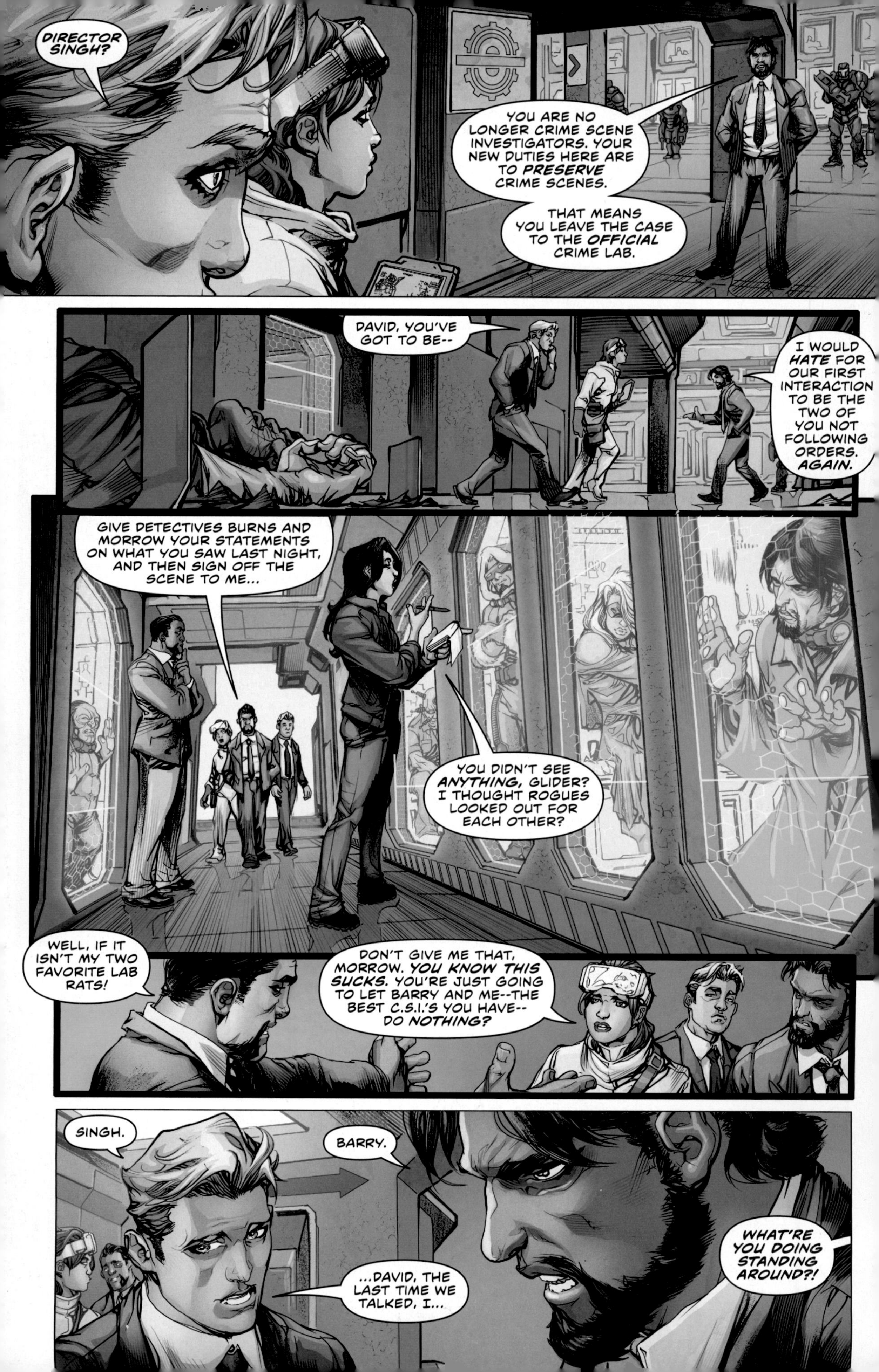
DIRECTOR SINGH?
YOU ARE NO LONGER CRIME SCENE INVESTIGATORS. YOUR NEW DUTIES HERE ARE TO PRESERVE CRIME SCENES.
THAT MEANS YOU LEAVE THE CASE TO THE OFFICIAL CRIME LAB.
DAVID, YOU'VE GOT TO BE--
I WOULD HATE FOR OUR FIRST INTERACTION TO BE THE TWO OF YOU NOT FOLLOWING ORDERS. AGAIN.
GIVE DETECTIVES BURNS AND MORROW YOUR STATEMENTS ON WHAT YOU SAW LAST NIGHT, AND THEN SIGN OFF THE SCENE TO ME...
YOU DIDN'T SEE ANYTHING, GLIDER? I THOUGHT ROGUES LOOKED OUT FOR EACH OTHER?
WELL, IF IT ISN'T MY TWO FAVORITE LAB RATS!
DON'T GIVE ME THAT, MORROW. YOU KNOW THIS SUCKS. YOU'RE JUST GOING TO LET BARRY AND ME--THE BEST C.S.I.'S YOU HAVE--DO NOTHING?
SINGH.
BARRY.
...DAVID, THE LAST TIME WE TALKED, I...
WHAT'RE YOU DOING STANDING AROUND?!

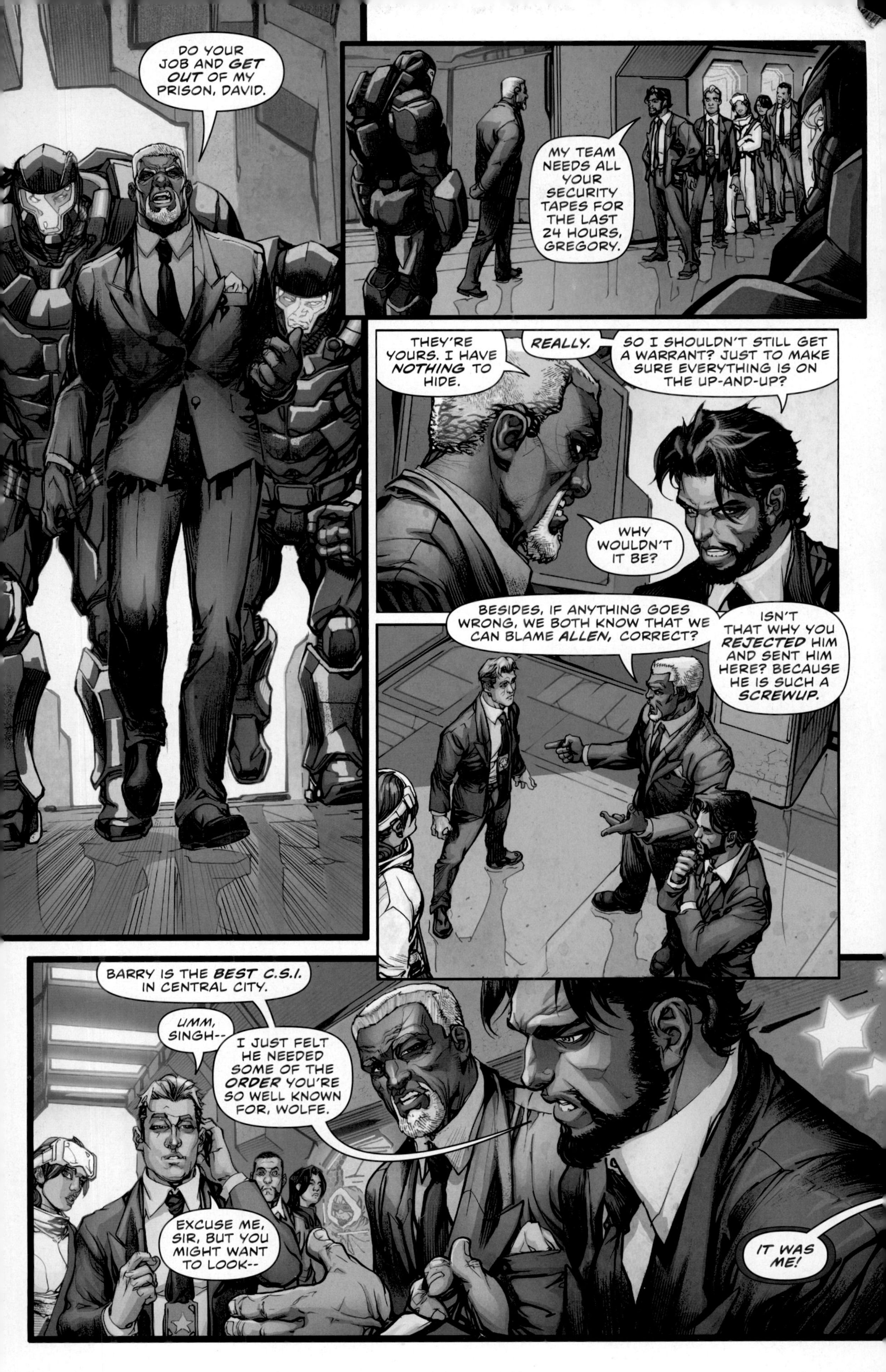
DO YOUR JOB AND GET OUT OF MY PRISON, DAVID.
MY TEAM NEEDS ALL YOUR SECURITY TAPES FOR THE LAST 24 HOURS, GREGORY.
THEY'RE YOURS. I HAVE NOTHING TO HIDE.
REALLY.
SO I SHOULDN'T STILL GET A WARRANT? JUST TO MAKE SURE EVERYTHING IS ON THE UP-AND-UP?
WHY WOULDN'T IT BE?
BESIDES, IF ANYTHING GOES WRONG, WE BOTH KNOW THAT WE CAN BLAME ALLEN, CORRECT?
ISN'T THAT WHY YOU REJECTED HIM AND SENT HIM HERE? BECAUSE HE IS SUCH A SCREWUP.
BARRY IS THE BEST C.S.I. IN CENTRAL CITY.
UMM, SINGH--
I JUST FELT HE NEEDED SOME OF THE ORDER YOU'RE SO WELL KNOWN FOR, WOLFE.
EXCUSE ME, SIR, BUT YOU MIGHT WANT TO LOOK--
IT WAS ME!

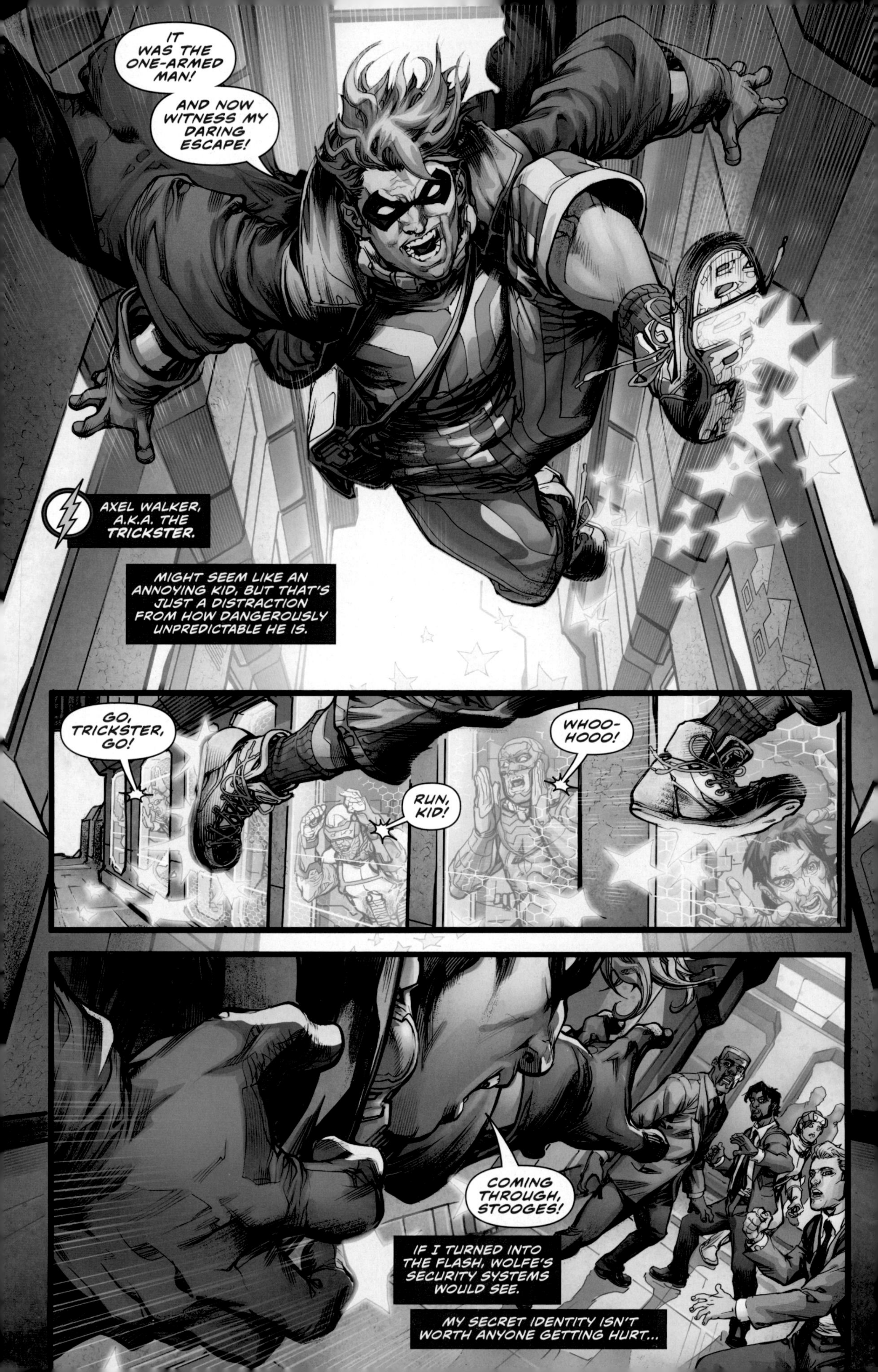
IT WAS THE ONE-ARMED MAN!
AND NOW WITNESS MY DARING ESCAPE!
AXEL WALKER, A.K.A. THE TRICKSTER.
MIGHT SEEM LIKE AN ANNOYING KID, BUT THAT'S JUST A DISTRACTION FROM HOW DANGEROUSLY UNPREDICTABLE HE IS.
GO, TRICKSTER, GO!
RUN, KID!
WHOO-HOOO!
COMING THROUGH, STOOGES!
IF I TURNED INTO THE FLASH, WOLFE'S SECURITY SYSTEMS WOULD SEE.
MY SECRET IDENTITY ISN'T WORTH ANYONE GETTING HURT...

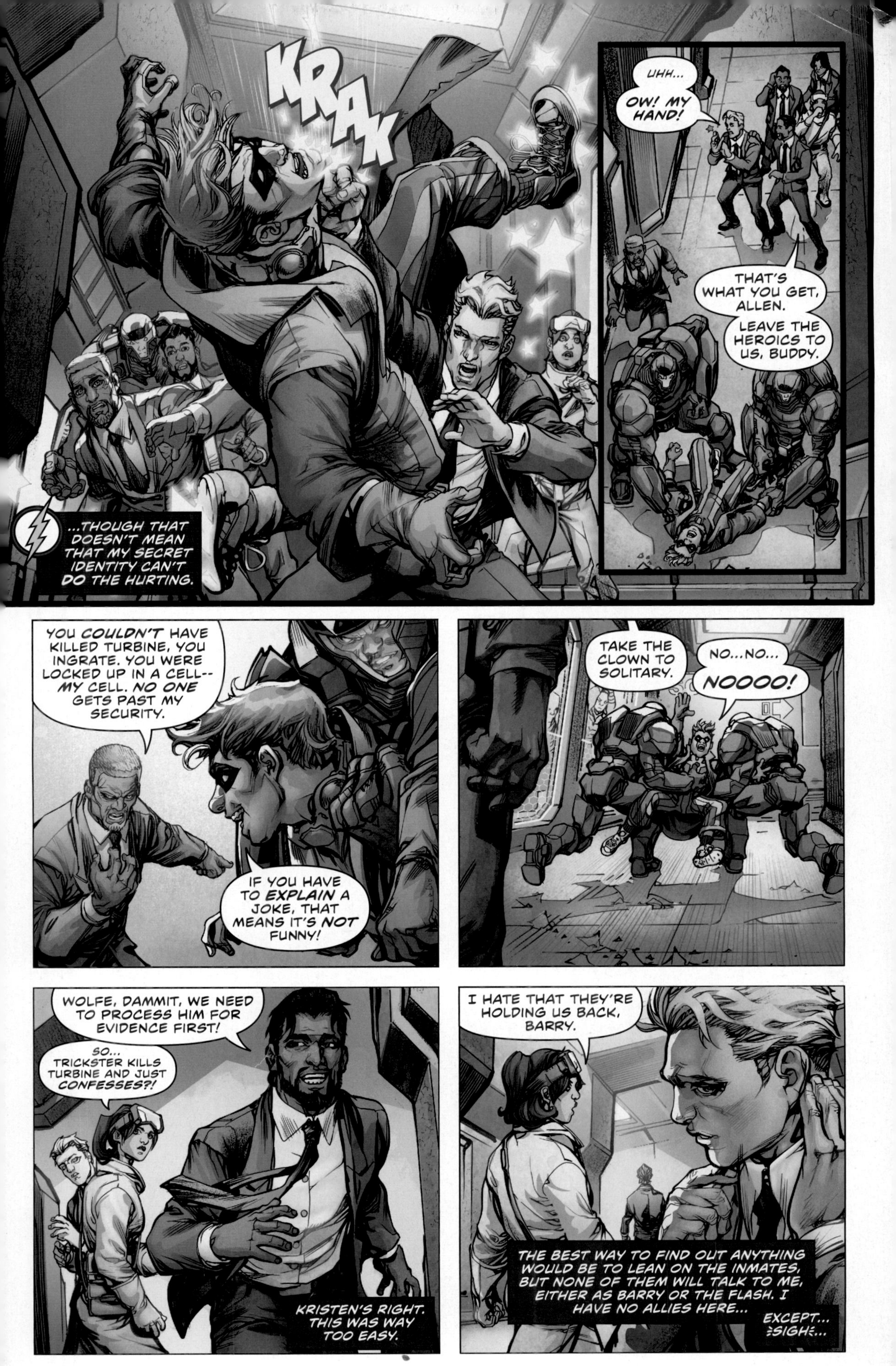
KRAK
...THOUGH THAT DOESN'T MEAN THAT MY SECRET IDENTITY CAN'T DO THE HURTING.
UHH...
OW! MY HAND!
THAT'S WHAT YOU GET, ALLEN.
LEAVE THE HEROICS TO US, BUDDY.
YOU COULDN'T HAVE KILLED TURBINE, YOU INGRATE. YOU WERE LOCKED UP IN A CELL-- MY CELL. NO ONE GETS PAST MY SECURITY.
IF YOU HAVE TO EXPLAIN A JOKE, THAT MEANS IT'S NOT FUNNY!
TAKE THE CLOWN TO SOLITARY.
NO...NO...
NOOOO!
WOLFE, DAMMIT, WE NEED TO PROCESS HIM FOR EVIDENCE FIRST!
SO... TRICKSTER KILLS TURBINE AND JUST CONFESSES?!
KRISTEN'S RIGHT. THIS WAS WAY TOO EASY.
I HATE THAT THEY'RE HOLDING US BACK, BARRY.
THE BEST WAY TO FIND OUT ANYTHING WOULD BE TO LEAN ON THE INMATES, BUT NONE OF THEM WILL TALK TO ME, EITHER AS BARRY OR THE FLASH. I HAVE NO ALLIES HERE...
EXCEPT... SIGH...

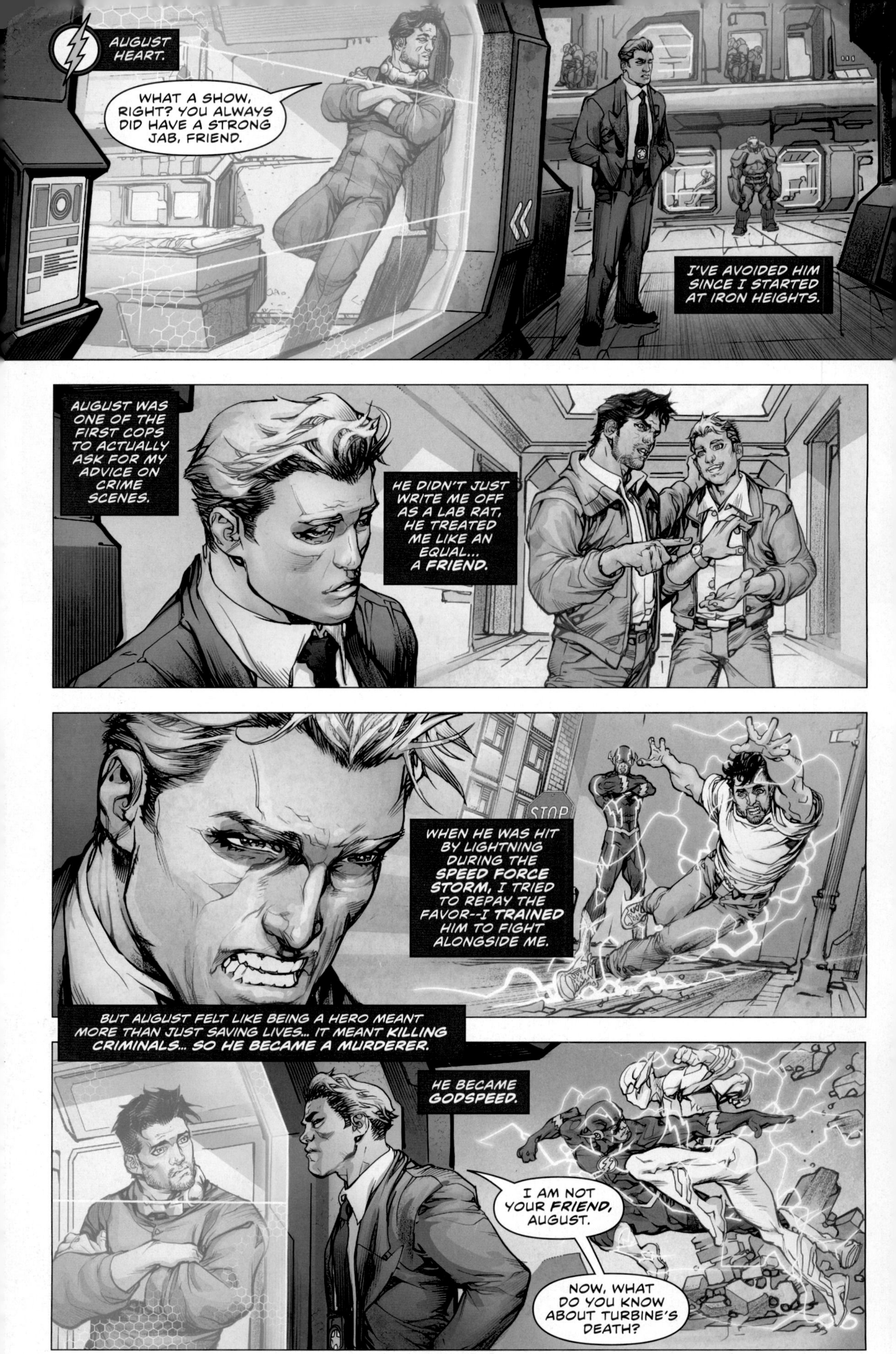
AUGUST HEART.
WHAT A SHOW, RIGHT? YOU ALWAYS DID HAVE A STRONG JAB, FRIEND.
I'VE AVOIDED HIM SINCE I STARTED AT IRON HEIGHTS.
AUGUST WAS ONE OF THE FIRST COPS TO ACTUALLY ASK FOR MY ADVICE ON CRIME SCENES.
HE DIDN'T JUST WRITE ME OFF AS A LAB RAT, HE TREATED ME LIKE AN EQUAL... A FRIEND.
STOP
WHEN HE WAS HIT BY LIGHTNING DURING THE SPEED FORCE STORM, I TRIED TO REPAY THE FAVOR--I TRAINED HIM TO FIGHT ALONGSIDE ME.
BUT AUGUST FELT LIKE BEING A HERO MEANT MORE THAN JUST SAVING LIVES... IT MEANT KILLING CRIMINALS... SO HE BECAME A MURDERER.
HE BECAME GODSPEED.
I AM NOT YOUR FRIEND, AUGUST.
NOW, WHAT DO YOU KNOW ABOUT TURBINE'S DEATH?

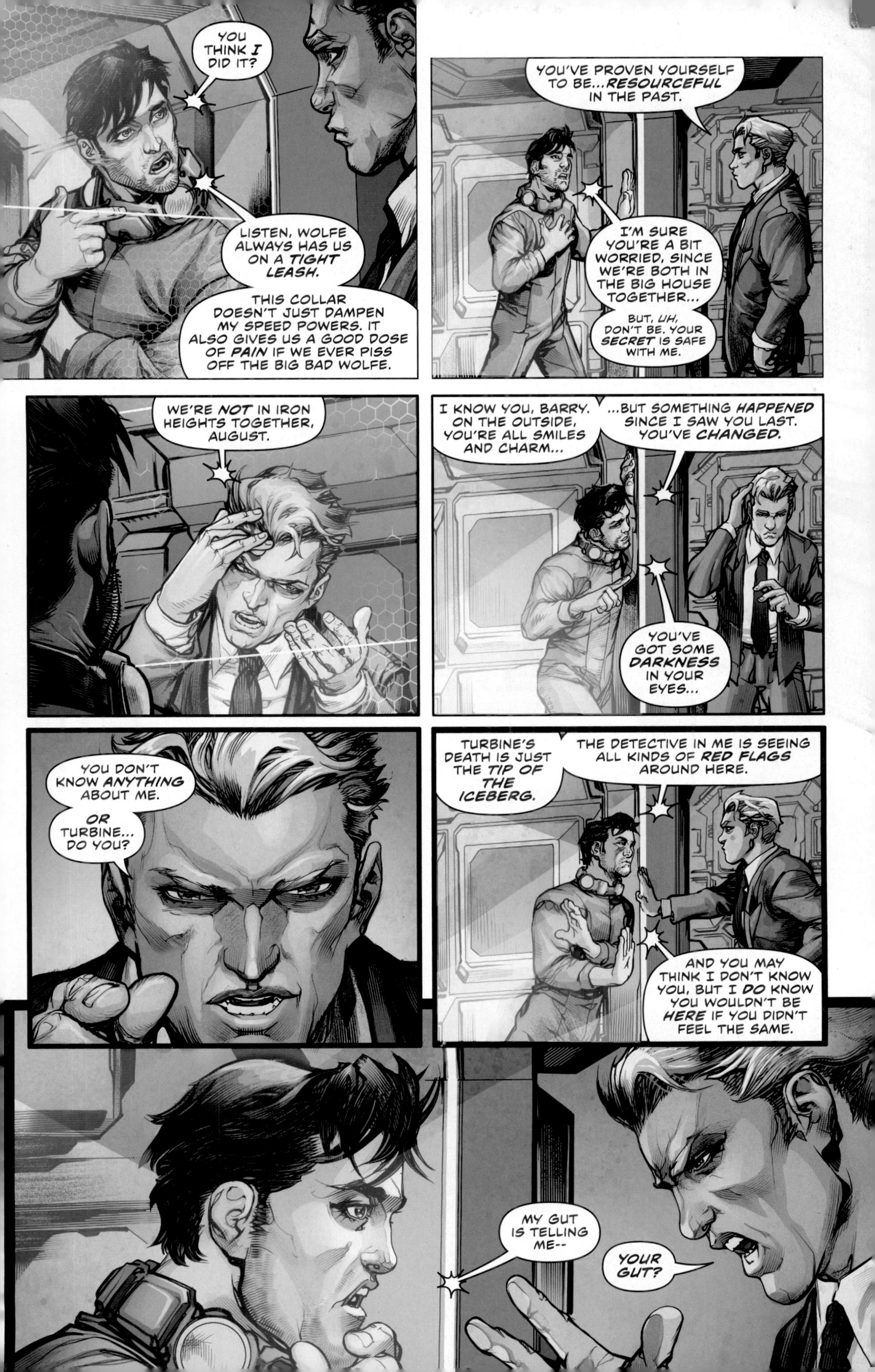

YOU THINK *I* DID IT?
LISTEN, WOLFE ALWAYS HAS US ON A *TIGHT LEASH.*
THIS COLLAR DOESN'T JUST DAMPEN MY SPEED POWERS. IT ALSO GIVES US A GOOD DOSE OF *PAIN* IF WE EVER PISS OFF THE BIG BAD WOLFE.
YOU'VE PROVEN YOURSELF TO BE...*RESOURCEFUL* IN THE PAST.
I'M SURE YOU'RE A BIT WORRIED, SINCE WE'RE BOTH IN THE BIG HOUSE TOGETHER...
BUT, *UH,* DON'T BE. YOUR *SECRET* IS SAFE WITH ME.
WE'RE *NOT* IN IRON HEIGHTS TOGETHER, AUGUST.
I KNOW YOU, BARRY. ON THE OUTSIDE, YOU'RE ALL SMILES AND CHARM...
...BUT SOMETHING *HAPPENED* SINCE I SAW YOU LAST. YOU'VE *CHANGED.*
YOU'VE GOT SOME *DARKNESS* IN YOUR EYES...
YOU DON'T KNOW *ANYTHING* ABOUT ME.
OR TURBINE... DO YOU?
TURBINE'S DEATH IS JUST THE *TIP OF THE ICEBERG.*
THE DETECTIVE IN ME IS SEEING ALL KINDS OF *RED FLAGS* AROUND HERE.
AND YOU MAY THINK I DON'T KNOW YOU, BUT I *DO* KNOW YOU WOULDN'T BE *HERE* IF YOU DIDN'T FEEL THE SAME.
MY GUT IS TELLING ME--
YOUR GUT?

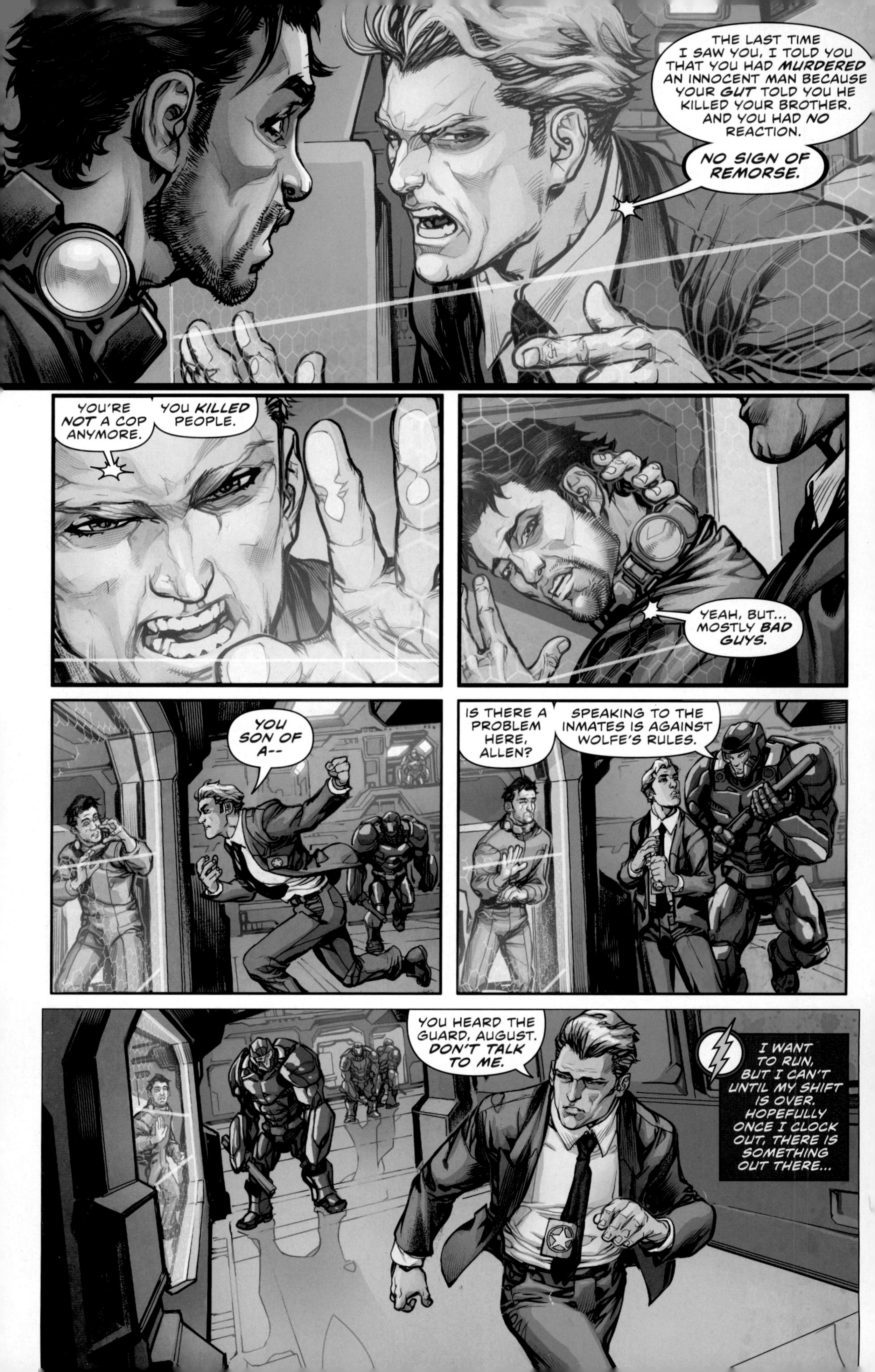
THE LAST TIME I SAW YOU, I TOLD YOU THAT YOU HAD MURDERED AN INNOCENT MAN BECAUSE YOUR GUT TOLD YOU HE KILLED YOUR BROTHER. AND YOU HAD NO REACTION.
NO SIGN OF REMORSE.
YOU'RE NOT A COP ANYMORE.
YOU KILLED PEOPLE.
YEAH, BUT... MOSTLY BAD GUYS.
YOU SON OF A--
IS THERE A PROBLEM HERE, ALLEN?
SPEAKING TO THE INMATES IS AGAINST WOLFE'S RULES.
YOU HEARD THE GUARD, AUGUST. DON'T TALK TO ME.
I WANT TO RUN, BUT I CAN'T UNTIL MY SHIFT IS OVER. HOPEFULLY ONCE I CLOCK OUT, THERE IS SOMETHING OUT THERE...

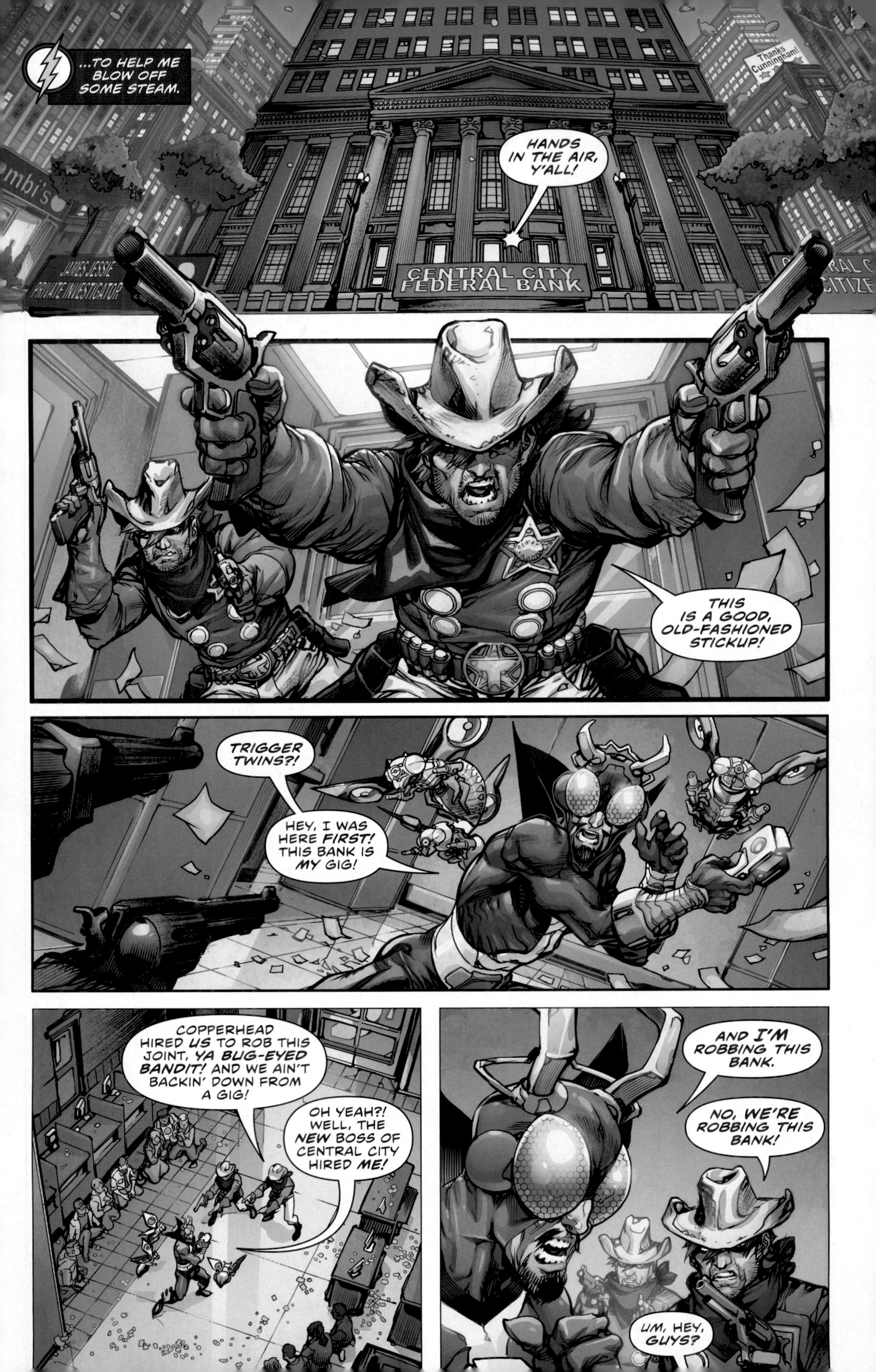

...TO HELP ME BLOW OFF SOME STEAM.
Thanks Cunningham!
HANDS IN THE AIR, Y'ALL!
JAMES JESSIE PRIVATE INVESTIGATOR
CENTRAL CITY FEDERAL BANK
THIS IS A GOOD, OLD-FASHIONED STICKUP!
TRIGGER TWINS?!
HEY, I WAS HERE FIRST! THIS BANK IS MY GIG!
COPPERHEAD HIRED US TO ROB THIS JOINT, YA BUG-EYED BANDIT! AND WE AIN'T BACKIN' DOWN FROM A GIG!
OH YEAH?! WELL, THE NEW BOSS OF CENTRAL CITY HIRED ME!
AND I'M ROBBING THIS BANK.
NO, WE'RE ROBBING THIS BANK!
UM, HEY, GUYS?

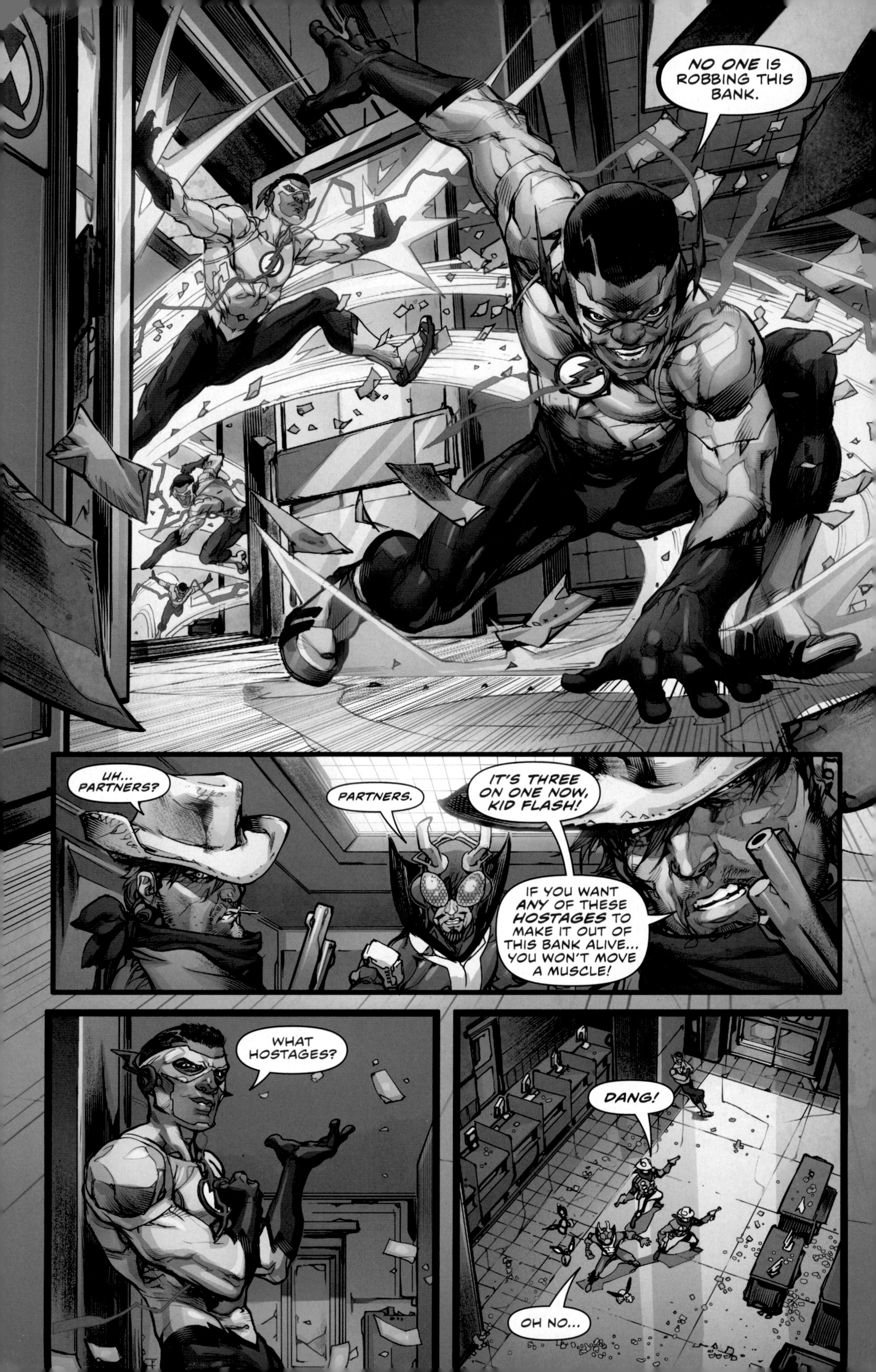
NO ONE IS ROBBING THIS BANK.
UH... PARTNERS?
PARTNERS.
IT'S THREE ON ONE NOW, KID FLASH!
IF YOU WANT ANY OF THESE HOSTAGES TO MAKE IT OUT OF THIS BANK ALIVE... YOU WON'T MOVE A MUSCLE!
WHAT HOSTAGES?
DANG!
OH NO...

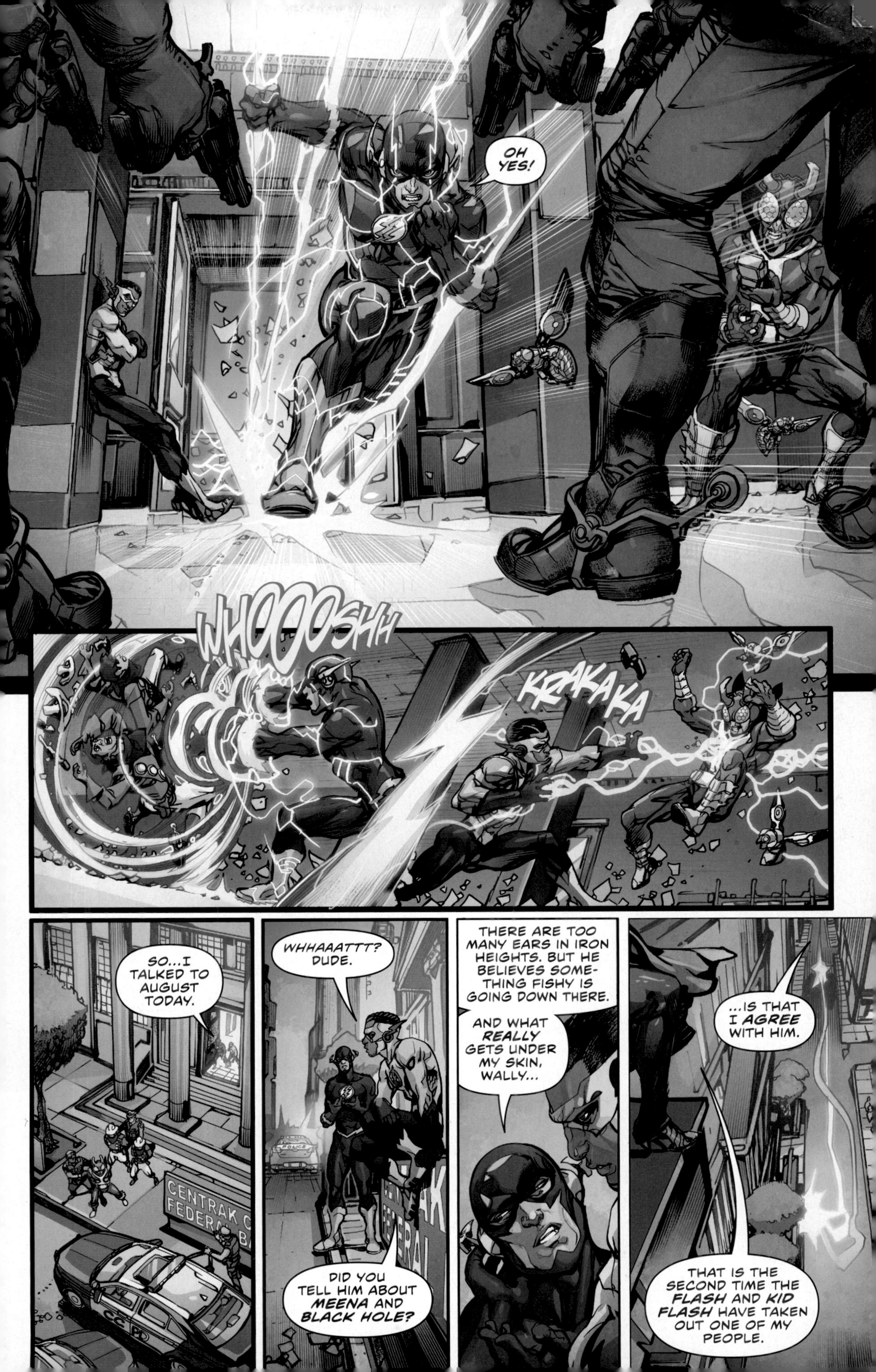
OH YES!
WHOOOOSHH
KRAKAKA
SO...I TALKED TO AUGUST TODAY.
CENTRAK C FEDERAL B
WHHAAATTT? DUDE.
POLICE
DID YOU TELL HIM ABOUT MEENA AND BLACK HOLE?
THERE ARE TOO MANY EARS IN IRON HEIGHTS. BUT HE BELIEVES SOMETHING FISHY IS GOING DOWN THERE.
AND WHAT REALLY GETS UNDER MY SKIN, WALLY...
...IS THAT I AGREE WITH HIM.
THAT IS THE SECOND TIME THE FLASH AND KID FLASH HAVE TAKEN OUT ONE OF MY PEOPLE.

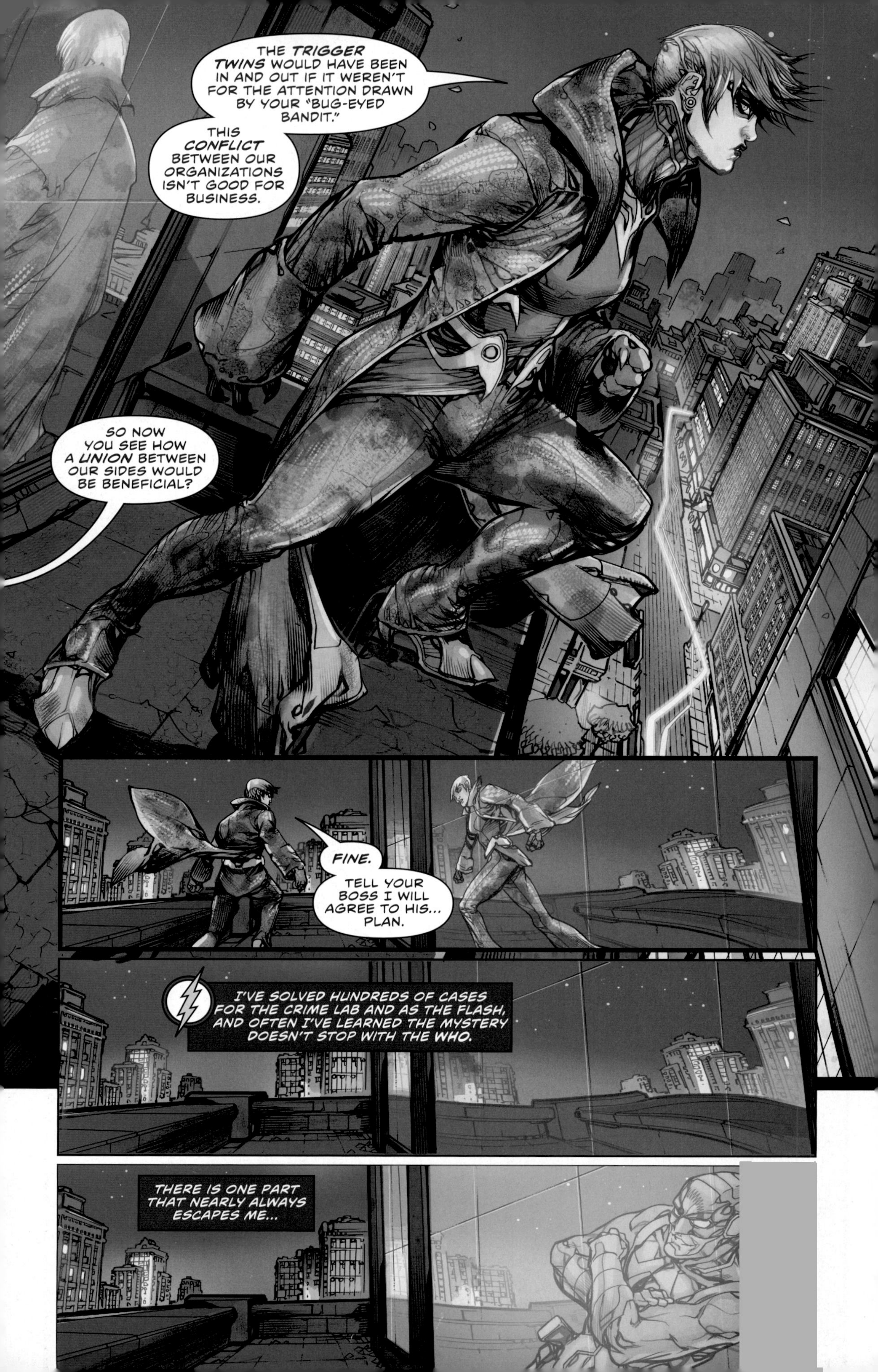
THE TRIGGER TWINS WOULD HAVE BEEN IN AND OUT IF IT WEREN'T FOR THE ATTENTION DRAWN BY YOUR "BUG-EYED BANDIT."
THIS CONFLICT BETWEEN OUR ORGANIZATIONS ISN'T GOOD FOR BUSINESS.
SO NOW YOU SEE HOW A UNION BETWEEN OUR SIDES WOULD BE BENEFICIAL?
FINE.
TELL YOUR BOSS I WILL AGREE TO HIS... PLAN.
I'VE SOLVED HUNDREDS OF CASES FOR THE CRIME LAB AND AS THE FLASH, AND OFTEN I'VE LEARNED THE MYSTERY DOESN'T STOP WITH THE WHO.
THERE IS ONE PART THAT NEARLY ALWAYS ESCAPES ME...

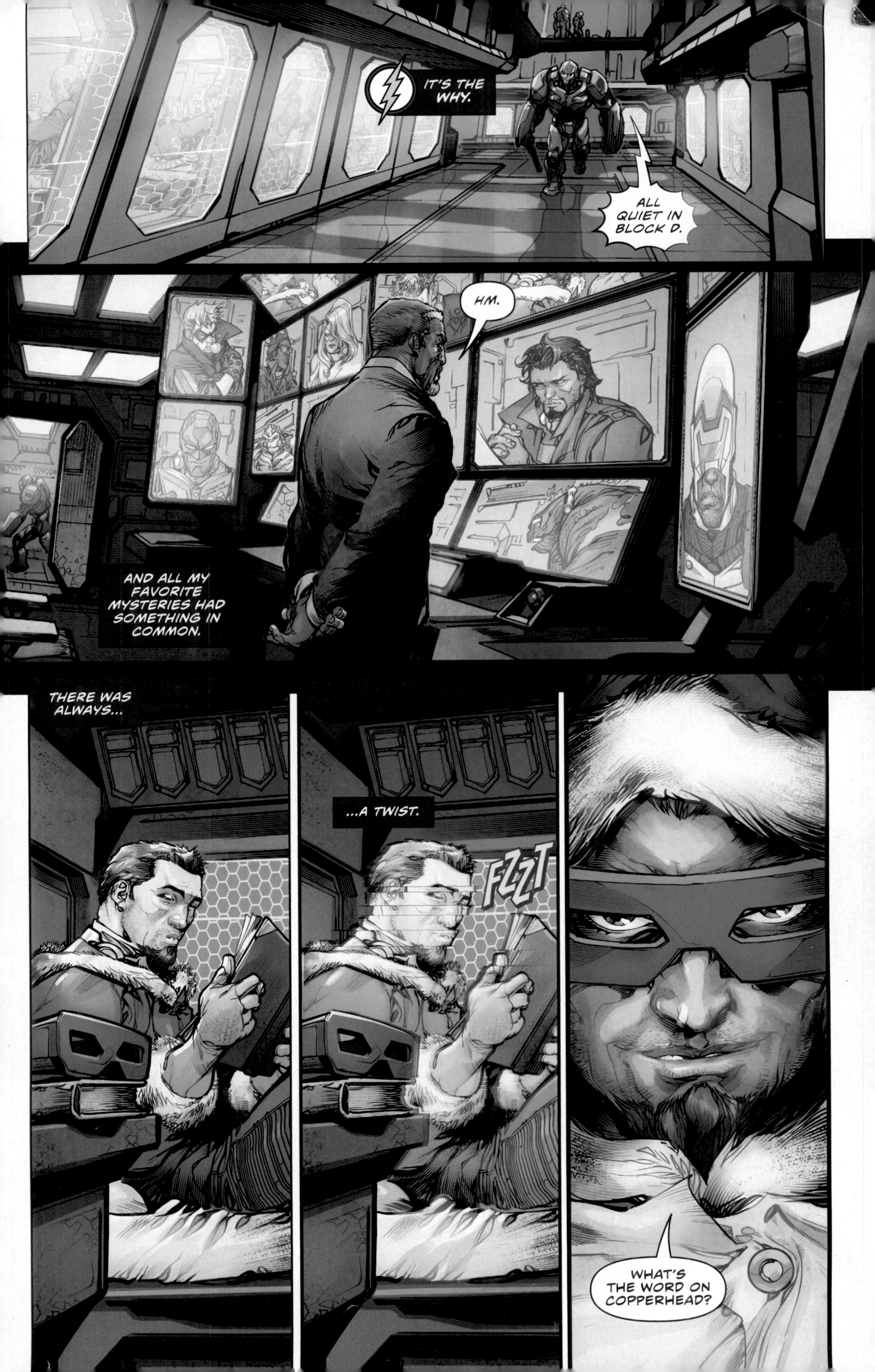
IT'S THE WHY.
ALL QUIET IN BLOCK D.
HM.
AND ALL MY FAVORITE MYSTERIES HAD SOMETHING IN COMMON.
THERE WAS ALWAYS...
...A TWIST.
FZZT
WHAT'S THE WORD ON COPPERHEAD?

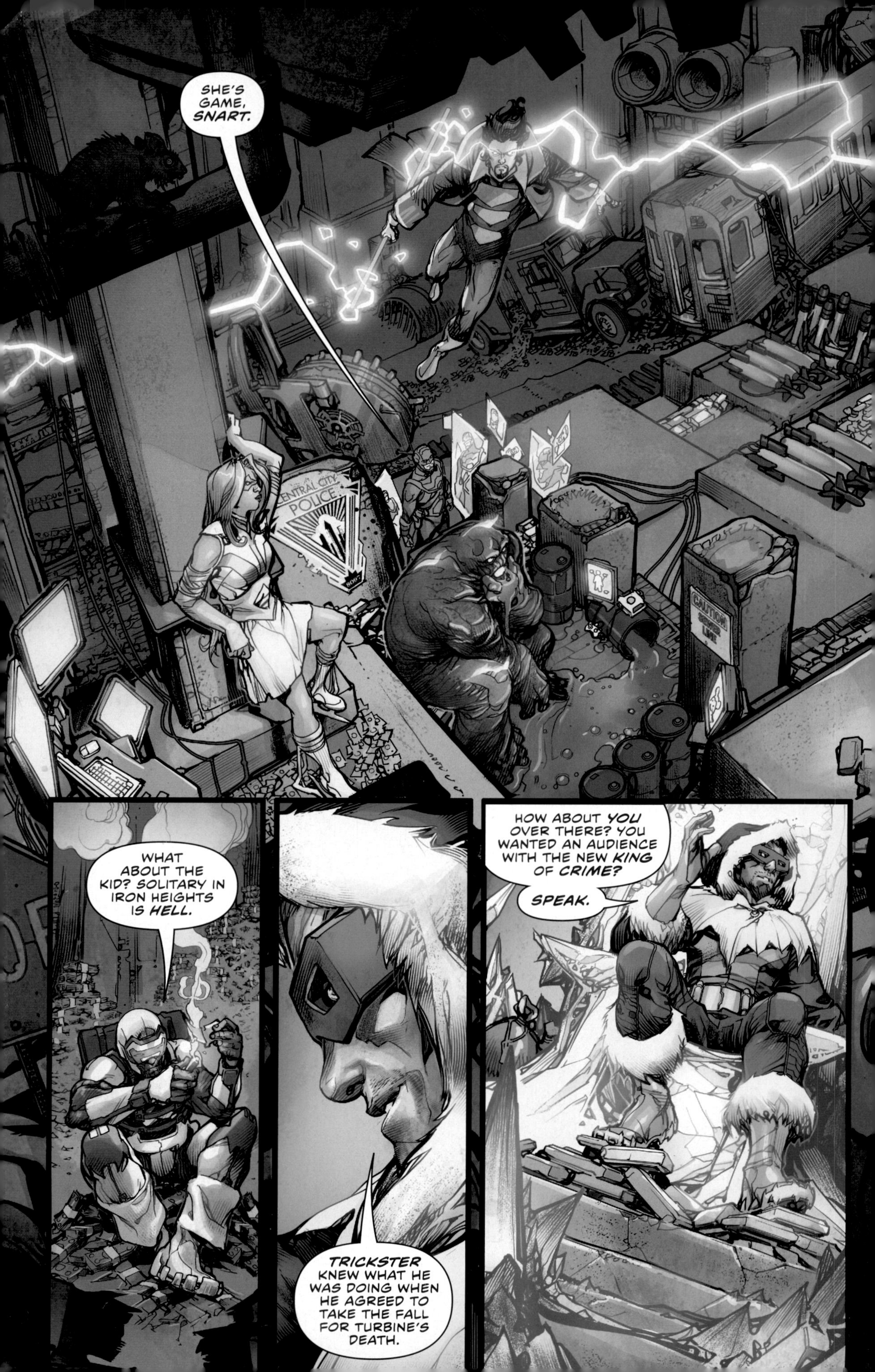
SHE'S GAME, SNART.
WHAT ABOUT THE KID? SOLITARY IN IRON HEIGHTS IS HELL.
TRICKSTER KNEW WHAT HE WAS DOING WHEN HE AGREED TO TAKE THE FALL FOR TURBINE'S DEATH.
HOW ABOUT YOU OVER THERE? YOU WANTED AN AUDIENCE WITH THE NEW KING OF CRIME?
SPEAK.
CENTRAL CITY POLICE
CAUTION

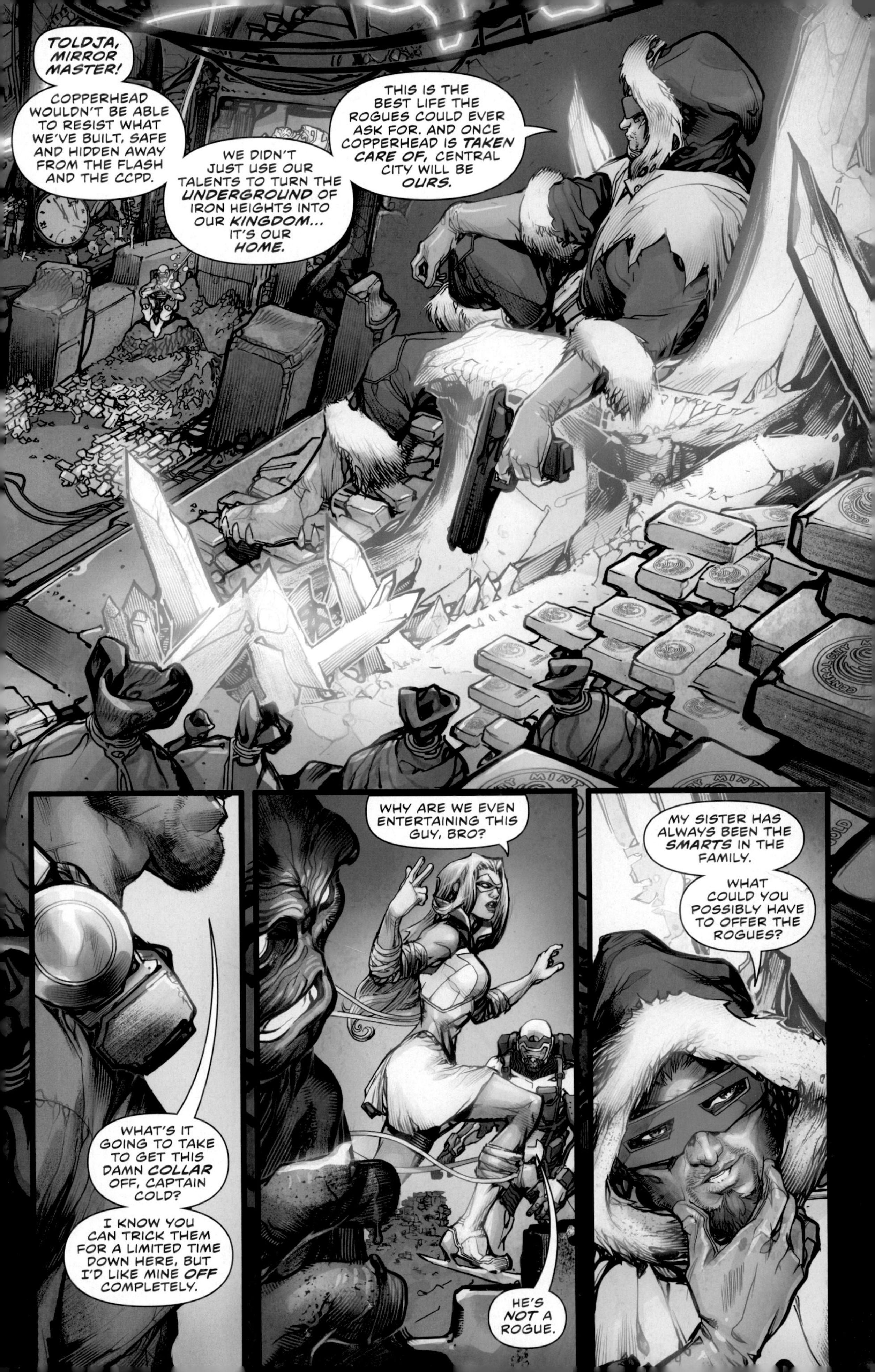
TOLDJA, MIRROR MASTER!
COPPERHEAD WOULDN'T BE ABLE TO RESIST WHAT WE'VE BUILT, SAFE AND HIDDEN AWAY FROM THE FLASH AND THE CCPD.
WE DIDN'T JUST USE OUR TALENTS TO TURN THE UNDERGROUND OF IRON HEIGHTS INTO OUR KINGDOM... IT'S OUR HOME.
THIS IS THE BEST LIFE THE ROGUES COULD EVER ASK FOR. AND ONCE COPPERHEAD IS TAKEN CARE OF, CENTRAL CITY WILL BE OURS.
WHAT'S IT GOING TO TAKE TO GET THIS DAMN COLLAR OFF, CAPTAIN COLD?
I KNOW YOU CAN TRICK THEM FOR A LIMITED TIME DOWN HERE, BUT I'D LIKE MINE OFF COMPLETELY.
WHY ARE WE EVEN ENTERTAINING THIS GUY, BRO?
HE'S NOT A ROGUE.
MY SISTER HAS ALWAYS BEEN THE SMARTS IN THE FAMILY.
WHAT COULD YOU POSSIBLY HAVE TO OFFER THE ROGUES?

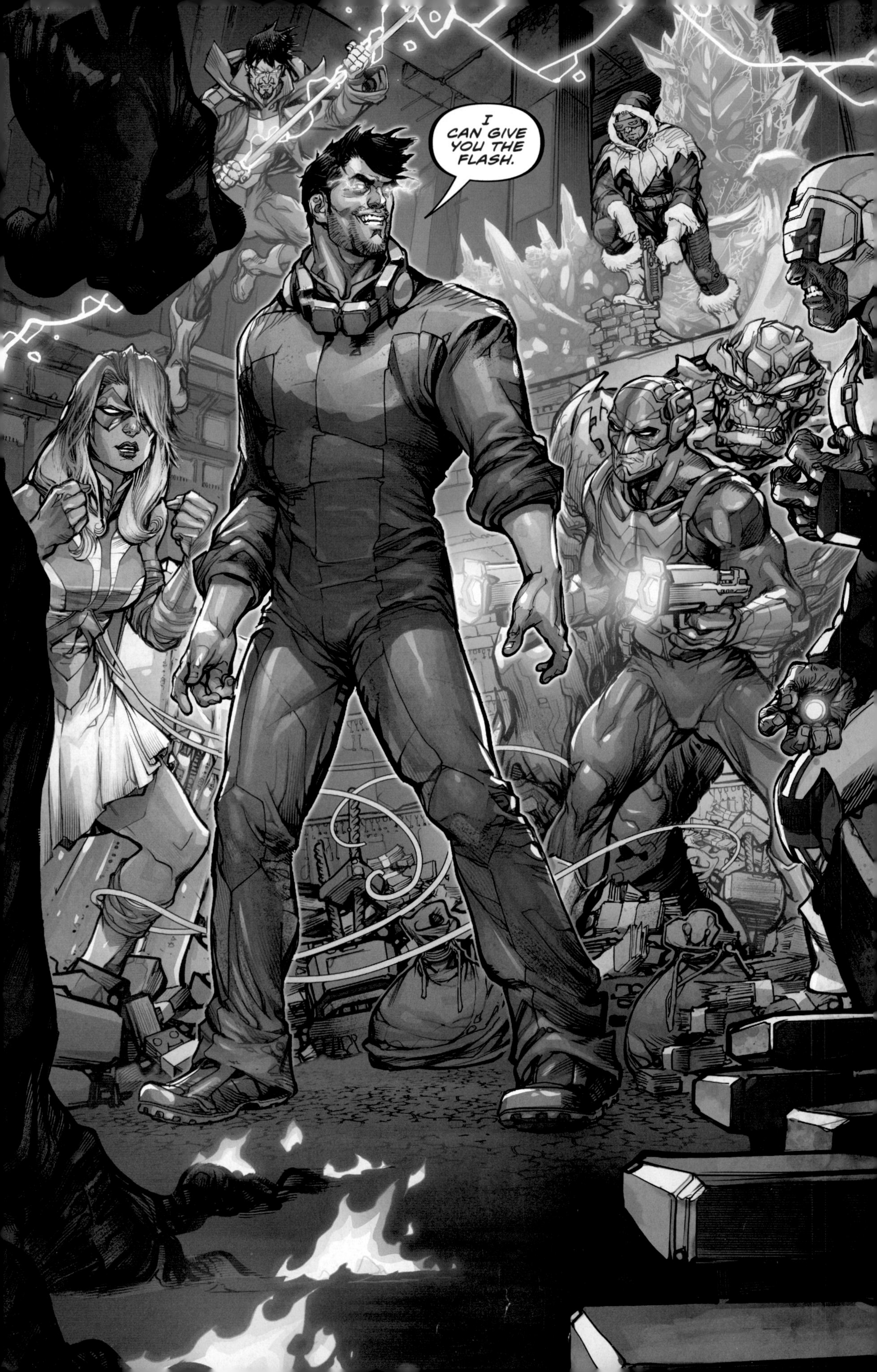
I CAN GIVE YOU THE FLASH.

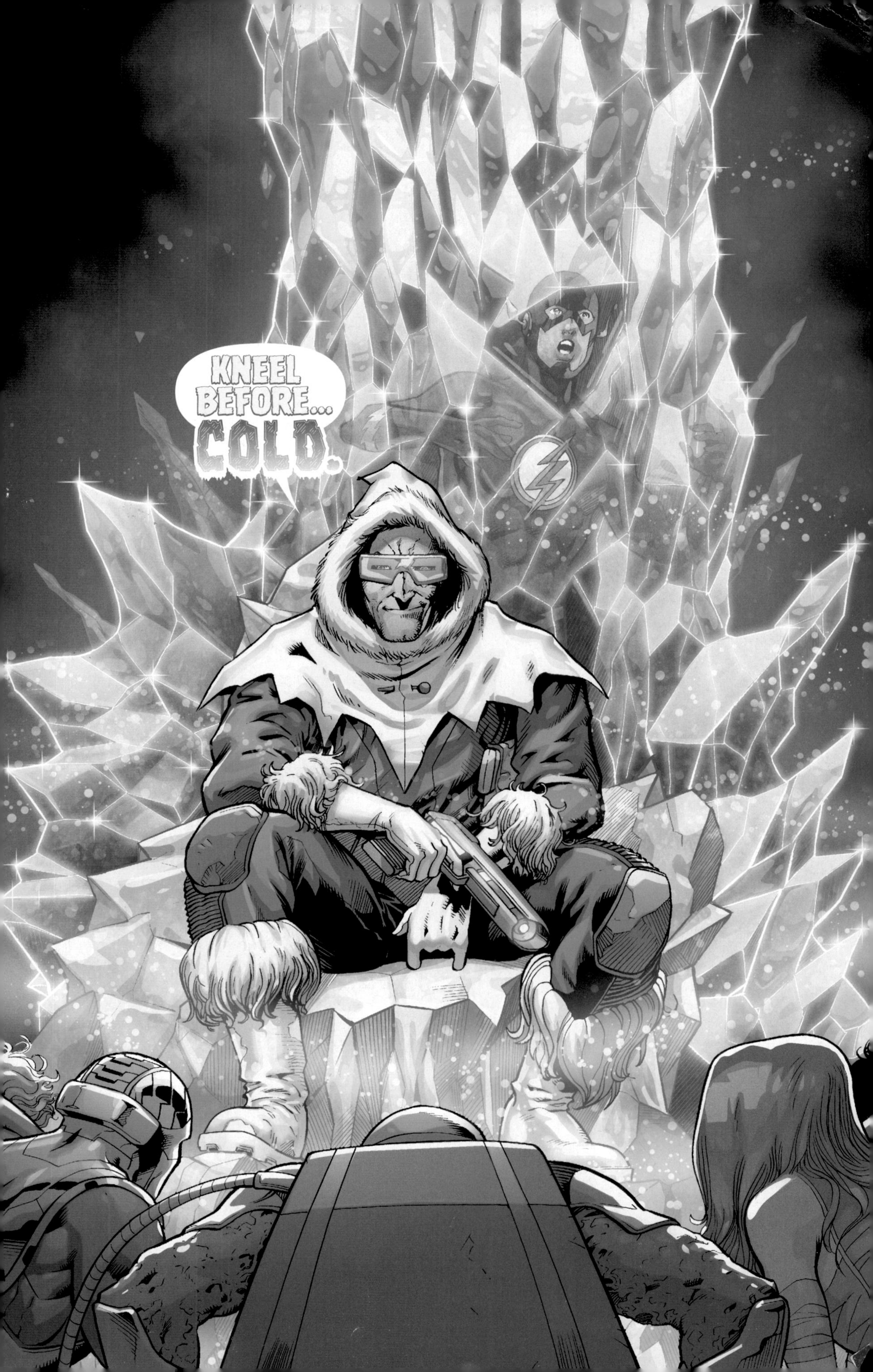
KNEEL BEFORE... COLD.

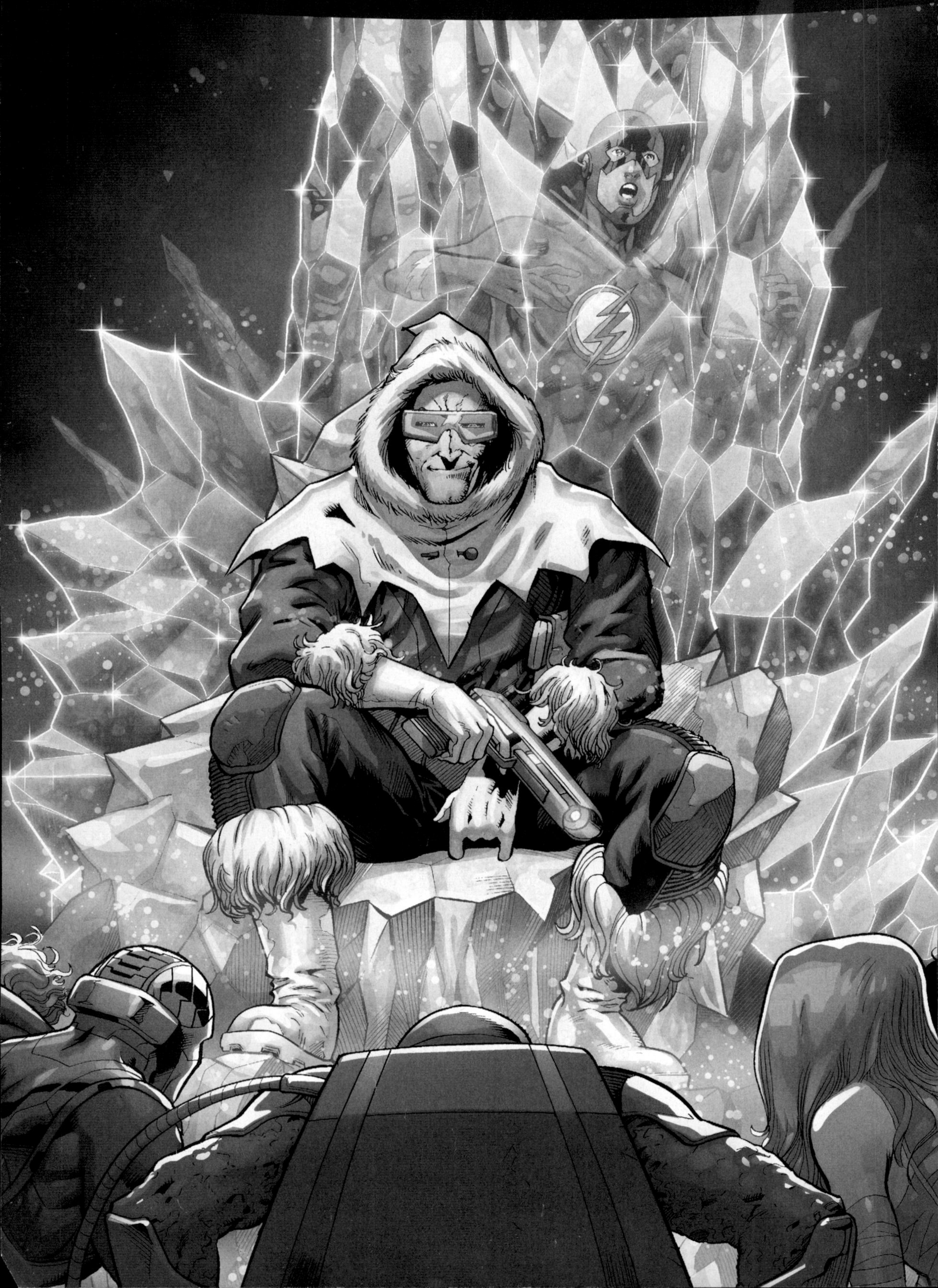

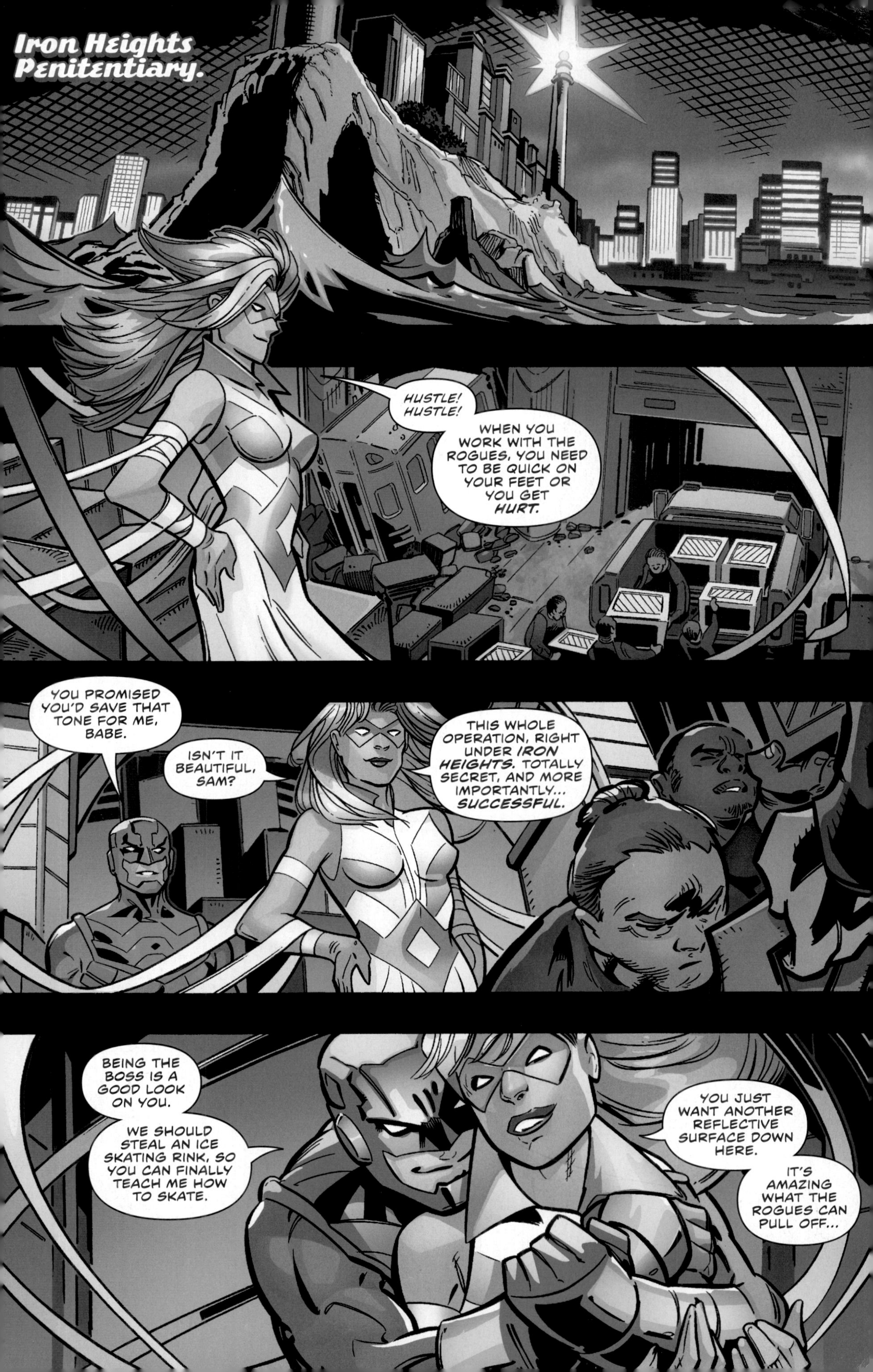
Iron Heights Penitentiary.
HUSTLE! HUSTLE!
WHEN YOU WORK WITH THE ROGUES, YOU NEED TO BE QUICK ON YOUR FEET OR YOU GET HURT.
YOU PROMISED YOU'D SAVE THAT TONE FOR ME, BABE.
ISN'T IT BEAUTIFUL, SAM?
THIS WHOLE OPERATION, RIGHT UNDER IRON HEIGHTS. TOTALLY SECRET, AND MORE IMPORTANTLY... SUCCESSFUL.
BEING THE BOSS IS A GOOD LOOK ON YOU.
WE SHOULD STEAL AN ICE SKATING RINK, SO YOU CAN FINALLY TEACH ME HOW TO SKATE.
YOU JUST WANT ANOTHER REFLECTIVE SURFACE DOWN HERE.
IT'S AMAZING WHAT THE ROGUES CAN PULL OFF...

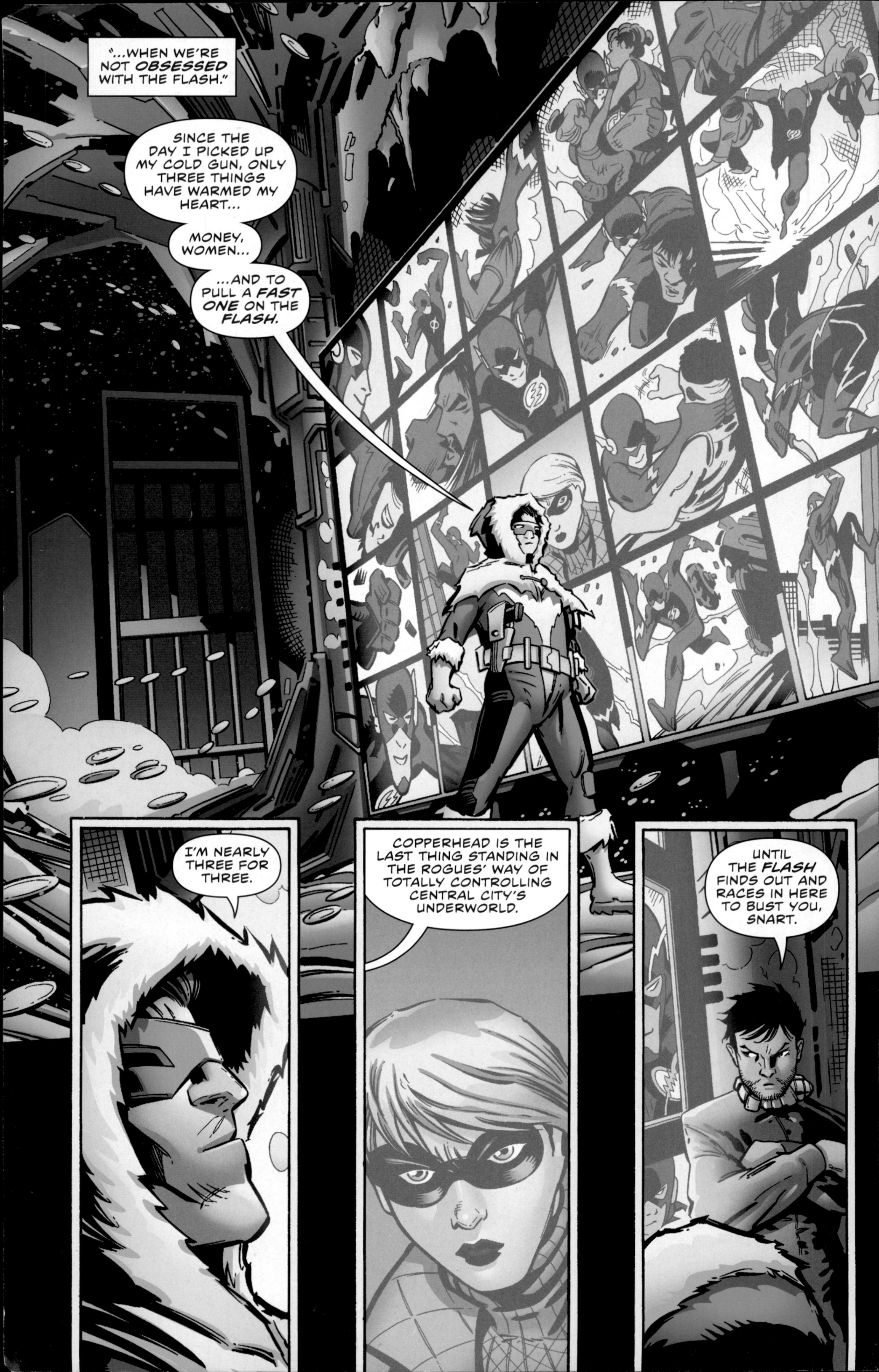
"...WHEN WE'RE NOT OBSESSED WITH THE FLASH."
SINCE THE DAY I PICKED UP MY COLD GUN, ONLY THREE THINGS HAVE WARMED MY HEART...
MONEY, WOMEN...
...AND TO PULL A FAST ONE ON THE FLASH.
I'M NEARLY THREE FOR THREE.
COPPERHEAD IS THE LAST THING STANDING IN THE ROGUES' WAY OF TOTALLY CONTROLLING CENTRAL CITY'S UNDERWORLD.
UNTIL THE FLASH FINDS OUT AND RACES IN HERE TO BUST YOU, SNART.

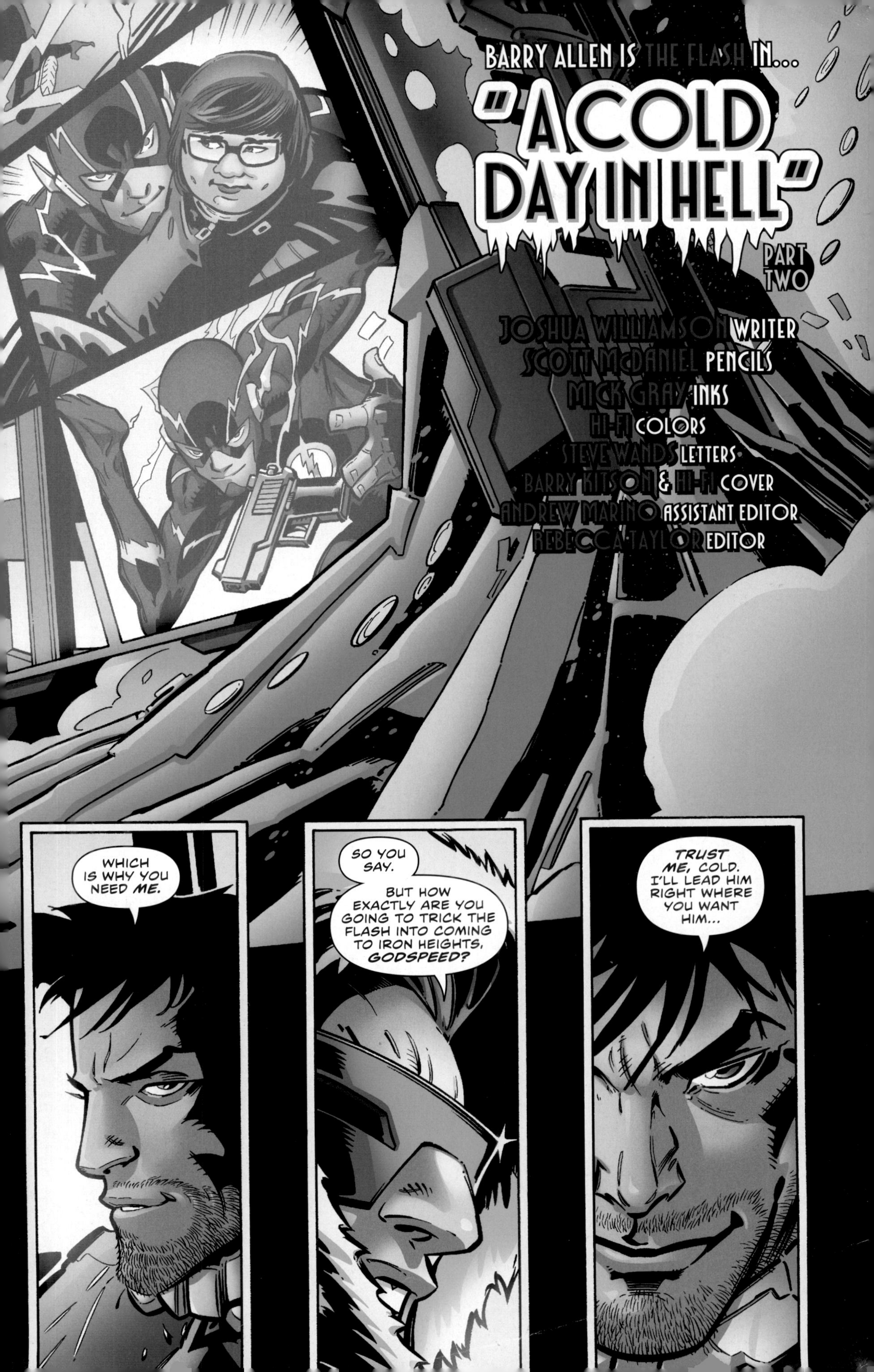

BARRY ALLEN IS THE FLASH IN...
"A COLD DAY IN HELL"
PART TWO
JOSHUA WILLIAMSON WRITER
SCOTT McDANIEL PENCILS
MICK GRAY INKS
HI-FI COLORS
STEVE WANDS LETTERS
BARRY KITSON & HI-FI COVER
ANDREW MARINO ASSISTANT EDITOR
REBECCA TAYLOR EDITOR
WHICH IS WHY YOU NEED *ME*.
SO YOU SAY.
BUT HOW EXACTLY ARE YOU GOING TO TRICK THE FLASH INTO COMING TO IRON HEIGHTS, *GODSPEED?*
TRUST ME, COLD. I'LL LEAD HIM RIGHT WHERE YOU WANT HIM...

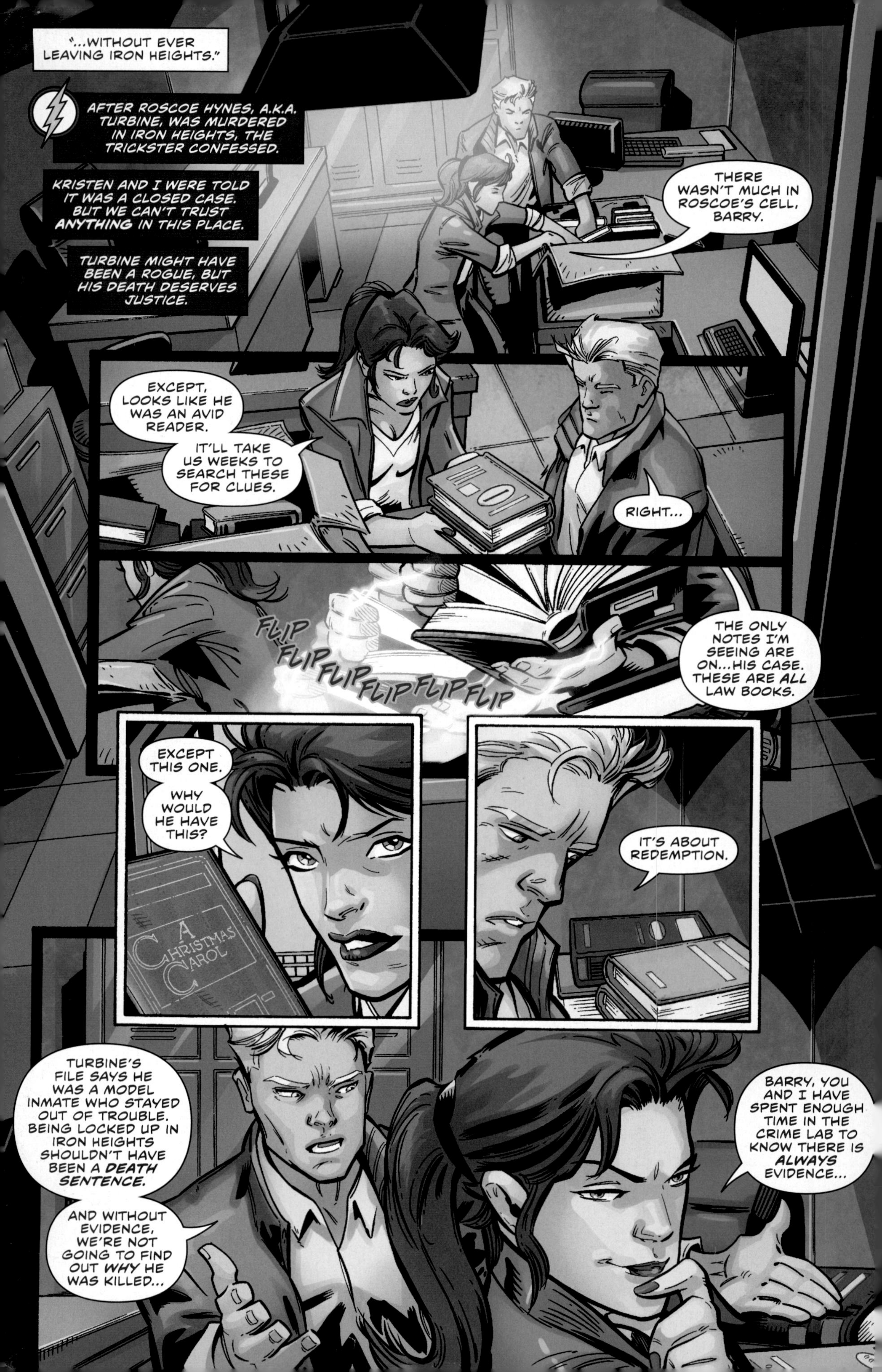
"...WITHOUT EVER LEAVING IRON HEIGHTS."
AFTER ROSCOE HYNES, A.K.A. TURBINE, WAS MURDERED IN IRON HEIGHTS, THE TRICKSTER CONFESSED.
KRISTEN AND I WERE TOLD IT WAS A CLOSED CASE. BUT WE CAN'T TRUST ANYTHING IN THIS PLACE.
TURBINE MIGHT HAVE BEEN A ROGUE, BUT HIS DEATH DESERVES JUSTICE.
THERE WASN'T MUCH IN ROSCOE'S CELL, BARRY.
EXCEPT, LOOKS LIKE HE WAS AN AVID READER.
IT'LL TAKE US WEEKS TO SEARCH THESE FOR CLUES.
RIGHT...
FLIP FLIP FLIP FLIP FLIP FLIP
THE ONLY NOTES I'M SEEING ARE ON...HIS CASE. THESE ARE ALL LAW BOOKS.
EXCEPT THIS ONE.
WHY WOULD HE HAVE THIS?
A CHRISTMAS CAROL
IT'S ABOUT REDEMPTION.
TURBINE'S FILE SAYS HE WAS A MODEL INMATE WHO STAYED OUT OF TROUBLE. BEING LOCKED UP IN IRON HEIGHTS SHOULDN'T HAVE BEEN A DEATH SENTENCE.
AND WITHOUT EVIDENCE, WE'RE NOT GOING TO FIND OUT WHY HE WAS KILLED...
BARRY, YOU AND I HAVE SPENT ENOUGH TIME IN THE CRIME LAB TO KNOW THERE IS ALWAYS EVIDENCE...

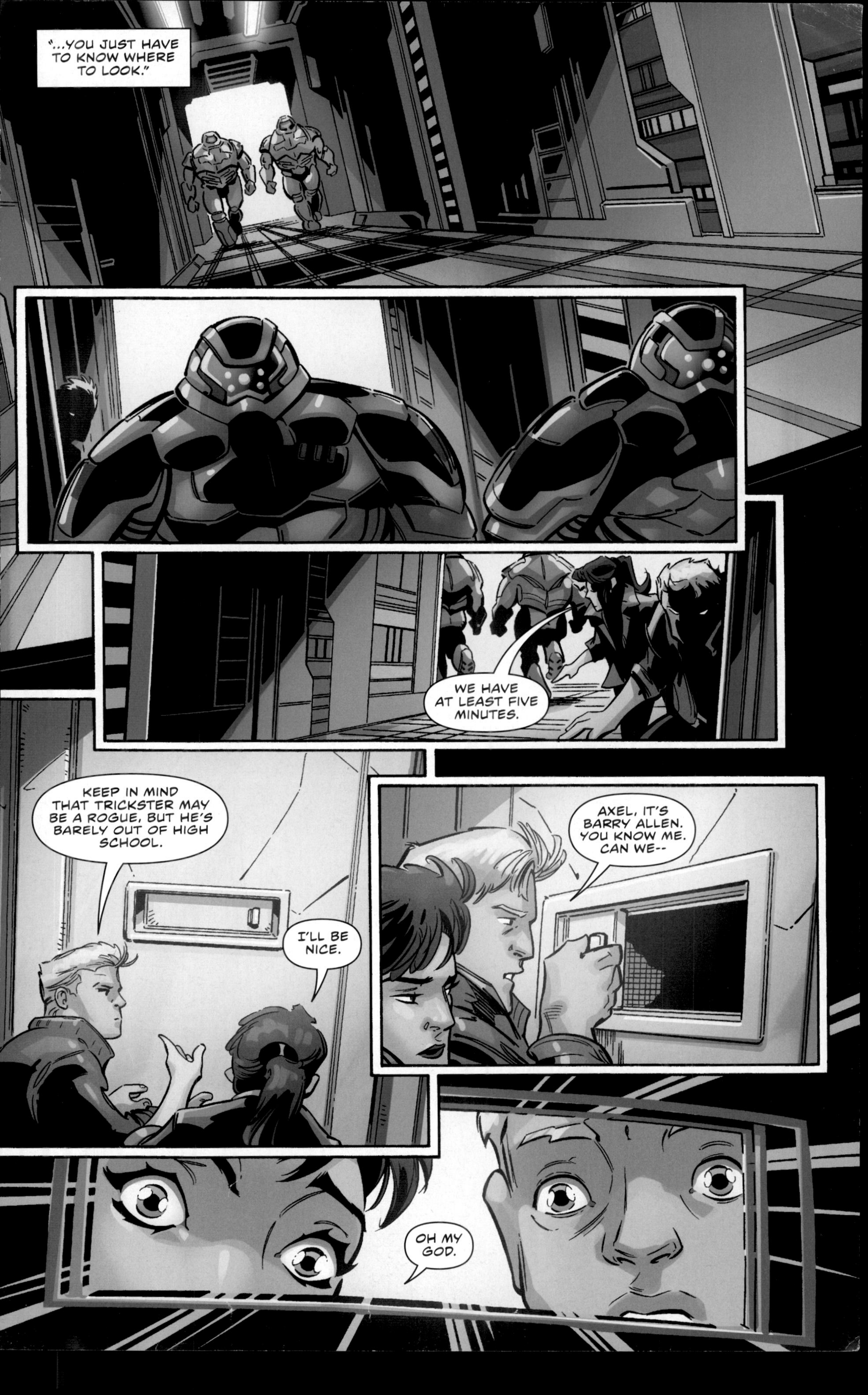
"...YOU JUST HAVE TO KNOW WHERE TO LOOK."
WE HAVE AT LEAST FIVE MINUTES.
KEEP IN MIND THAT TRICKSTER MAY BE A ROGUE, BUT HE'S BARELY OUT OF HIGH SCHOOL.
I'LL BE NICE.
AXEL, IT'S BARRY ALLEN. YOU KNOW ME. CAN WE--
OH MY GOD.

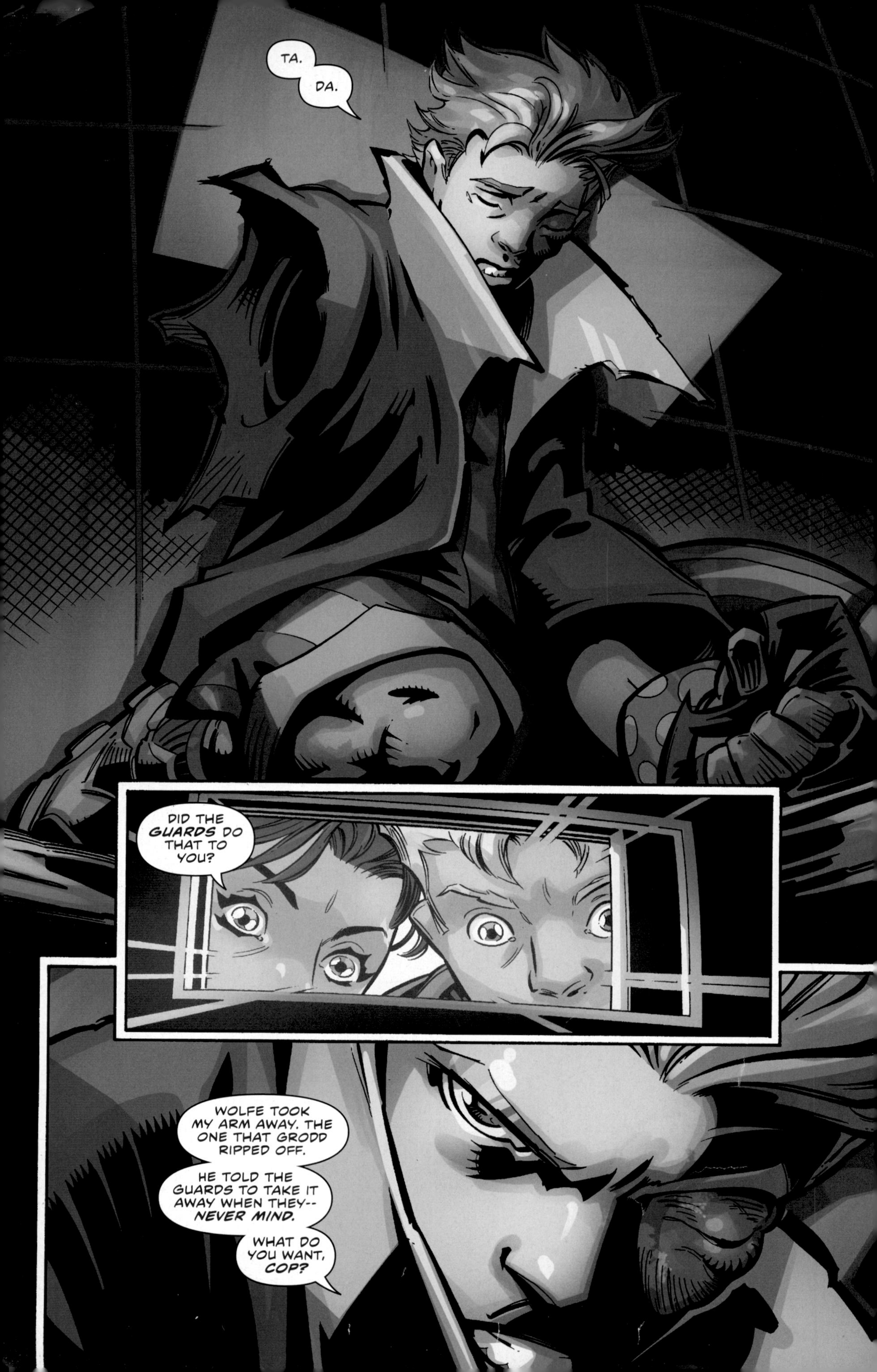

TA.
DA.
DID THE GUARDS DO THAT TO YOU?
WOLFE TOOK MY ARM AWAY. THE ONE THAT GRODD RIPPED OFF.
HE TOLD THE GUARDS TO TAKE IT AWAY WHEN THEY-- NEVER MIND.
WHAT DO YOU WANT, COP?

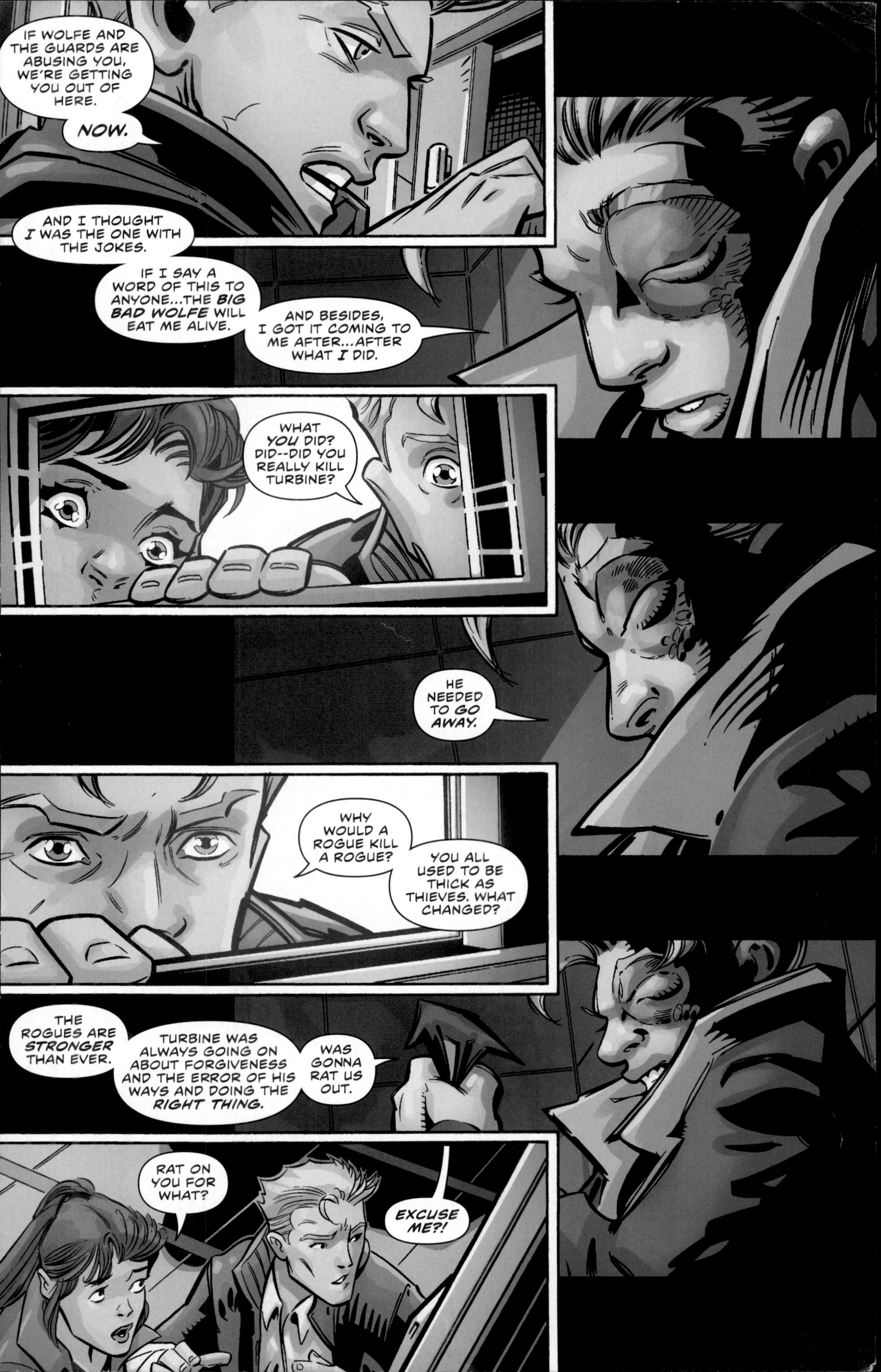

IF WOLFE AND THE GUARDS ARE ABUSING YOU, WE'RE GETTING YOU OUT OF HERE.
NOW.
AND I THOUGHT I WAS THE ONE WITH THE JOKES.
IF I SAY A WORD OF THIS TO ANYONE...THE BIG BAD WOLFE WILL EAT ME ALIVE.
AND BESIDES, I GOT IT COMING TO ME AFTER...AFTER WHAT I DID.
WHAT YOU DID? DID--DID YOU REALLY KILL TURBINE?
HE NEEDED TO GO AWAY.
WHY WOULD A ROGUE KILL A ROGUE?
YOU ALL USED TO BE THICK AS THIEVES. WHAT CHANGED?
THE ROGUES ARE STRONGER THAN EVER.
TURBINE WAS ALWAYS GOING ON ABOUT FORGIVENESS AND THE ERROR OF HIS WAYS AND DOING THE RIGHT THING.
WAS GONNA RAT US OUT.
RAT ON YOU FOR WHAT?
EXCUSE ME?!

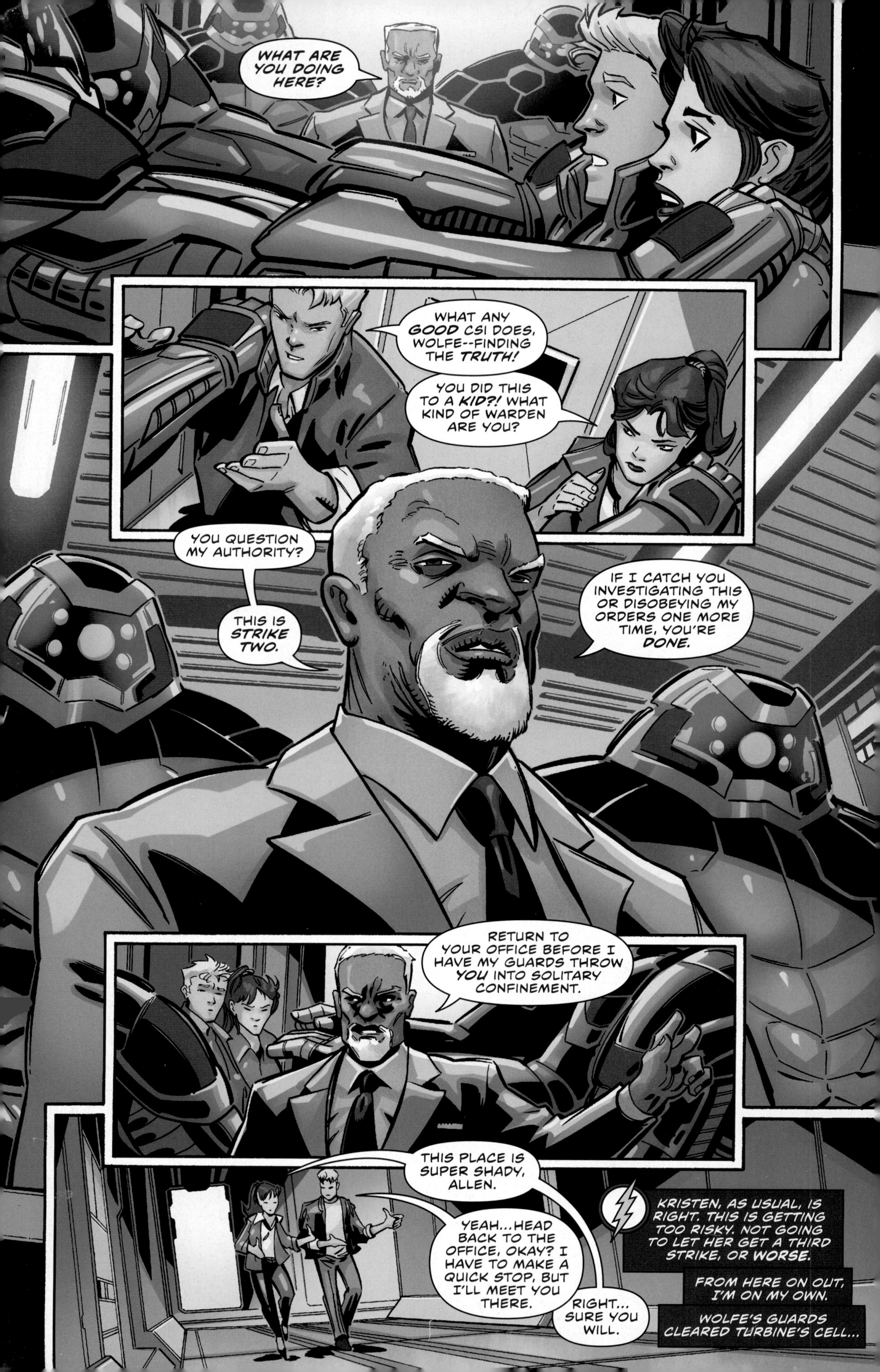
WHAT ARE YOU DOING HERE?
WHAT ANY GOOD CSI DOES, WOLFE--FINDING THE TRUTH!
YOU DID THIS TO A KID?! WHAT KIND OF WARDEN ARE YOU?
YOU QUESTION MY AUTHORITY?
THIS IS STRIKE TWO.
IF I CATCH YOU INVESTIGATING THIS OR DISOBEYING MY ORDERS ONE MORE TIME, YOU'RE DONE.
RETURN TO YOUR OFFICE BEFORE I HAVE MY GUARDS THROW YOU INTO SOLITARY CONFINEMENT.
THIS PLACE IS SUPER SHADY, ALLEN.
YEAH...HEAD BACK TO THE OFFICE, OKAY? I HAVE TO MAKE A QUICK STOP, BUT I'LL MEET YOU THERE.
RIGHT... SURE YOU WILL.
KRISTEN, AS USUAL, IS RIGHT. THIS IS GETTING TOO RISKY. NOT GOING TO LET HER GET A THIRD STRIKE, OR WORSE.
FROM HERE ON OUT, I'M ON MY OWN.
WOLFE'S GUARDS CLEARED TURBINE'S CELL...

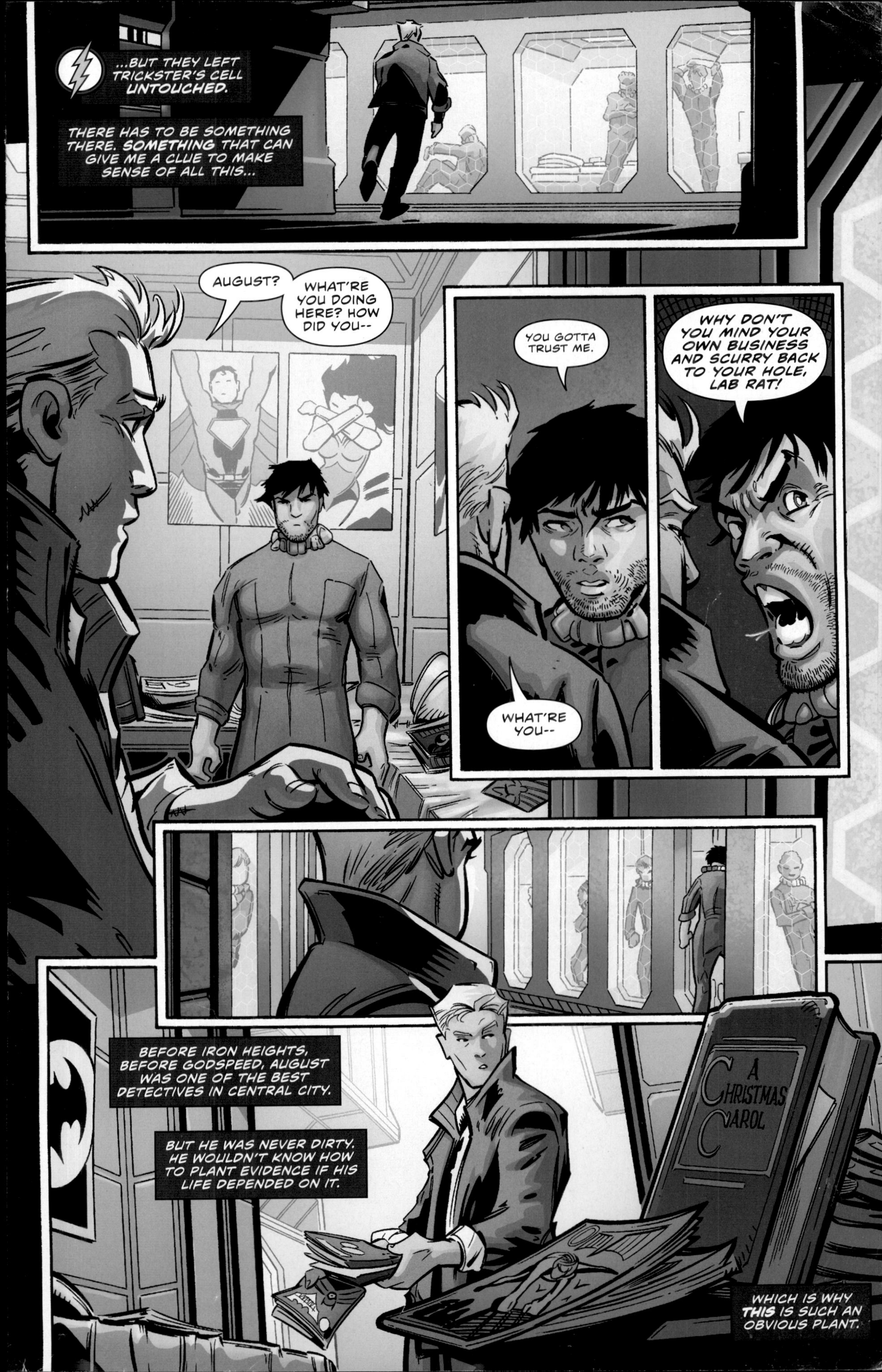
...BUT THEY LEFT TRICKSTER'S CELL UNTOUCHED.
THERE HAS TO BE SOMETHING THERE. SOMETHING THAT CAN GIVE ME A CLUE TO MAKE SENSE OF ALL THIS...
AUGUST?
WHAT'RE YOU DOING HERE? HOW DID YOU--
YOU GOTTA TRUST ME.
WHAT'RE YOU--
WHY DON'T YOU MIND YOUR OWN BUSINESS AND SCURRY BACK TO YOUR HOLE, LAB RAT!
BEFORE IRON HEIGHTS, BEFORE GODSPEED, AUGUST WAS ONE OF THE BEST DETECTIVES IN CENTRAL CITY.
BUT HE WAS NEVER DIRTY. HE WOULDN'T KNOW HOW TO PLANT EVIDENCE IF HIS LIFE DEPENDED ON IT.
A CHRISTMAS CAROL
WHICH IS WHY THIS IS SUCH AN OBVIOUS PLANT.

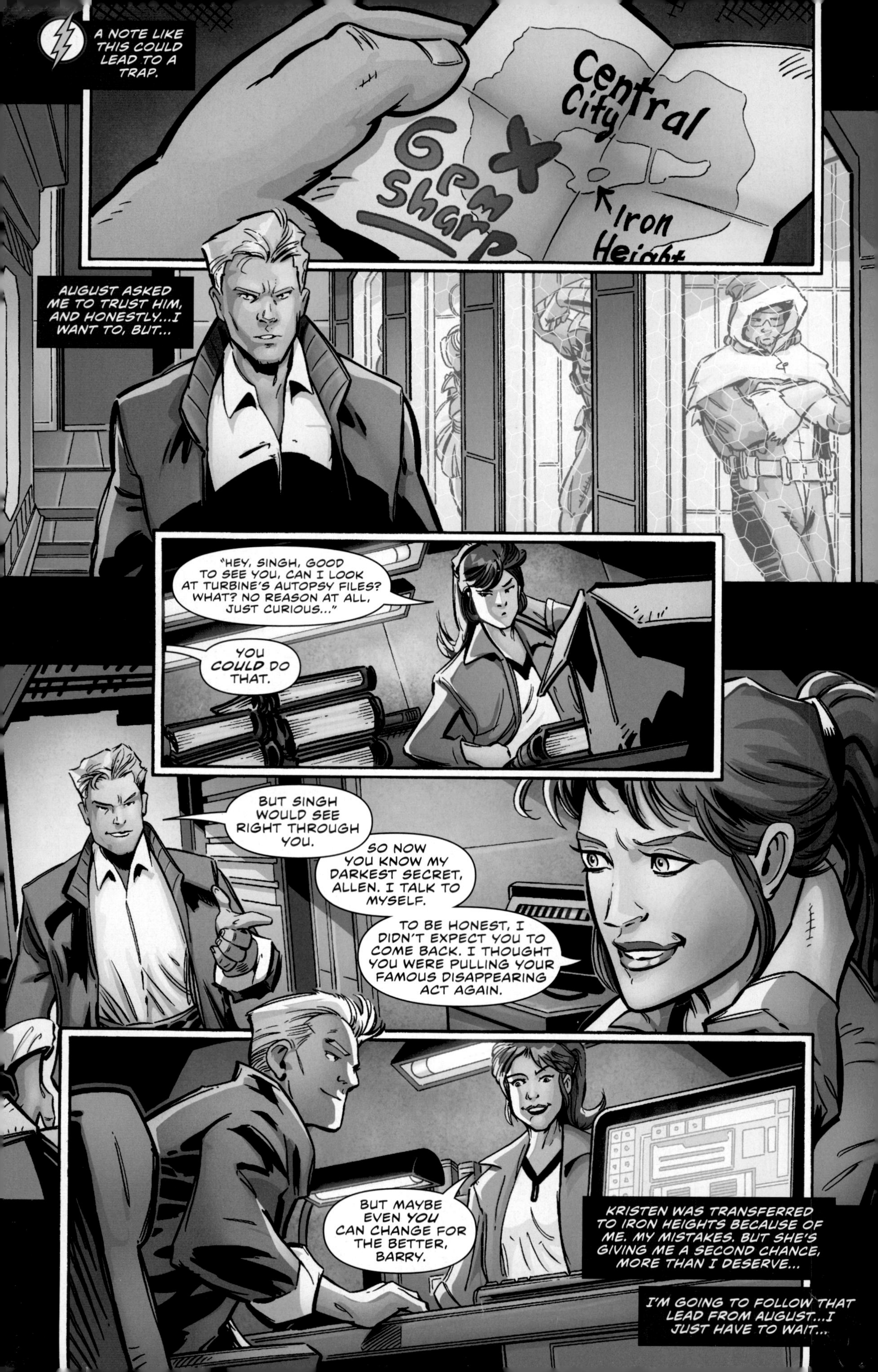
A NOTE LIKE THIS COULD LEAD TO A TRAP.
Central City
6pm
Gem Sharp
Iron Height
AUGUST ASKED ME TO TRUST HIM, AND HONESTLY...I WANT TO, BUT...
"HEY, SINGH, GOOD TO SEE YOU, CAN I LOOK AT TURBINE'S AUTOPSY FILES? WHAT? NO REASON AT ALL, JUST CURIOUS..."
YOU COULD DO THAT.
BUT SINGH WOULD SEE RIGHT THROUGH YOU.
SO NOW YOU KNOW MY DARKEST SECRET, ALLEN. I TALK TO MYSELF.
TO BE HONEST, I DIDN'T EXPECT YOU TO COME BACK. I THOUGHT YOU WERE PULLING YOUR FAMOUS DISAPPEARING ACT AGAIN.
BUT MAYBE EVEN YOU CAN CHANGE FOR THE BETTER, BARRY.
KRISTEN WAS TRANSFERRED TO IRON HEIGHTS BECAUSE OF ME. MY MISTAKES. BUT SHE'S GIVING ME A SECOND CHANCE, MORE THAN I DESERVE...
I'M GOING TO FOLLOW THAT LEAD FROM AUGUST...I JUST HAVE TO WAIT...

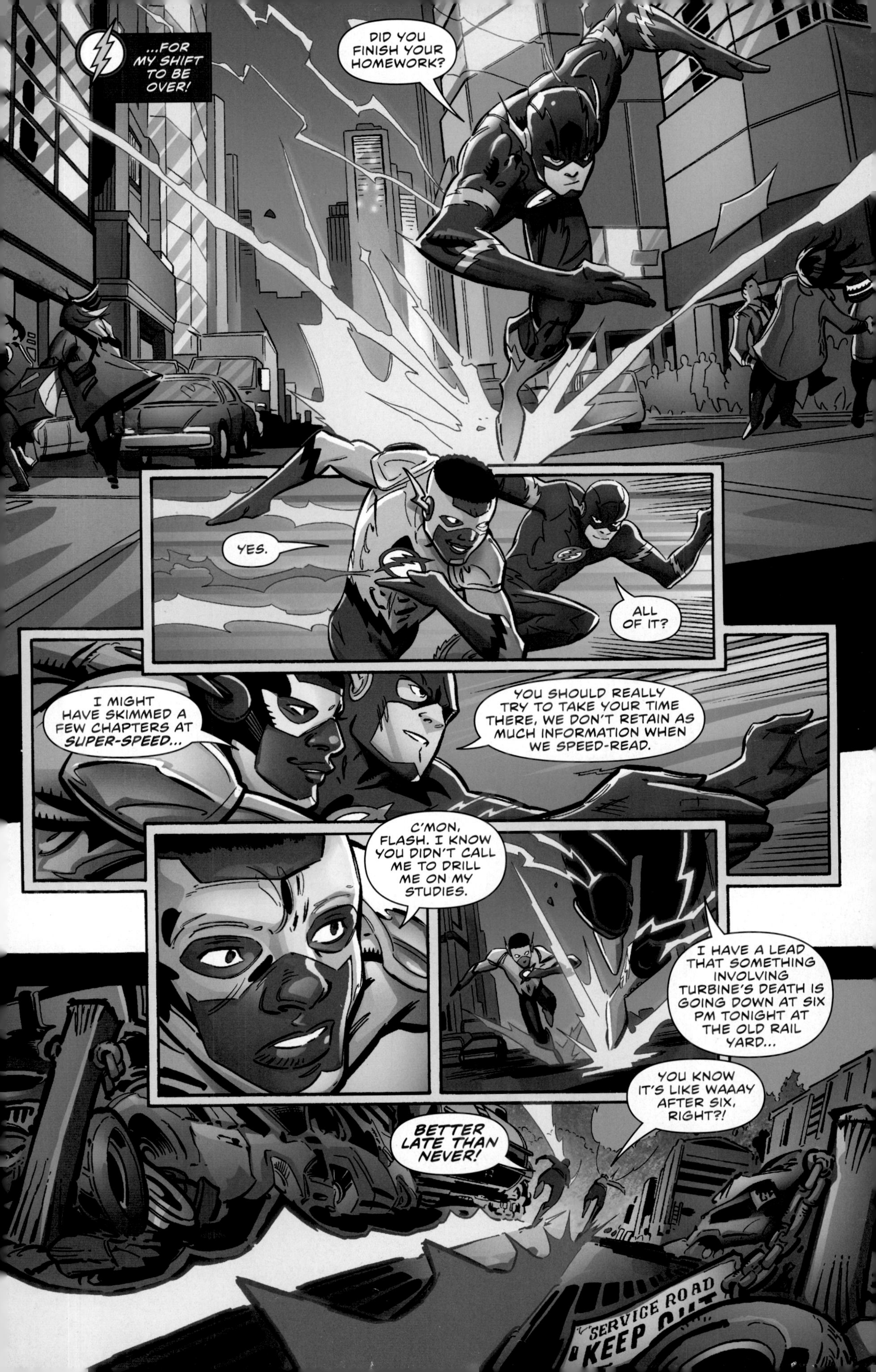
...FOR MY SHIFT TO BE OVER!
DID YOU FINISH YOUR HOMEWORK?
YES.
ALL OF IT?
I MIGHT HAVE SKIMMED A FEW CHAPTERS AT SUPER-SPEED...
YOU SHOULD REALLY TRY TO TAKE YOUR TIME THERE, WE DON'T RETAIN AS MUCH INFORMATION WHEN WE SPEED-READ.
C'MON, FLASH. I KNOW YOU DIDN'T CALL ME TO DRILL ME ON MY STUDIES.
I HAVE A LEAD THAT SOMETHING INVOLVING TURBINE'S DEATH IS GOING DOWN AT SIX PM TONIGHT AT THE OLD RAIL YARD...
YOU KNOW IT'S LIKE WAAAY AFTER SIX, RIGHT?!
BETTER LATE THAN NEVER!
SERVICE ROAD
KEEP OUT

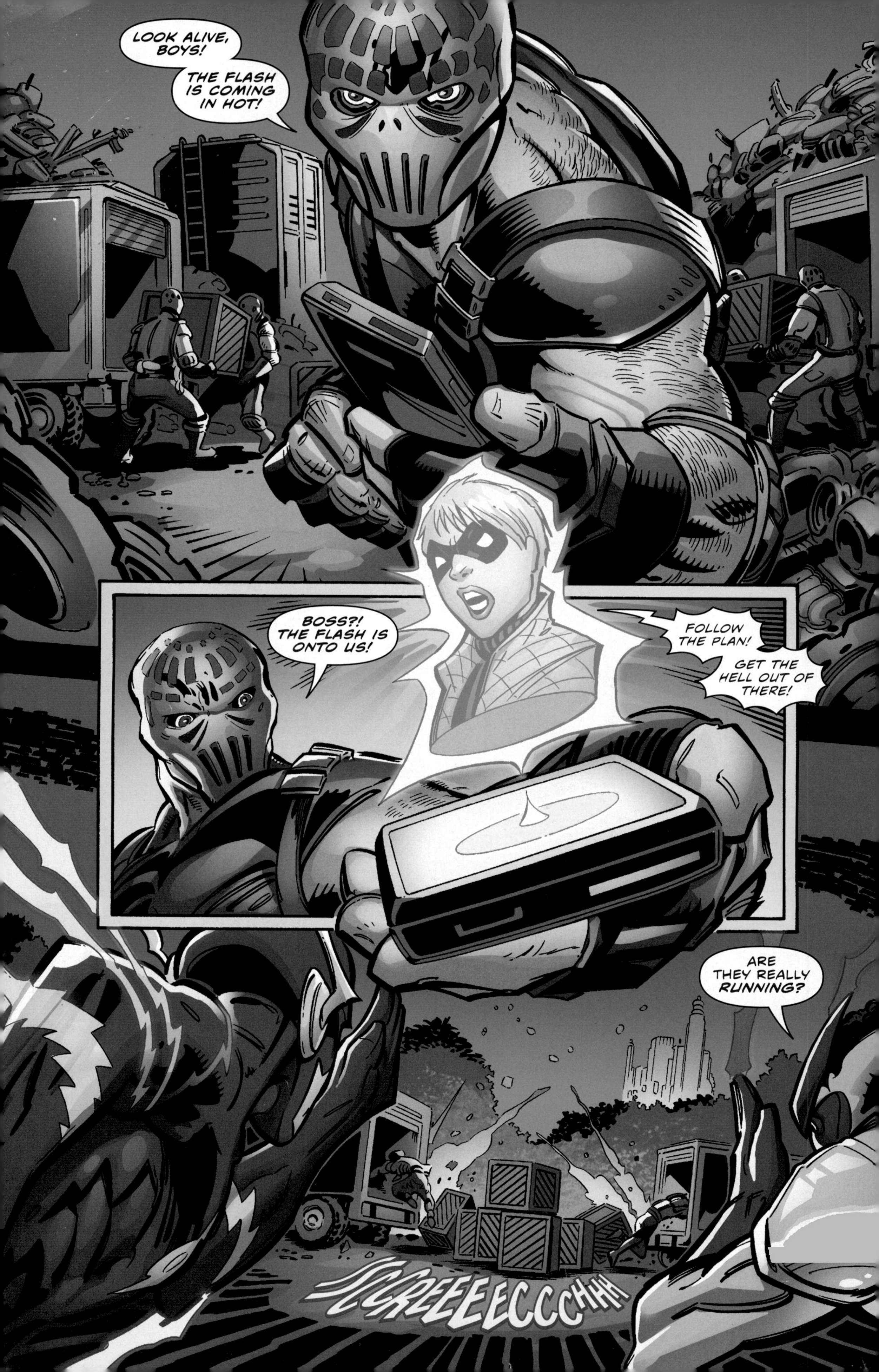
LOOK ALIVE, BOYS!
THE FLASH IS COMING IN HOT!
BOSS?! THE FLASH IS ONTO US!
FOLLOW THE PLAN!
GET THE HELL OUT OF THERE!
ARE THEY REALLY RUNNING?
SCREEEEECCCCHHH

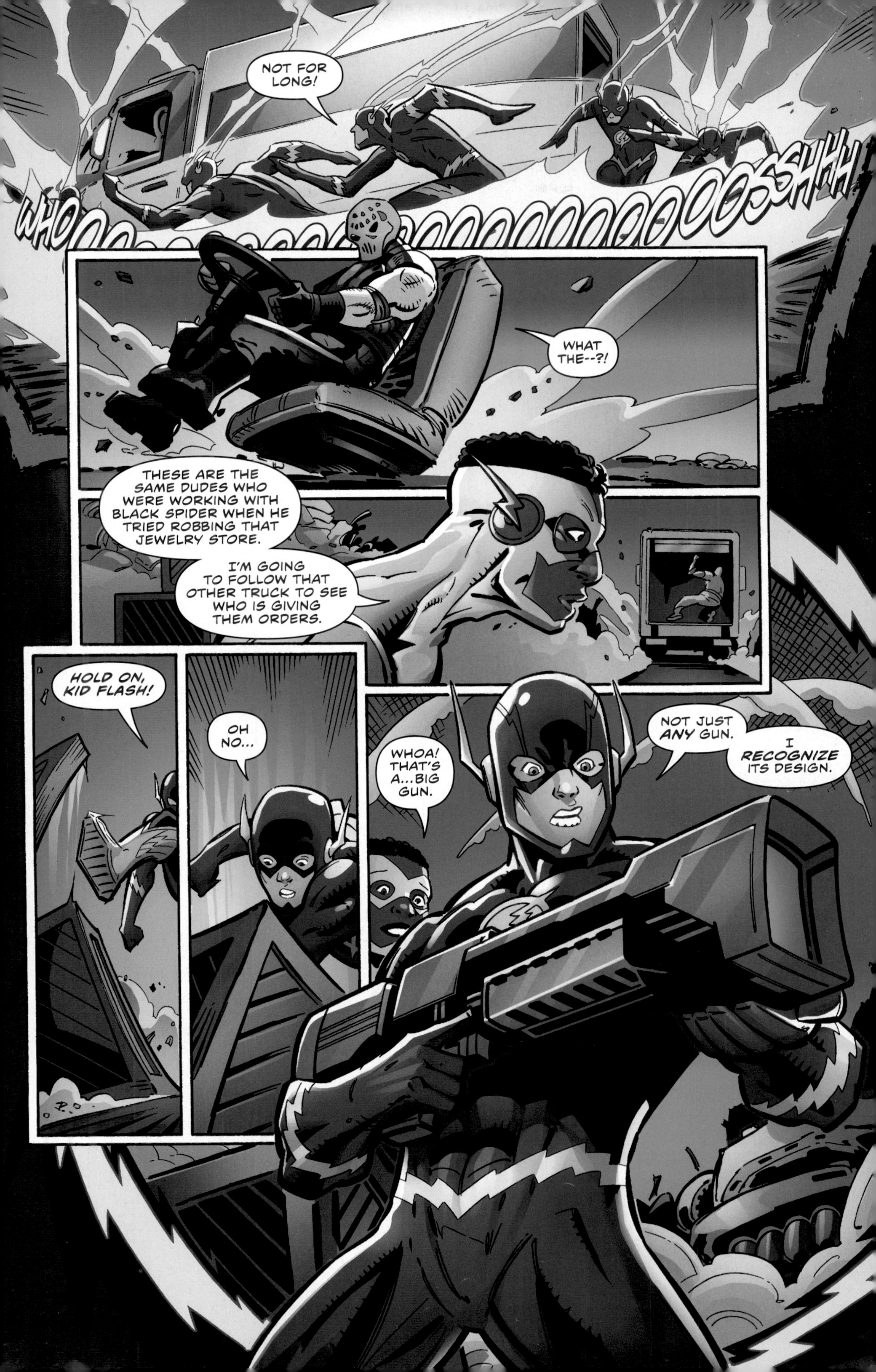
NOT FOR LONG!
WHOOOOOOOOOOOOOOOOOOOOOOOOOOOSSHHH
WHAT THE--?!
THESE ARE THE SAME DUDES WHO WERE WORKING WITH BLACK SPIDER WHEN HE TRIED ROBBING THAT JEWELRY STORE.
I'M GOING TO FOLLOW THAT OTHER TRUCK TO SEE WHO IS GIVING THEM ORDERS.
HOLD ON, KID FLASH!
OH NO...
WHOA! THAT'S A...BIG GUN.
NOT JUST ANY GUN.
I RECOGNIZE ITS DESIGN.

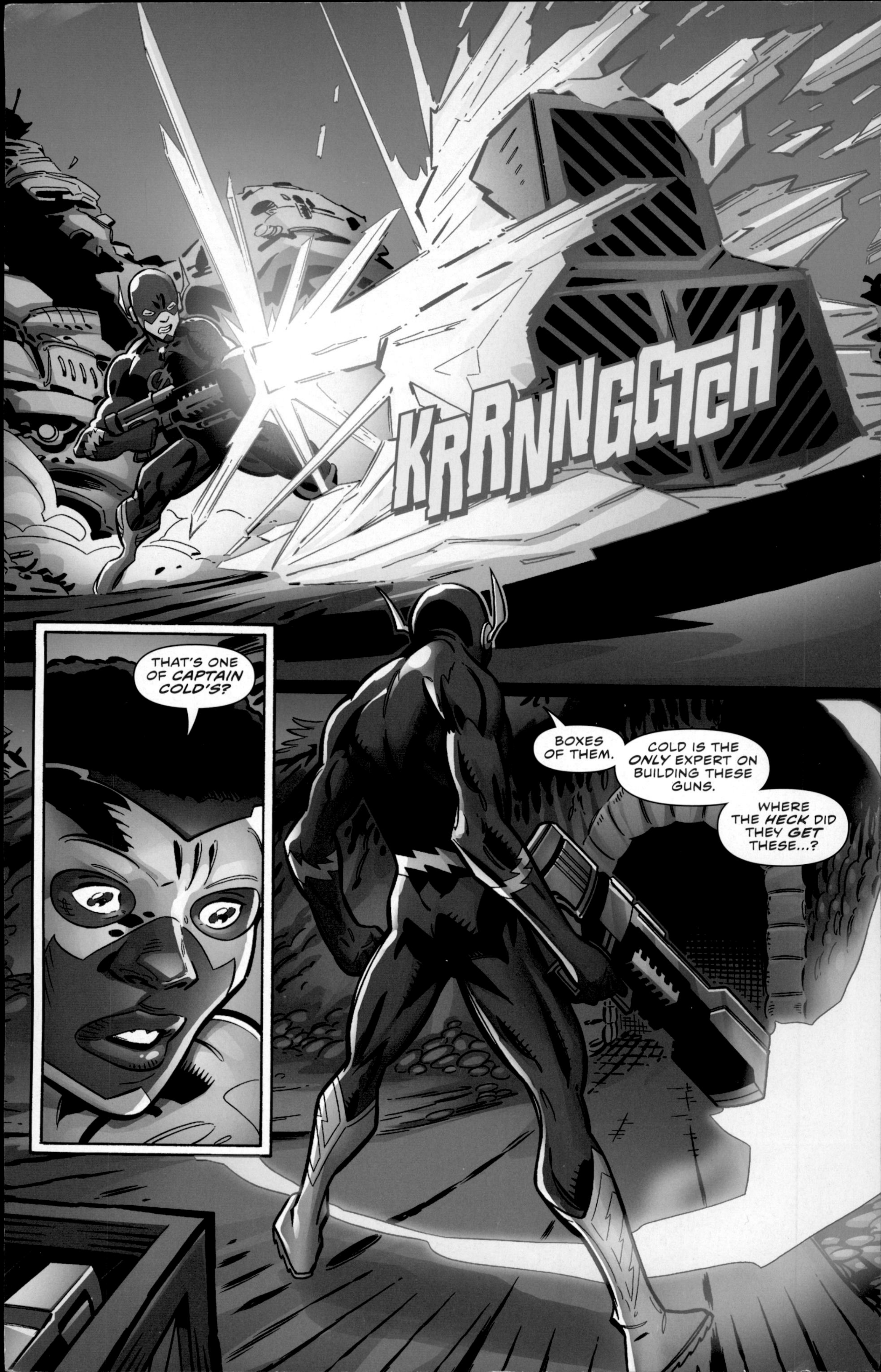
KRRNNGGTCH
THAT'S ONE OF CAPTAIN COLD'S?
BOXES OF THEM.
COLD IS THE ONLY EXPERT ON BUILDING THESE GUNS.
WHERE THE HECK DID THEY GET THESE...?

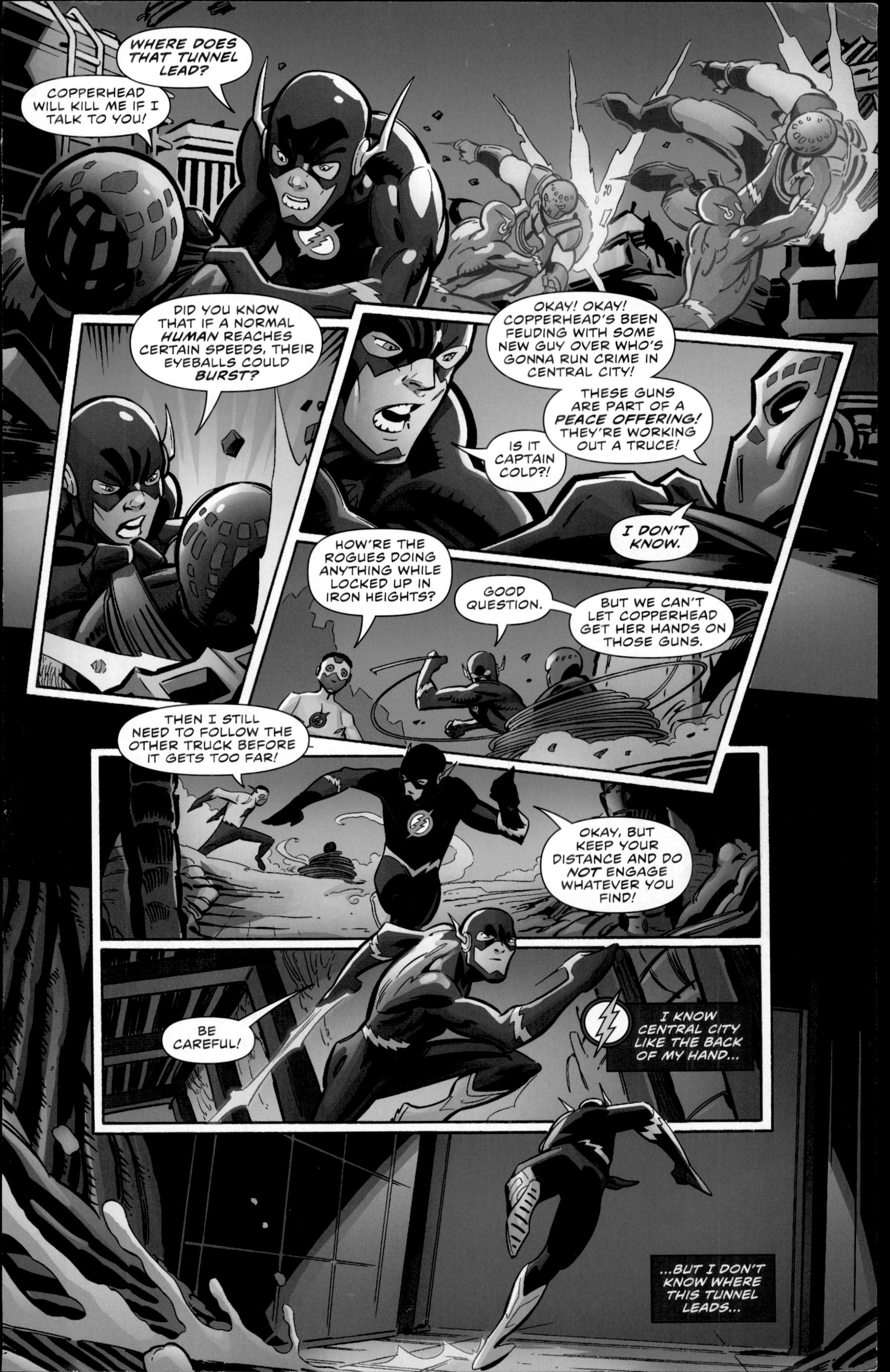
WHERE DOES THAT TUNNEL LEAD?
COPPERHEAD WILL KILL ME IF I TALK TO YOU!
DID YOU KNOW THAT IF A NORMAL HUMAN REACHES CERTAIN SPEEDS, THEIR EYEBALLS COULD BURST?
OKAY! OKAY! COPPERHEAD'S BEEN FEUDING WITH SOME NEW GUY OVER WHO'S GONNA RUN CRIME IN CENTRAL CITY!
THESE GUNS ARE PART OF A PEACE OFFERING! THEY'RE WORKING OUT A TRUCE!
IS IT CAPTAIN COLD?!
I DON'T KNOW.
HOW'RE THE ROGUES DOING ANYTHING WHILE LOCKED UP IN IRON HEIGHTS?
GOOD QUESTION.
BUT WE CAN'T LET COPPERHEAD GET HER HANDS ON THOSE GUNS.
THEN I STILL NEED TO FOLLOW THE OTHER TRUCK BEFORE IT GETS TOO FAR!
OKAY, BUT KEEP YOUR DISTANCE AND DO NOT ENGAGE WHATEVER YOU FIND!
BE CAREFUL!
I KNOW CENTRAL CITY LIKE THE BACK OF MY HAND...
...BUT I DON'T KNOW WHERE THIS TUNNEL LEADS...

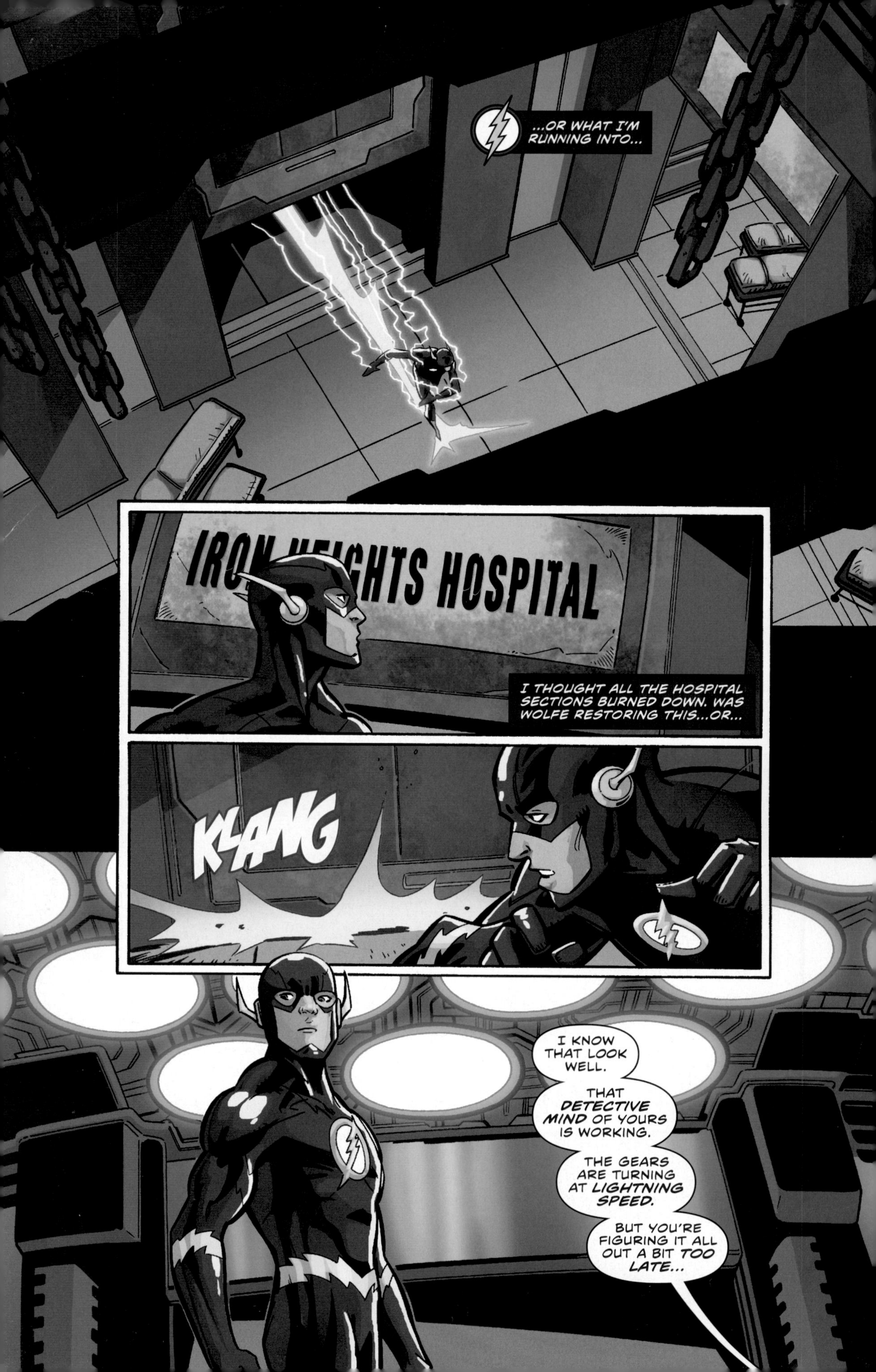
...OR WHAT I'M RUNNING INTO...
IRON HEIGHTS HOSPITAL
I THOUGHT ALL THE HOSPITAL SECTIONS BURNED DOWN. WAS WOLFE RESTORING THIS...OR...
KLANG
I KNOW THAT LOOK WELL.
THAT DETECTIVE MIND OF YOURS IS WORKING.
THE GEARS ARE TURNING AT LIGHTNING SPEED.
BUT YOU'RE FIGURING IT ALL OUT A BIT TOO LATE...

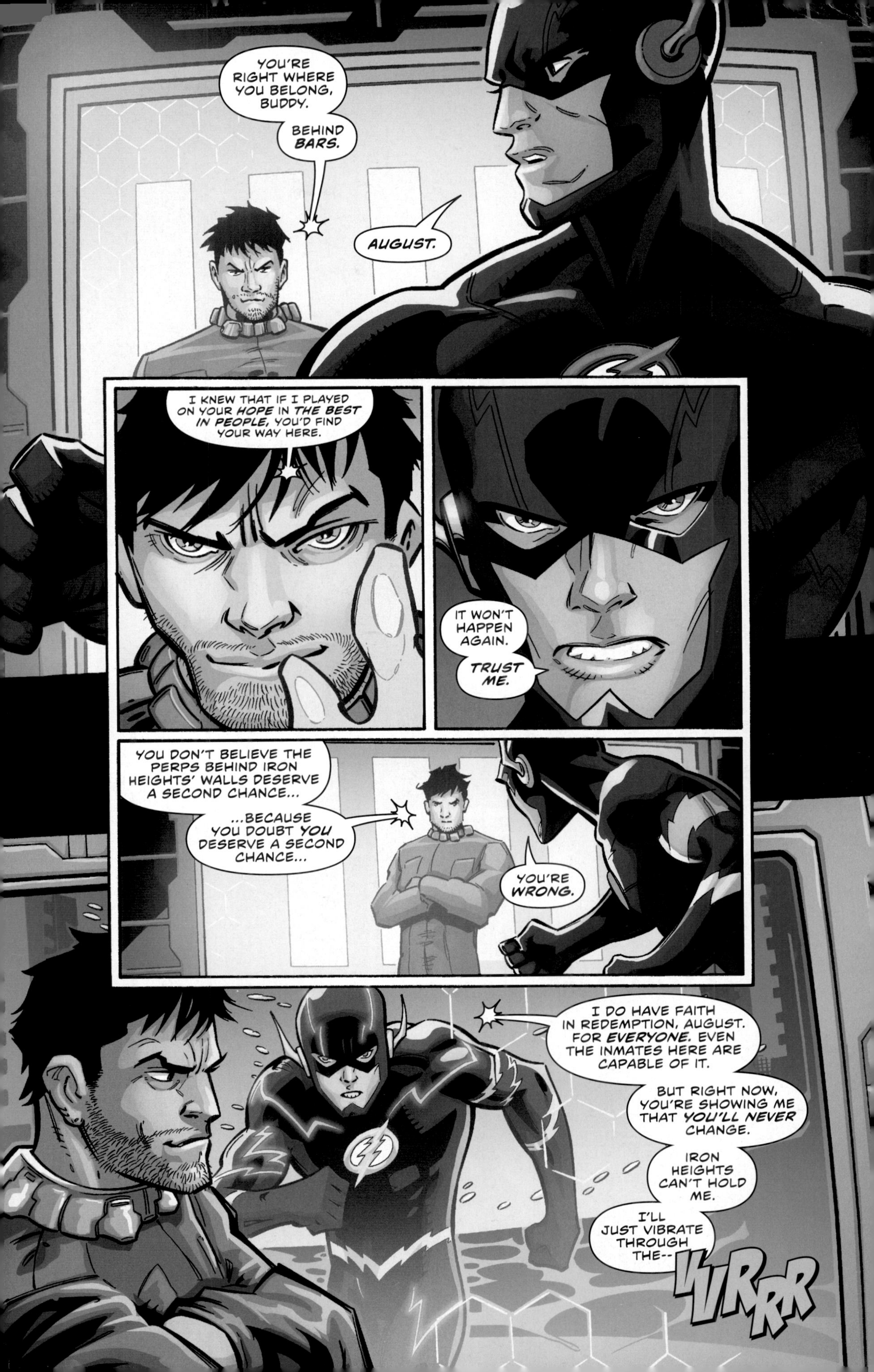
YOU'RE RIGHT WHERE YOU BELONG, BUDDY.
BEHIND BARS.
AUGUST.
I KNEW THAT IF I PLAYED ON YOUR HOPE IN THE BEST IN PEOPLE, YOU'D FIND YOUR WAY HERE.
IT WON'T HAPPEN AGAIN.
TRUST ME.
YOU DON'T BELIEVE THE PERPS BEHIND IRON HEIGHTS' WALLS DESERVE A SECOND CHANCE...
...BECAUSE YOU DOUBT YOU DESERVE A SECOND CHANCE...
YOU'RE WRONG.
I DO HAVE FAITH IN REDEMPTION, AUGUST. FOR EVERYONE. EVEN THE INMATES HERE ARE CAPABLE OF IT.
BUT RIGHT NOW, YOU'RE SHOWING ME THAT YOU'LL NEVER CHANGE.
IRON HEIGHTS CAN'T HOLD ME.
I'LL JUST VIBRATE THROUGH THE--
VVRRR

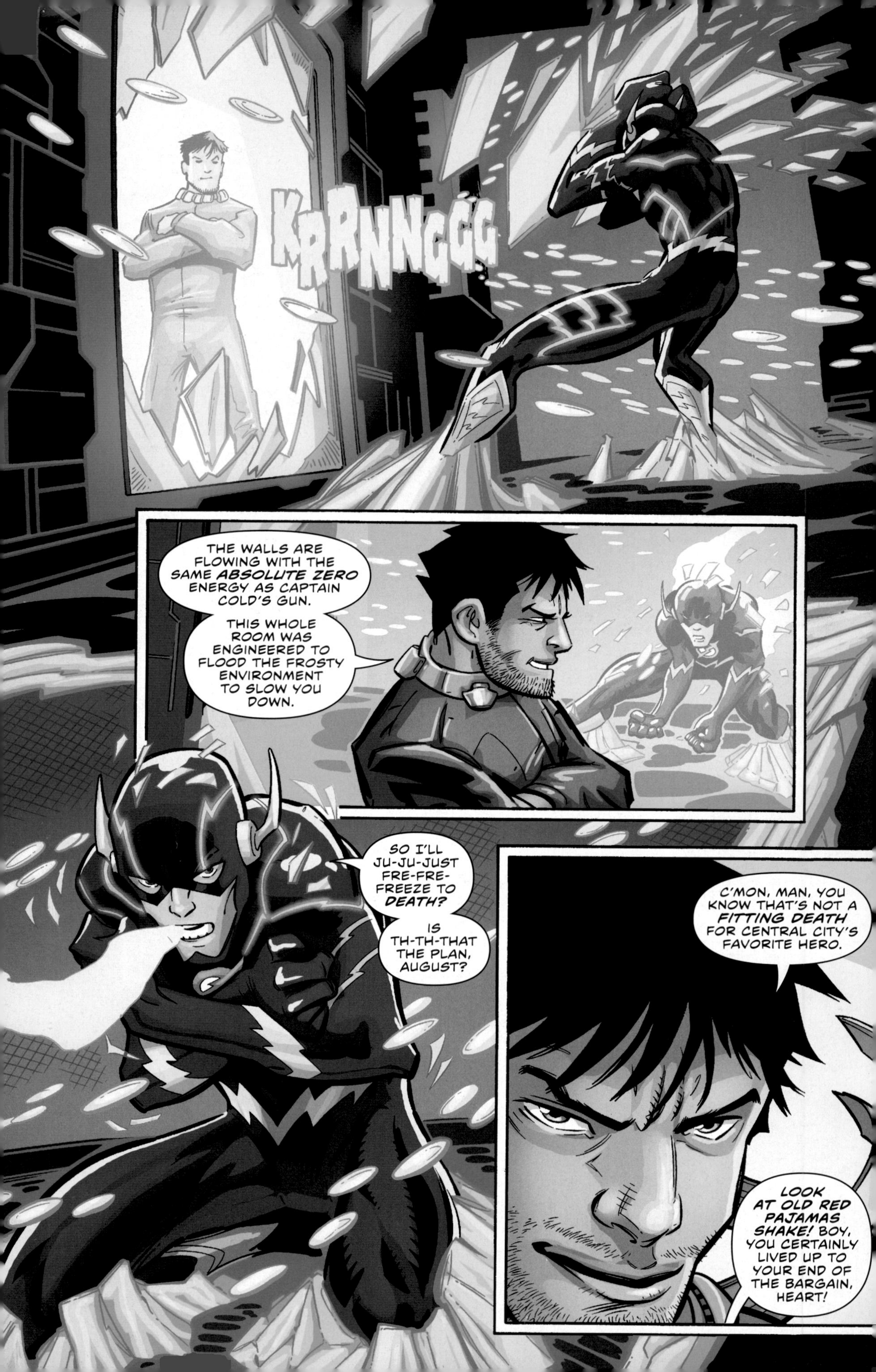
KRRNNGGG
THE WALLS ARE FLOWING WITH THE SAME ABSOLUTE ZERO ENERGY AS CAPTAIN COLD'S GUN.
THIS WHOLE ROOM WAS ENGINEERED TO FLOOD THE FROSTY ENVIRONMENT TO SLOW YOU DOWN.
SO I'LL JU-JU-JUST FRE-FRE-FREEZE TO DEATH?
IS TH-TH-THAT THE PLAN, AUGUST?
C'MON, MAN, YOU KNOW THAT'S NOT A FITTING DEATH FOR CENTRAL CITY'S FAVORITE HERO.
LOOK AT OLD RED PAJAMAS SHAKE! BOY, YOU CERTAINLY LIVED UP TO YOUR END OF THE BARGAIN, HEART!

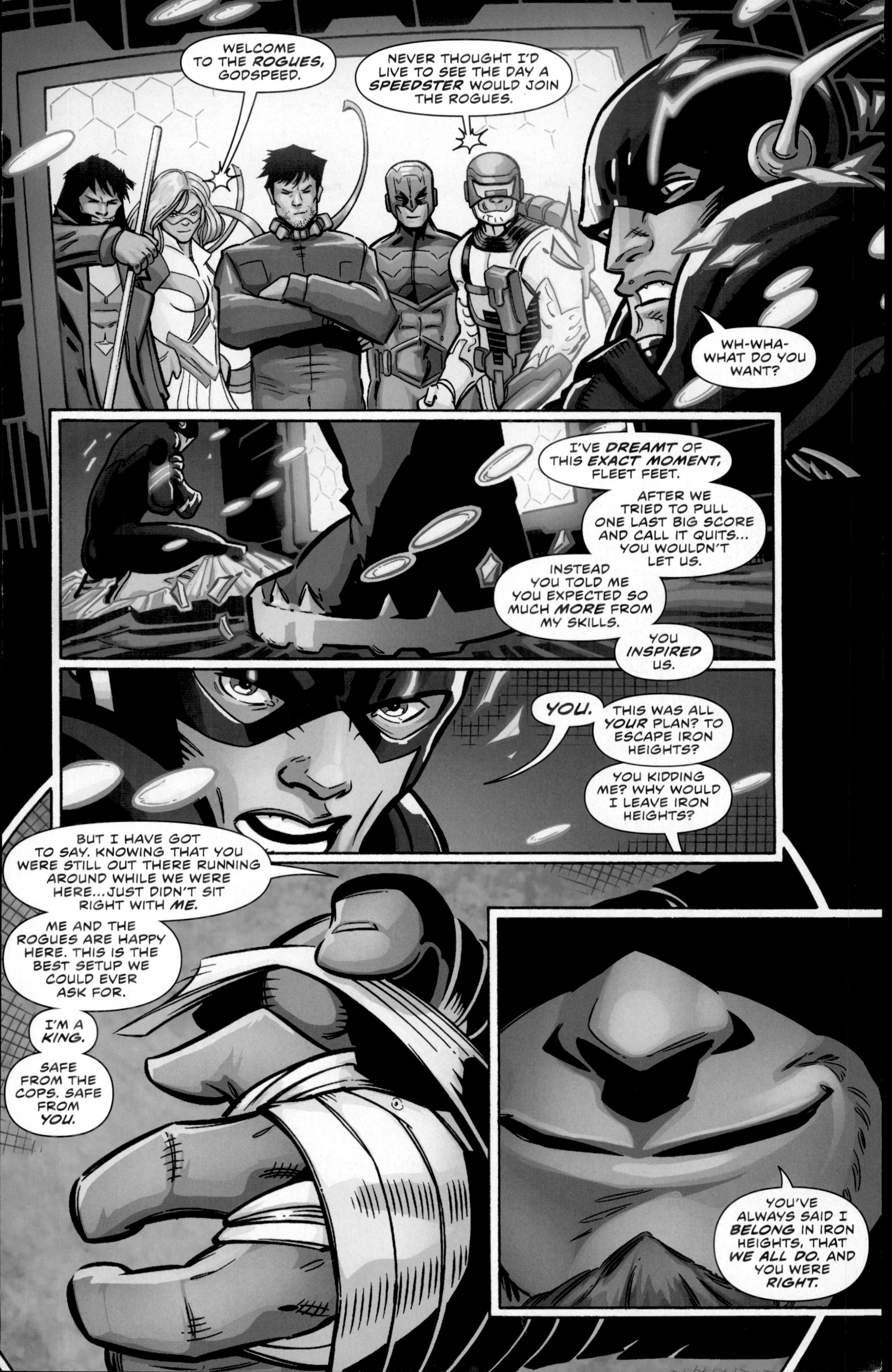
WELCOME TO THE ROGUES, GODSPEED.
NEVER THOUGHT I'D LIVE TO SEE THE DAY A SPEEDSTER WOULD JOIN THE ROGUES.
WH-WHA- WHAT DO YOU WANT?
I'VE DREAMT OF THIS EXACT MOMENT, FLEET FEET.
AFTER WE TRIED TO PULL ONE LAST BIG SCORE AND CALL IT QUITS... YOU WOULDN'T LET US.
INSTEAD YOU TOLD ME YOU EXPECTED SO MUCH MORE FROM MY SKILLS.
YOU INSPIRED US.
YOU.
THIS WAS ALL YOUR PLAN? TO ESCAPE IRON HEIGHTS?
YOU KIDDING ME? WHY WOULD I LEAVE IRON HEIGHTS?
BUT I HAVE GOT TO SAY. KNOWING THAT YOU WERE STILL OUT THERE RUNNING AROUND WHILE WE WERE HERE...JUST DIDN'T SIT RIGHT WITH ME.
ME AND THE ROGUES ARE HAPPY HERE. THIS IS THE BEST SETUP WE COULD EVER ASK FOR.
I'M A KING.
SAFE FROM THE COPS. SAFE FROM YOU.
YOU'VE ALWAYS SAID I BELONG IN IRON HEIGHTS, THAT WE ALL DO. AND YOU WERE RIGHT.

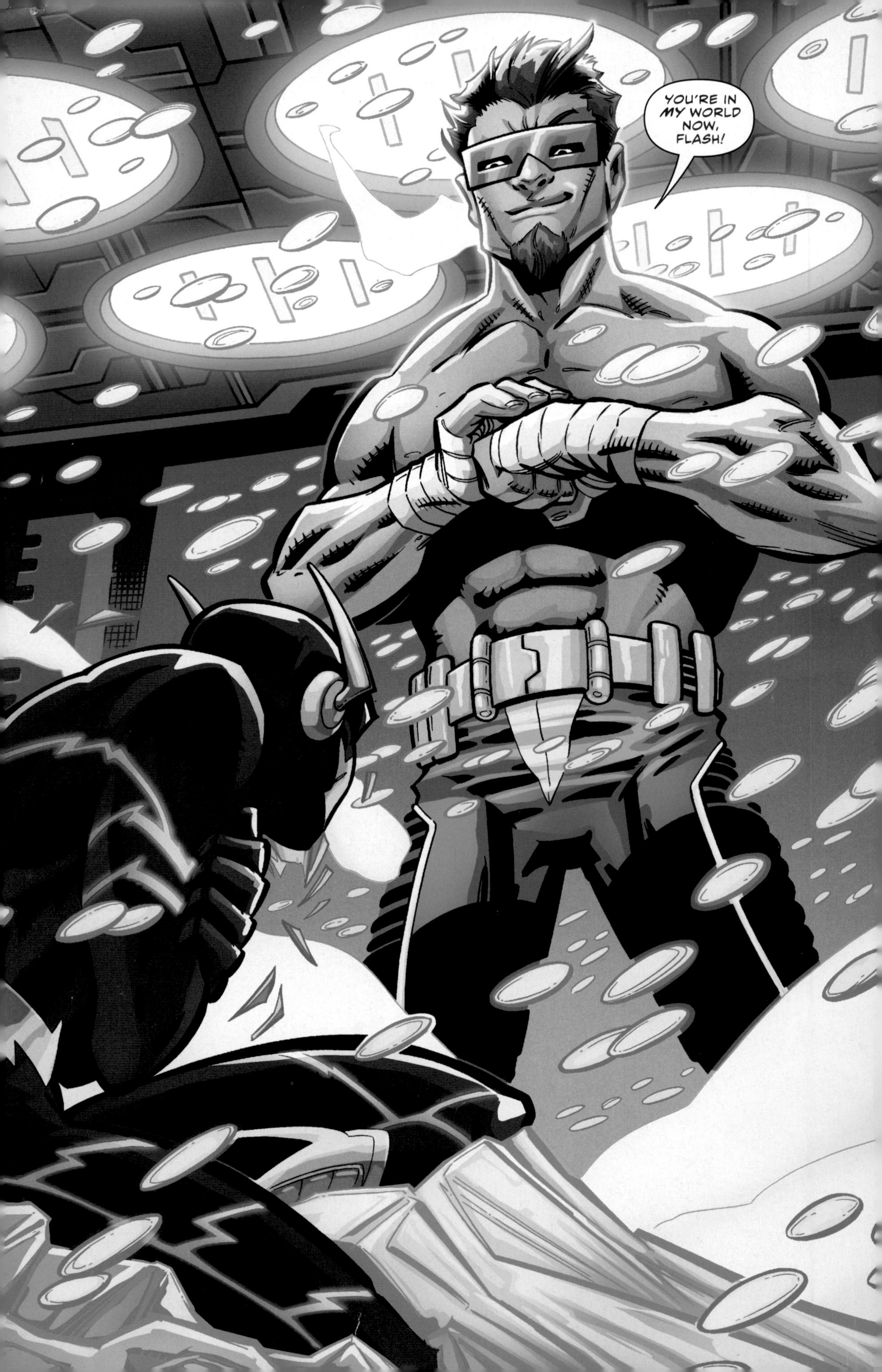
YOU'RE IN MY WORLD NOW, FLASH!

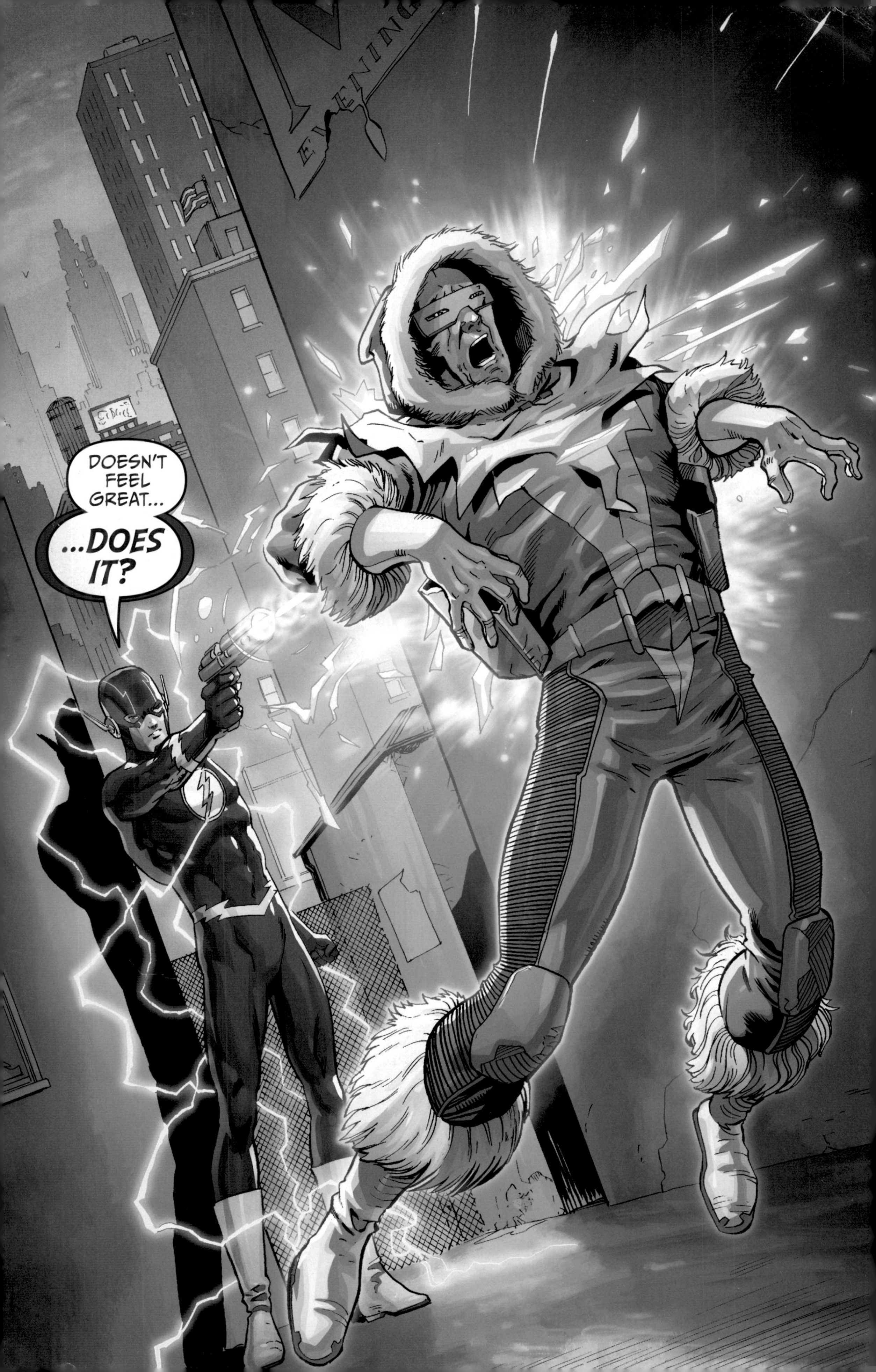
DOESN'T FEEL GREAT...
...DOES IT?

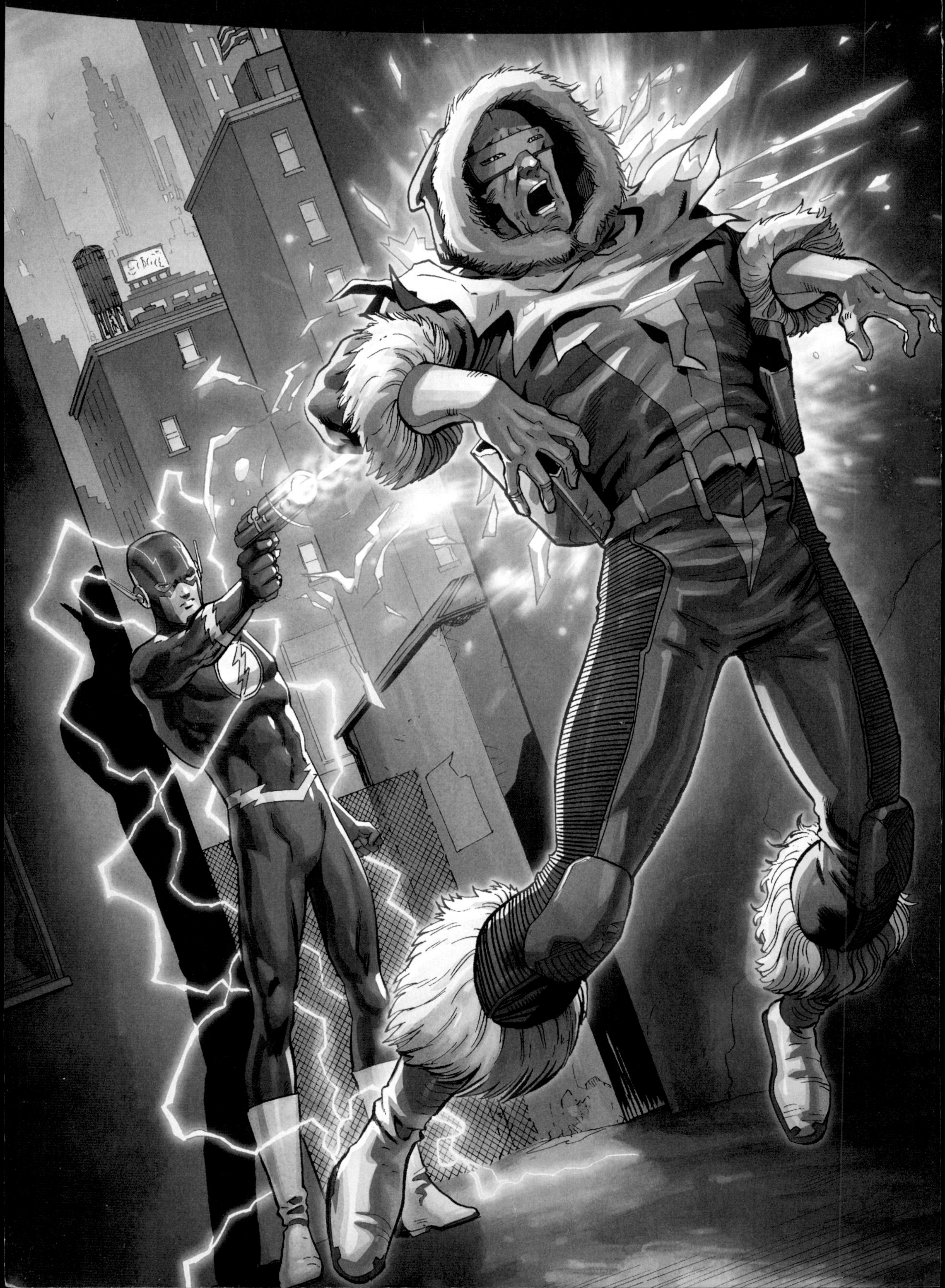

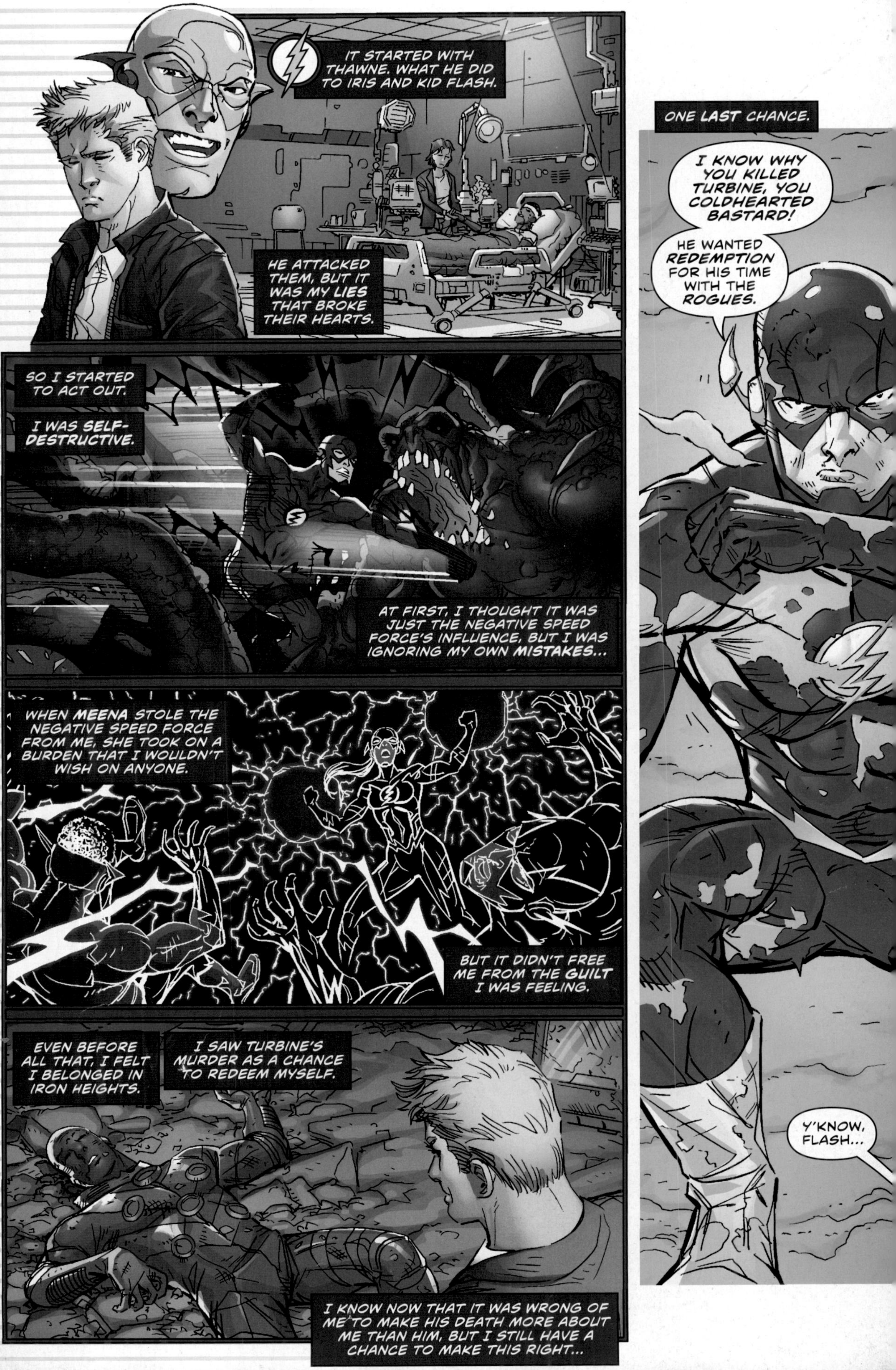

IT STARTED WITH THAWNE. WHAT HE DID TO IRIS AND KID FLASH.
HE ATTACKED THEM, BUT IT WAS MY LIES THAT BROKE THEIR HEARTS.
SO I STARTED TO ACT OUT.
I WAS SELF-DESTRUCTIVE.
AT FIRST, I THOUGHT IT WAS JUST THE NEGATIVE SPEED FORCE'S INFLUENCE, BUT I WAS IGNORING MY OWN MISTAKES...
WHEN MEENA STOLE THE NEGATIVE SPEED FORCE FROM ME, SHE TOOK ON A BURDEN THAT I WOULDN'T WISH ON ANYONE.
BUT IT DIDN'T FREE ME FROM THE GUILT I WAS FEELING.
EVEN BEFORE ALL THAT, I FELT I BELONGED IN IRON HEIGHTS.
I SAW TURBINE'S MURDER AS A CHANCE TO REDEEM MYSELF.
I KNOW NOW THAT IT WAS WRONG OF ME TO MAKE HIS DEATH MORE ABOUT ME THAN HIM, BUT I STILL HAVE A CHANCE TO MAKE THIS RIGHT...
ONE LAST CHANCE.
I KNOW WHY YOU KILLED TURBINE, YOU COLDHEARTED BASTARD!
HE WANTED REDEMPTION FOR HIS TIME WITH THE ROGUES.
Y'KNOW, FLASH...

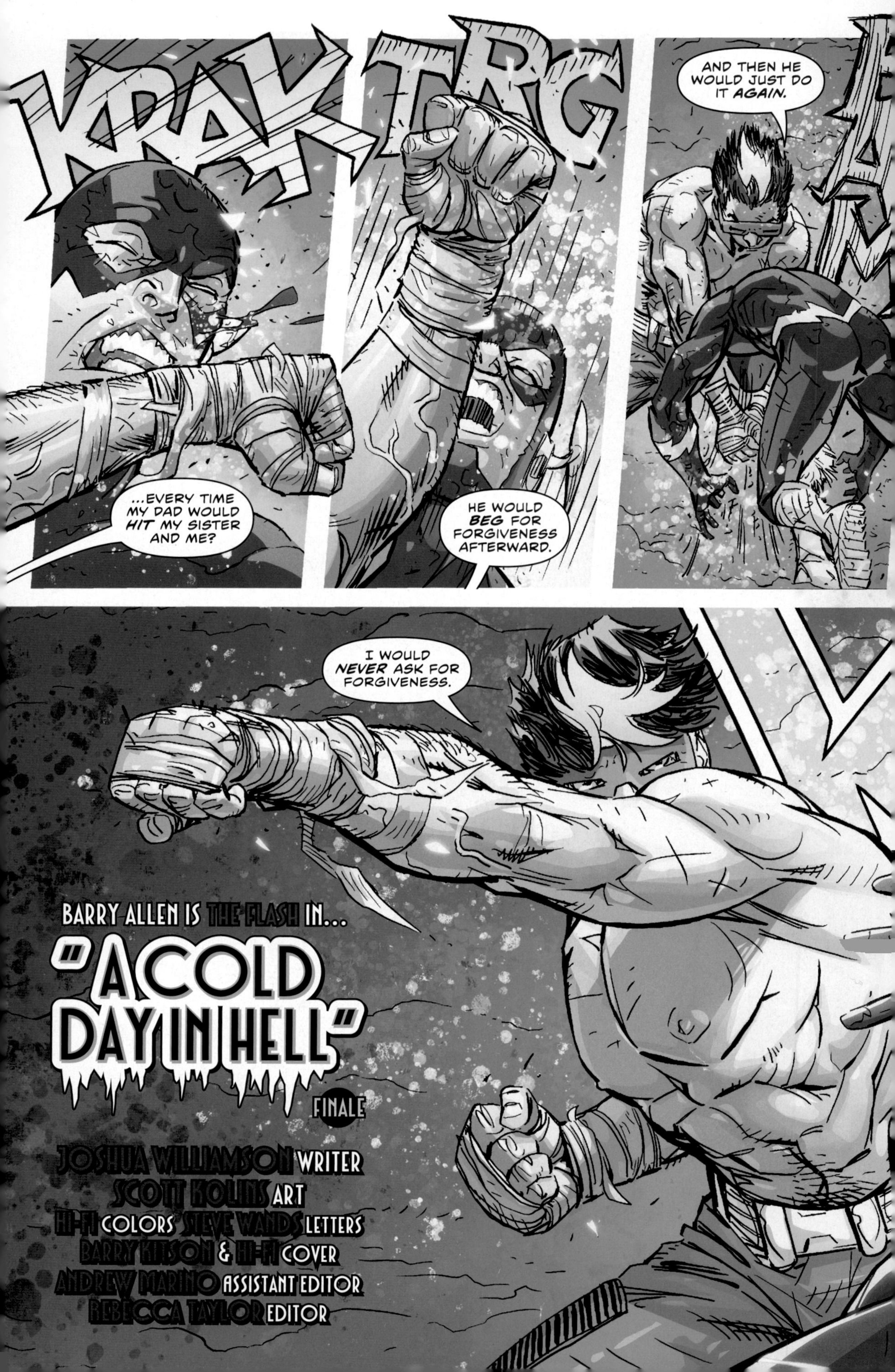
KRAK
...EVERY TIME MY DAD WOULD *HIT* MY SISTER AND ME?
TRG
HE WOULD *BEG* FOR FORGIVENESS AFTERWARD.
AND THEN HE WOULD JUST DO IT *AGAIN.*
I WOULD *NEVER* ASK FOR FORGIVENESS.
BARRY ALLEN IS THE FLASH IN...
"A COLD DAY IN HELL"
FINALE
JOSHUA WILLIAMSON WRITER
SCOTT KOLINS ART
HI-FI COLORS STEVE WANDS LETTERS
BARRY KITSON & HI-FI COVER
ANDREW MARINO ASSISTANT EDITOR
REBECCA TAYLOR EDITOR

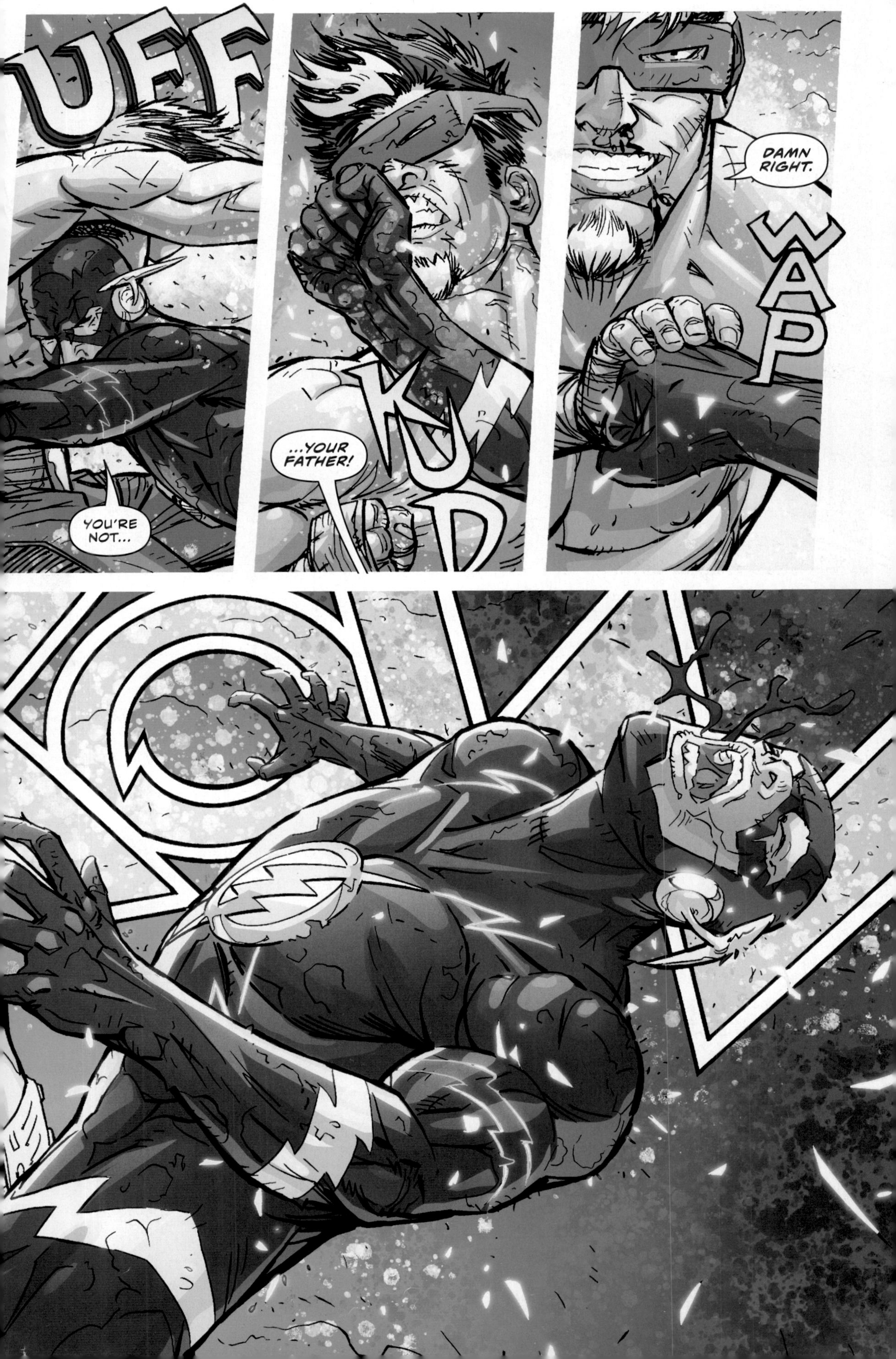
UFF
YOU'RE NOT...
...YOUR FATHER!
KUD
DAMN RIGHT.
WAP

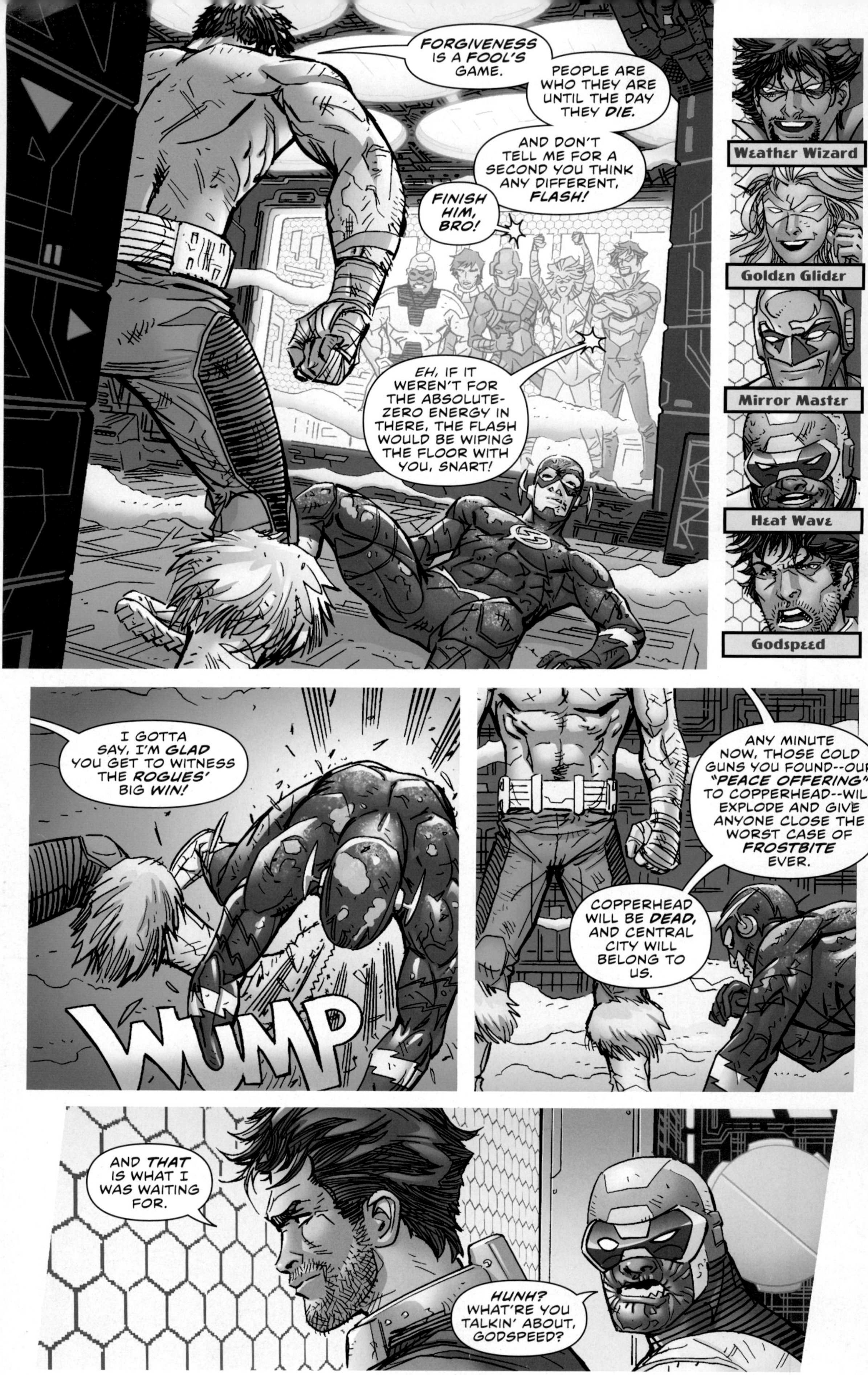
FORGIVENESS IS A FOOL'S GAME.
PEOPLE ARE WHO THEY ARE UNTIL THE DAY THEY DIE.
AND DON'T TELL ME FOR A SECOND YOU THINK ANY DIFFERENT, FLASH!
FINISH HIM, BRO!
EH, IF IT WEREN'T FOR THE ABSOLUTE-ZERO ENERGY IN THERE, THE FLASH WOULD BE WIPING THE FLOOR WITH YOU, SNART!
Weather Wizard
Golden Glider
Mirror Master
Heat Wave
Godspeed
I GOTTA SAY, I'M GLAD YOU GET TO WITNESS THE ROGUES' BIG WIN!
WUMP
ANY MINUTE NOW, THOSE COLD GUNS YOU FOUND--OUR "PEACE OFFERING" TO COPPERHEAD--WILL EXPLODE AND GIVE ANYONE CLOSE THE WORST CASE OF FROSTBITE EVER.
COPPERHEAD WILL BE DEAD, AND CENTRAL CITY WILL BELONG TO US.
AND THAT IS WHAT I WAS WAITING FOR.
HUNH? WHAT'RE YOU TALKIN' ABOUT, GODSPEED?

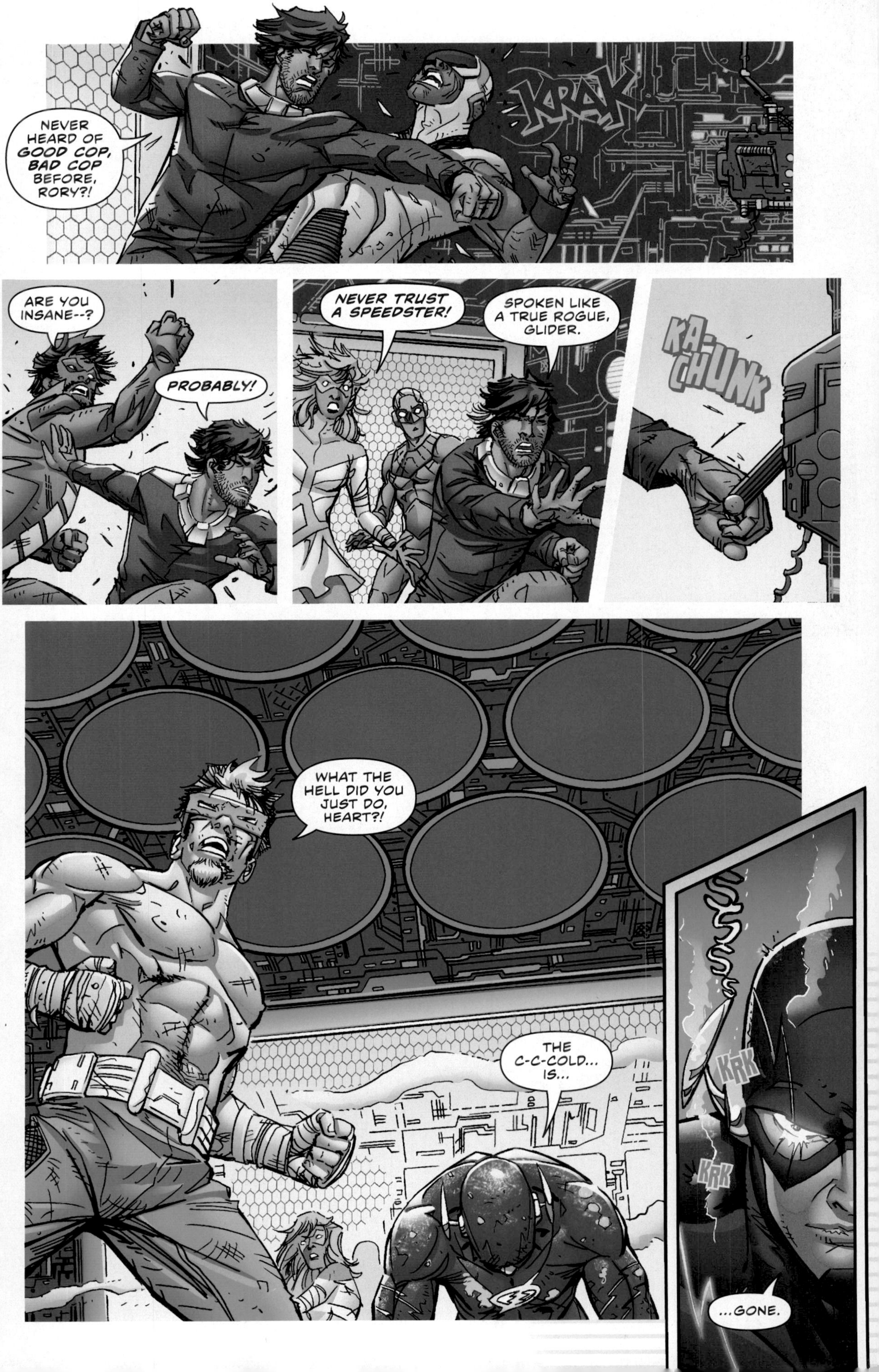
NEVER HEARD OF GOOD COP, BAD COP BEFORE, RORY?!
KRAK
ARE YOU INSANE--?
PROBABLY!
NEVER TRUST A SPEEDSTER!
SPOKEN LIKE A TRUE ROGUE, GLIDER.
KA-CHUNK
WHAT THE HELL DID YOU JUST DO, HEART?!
THE C-C-COLD... IS...
KRK
KRK
...GONE.

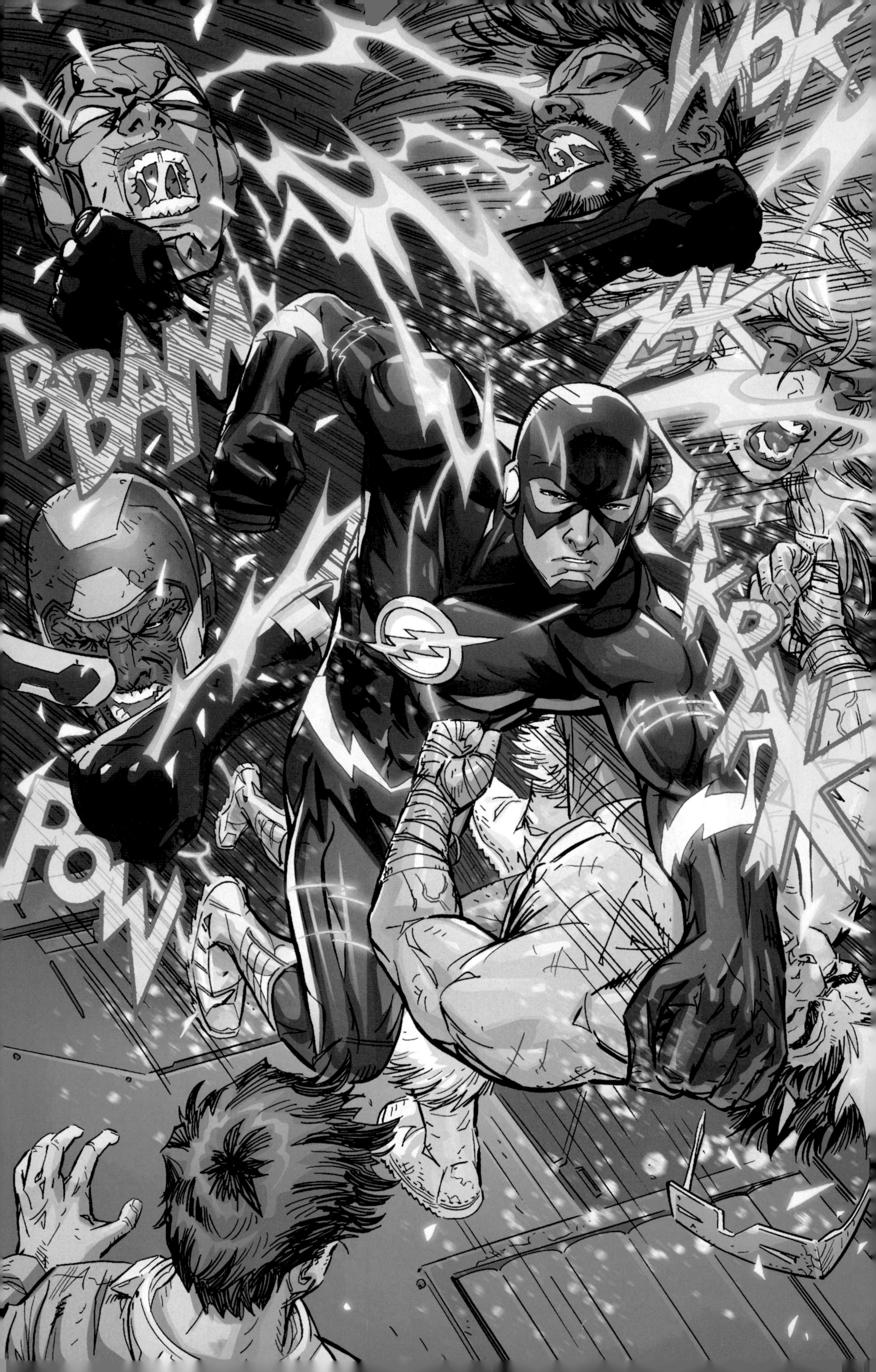
BBAM
POW

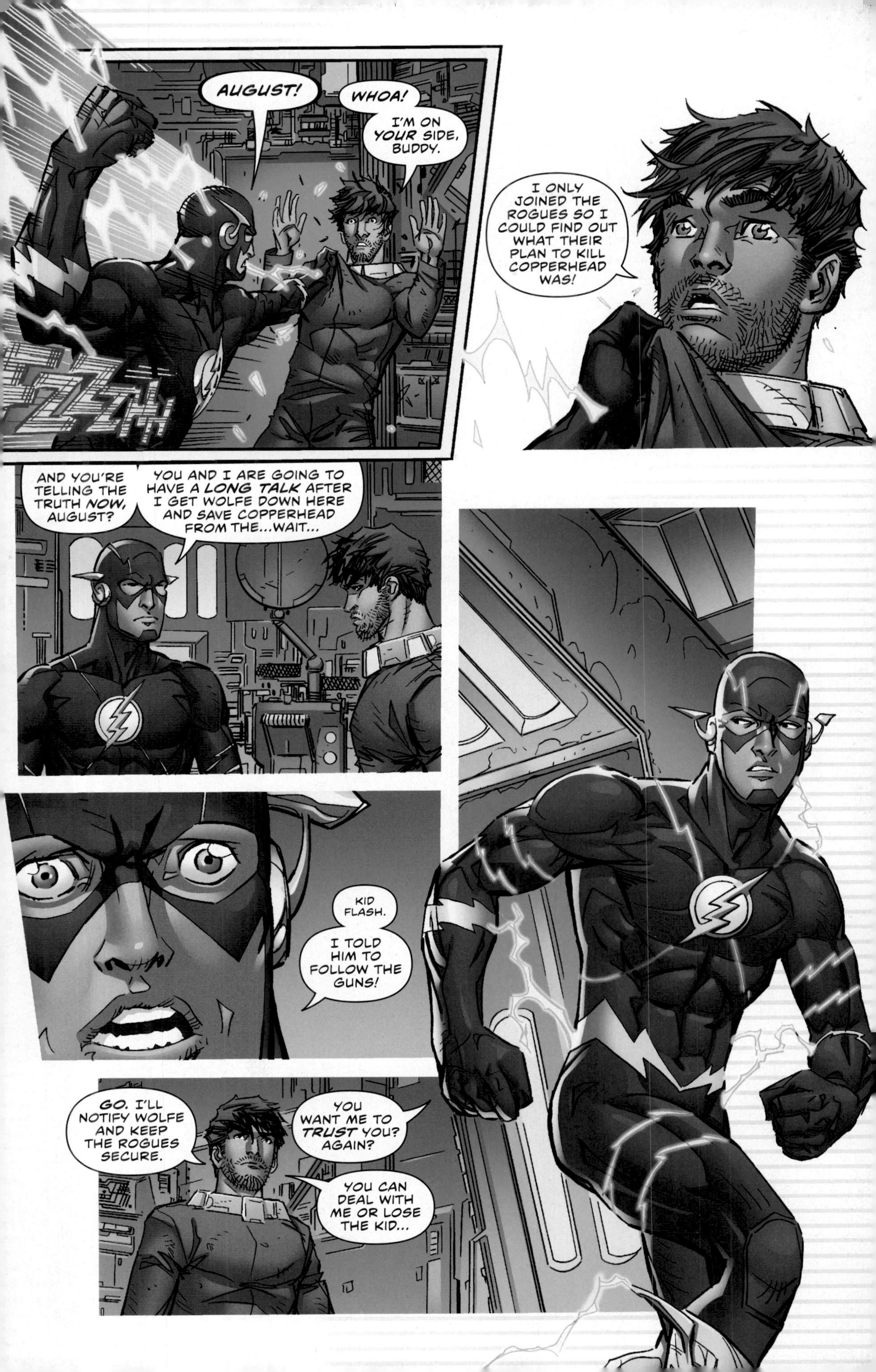
AUGUST!
WHOA!
I'M ON YOUR SIDE, BUDDY.
I ONLY JOINED THE ROGUES SO I COULD FIND OUT WHAT THEIR PLAN TO KILL COPPERHEAD WAS!
AND YOU'RE TELLING THE TRUTH NOW, AUGUST?
YOU AND I ARE GOING TO HAVE A LONG TALK AFTER I GET WOLFE DOWN HERE AND SAVE COPPERHEAD FROM THE...WAIT...
KID FLASH.
I TOLD HIM TO FOLLOW THE GUNS!
GO. I'LL NOTIFY WOLFE AND KEEP THE ROGUES SECURE.
YOU WANT ME TO TRUST YOU? AGAIN?
YOU CAN DEAL WITH ME OR LOSE THE KID...

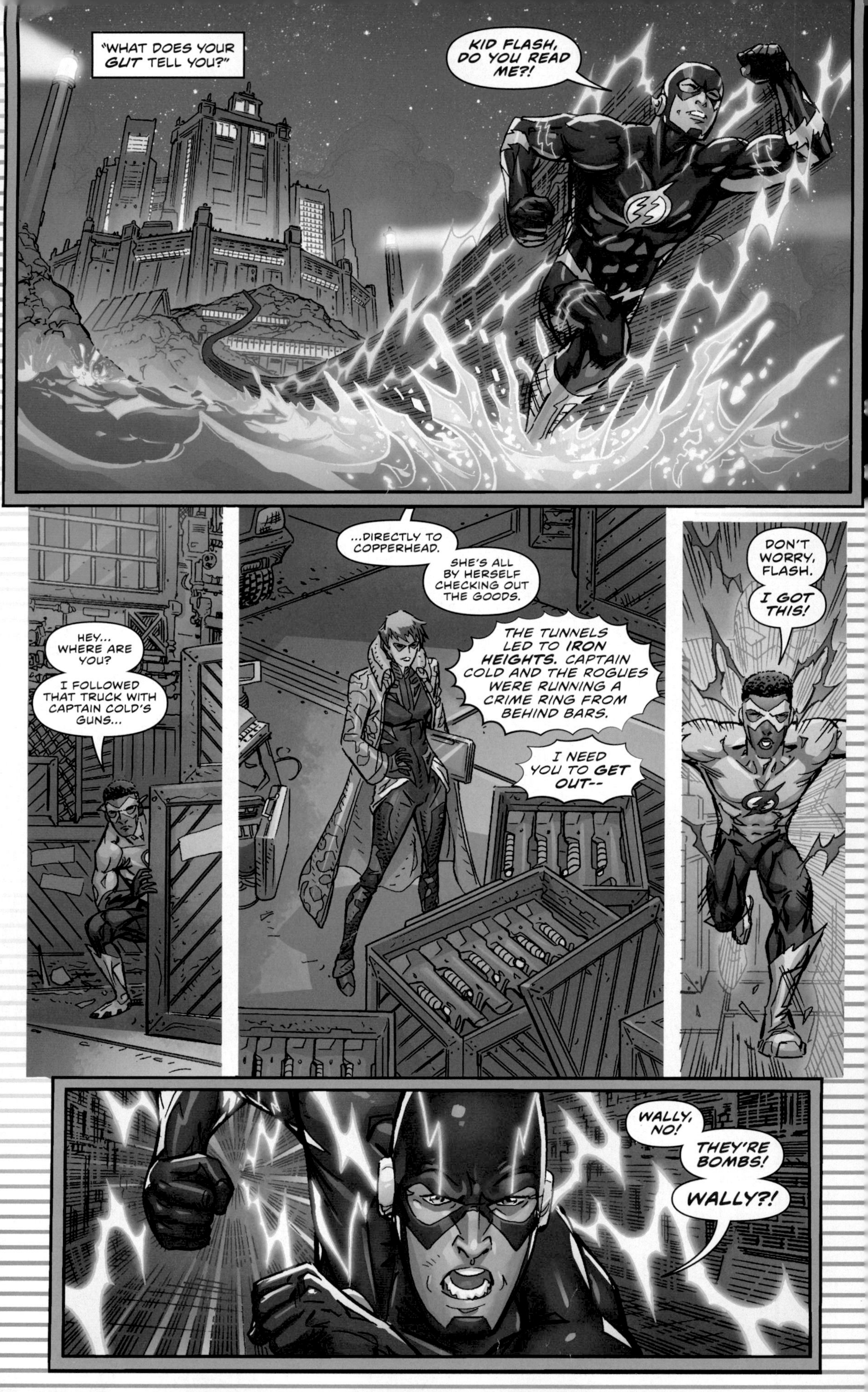
"WHAT DOES YOUR GUT TELL YOU?"
KID FLASH, DO YOU READ ME?!
HEY... WHERE ARE YOU?
I FOLLOWED THAT TRUCK WITH CAPTAIN COLD'S GUNS...
...DIRECTLY TO COPPERHEAD.
SHE'S ALL BY HERSELF CHECKING OUT THE GOODS.
THE TUNNELS LED TO IRON HEIGHTS. CAPTAIN COLD AND THE ROGUES WERE RUNNING A CRIME RING FROM BEHIND BARS.
I NEED YOU TO GET OUT--
DON'T WORRY, FLASH.
I GOT THIS!
WALLY, NO!
THEY'RE BOMBS!
WALLY?!

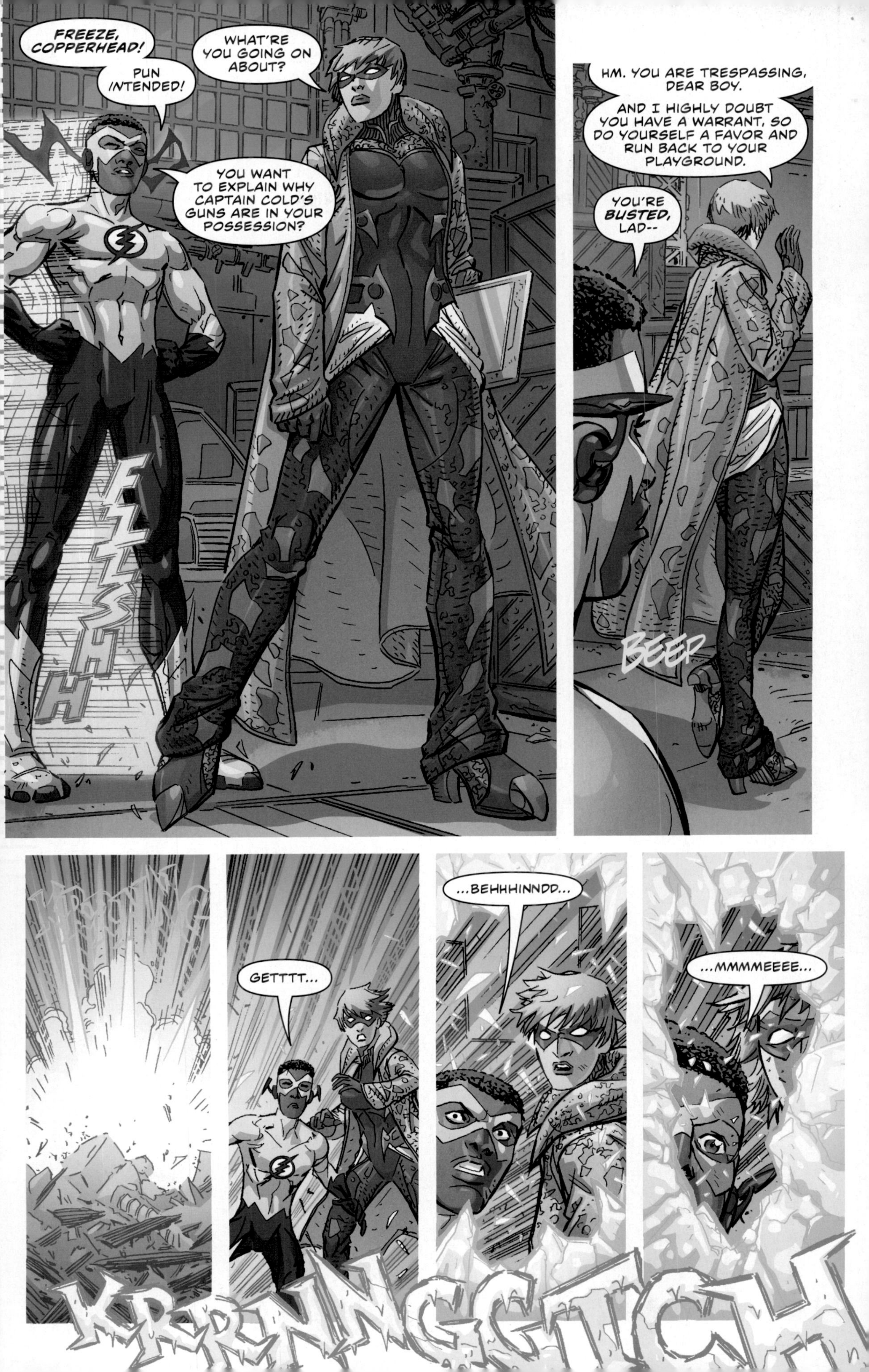
FREEZE, COPPERHEAD!
PUN INTENDED!
WHAT'RE YOU GOING ON ABOUT?
YOU WANT TO EXPLAIN WHY CAPTAIN COLD'S GUNS ARE IN YOUR POSSESSION?
FFLLSSHHH
HM. YOU ARE TRESPASSING, DEAR BOY.
AND I HIGHLY DOUBT YOU HAVE A WARRANT, SO DO YOURSELF A FAVOR AND RUN BACK TO YOUR PLAYGROUND.
YOU'RE BUSTED, LAD--
BEEP
GETTTT...
...BEHHHINNDD...
...MMMMEEEE...

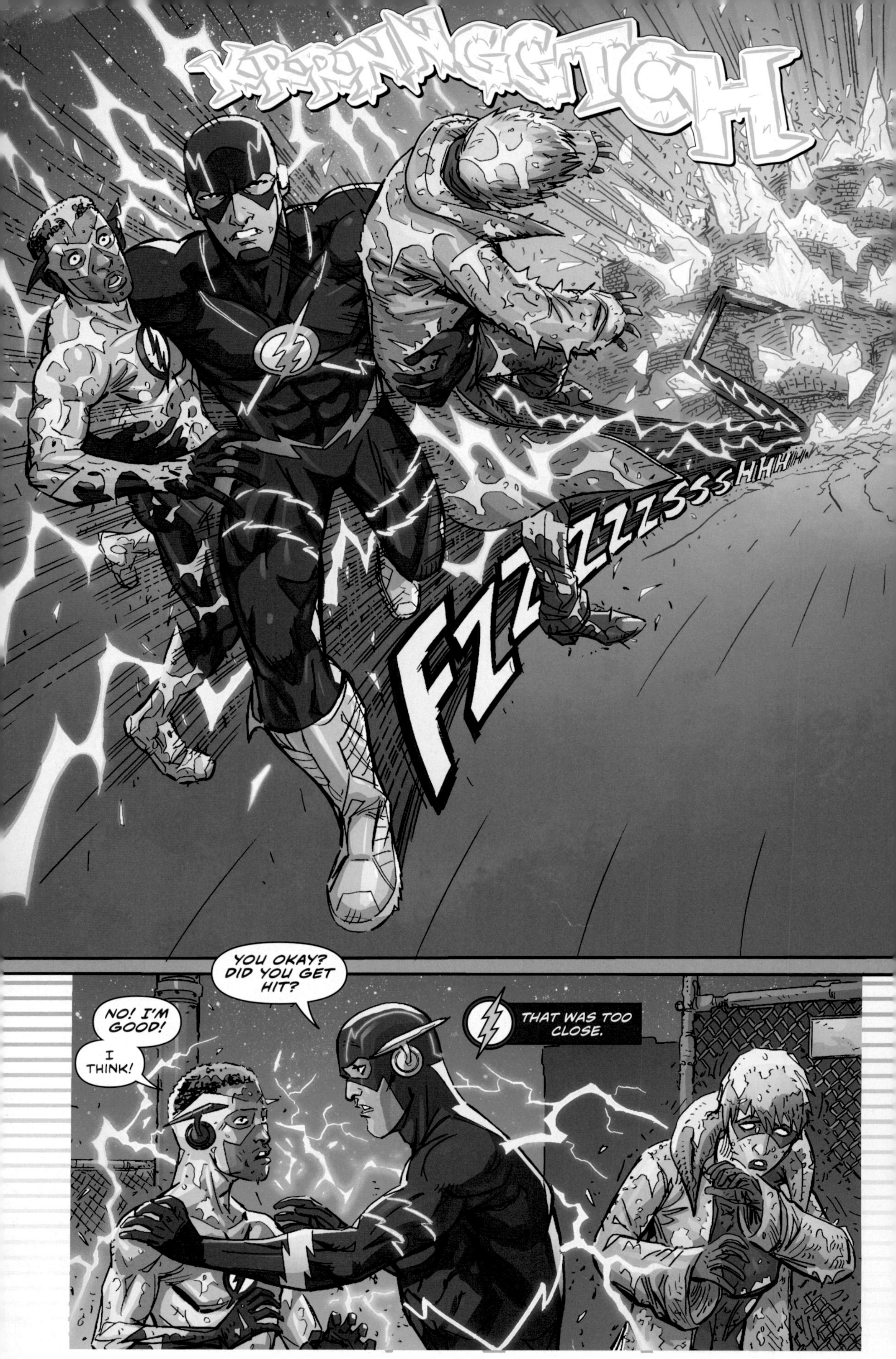
KRRNNGGTCH
FZZZZZZZSSSSHHHH
YOU OKAY? DID YOU GET HIT?
NO! I'M GOOD!
I THINK!
THAT WAS TOO CLOSE.

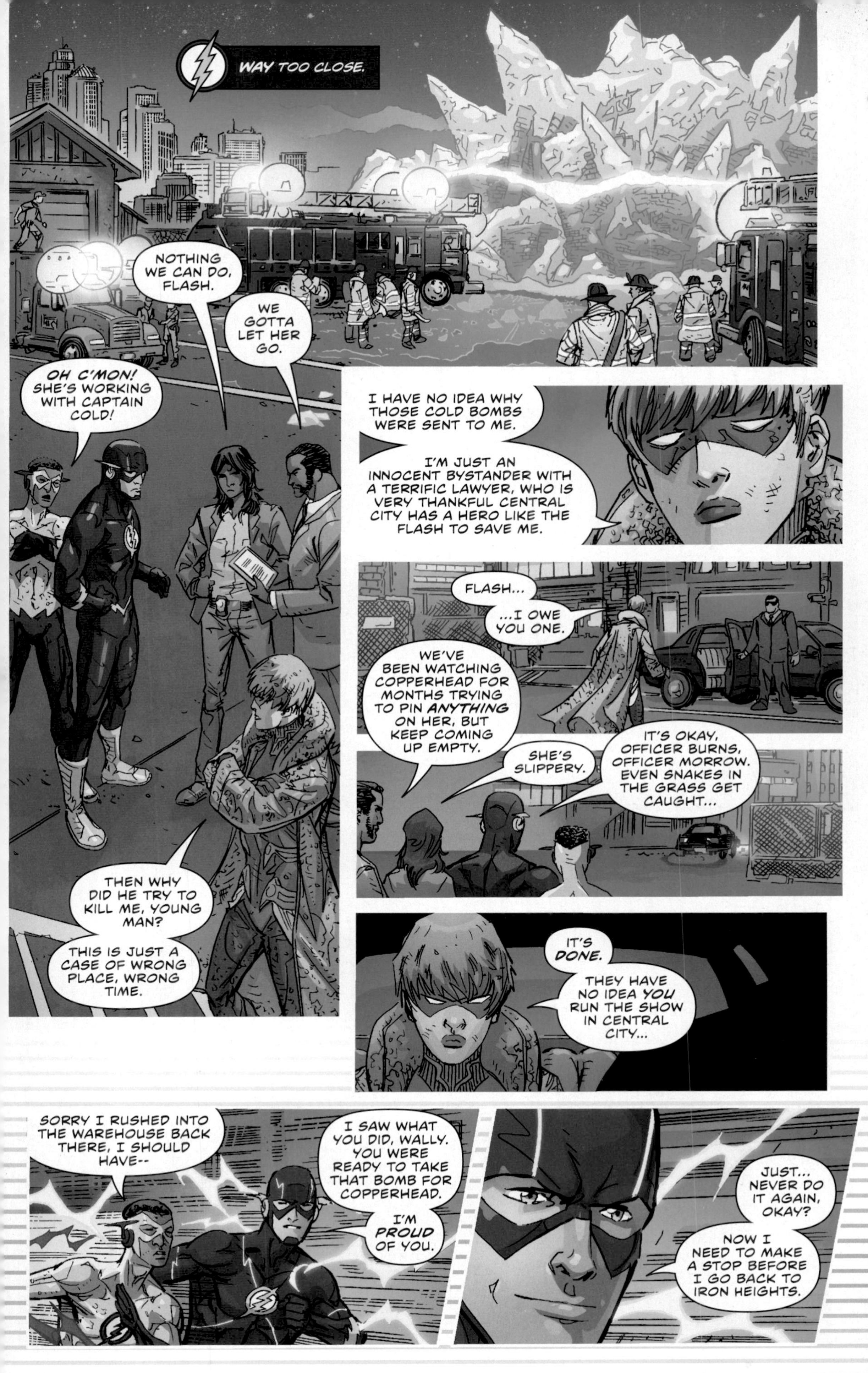
WAY TOO CLOSE.
NOTHING WE CAN DO, FLASH.
WE GOTTA LET HER GO.
OH C'MON! SHE'S WORKING WITH CAPTAIN COLD!
I HAVE NO IDEA WHY THOSE COLD BOMBS WERE SENT TO ME.
I'M JUST AN INNOCENT BYSTANDER WITH A TERRIFIC LAWYER, WHO IS VERY THANKFUL CENTRAL CITY HAS A HERO LIKE THE FLASH TO SAVE ME.
THEN WHY DID HE TRY TO KILL ME, YOUNG MAN?
THIS IS JUST A CASE OF WRONG PLACE, WRONG TIME.
FLASH...
...I OWE YOU ONE.
WE'VE BEEN WATCHING COPPERHEAD FOR MONTHS TRYING TO PIN ANYTHING ON HER, BUT KEEP COMING UP EMPTY.
SHE'S SLIPPERY.
IT'S OKAY, OFFICER BURNS, OFFICER MORROW. EVEN SNAKES IN THE GRASS GET CAUGHT...
IT'S DONE.
THEY HAVE NO IDEA YOU RUN THE SHOW IN CENTRAL CITY...
SORRY I RUSHED INTO THE WAREHOUSE BACK THERE, I SHOULD HAVE--
I SAW WHAT YOU DID, WALLY. YOU WERE READY TO TAKE THAT BOMB FOR COPPERHEAD.
I'M PROUD OF YOU.
JUST... NEVER DO IT AGAIN, OKAY?
NOW I NEED TO MAKE A STOP BEFORE I GO BACK TO IRON HEIGHTS.

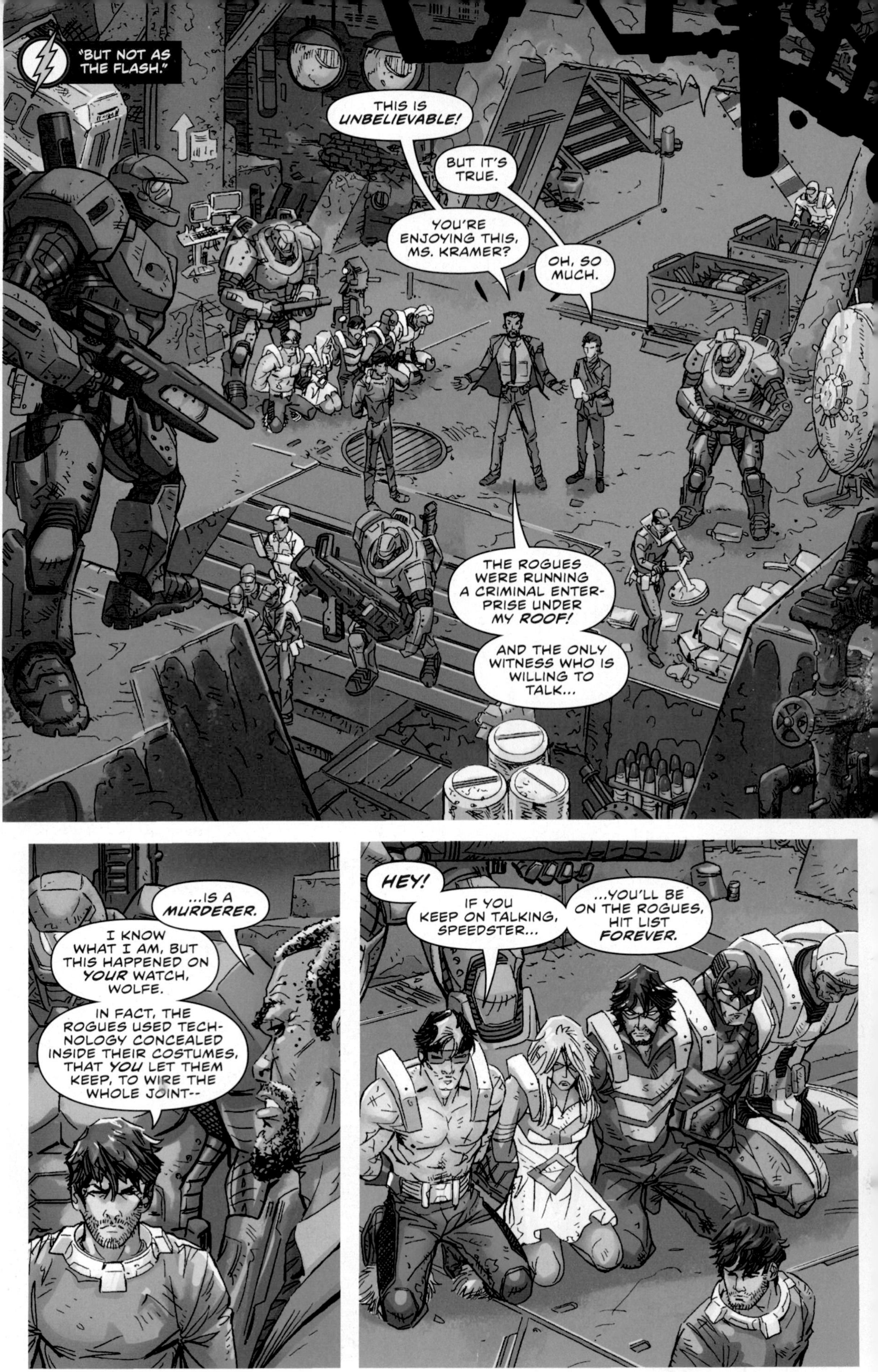
"BUT NOT AS THE FLASH."
THIS IS UNBELIEVABLE!
YOU'RE ENJOYING THIS, MS. KRAMER?
BUT IT'S TRUE.
OH, SO MUCH.
THE ROGUES WERE RUNNING A CRIMINAL ENTER-PRISE UNDER MY ROOF!
AND THE ONLY WITNESS WHO IS WILLING TO TALK...
...IS A MURDERER.
I KNOW WHAT I AM, BUT THIS HAPPENED ON YOUR WATCH, WOLFE.
IN FACT, THE ROGUES USED TECH-NOLOGY CONCEALED INSIDE THEIR COSTUMES, THAT YOU LET THEM KEEP, TO WIRE THE WHOLE JOINT--
HEY!
IF YOU KEEP ON TALKING, SPEEDSTER...
...YOU'LL BE ON THE ROGUES' HIT LIST FOREVER.

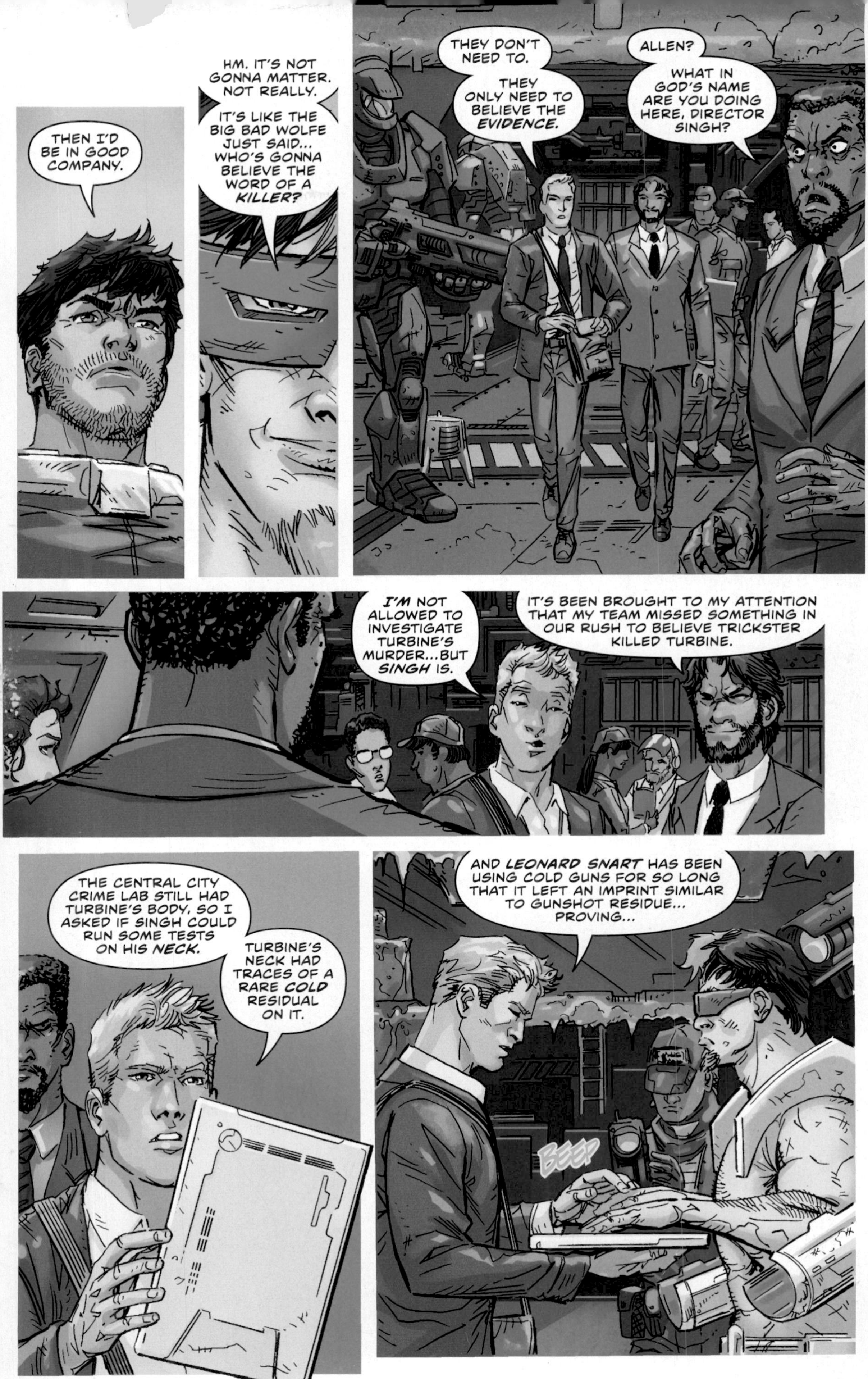
THEN I'D BE IN GOOD COMPANY.
HM. IT'S NOT GONNA MATTER. NOT REALLY.
IT'S LIKE THE BIG BAD WOLFE JUST SAID... WHO'S GONNA BELIEVE THE WORD OF A *KILLER?*
THEY DON'T NEED TO.
THEY ONLY NEED TO BELIEVE THE *EVIDENCE.*
ALLEN?
WHAT IN GOD'S NAME ARE YOU DOING HERE, DIRECTOR SINGH?
I'M NOT ALLOWED TO INVESTIGATE TURBINE'S MURDER...BUT *SINGH* IS.
IT'S BEEN BROUGHT TO MY ATTENTION THAT MY TEAM MISSED SOMETHING IN OUR RUSH TO BELIEVE TRICKSTER KILLED TURBINE.
THE CENTRAL CITY CRIME LAB STILL HAD TURBINE'S BODY, SO I ASKED IF SINGH COULD RUN SOME TESTS ON HIS *NECK.*
TURBINE'S NECK HAD TRACES OF A RARE *COLD* RESIDUAL ON IT.
AND *LEONARD SNART* HAS BEEN USING COLD GUNS FOR SO LONG THAT IT LEFT AN IMPRINT SIMILAR TO GUNSHOT RESIDUE... PROVING...
BEEP

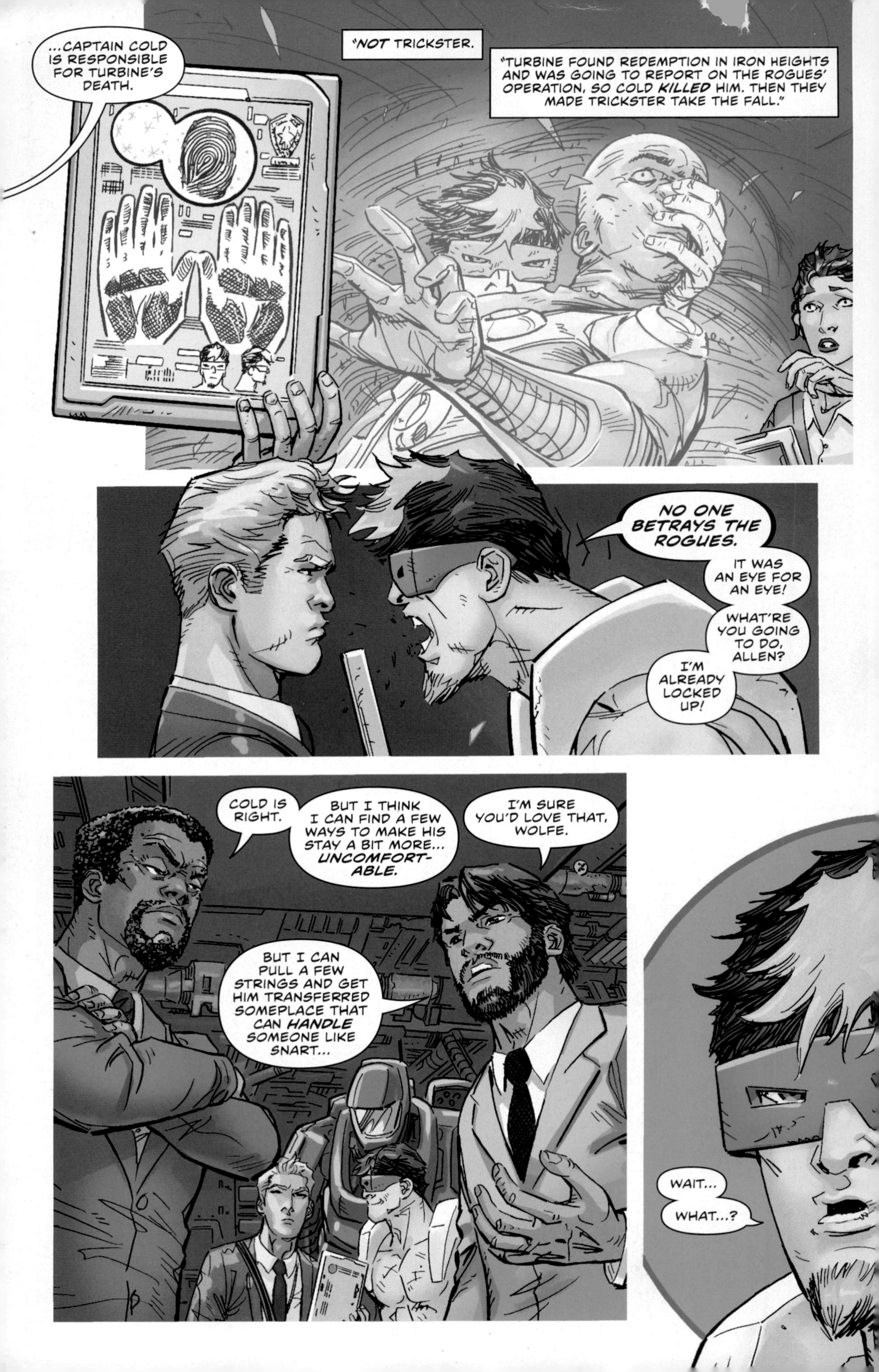

...CAPTAIN COLD IS RESPONSIBLE FOR TURBINE'S DEATH.
"NOT TRICKSTER.
"TURBINE FOUND REDEMPTION IN IRON HEIGHTS AND WAS GOING TO REPORT ON THE ROGUES' OPERATION, SO COLD KILLED HIM. THEN THEY MADE TRICKSTER TAKE THE FALL."
NO ONE BETRAYS THE ROGUES.
IT WAS AN EYE FOR AN EYE!
WHAT'RE YOU GOING TO DO, ALLEN?
I'M ALREADY LOCKED UP!
COLD IS RIGHT.
BUT I THINK I CAN FIND A FEW WAYS TO MAKE HIS STAY A BIT MORE... UNCOMFORTABLE.
I'M SURE YOU'D LOVE THAT, WOLFE.
BUT I CAN PULL A FEW STRINGS AND GET HIM TRANSFERRED SOMEPLACE THAT CAN HANDLE SOMEONE LIKE SNART...
WAIT...
WHAT...?

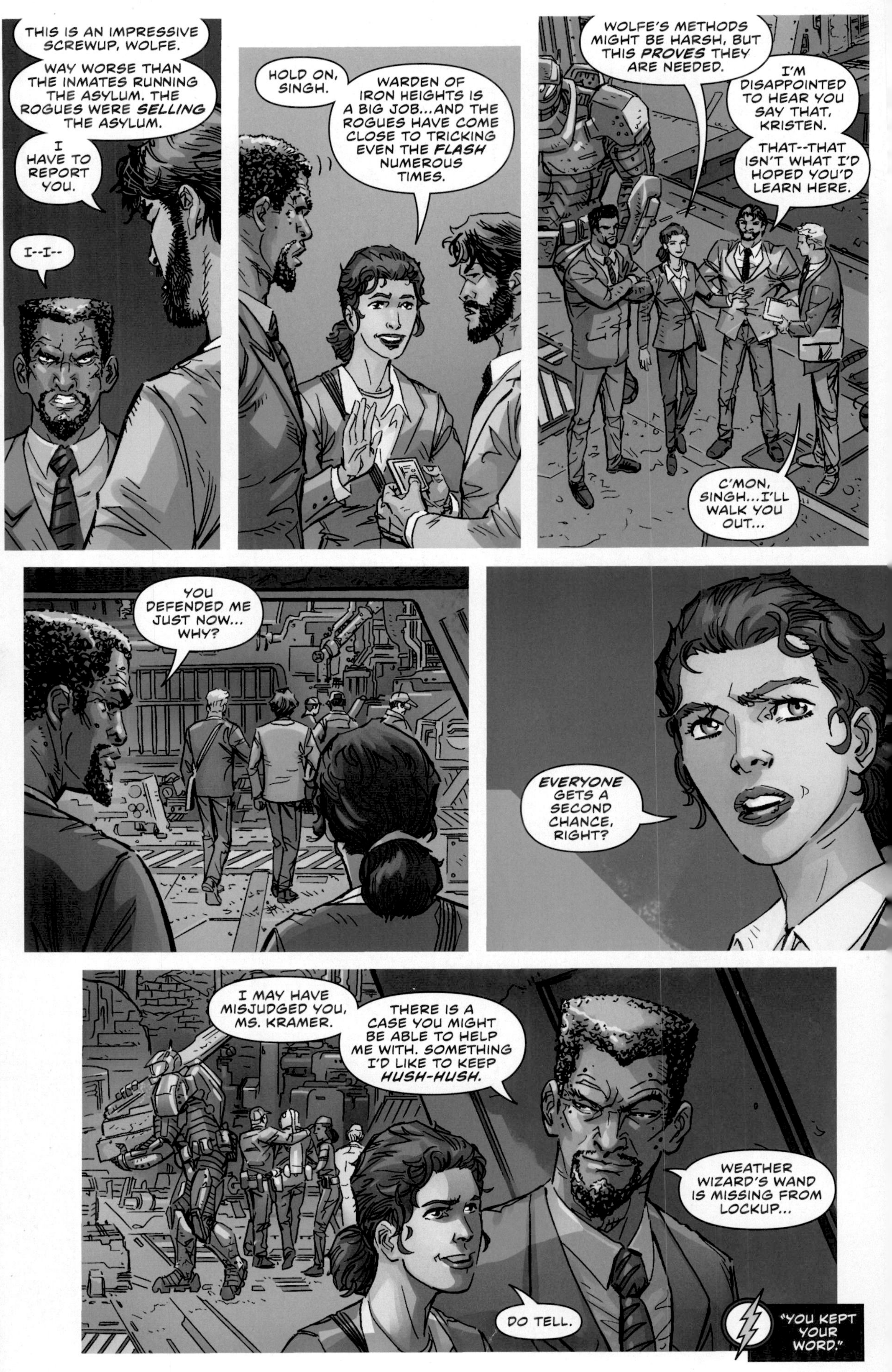
THIS IS AN IMPRESSIVE SCREWUP, WOLFE.
WAY WORSE THAN THE INMATES RUNNING THE ASYLUM. THE ROGUES WERE *SELLING* THE ASYLUM.
I HAVE TO REPORT YOU.
I--I--
HOLD ON, SINGH.
WARDEN OF IRON HEIGHTS IS A BIG JOB...AND THE ROGUES HAVE COME CLOSE TO TRICKING EVEN THE *FLASH* NUMEROUS TIMES.
WOLFE'S METHODS MIGHT BE HARSH, BUT THIS *PROVES* THEY ARE NEEDED.
I'M DISAPPOINTED TO HEAR YOU SAY THAT, KRISTEN.
THAT--THAT ISN'T WHAT I'D HOPED YOU'D LEARN HERE.
C'MON, SINGH...I'LL WALK YOU OUT...
YOU DEFENDED ME JUST NOW... WHY?
EVERYONE GETS A SECOND CHANCE, RIGHT?
I MAY HAVE MISJUDGED YOU, MS. KRAMER.
THERE IS A CASE YOU MIGHT BE ABLE TO HELP ME WITH. SOMETHING I'D LIKE TO KEEP *HUSH-HUSH.*
WEATHER WIZARD'S WAND IS MISSING FROM LOCKUP...
DO TELL.
"YOU KEPT YOUR WORD."

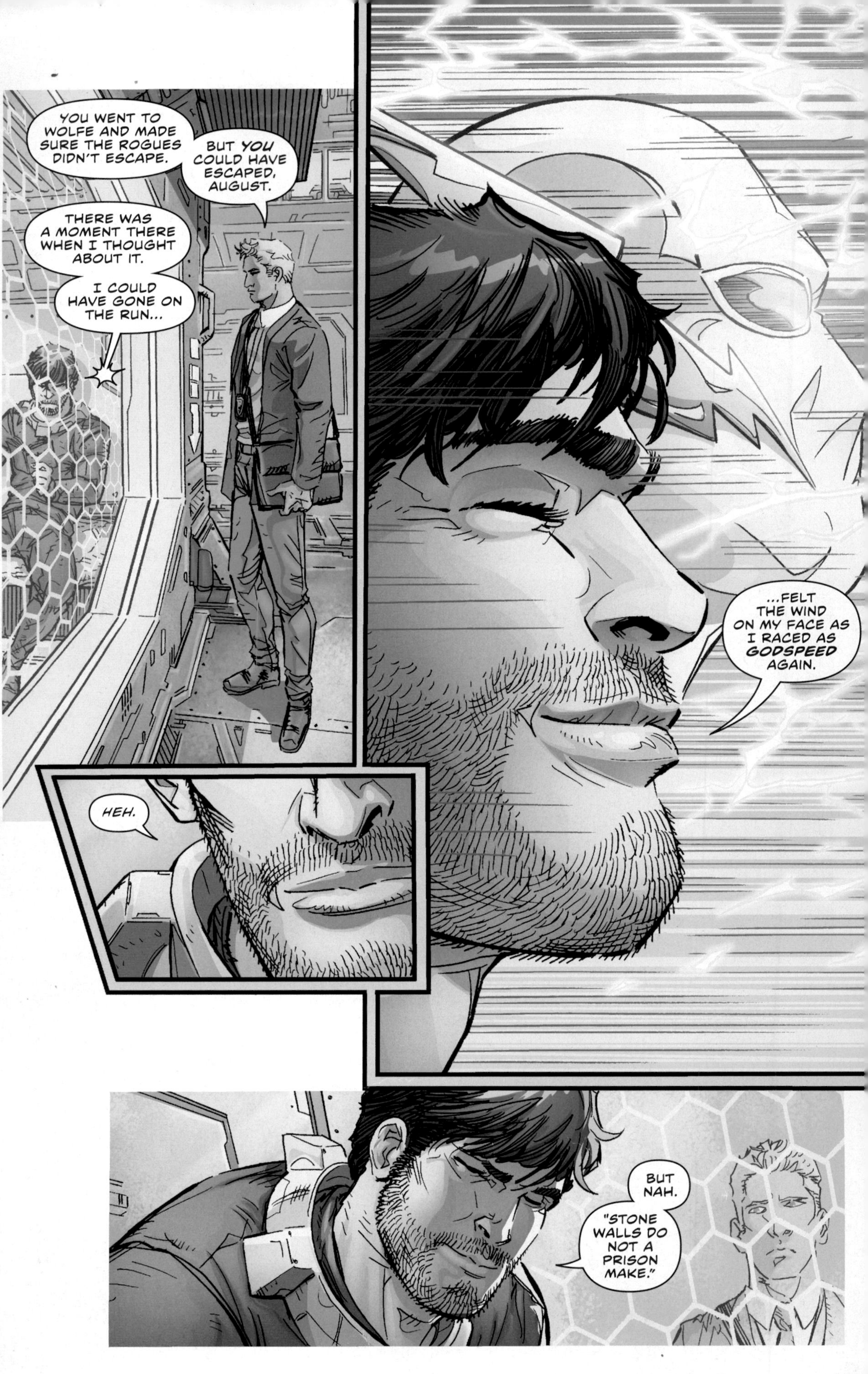
YOU WENT TO WOLFE AND MADE SURE THE ROGUES DIDN'T ESCAPE.
BUT *YOU* COULD HAVE ESCAPED, AUGUST.
THERE WAS A MOMENT THERE WHEN I THOUGHT ABOUT IT.
I COULD HAVE GONE ON THE RUN...
...FELT THE WIND ON MY FACE AS I RACED AS **GODSPEED** AGAIN.
HEH.
BUT NAH.
"STONE WALLS DO NOT A PRISON MAKE."

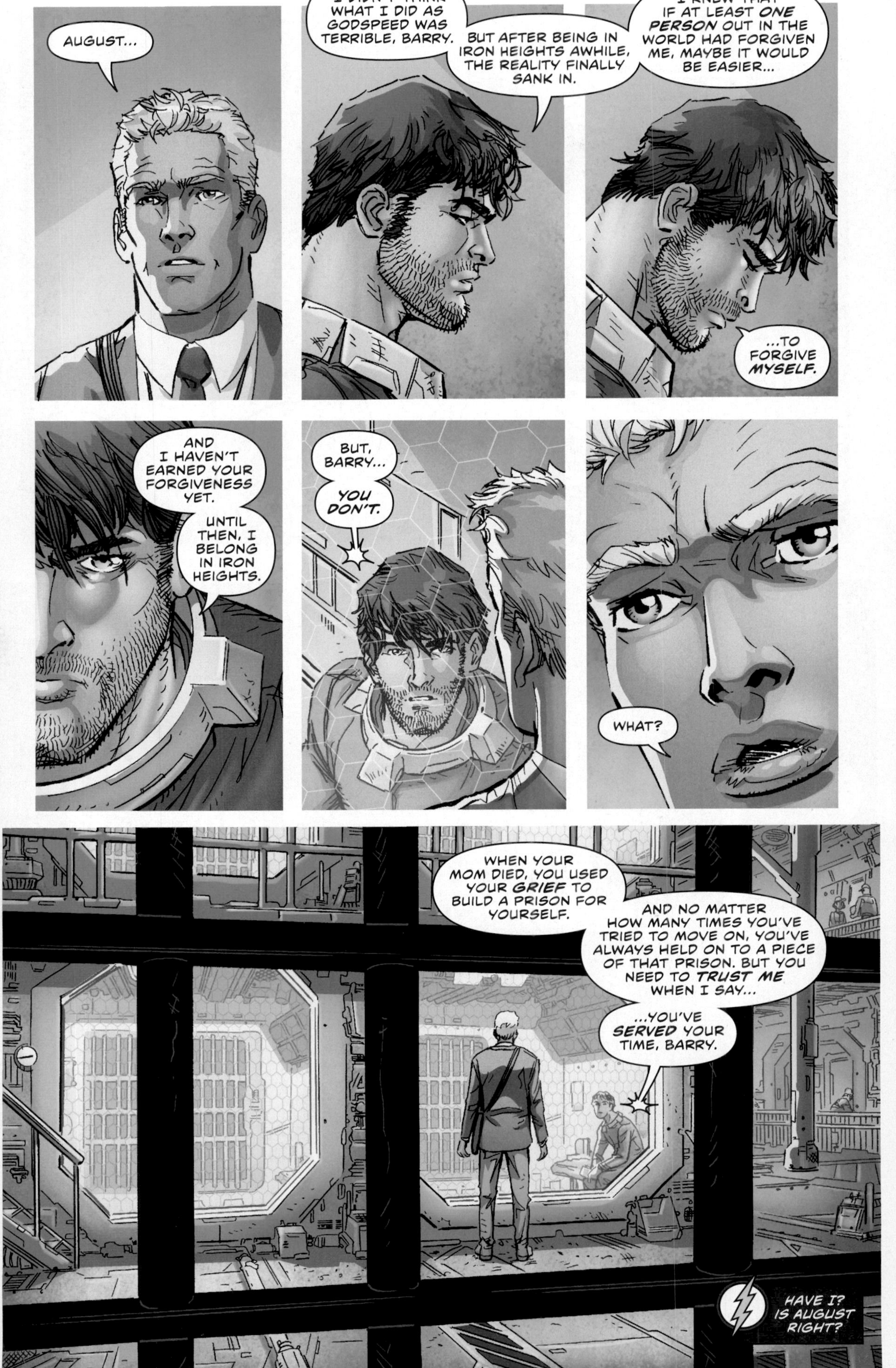
AUGUST...
I DIDN'T THINK WHAT I DID AS GODSPEED WAS TERRIBLE, BARRY.
BUT AFTER BEING IN IRON HEIGHTS AWHILE, THE REALITY FINALLY SANK IN.
I KNEW THAT IF AT LEAST ONE PERSON OUT IN THE WORLD HAD FORGIVEN ME, MAYBE IT WOULD BE EASIER...
...TO FORGIVE MYSELF.
AND I HAVEN'T EARNED YOUR FORGIVENESS YET.
UNTIL THEN, I BELONG IN IRON HEIGHTS.
BUT, BARRY...
YOU DON'T.
WHAT?
WHEN YOUR MOM DIED, YOU USED YOUR GRIEF TO BUILD A PRISON FOR YOURSELF.
AND NO MATTER HOW MANY TIMES YOU'VE TRIED TO MOVE ON, YOU'VE ALWAYS HELD ON TO A PIECE OF THAT PRISON. BUT YOU NEED TO TRUST ME WHEN I SAY...
...YOU'VE SERVED YOUR TIME, BARRY.
HAVE I? IS AUGUST RIGHT?

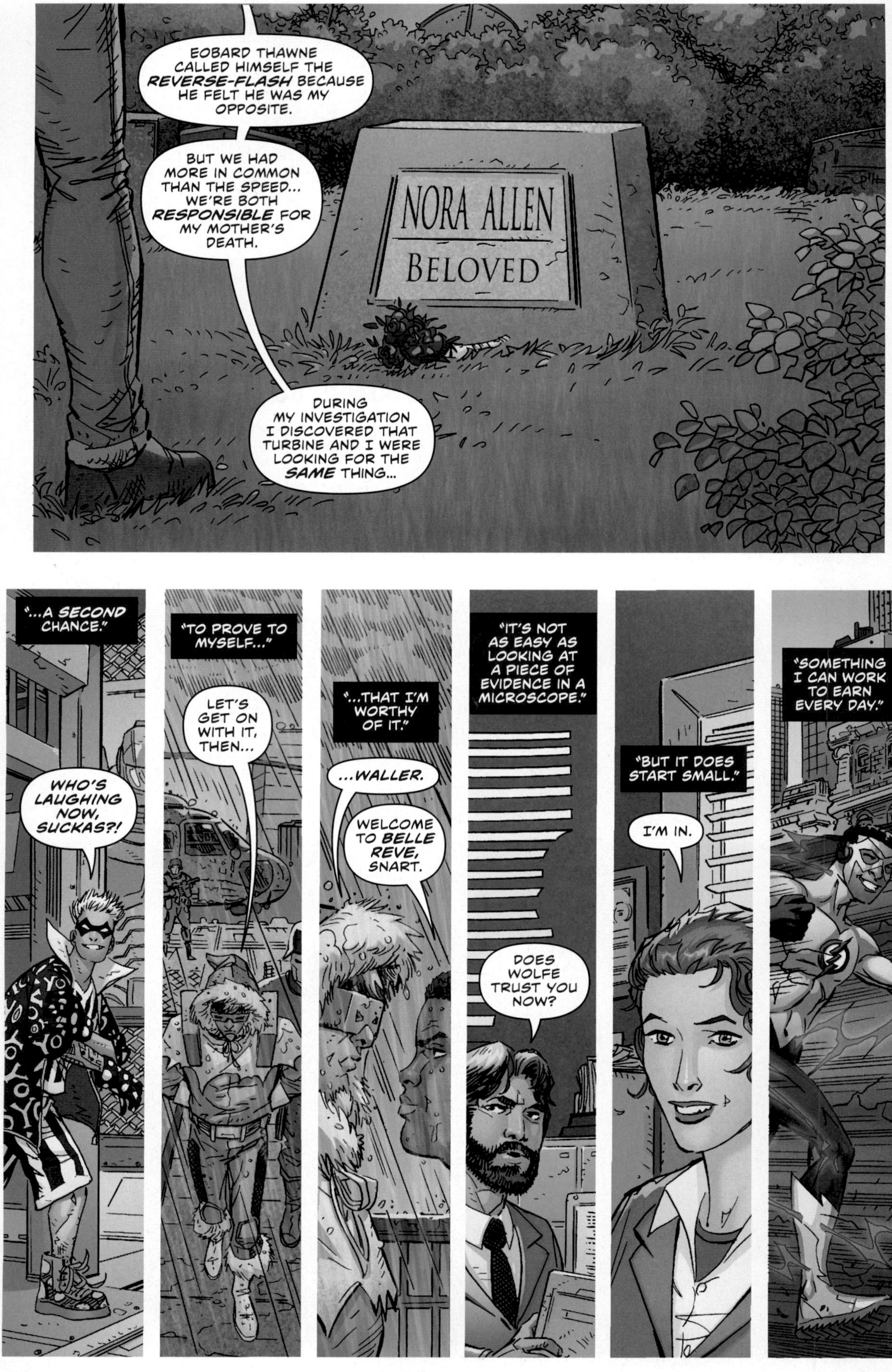
EOBARD THAWNE CALLED HIMSELF THE *REVERSE-FLASH* BECAUSE HE FELT HE WAS MY OPPOSITE.
BUT WE HAD MORE IN COMMON THAN THE SPEED... WE'RE BOTH *RESPONSIBLE* FOR MY MOTHER'S DEATH.
NORA ALLEN
BELOVED
DURING MY INVESTIGATION I DISCOVERED THAT TURBINE AND I WERE LOOKING FOR THE *SAME* THING...
"...A *SECOND* CHANCE."
WHO'S LAUGHING NOW, SUCKAS?!
"TO PROVE TO MYSELF..."
LET'S GET ON WITH IT, THEN...
"...THAT I'M WORTHY OF IT."
...WALLER.
WELCOME TO *BELLE REVE,* SNART.
"IT'S NOT AS EASY AS LOOKING AT A PIECE OF EVIDENCE IN A MICROSCOPE."
DOES WOLFE TRUST YOU NOW?
"BUT IT DOES START SMALL."
I'M IN.
"SOMETHING I CAN WORK TO EARN EVERY DAY."

I KNOW I'D LIKE TO BE FORGIVEN.

FOR THE LIES I TOLD.

THE MISTAKES I MADE.

THE PEOPLE I'VE HURT.

THERE ARE SO MANY PEOPLE I WANT TO TELL I'M SORRY, BUT--

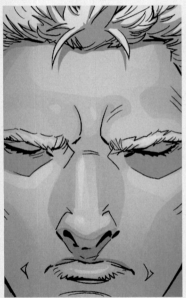

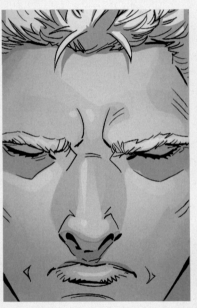

BUT I KNOW NOW THAT FORGIVENESS ISN'T CUT-AND-DRY.

IT'S A MYSTERY.

ONE THAT I DON'T KNOW IF I CAN EVER SOLVE.

BUT I CAN STILL TRY.

AND THE ONLY PERSON I WANT TO TRY TO SOLVE IT WITH...

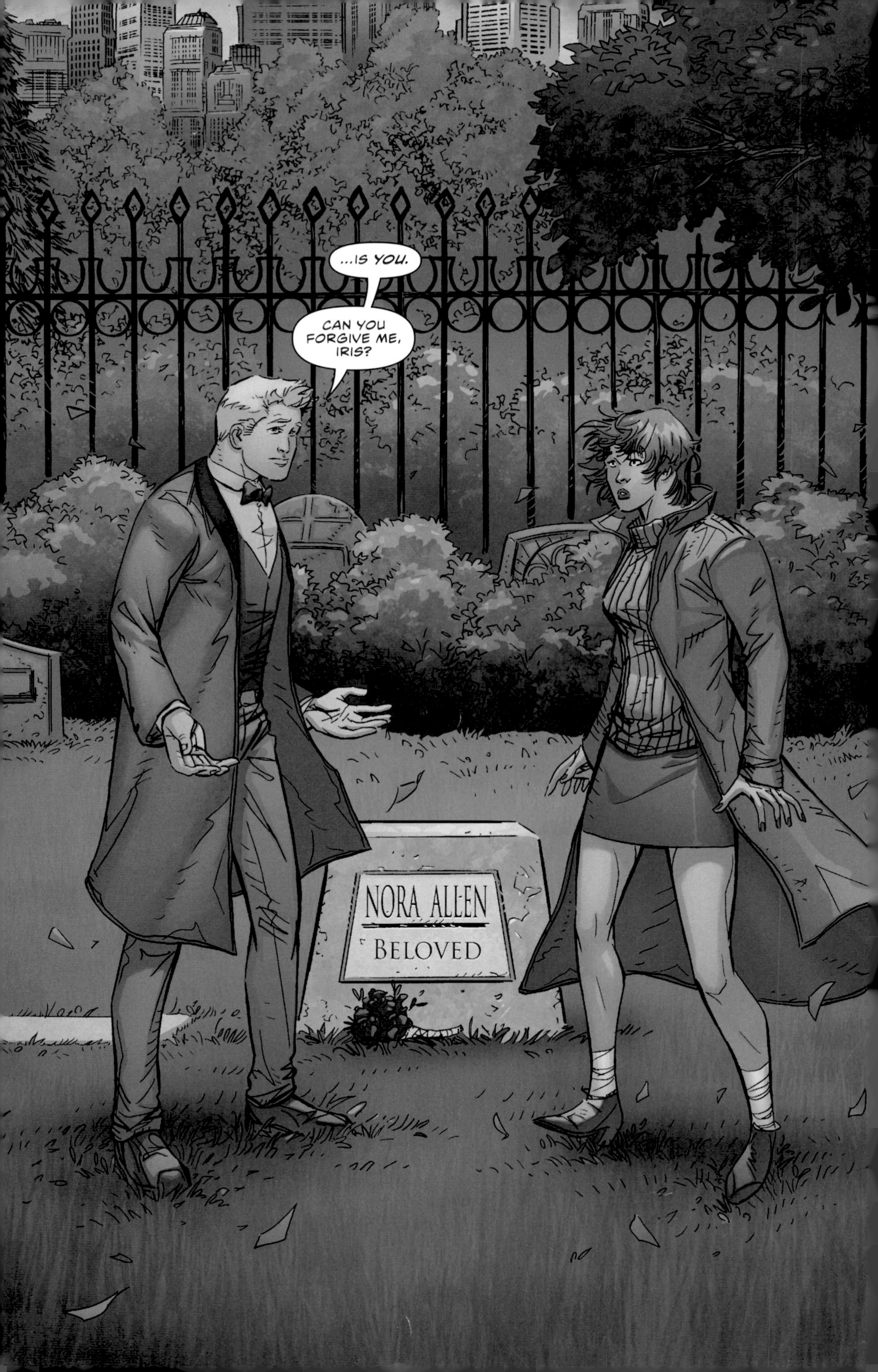
...IS YOU.
CAN YOU FORGIVE ME, IRIS?
NORA ALLEN
BELOVED

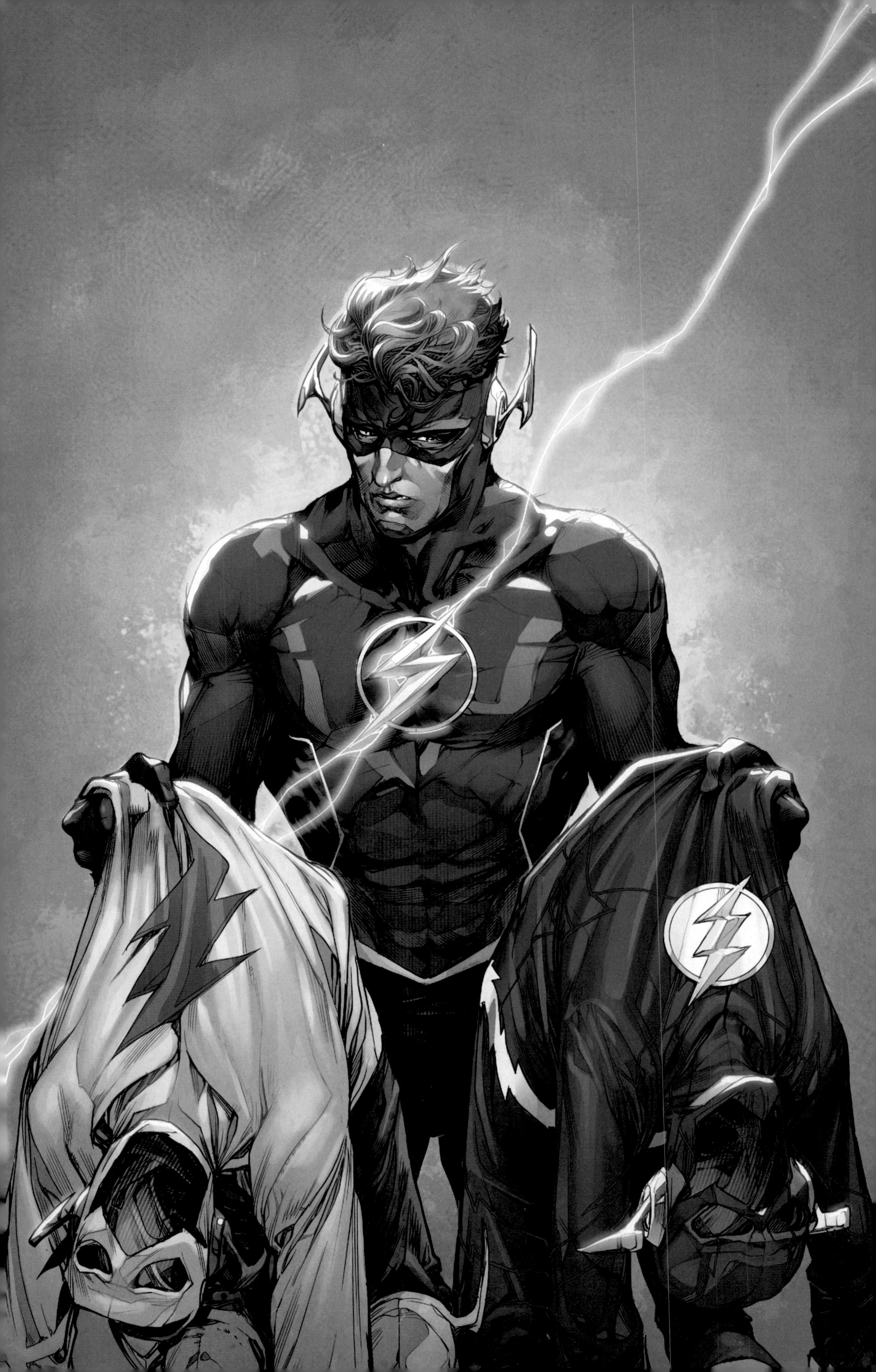

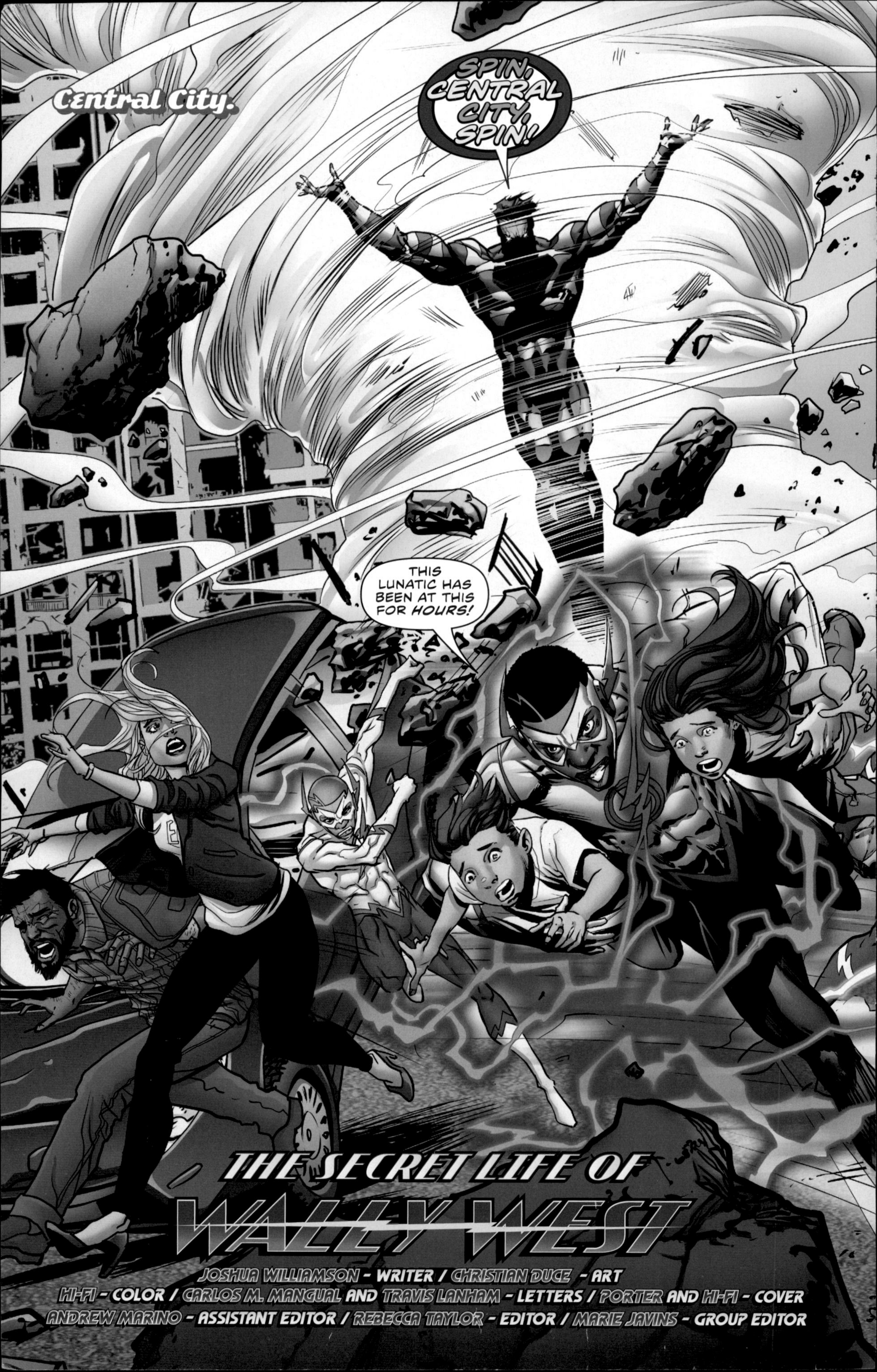
Central City.
SPIN, CENTRAL CITY, SPIN!
THIS LUNATIC HAS BEEN AT THIS FOR HOURS!
THE SECRET LIFE OF
WALLY WEST
JOSHUA WILLIAMSON - WRITER / CHRISTIAN DUCE - ART
HI-FI - COLOR / CARLOS M. MANGUAL AND TRAVIS LANHAM - LETTERS / PORTER AND HI-FI - COVER
ANDREW MARINO - ASSISTANT EDITOR / REBECCA TAYLOR - EDITOR / MARIE JAVINS - GROUP EDITOR

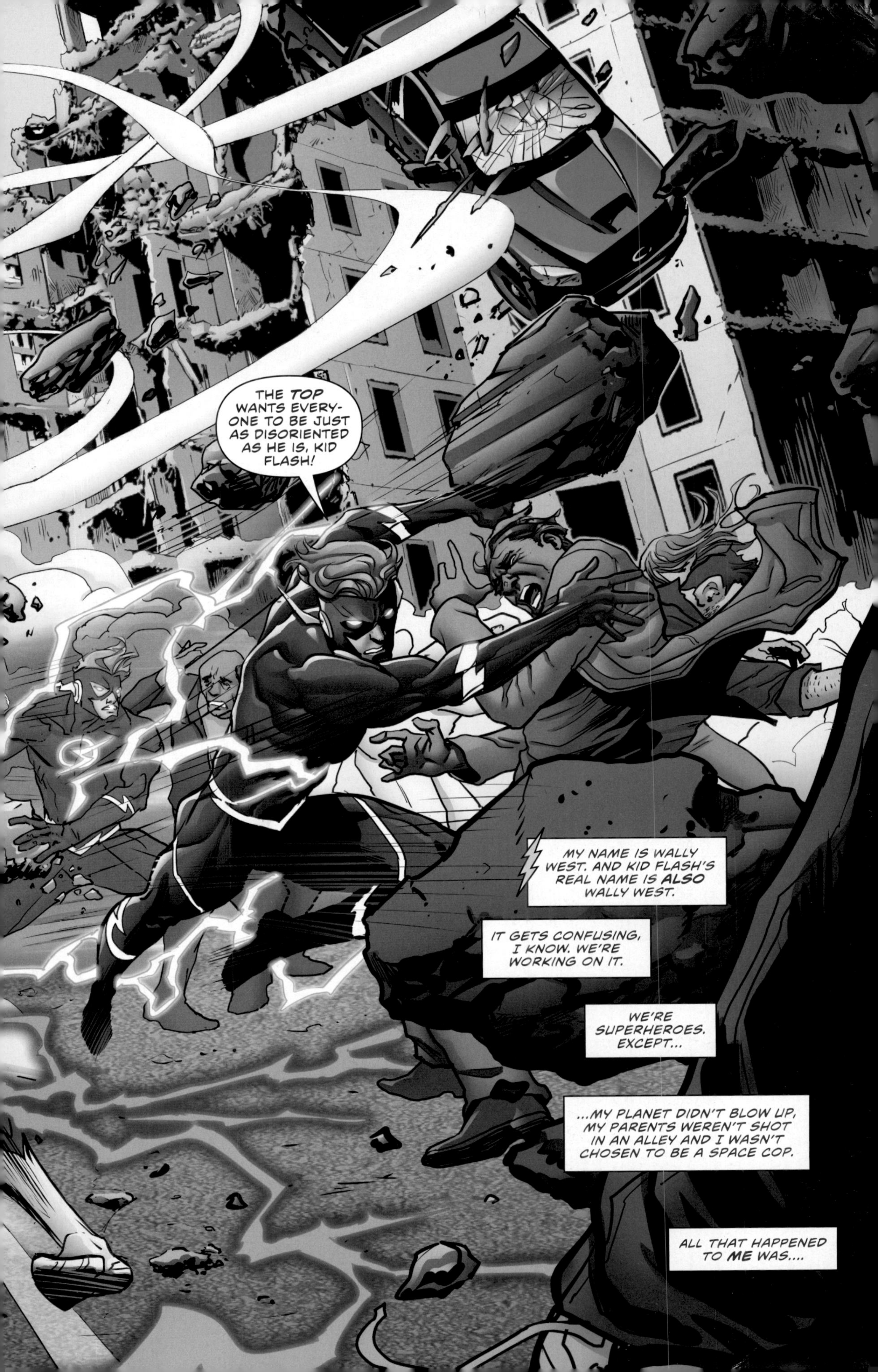
THE TOP WANTS EVERY-ONE TO BE JUST AS DISORIENTED AS HE IS, KID FLASH!
MY NAME IS WALLY WEST. AND KID FLASH'S REAL NAME IS ALSO WALLY WEST.
IT GETS CONFUSING, I KNOW. WE'RE WORKING ON IT.
WE'RE SUPERHEROES. EXCEPT...
...MY PLANET DIDN'T BLOW UP, MY PARENTS WEREN'T SHOT IN AN ALLEY AND I WASN'T CHOSEN TO BE A SPACE COP.
ALL THAT HAPPENED TO ME WAS....

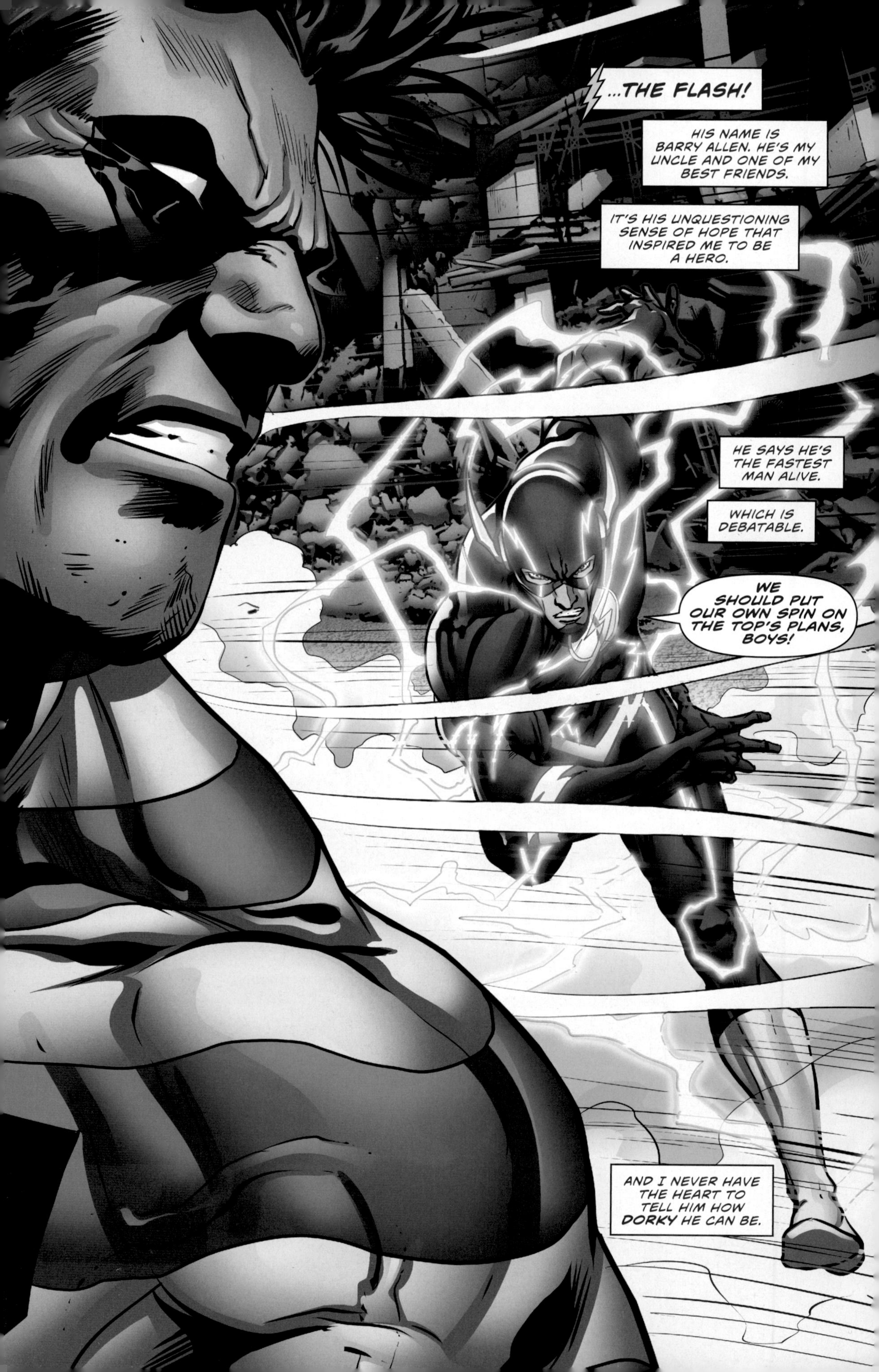
...THE FLASH!
HIS NAME IS BARRY ALLEN. HE'S MY UNCLE AND ONE OF MY BEST FRIENDS.
IT'S HIS UNQUESTIONING SENSE OF HOPE THAT INSPIRED ME TO BE A HERO.
HE SAYS HE'S THE FASTEST MAN ALIVE.
WHICH IS DEBATABLE.
WE SHOULD PUT OUR OWN SPIN ON THE TOP'S PLANS, BOYS!
AND I NEVER HAVE THE HEART TO TELL HIM HOW DORKY HE CAN BE.

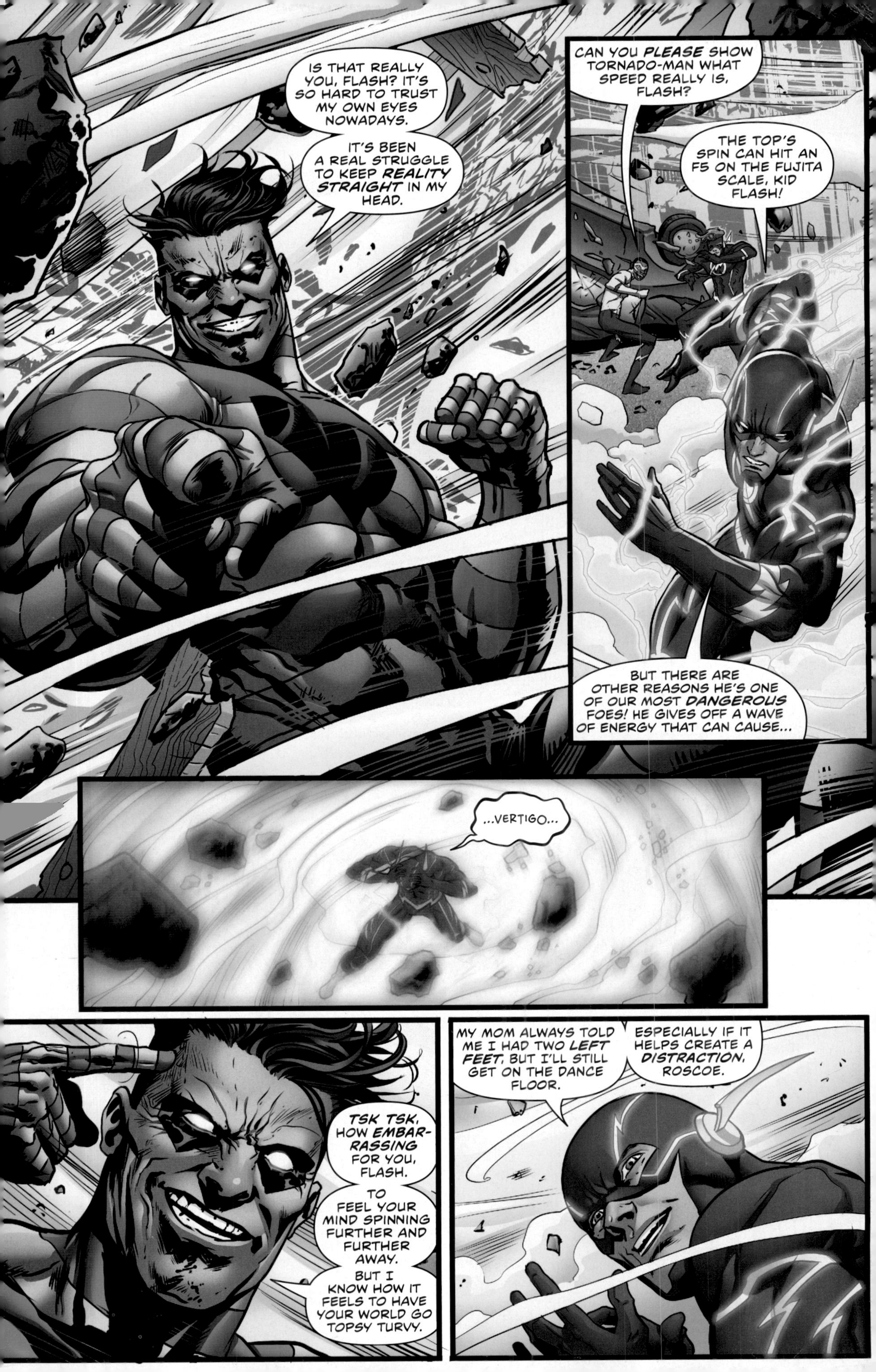
IS THAT REALLY YOU, FLASH? IT'S SO HARD TO TRUST MY OWN EYES NOWADAYS.
IT'S BEEN A REAL STRUGGLE TO KEEP REALITY STRAIGHT IN MY HEAD.
CAN YOU PLEASE SHOW TORNADO-MAN WHAT SPEED REALLY IS, FLASH?
THE TOP'S SPIN CAN HIT AN F5 ON THE FUJITA SCALE, KID FLASH!
BUT THERE ARE OTHER REASONS HE'S ONE OF OUR MOST DANGEROUS FOES! HE GIVES OFF A WAVE OF ENERGY THAT CAN CAUSE...
...VERTIGO...
TSK TSK, HOW EMBARRASSING FOR YOU, FLASH.
TO FEEL YOUR MIND SPINNING FURTHER AND FURTHER AWAY.
BUT I KNOW HOW IT FEELS TO HAVE YOUR WORLD GO TOPSY TURVY.
MY MOM ALWAYS TOLD ME I HAD TWO LEFT FEET, BUT I'LL STILL GET ON THE DANCE FLOOR.
ESPECIALLY IF IT HELPS CREATE A DISTRACTION, ROSCOE.

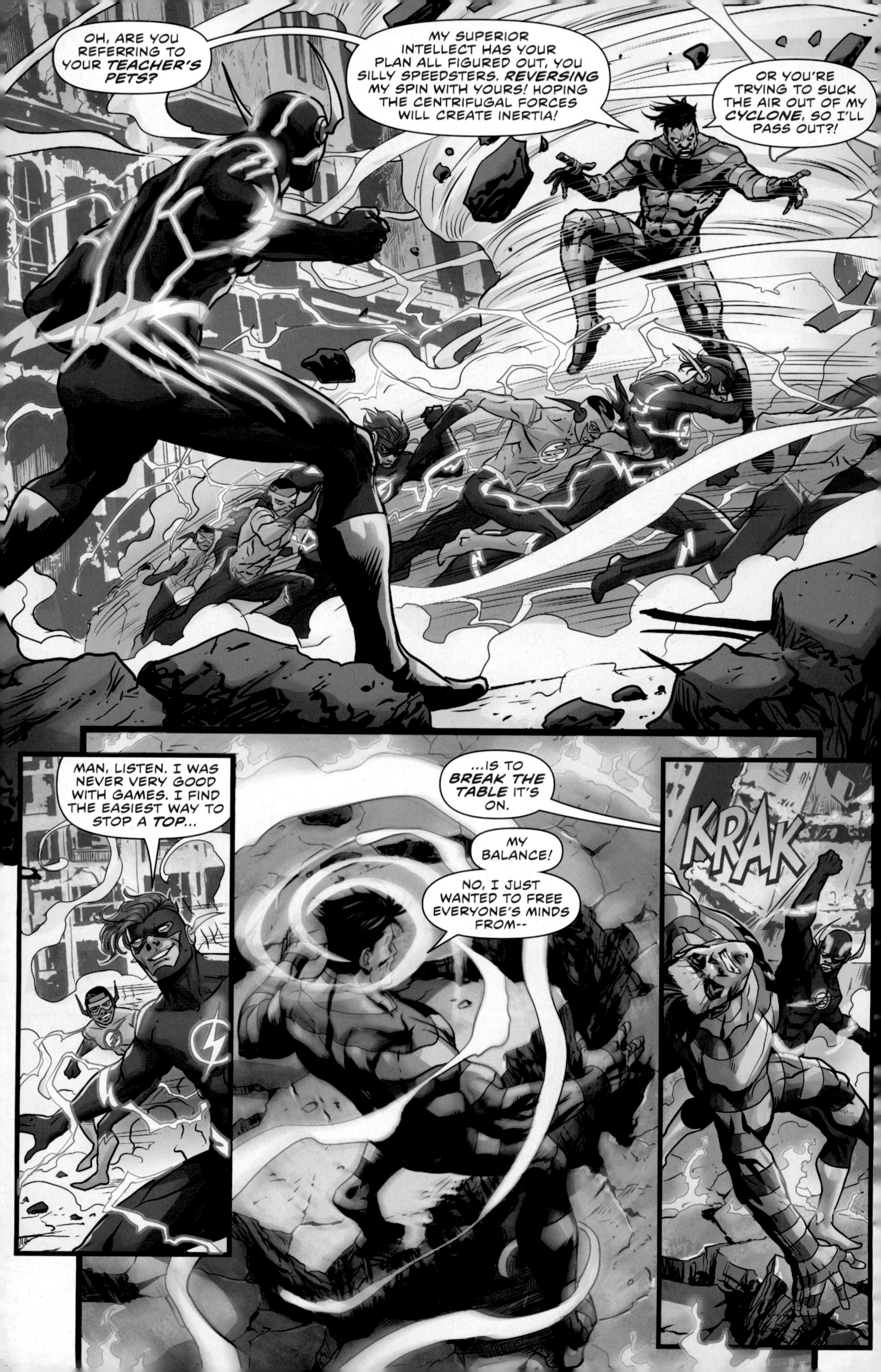
OH, ARE YOU REFERRING TO YOUR TEACHER'S PETS?
MY SUPERIOR INTELLECT HAS YOUR PLAN ALL FIGURED OUT, YOU SILLY SPEEDSTERS. REVERSING MY SPIN WITH YOURS! HOPING THE CENTRIFUGAL FORCES WILL CREATE INERTIA!
OR YOU'RE TRYING TO SUCK THE AIR OUT OF MY CYCLONE, SO I'LL PASS OUT?!
MAN, LISTEN. I WAS NEVER VERY GOOD WITH GAMES. I FIND THE EASIEST WAY TO STOP A TOP...
...IS TO BREAK THE TABLE IT'S ON.
MY BALANCE!
NO, I JUST WANTED TO FREE EVERYONE'S MINDS FROM--
KRAK

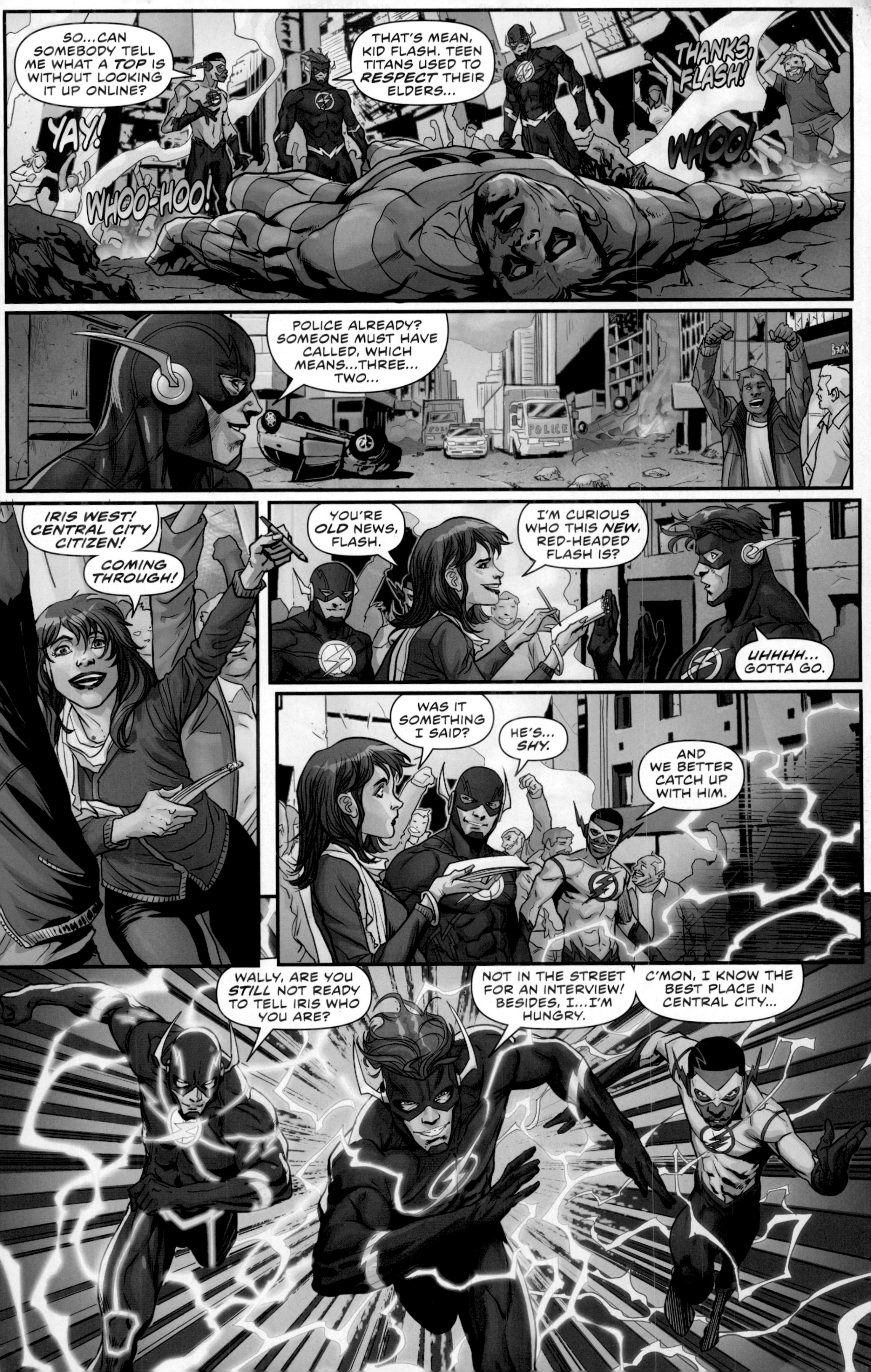
SO...CAN SOMEBODY TELL ME WHAT A *TOP* IS WITHOUT LOOKING IT UP ONLINE?
THAT'S MEAN, KID FLASH. TEEN TITANS USED TO *RESPECT* THEIR ELDERS...
THANKS, FLASH!
YAY!
WHOO!
WHOO-HOO!
POLICE ALREADY? SOMEONE MUST HAVE CALLED, WHICH MEANS...THREE... TWO...
POLICE
BANK
IRIS WEST! CENTRAL CITY CITIZEN!
COMING THROUGH!
YOU'RE *OLD* NEWS, FLASH.
I'M CURIOUS WHO THIS *NEW*, RED-HEADED FLASH IS?
UHHHH... GOTTA GO.
WAS IT SOMETHING I SAID?
HE'S... *SHY.*
AND WE BETTER CATCH UP WITH HIM.
WALLY, ARE YOU *STILL* NOT READY TO TELL IRIS WHO YOU ARE?
NOT IN THE STREET FOR AN INTERVIEW! BESIDES, I...I'M HUNGRY.
C'MON, I KNOW THE BEST PLACE IN CENTRAL CITY...

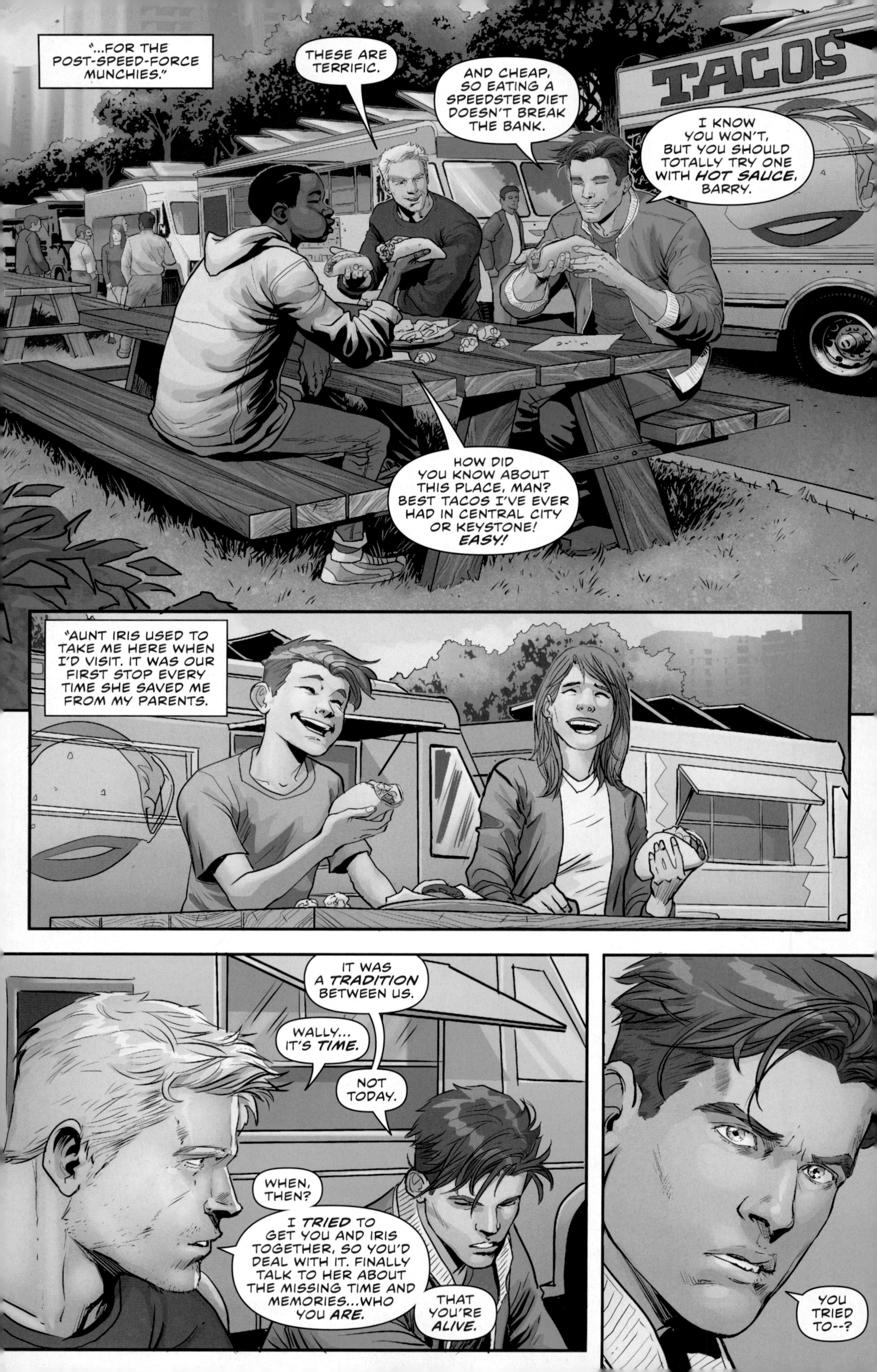
"...FOR THE POST-SPEED-FORCE MUNCHIES."
THESE ARE TERRIFIC.
AND CHEAP, SO EATING A SPEEDSTER DIET DOESN'T BREAK THE BANK.
I KNOW YOU WON'T, BUT YOU SHOULD TOTALLY TRY ONE WITH HOT SAUCE, BARRY.
TACOS
HOW DID YOU KNOW ABOUT THIS PLACE, MAN? BEST TACOS I'VE EVER HAD IN CENTRAL CITY OR KEYSTONE! EASY!
"AUNT IRIS USED TO TAKE ME HERE WHEN I'D VISIT. IT WAS OUR FIRST STOP EVERY TIME SHE SAVED ME FROM MY PARENTS.
IT WAS A TRADITION BETWEEN US.
WALLY... IT'S TIME.
NOT TODAY.
WHEN, THEN?
I TRIED TO GET YOU AND IRIS TOGETHER, SO YOU'D DEAL WITH IT. FINALLY TALK TO HER ABOUT THE MISSING TIME AND MEMORIES...WHO YOU ARE.
THAT YOU'RE ALIVE.
YOU TRIED TO--?

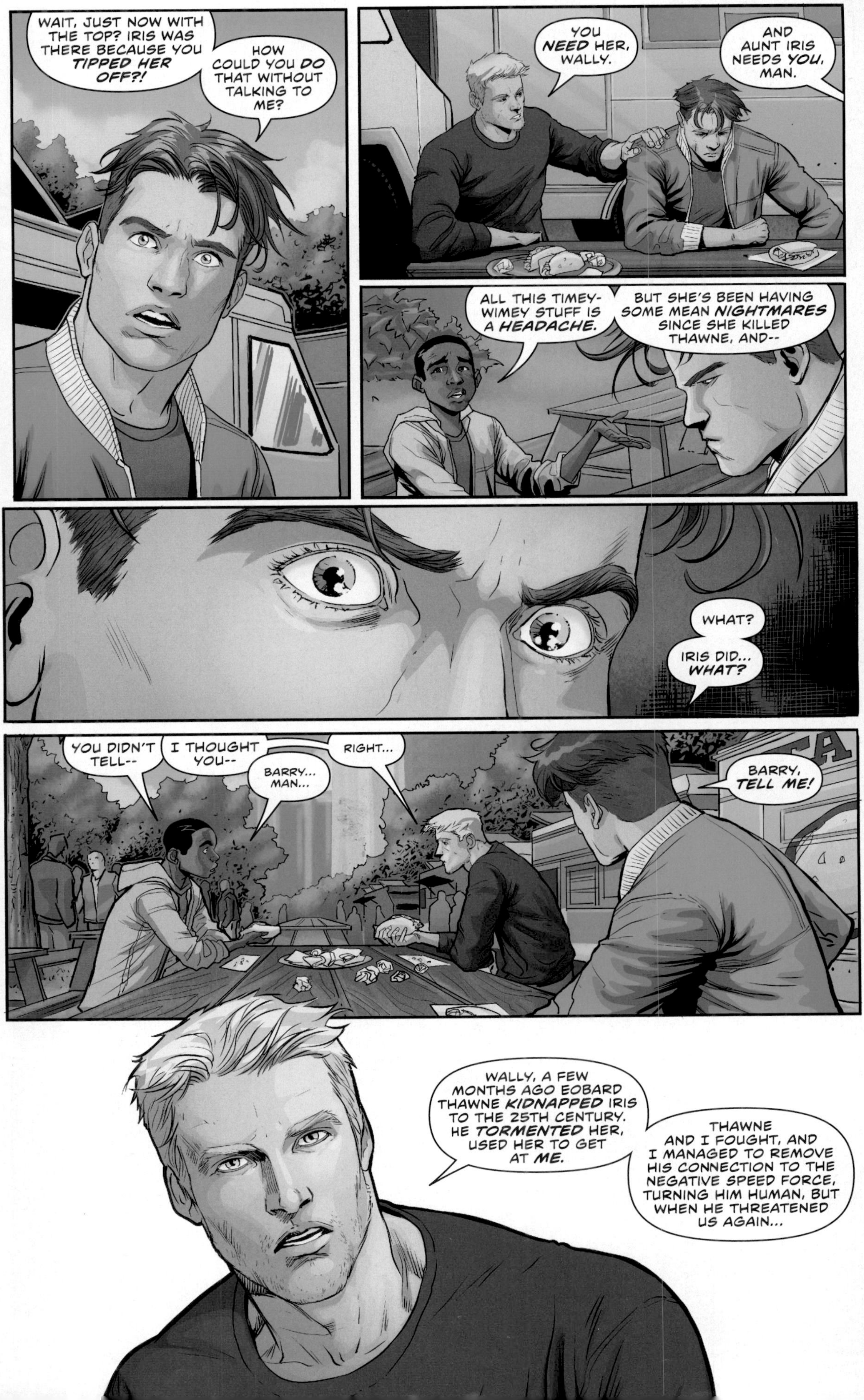
WAIT, JUST NOW WITH THE TOP? IRIS WAS THERE BECAUSE YOU TIPPED HER OFF?!
HOW COULD YOU DO THAT WITHOUT TALKING TO ME?
YOU NEED HER, WALLY.
AND AUNT IRIS NEEDS YOU, MAN.
ALL THIS TIMEY-WIMEY STUFF IS A HEADACHE.
BUT SHE'S BEEN HAVING SOME MEAN NIGHTMARES SINCE SHE KILLED THAWNE, AND--
WHAT?
IRIS DID... WHAT?
YOU DIDN'T TELL--
I THOUGHT YOU--
BARRY... MAN...
RIGHT...
BARRY, TELL ME!
WALLY, A FEW MONTHS AGO EOBARD THAWNE KIDNAPPED IRIS TO THE 25TH CENTURY. HE TORMENTED HER, USED HER TO GET AT ME.
THAWNE AND I FOUGHT, AND I MANAGED TO REMOVE HIS CONNECTION TO THE NEGATIVE SPEED FORCE, TURNING HIM HUMAN, BUT WHEN HE THREATENED US AGAIN...

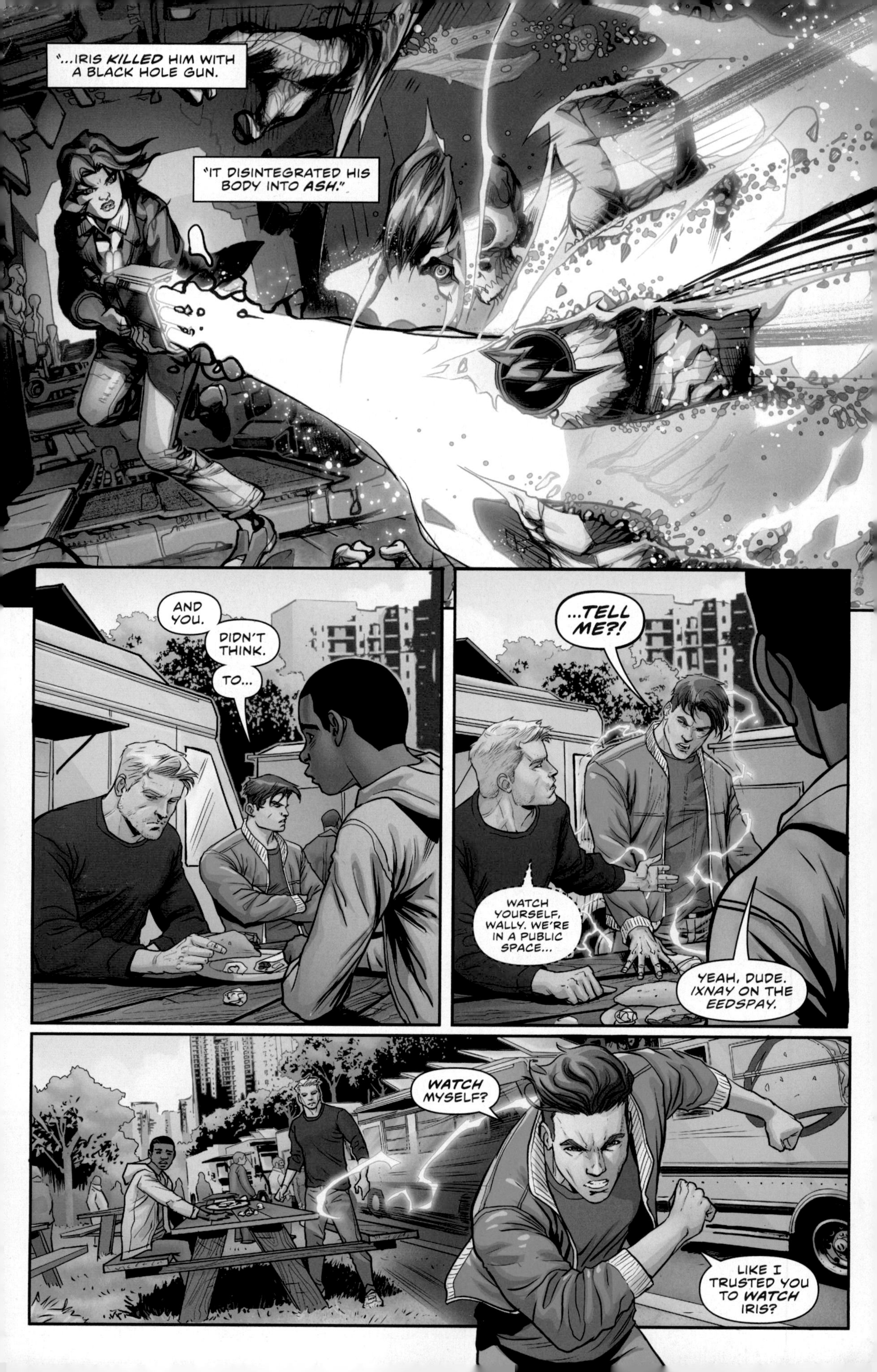
"...IRIS KILLED HIM WITH A BLACK HOLE GUN.
"IT DISINTEGRATED HIS BODY INTO ASH."
AND YOU.
DIDN'T THINK.
TO...
...TELL ME?!
WATCH YOURSELF, WALLY. WE'RE IN A PUBLIC SPACE...
YEAH, DUDE. IXNAY ON THE EEDSPAY.
WATCH MYSELF?
LIKE I TRUSTED YOU TO WATCH IRIS?

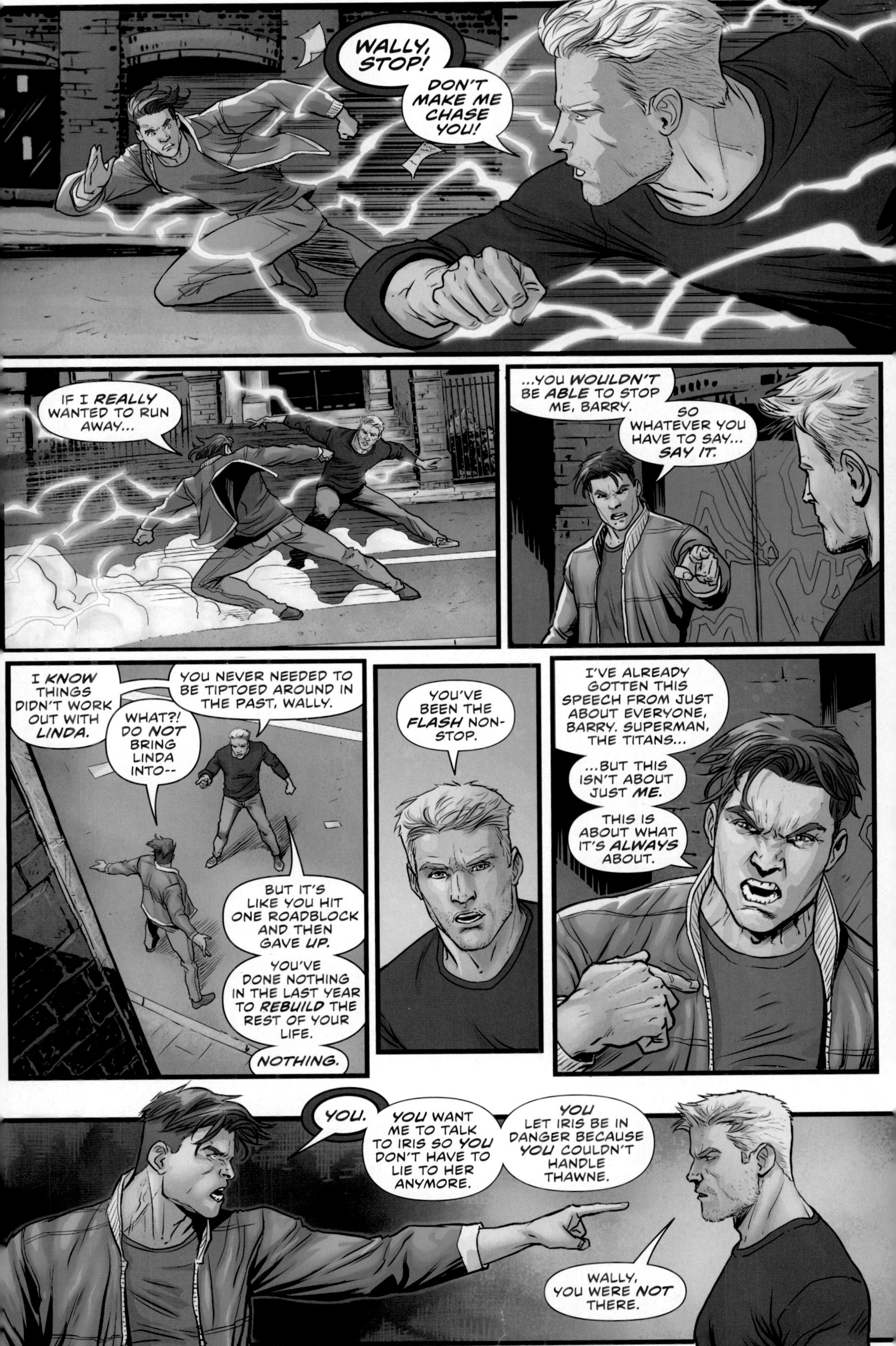
WALLY, STOP!
DON'T MAKE ME CHASE YOU!
IF I REALLY WANTED TO RUN AWAY...
...YOU WOULDN'T BE ABLE TO STOP ME, BARRY.
SO WHATEVER YOU HAVE TO SAY... SAY IT.
I KNOW THINGS DIDN'T WORK OUT WITH LINDA.
WHAT?! DO NOT BRING LINDA INTO--
YOU NEVER NEEDED TO BE TIPTOED AROUND IN THE PAST, WALLY.
BUT IT'S LIKE YOU HIT ONE ROADBLOCK AND THEN GAVE UP.
YOU'VE DONE NOTHING IN THE LAST YEAR TO REBUILD THE REST OF YOUR LIFE.
NOTHING.
YOU'VE BEEN THE FLASH NON-STOP.
I'VE ALREADY GOTTEN THIS SPEECH FROM JUST ABOUT EVERYONE, BARRY. SUPERMAN, THE TITANS...
...BUT THIS ISN'T ABOUT JUST ME.
THIS IS ABOUT WHAT IT'S ALWAYS ABOUT.
YOU.
YOU WANT ME TO TALK TO IRIS SO YOU DON'T HAVE TO LIE TO HER ANYMORE.
YOU LET IRIS BE IN DANGER BECAUSE YOU COULDN'T HANDLE THAWNE.
WALLY, YOU WERE NOT THERE.

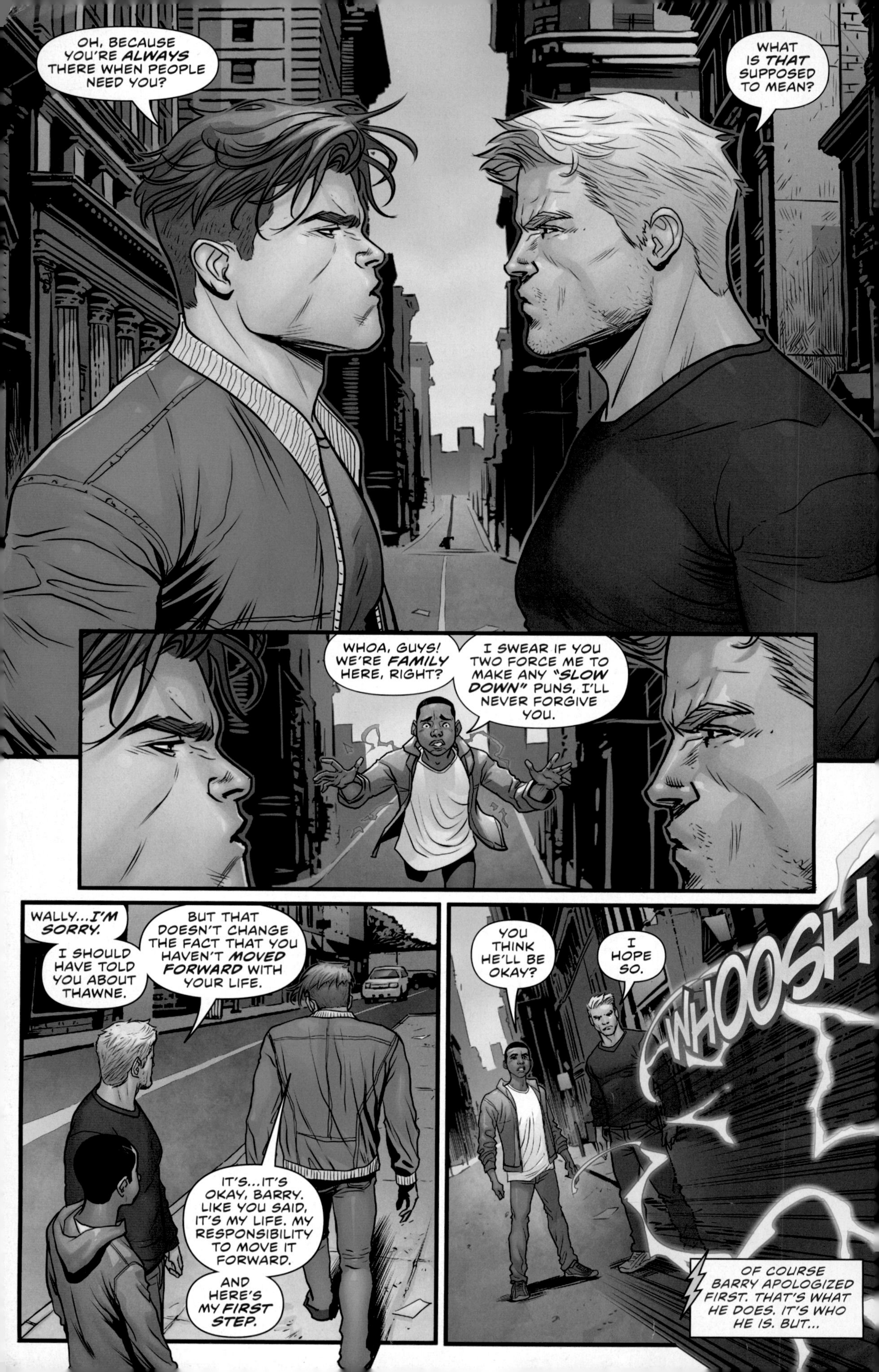
OH, BECAUSE YOU'RE *ALWAYS* THERE WHEN PEOPLE NEED YOU?
WHAT IS *THAT* SUPPOSED TO MEAN?
WHOA, GUYS! WE'RE *FAMILY* HERE, RIGHT?
I SWEAR IF YOU TWO FORCE ME TO MAKE ANY *"SLOW DOWN"* PUNS, I'LL NEVER FORGIVE YOU.
WALLY...*I'M SORRY.*
I SHOULD HAVE TOLD YOU ABOUT THAWNE.
BUT THAT DOESN'T CHANGE THE FACT THAT YOU HAVEN'T *MOVED FORWARD* WITH YOUR LIFE.
IT'S...IT'S OKAY, BARRY. LIKE YOU SAID, IT'S MY LIFE. MY RESPONSIBILITY TO MOVE IT FORWARD.
AND HERE'S MY *FIRST STEP.*
WHOOSH
YOU THINK HE'LL BE OKAY?
I HOPE SO.
OF COURSE BARRY APOLOGIZED FIRST. THAT'S WHAT HE DOES. IT'S WHO HE IS. BUT...

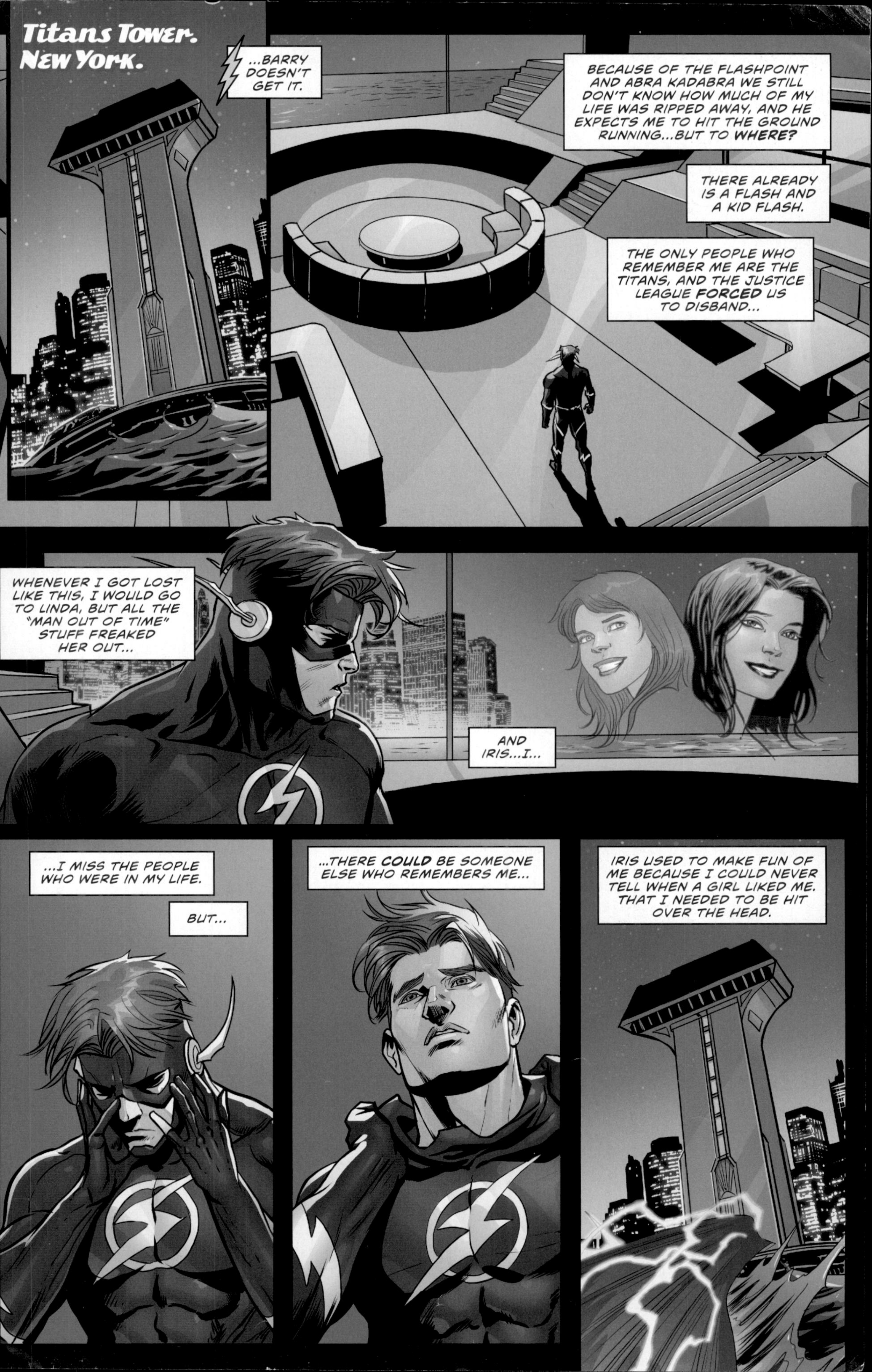
Titans Tower. New York.
...BARRY DOESN'T GET IT.
BECAUSE OF THE FLASHPOINT AND ABRA KADABRA WE STILL DON'T KNOW HOW MUCH OF MY LIFE WAS RIPPED AWAY, AND HE EXPECTS ME TO HIT THE GROUND RUNNING...BUT TO WHERE?
THERE ALREADY IS A FLASH AND A KID FLASH.
THE ONLY PEOPLE WHO REMEMBER ME ARE THE TITANS, AND THE JUSTICE LEAGUE FORCED US TO DISBAND...
WHENEVER I GOT LOST LIKE THIS, I WOULD GO TO LINDA, BUT ALL THE "MAN OUT OF TIME" STUFF FREAKED HER OUT...
AND IRIS...I...
...I MISS THE PEOPLE WHO WERE IN MY LIFE.
BUT...
...THERE COULD BE SOMEONE ELSE WHO REMEMBERS ME...
IRIS USED TO MAKE FUN OF ME BECAUSE I COULD NEVER TELL WHEN A GIRL LIKED ME. THAT I NEEDED TO BE HIT OVER THE HEAD.

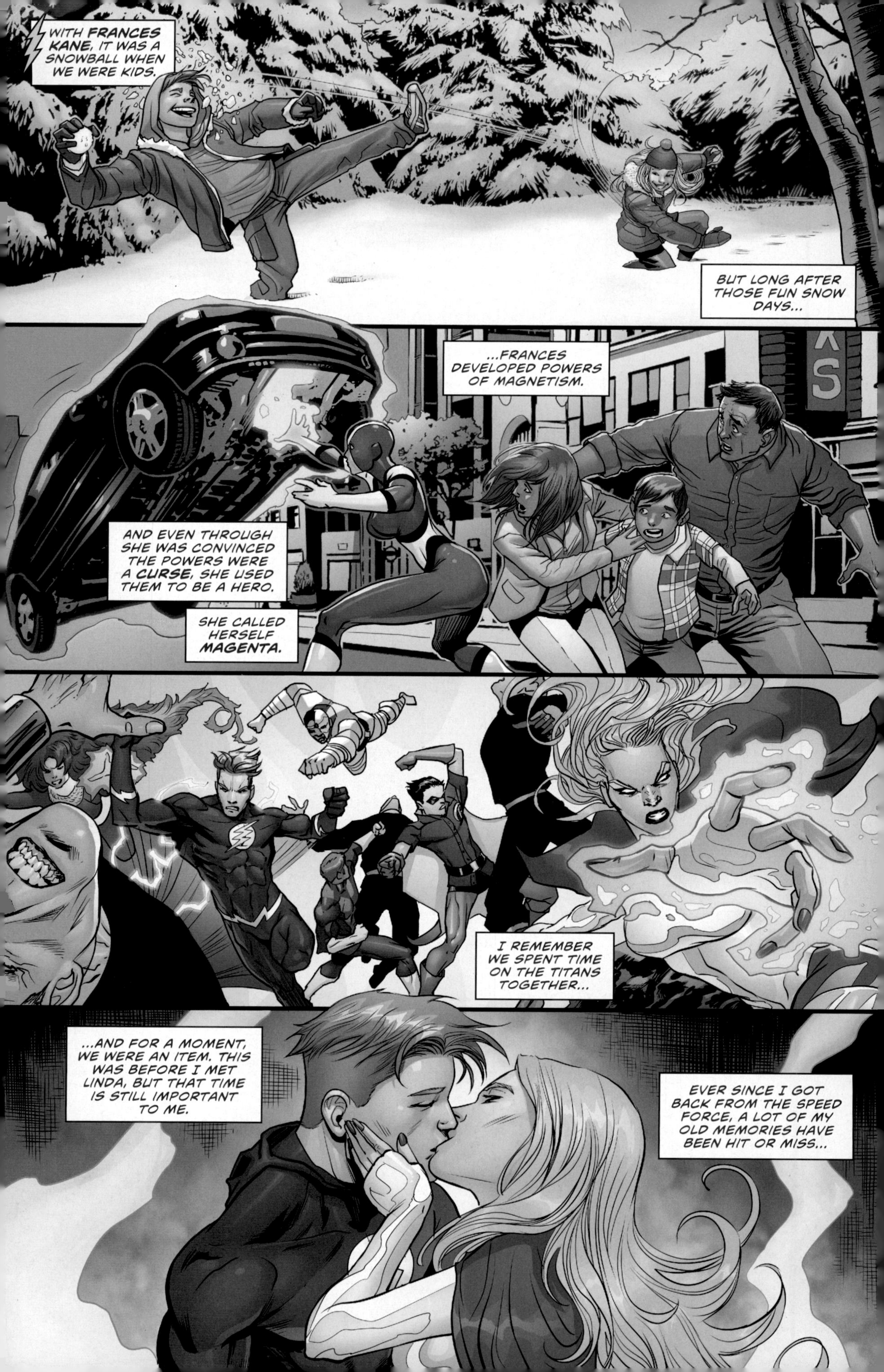

WITH FRANCES KANE, IT WAS A SNOWBALL WHEN WE WERE KIDS.
BUT LONG AFTER THOSE FUN SNOW DAYS...
...FRANCES DEVELOPED POWERS OF MAGNETISM.
AND EVEN THROUGH SHE WAS CONVINCED THE POWERS WERE A CURSE, SHE USED THEM TO BE A HERO.
SHE CALLED HERSELF MAGENTA.
I REMEMBER WE SPENT TIME ON THE TITANS TOGETHER...
...AND FOR A MOMENT, WE WERE AN ITEM. THIS WAS BEFORE I MET LINDA, BUT THAT TIME IS STILL IMPORTANT TO ME.
EVER SINCE I GOT BACK FROM THE SPEED FORCE, A LOT OF MY OLD MEMORIES HAVE BEEN HIT OR MISS...

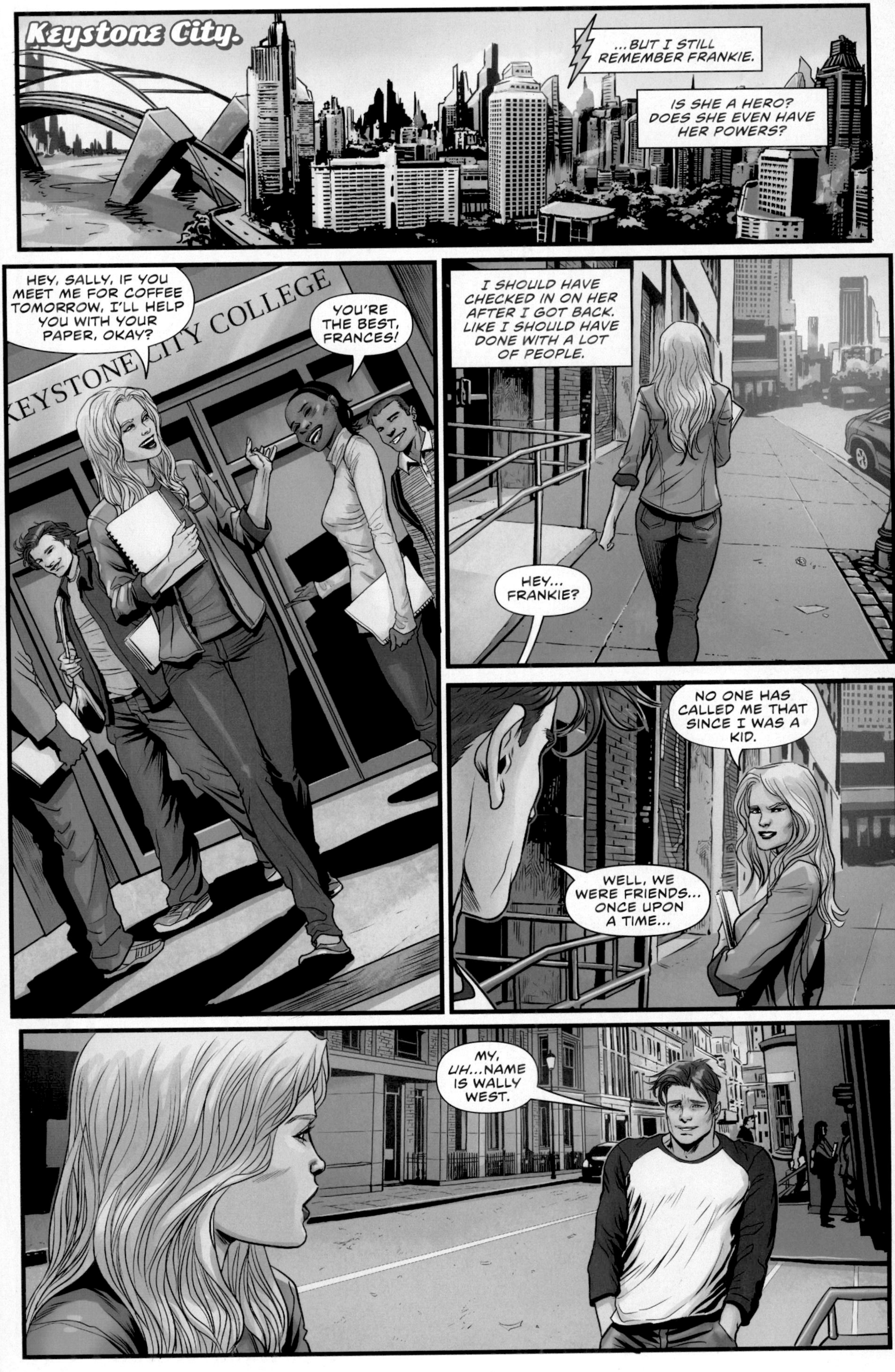
Keystone City.
...BUT I STILL REMEMBER FRANKIE.
IS SHE A HERO? DOES SHE EVEN HAVE HER POWERS?
KEYSTONE CITY COLLEGE
HEY, SALLY, IF YOU MEET ME FOR COFFEE TOMORROW, I'LL HELP YOU WITH YOUR PAPER, OKAY?
YOU'RE THE BEST, FRANCES!
I SHOULD HAVE CHECKED IN ON HER AFTER I GOT BACK. LIKE I SHOULD HAVE DONE WITH A LOT OF PEOPLE.
HEY... FRANKIE?
NO ONE HAS CALLED ME THAT SINCE I WAS A KID.
WELL, WE WERE FRIENDS... ONCE UPON A TIME...
MY, UH...NAME IS WALLY WEST.

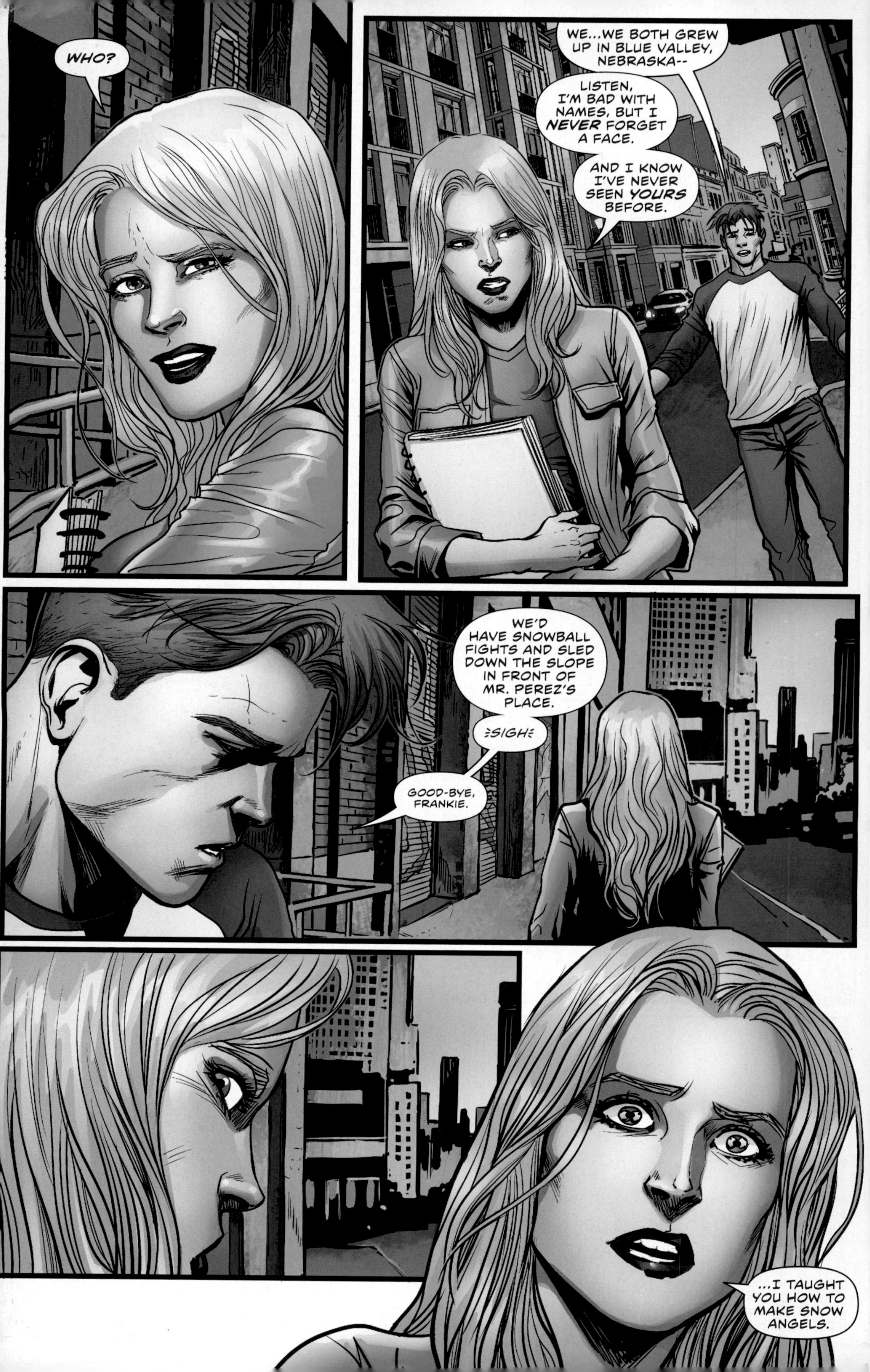
WHO?
WE...WE BOTH GREW UP IN BLUE VALLEY, NEBRASKA--
LISTEN, I'M BAD WITH NAMES, BUT I NEVER FORGET A FACE.
AND I KNOW I'VE NEVER SEEN YOURS BEFORE.
WE'D HAVE SNOWBALL FIGHTS AND SLED DOWN THE SLOPE IN FRONT OF MR. PEREZ'S PLACE.
SIGH
GOOD-BYE, FRANKIE.
...I TAUGHT YOU HOW TO MAKE SNOW ANGELS.

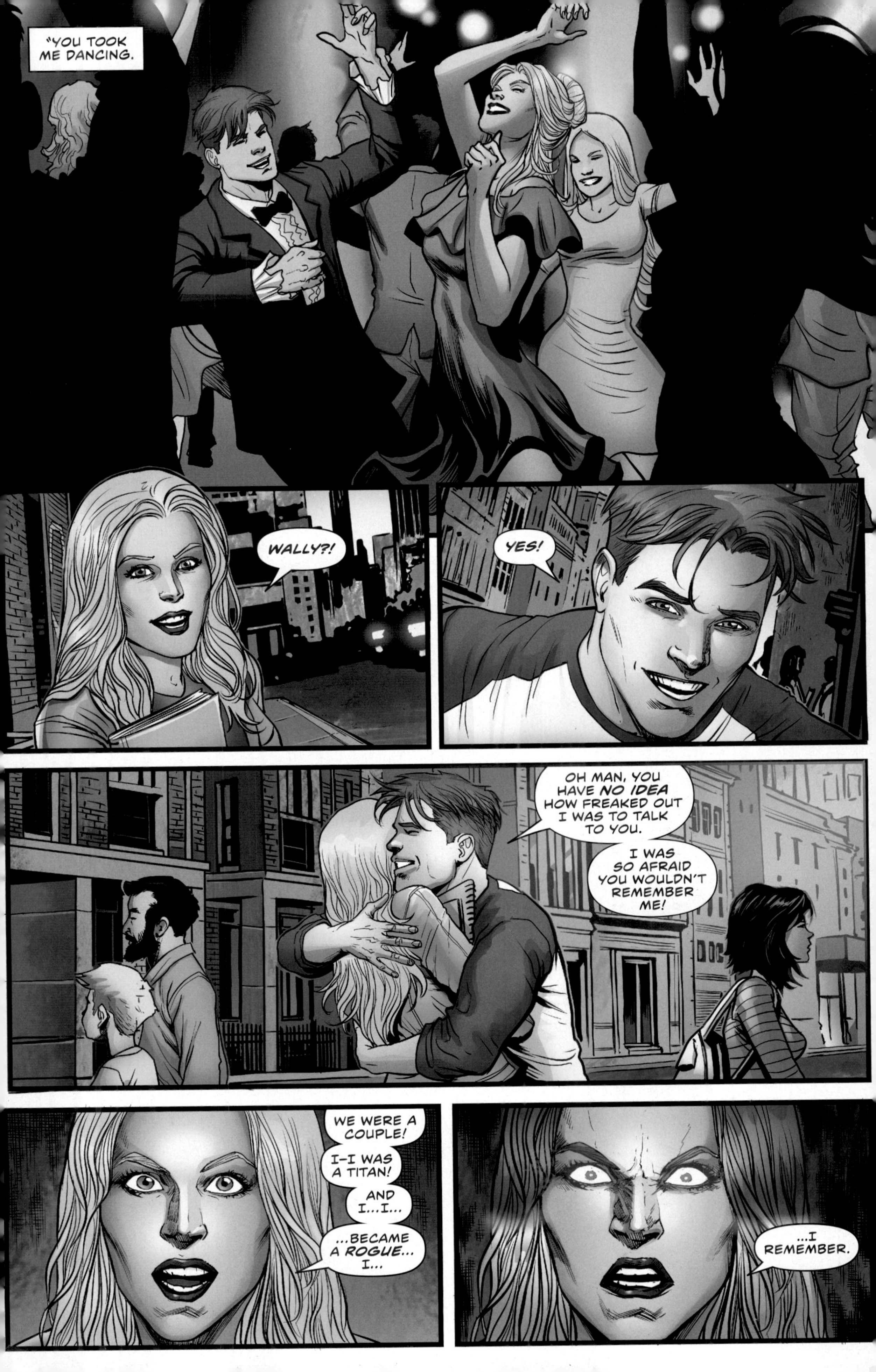
"YOU TOOK ME DANCING.
WALLY?!
YES!
OH MAN, YOU HAVE NO IDEA HOW FREAKED OUT I WAS TO TALK TO YOU.
I WAS SO AFRAID YOU WOULDN'T REMEMBER ME!
WE WERE A COUPLE!
I-I WAS A TITAN!
AND I...I...
...BECAME A ROGUE... I...
...I REMEMBER.

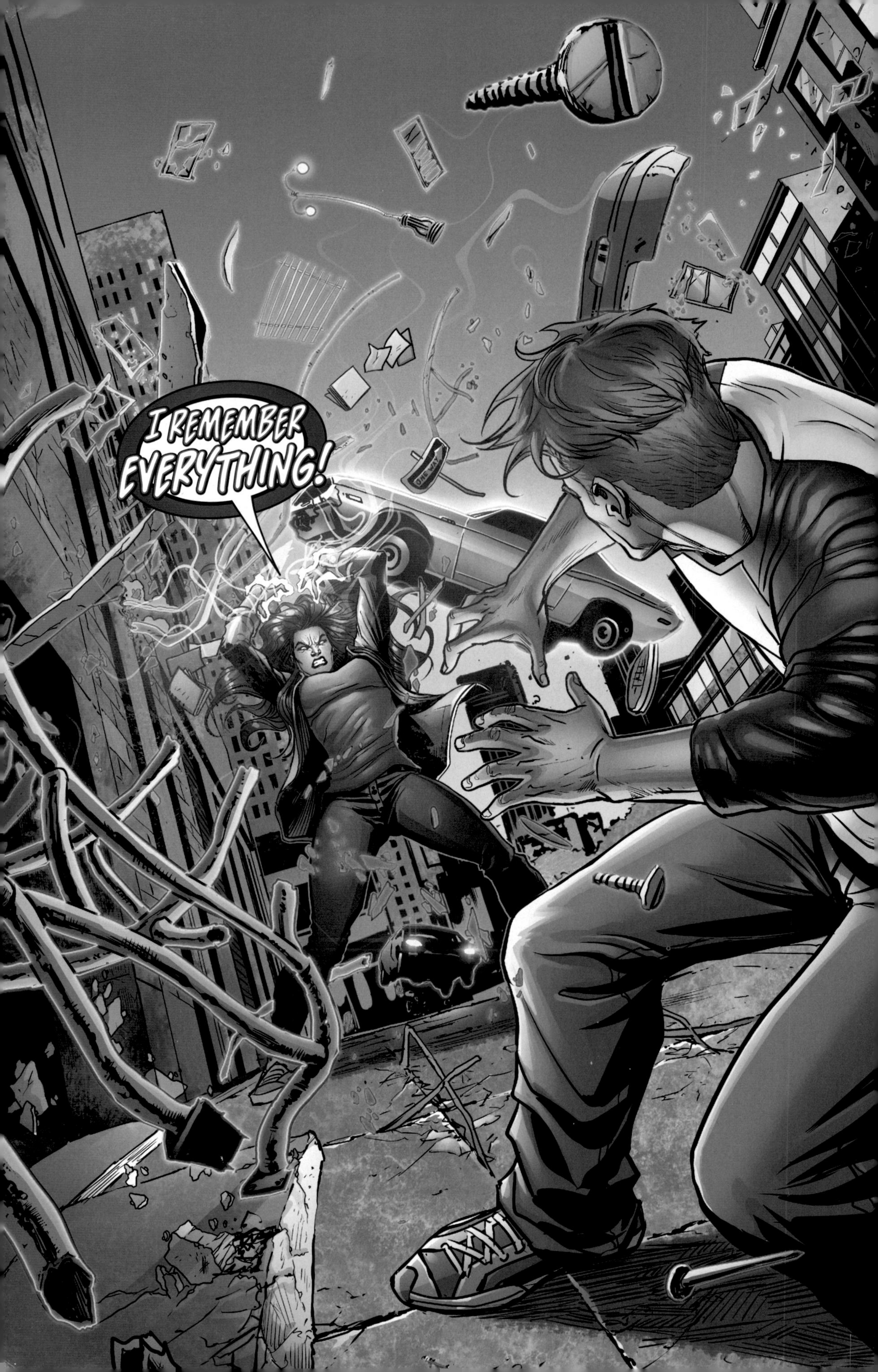
I REMEMBER EVERYTHING!

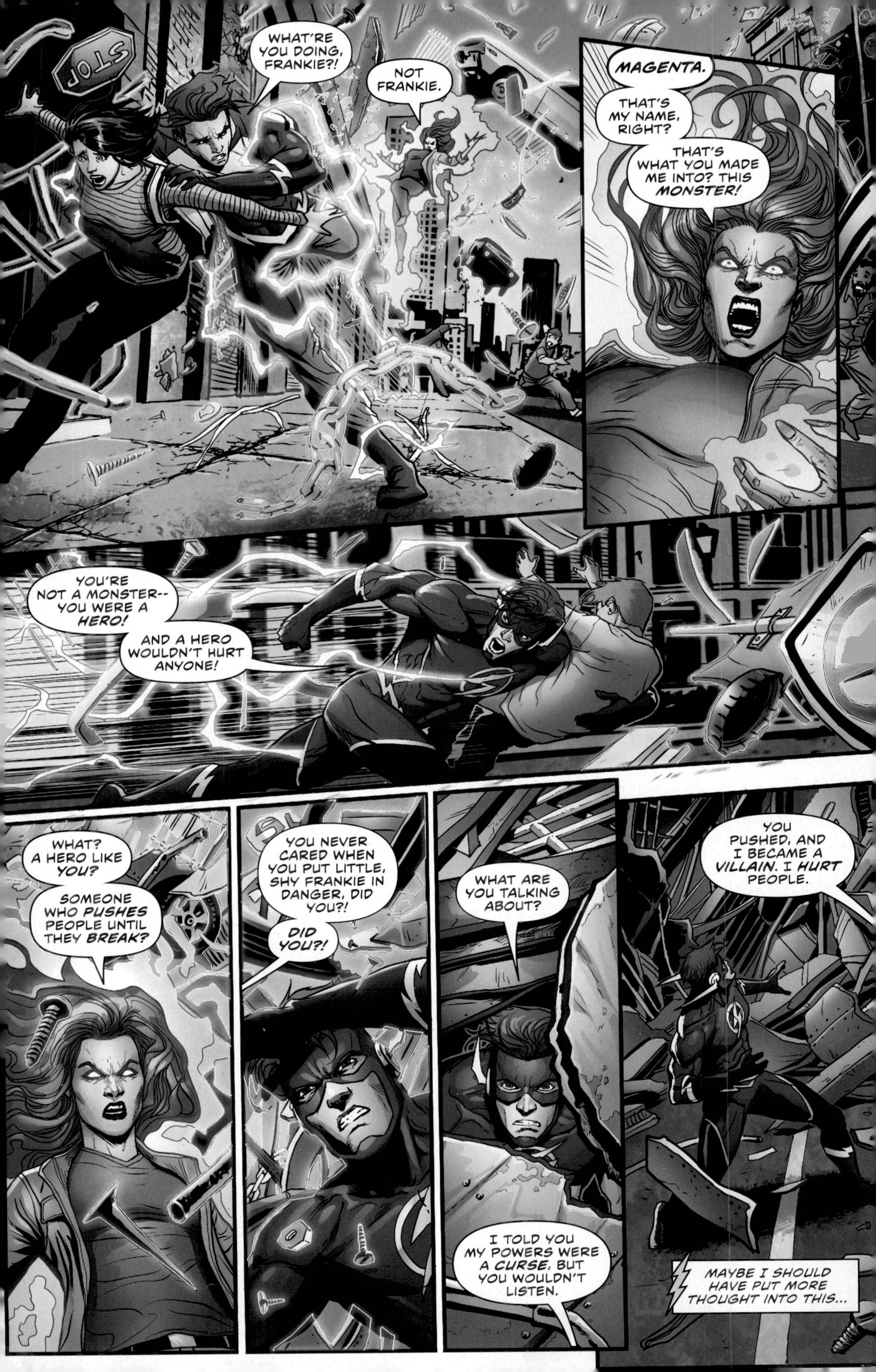
STOP
WHAT'RE YOU DOING, FRANKIE?!
NOT FRANKIE.
MAGENTA.
THAT'S MY NAME, RIGHT?
THAT'S WHAT YOU MADE ME INTO? THIS MONSTER!
YOU'RE NOT A MONSTER-- YOU WERE A HERO!
AND A HERO WOULDN'T HURT ANYONE!
WHAT? A HERO LIKE YOU?
SOMEONE WHO PUSHES PEOPLE UNTIL THEY BREAK?
YOU NEVER CARED WHEN YOU PUT LITTLE, SHY FRANKIE IN DANGER, DID YOU?!
DID YOU?!
WHAT ARE YOU TALKING ABOUT?
I TOLD YOU MY POWERS WERE A CURSE, BUT YOU WOULDN'T LISTEN.
YOU PUSHED, AND I BECAME A VILLAIN. I HURT PEOPLE.
MAYBE I SHOULD HAVE PUT MORE THOUGHT INTO THIS...

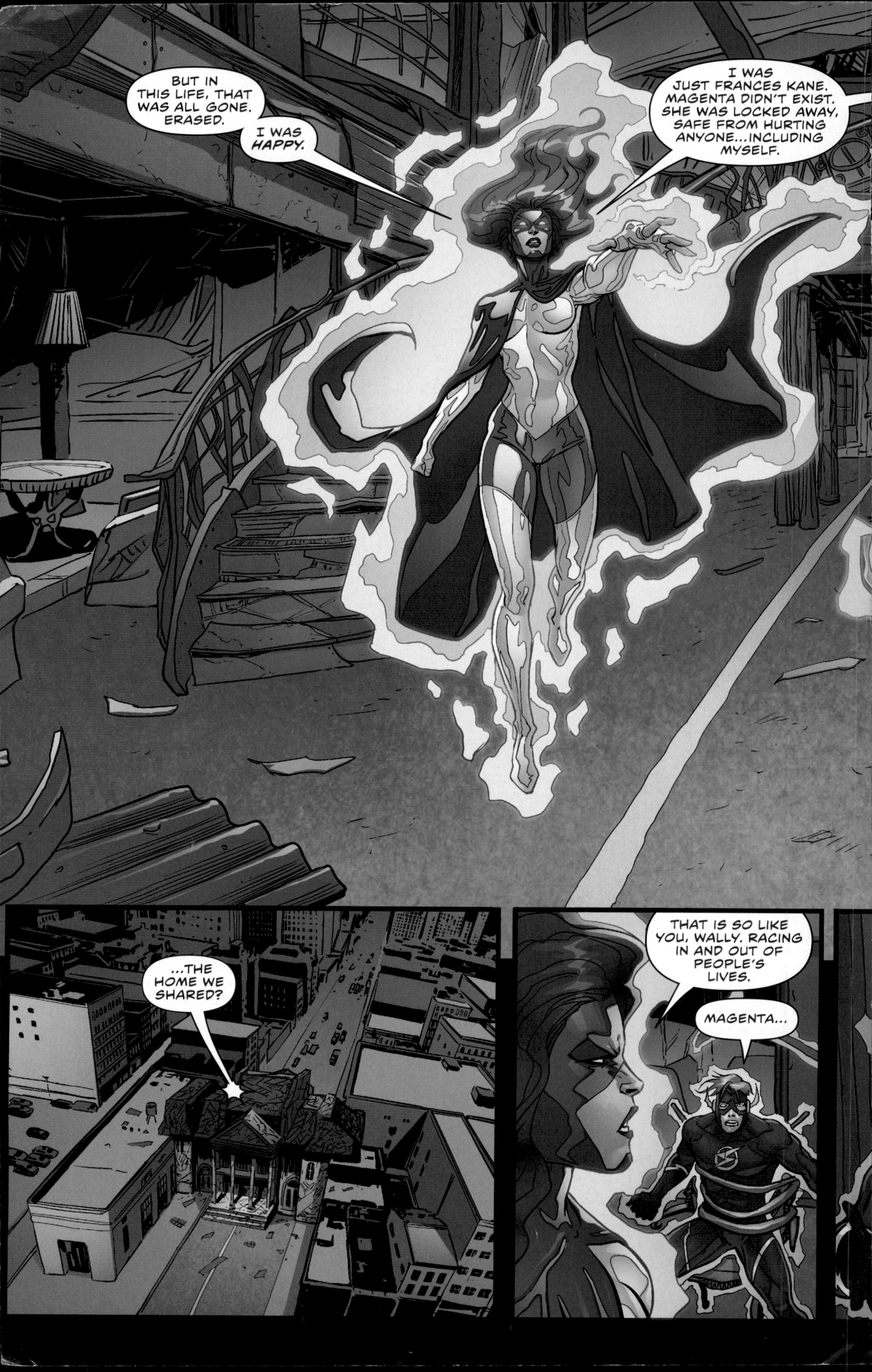
BUT IN THIS LIFE, THAT WAS ALL GONE. ERASED.
I WAS *HAPPY.*
I WAS JUST FRANCES KANE. MAGENTA DIDN'T EXIST. SHE WAS LOCKED AWAY, SAFE FROM HURTING ANYONE...INCLUDING MYSELF.
...THE HOME WE SHARED?
THAT IS SO LIKE YOU, WALLY. RACING IN AND OUT OF PEOPLE'S LIVES.
MAGENTA...

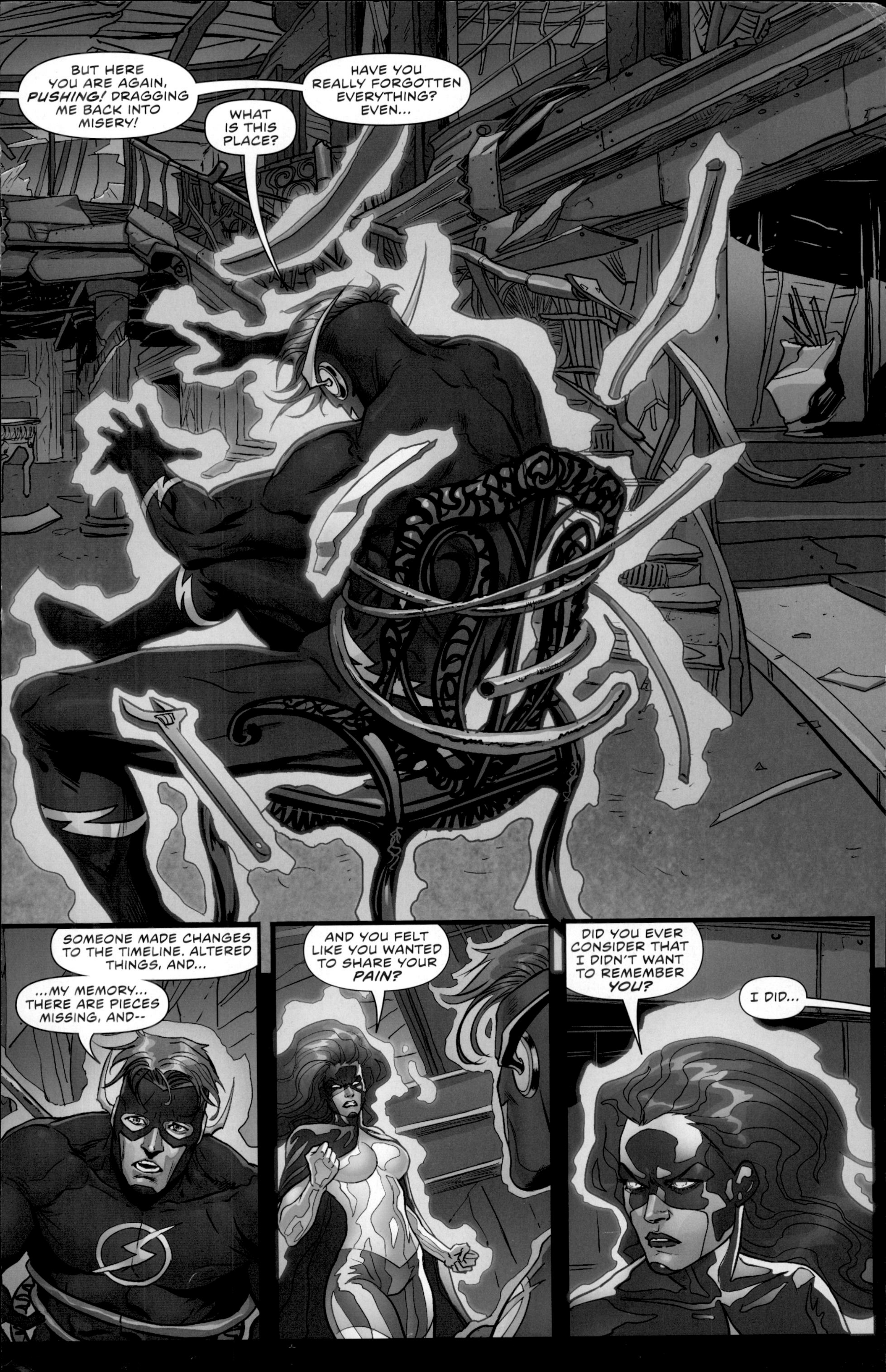
BUT HERE YOU ARE AGAIN, PUSHING! DRAGGING ME BACK INTO MISERY!
HAVE YOU REALLY FORGOTTEN EVERYTHING? EVEN...
WHAT IS THIS PLACE?
SOMEONE MADE CHANGES TO THE TIMELINE. ALTERED THINGS, AND...
...MY MEMORY... THERE ARE PIECES MISSING, AND--
AND YOU FELT LIKE YOU WANTED TO SHARE YOUR PAIN?
DID YOU EVER CONSIDER THAT I DIDN'T WANT TO REMEMBER YOU?
I DID...

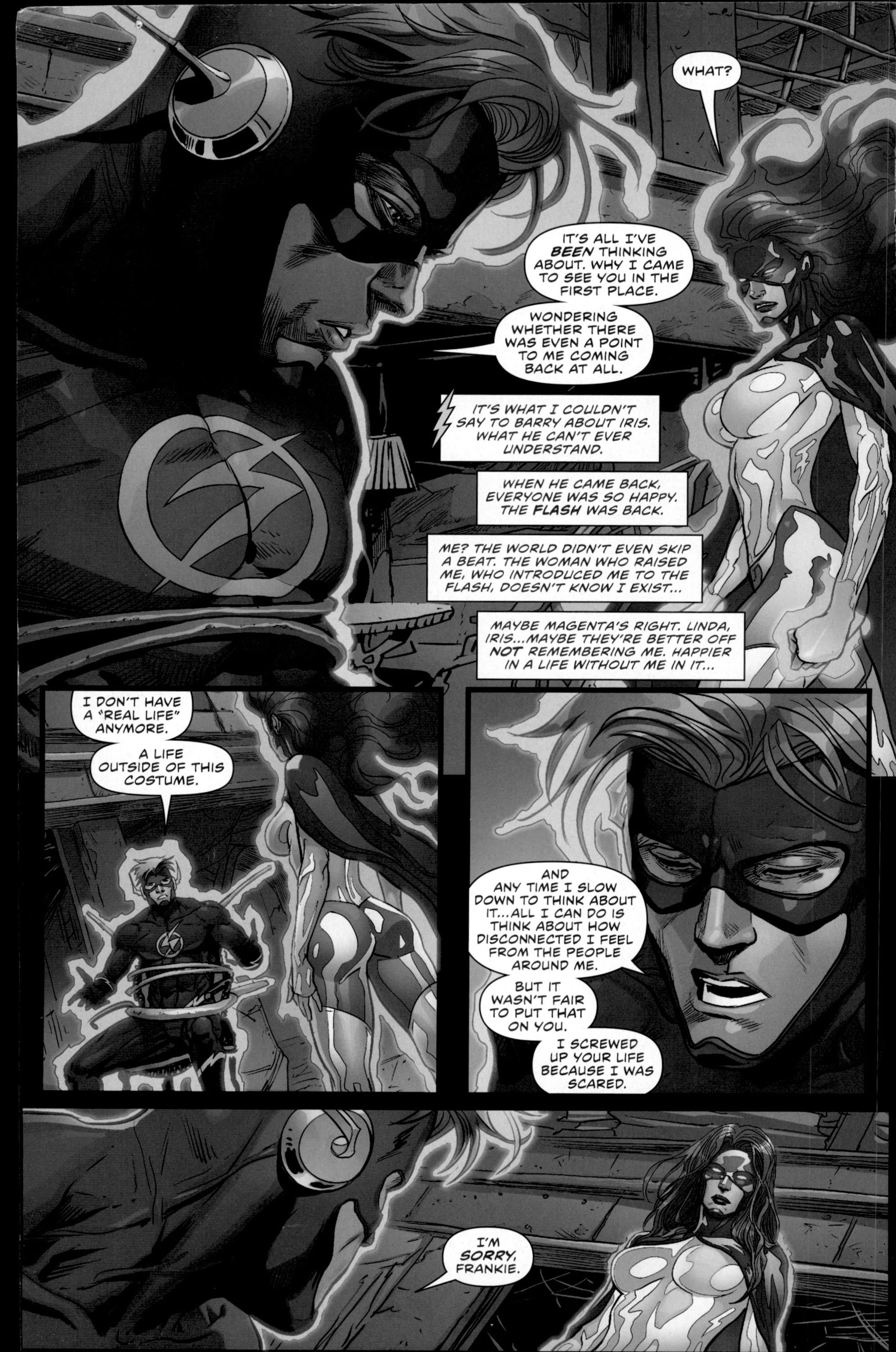
WHAT?
IT'S ALL I'VE BEEN THINKING ABOUT. WHY I CAME TO SEE YOU IN THE FIRST PLACE.
WONDERING WHETHER THERE WAS EVEN A POINT TO ME COMING BACK AT ALL.
IT'S WHAT I COULDN'T SAY TO BARRY ABOUT IRIS. WHAT HE CAN'T EVER UNDERSTAND.
WHEN HE CAME BACK, EVERYONE WAS SO HAPPY. THE FLASH WAS BACK.
ME? THE WORLD DIDN'T EVEN SKIP A BEAT. THE WOMAN WHO RAISED ME, WHO INTRODUCED ME TO THE FLASH, DOESN'T KNOW I EXIST...
MAYBE MAGENTA'S RIGHT. LINDA, IRIS...MAYBE THEY'RE BETTER OFF NOT REMEMBERING ME. HAPPIER IN A LIFE WITHOUT ME IN IT...
I DON'T HAVE A "REAL LIFE" ANYMORE.
A LIFE OUTSIDE OF THIS COSTUME.
AND ANY TIME I SLOW DOWN TO THINK ABOUT IT...ALL I CAN DO IS THINK ABOUT HOW DISCONNECTED I FEEL FROM THE PEOPLE AROUND ME.
BUT IT WASN'T FAIR TO PUT THAT ON YOU.
I SCREWED UP YOUR LIFE BECAUSE I WAS SCARED.
I'M SORRY, FRANKIE.

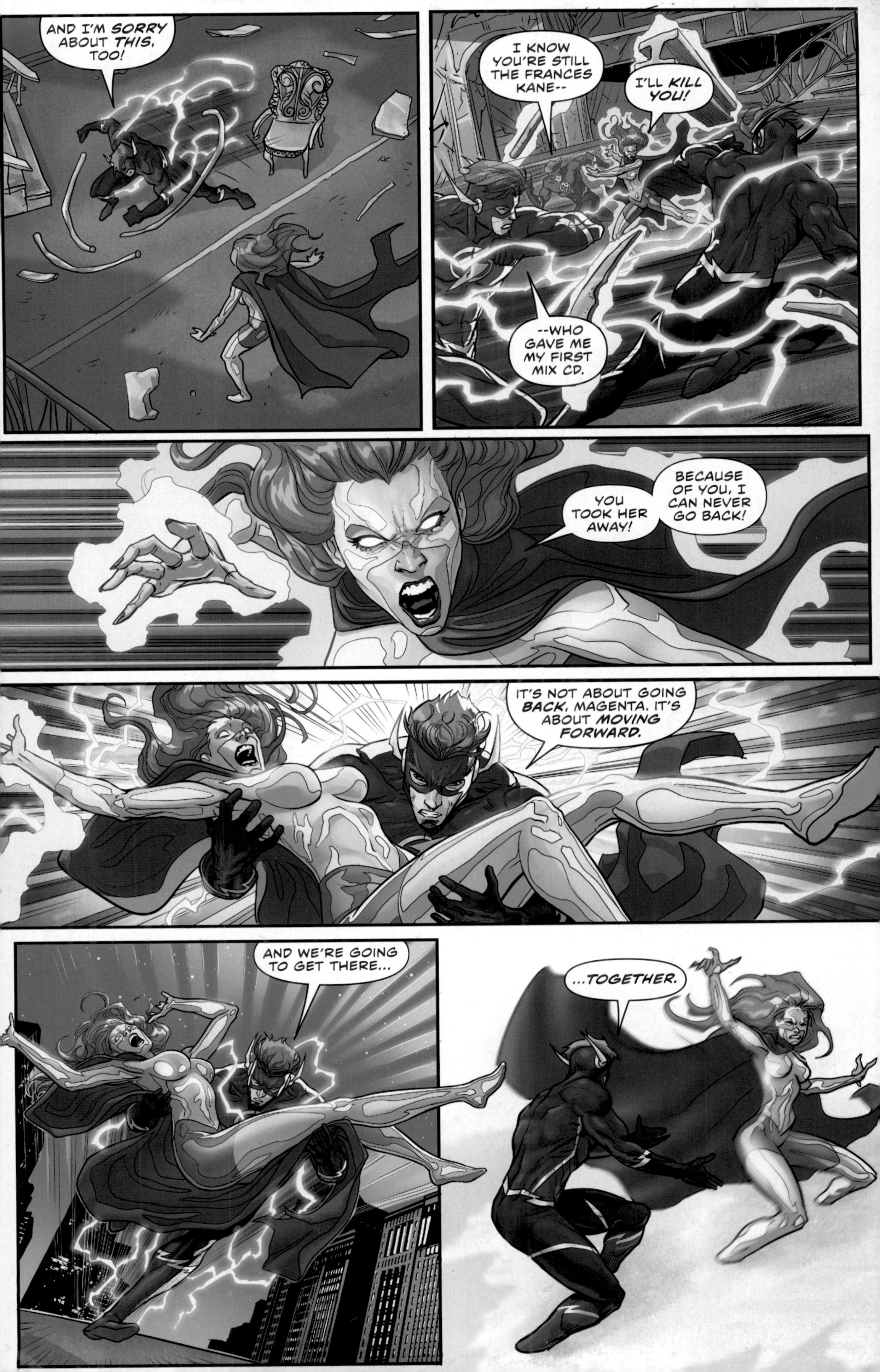
AND I'M *SORRY* ABOUT *THIS*, TOO!
I KNOW YOU'RE STILL THE FRANCES KANE--
I'LL *KILL YOU!*
--WHO GAVE ME MY FIRST MIX CD.
YOU TOOK HER AWAY!
BECAUSE OF YOU, I CAN NEVER GO BACK!
IT'S NOT ABOUT GOING *BACK*, MAGENTA. IT'S ABOUT *MOVING FORWARD*.
AND WE'RE GOING TO GET THERE...
...*TOGETHER*.

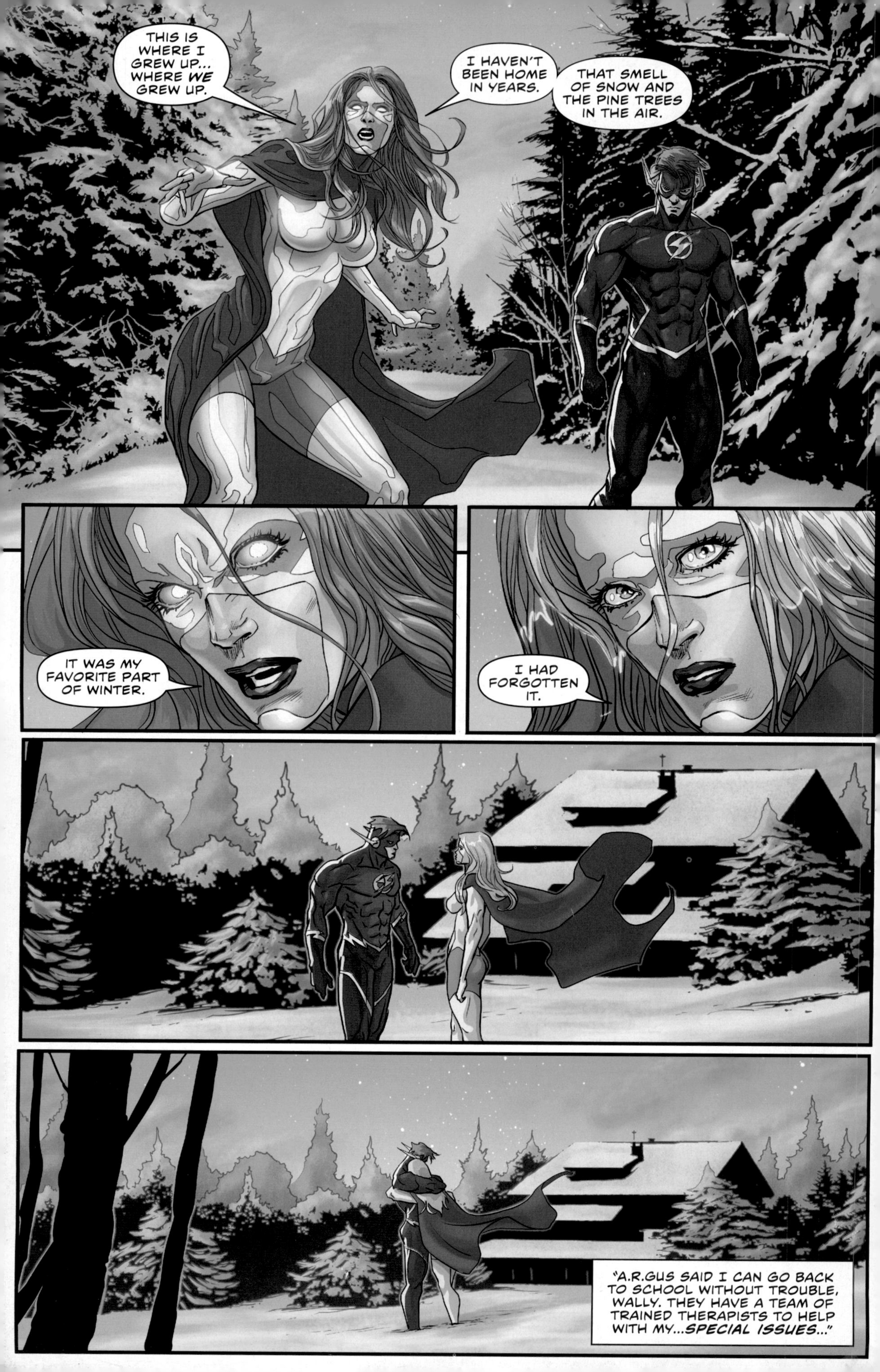
THIS IS WHERE I GREW UP... WHERE *WE* GREW UP.
I HAVEN'T BEEN HOME IN YEARS.
THAT SMELL OF SNOW AND THE PINE TREES IN THE AIR.
IT WAS MY FAVORITE PART OF WINTER.
I HAD FORGOTTEN IT.
"A.R.GUS SAID I CAN GO BACK TO SCHOOL WITHOUT TROUBLE, WALLY. THEY HAVE A TEAM OF TRAINED THERAPISTS TO HELP WITH MY...*SPECIAL ISSUES*..."

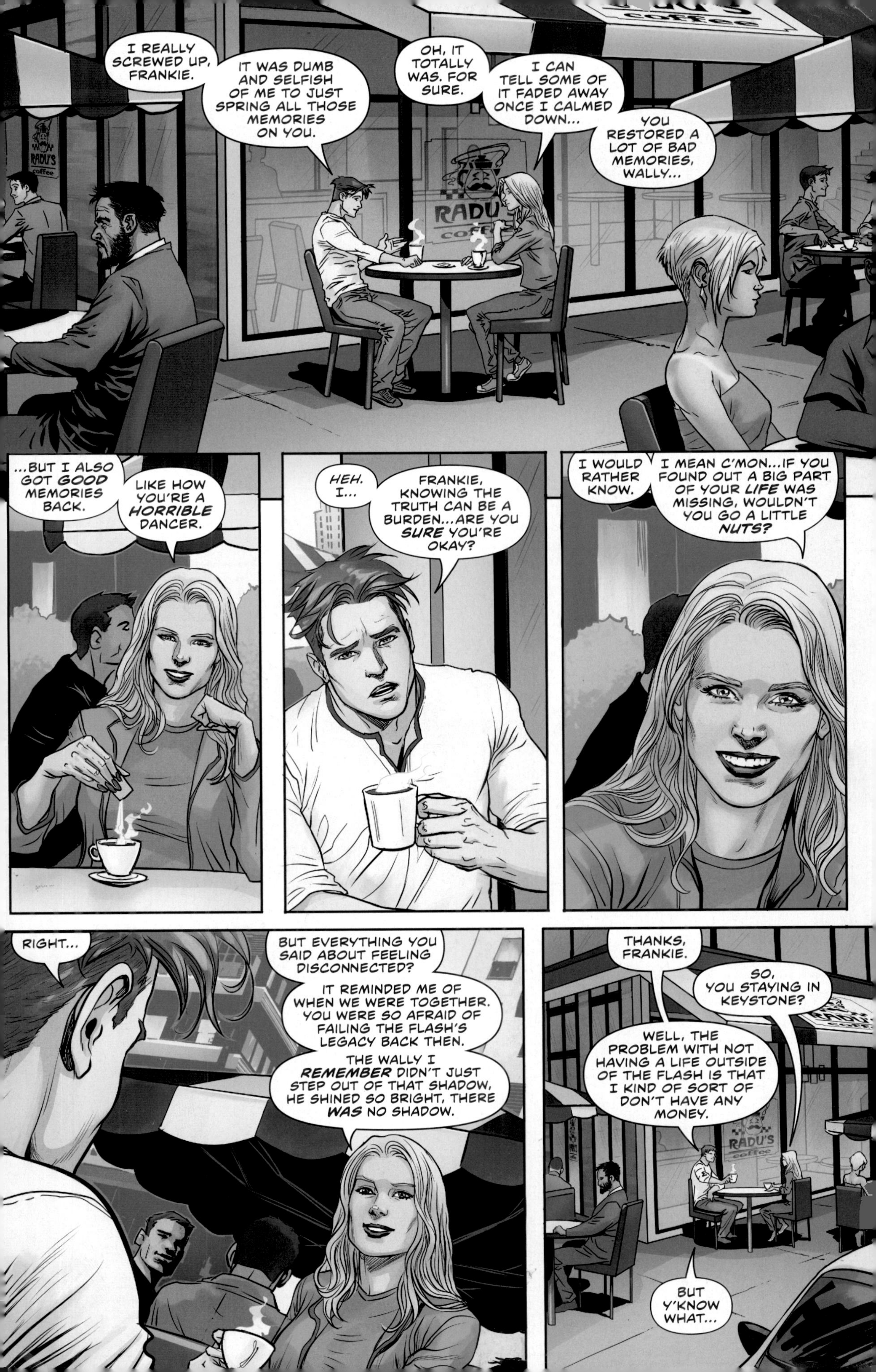
I REALLY SCREWED UP, FRANKIE.
IT WAS DUMB AND SELFISH OF ME TO JUST SPRING ALL THOSE MEMORIES ON YOU.
OH, IT TOTALLY WAS. FOR SURE.
I CAN TELL SOME OF IT FADED AWAY ONCE I CALMED DOWN...
YOU RESTORED A LOT OF BAD MEMORIES, WALLY...
RADU'S coffee
...BUT I ALSO GOT GOOD MEMORIES BACK.
LIKE HOW YOU'RE A HORRIBLE DANCER.
HEH. I...
FRANKIE, KNOWING THE TRUTH CAN BE A BURDEN...ARE YOU SURE YOU'RE OKAY?
I WOULD RATHER KNOW.
I MEAN C'MON...IF YOU FOUND OUT A BIG PART OF YOUR LIFE WAS MISSING, WOULDN'T YOU GO A LITTLE NUTS?
RIGHT...
BUT EVERYTHING YOU SAID ABOUT FEELING DISCONNECTED?
IT REMINDED ME OF WHEN WE WERE TOGETHER. YOU WERE SO AFRAID OF FAILING THE FLASH'S LEGACY BACK THEN.
THE WALLY I REMEMBER DIDN'T JUST STEP OUT OF THAT SHADOW, HE SHINED SO BRIGHT, THERE WAS NO SHADOW.
THANKS, FRANKIE.
SO, YOU STAYING IN KEYSTONE?
WELL, THE PROBLEM WITH NOT HAVING A LIFE OUTSIDE OF THE FLASH IS THAT I KIND OF SORT OF DON'T HAVE ANY MONEY.
BUT Y'KNOW WHAT...

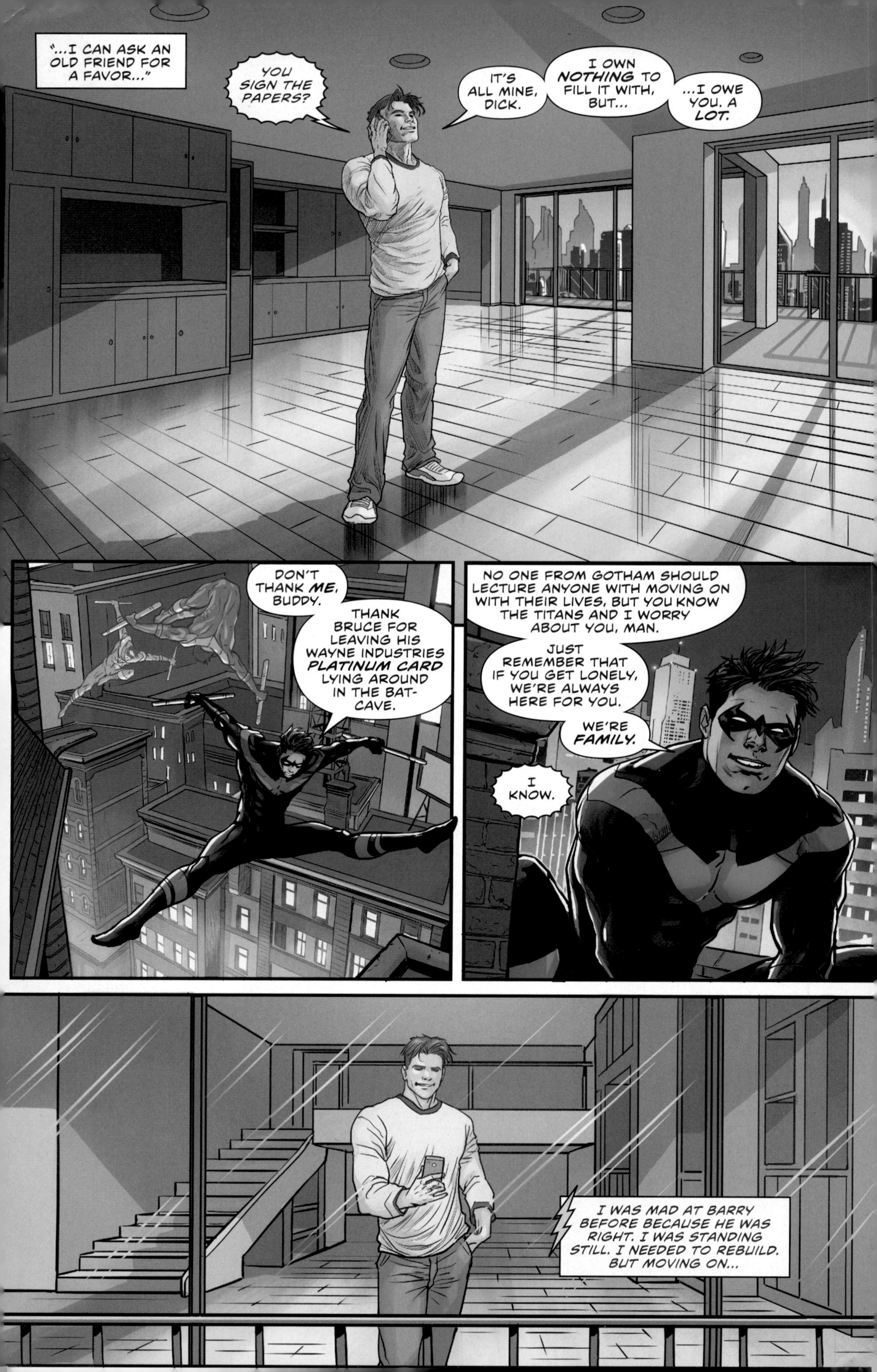
"...I CAN ASK AN OLD FRIEND FOR A FAVOR..."
YOU SIGN THE PAPERS?
IT'S ALL MINE, DICK.
I OWN NOTHING TO FILL IT WITH, BUT...
...I OWE YOU. A LOT.
DON'T THANK ME, BUDDY.
THANK BRUCE FOR LEAVING HIS WAYNE INDUSTRIES PLATINUM CARD LYING AROUND IN THE BAT-CAVE.
NO ONE FROM GOTHAM SHOULD LECTURE ANYONE WITH MOVING ON WITH THEIR LIVES, BUT YOU KNOW THE TITANS AND I WORRY ABOUT YOU, MAN.
JUST REMEMBER THAT IF YOU GET LONELY, WE'RE ALWAYS HERE FOR YOU.
WE'RE FAMILY.
I KNOW.
I WAS MAD AT BARRY BEFORE BECAUSE HE WAS RIGHT. I WAS STANDING STILL. I NEEDED TO REBUILD. BUT MOVING ON...

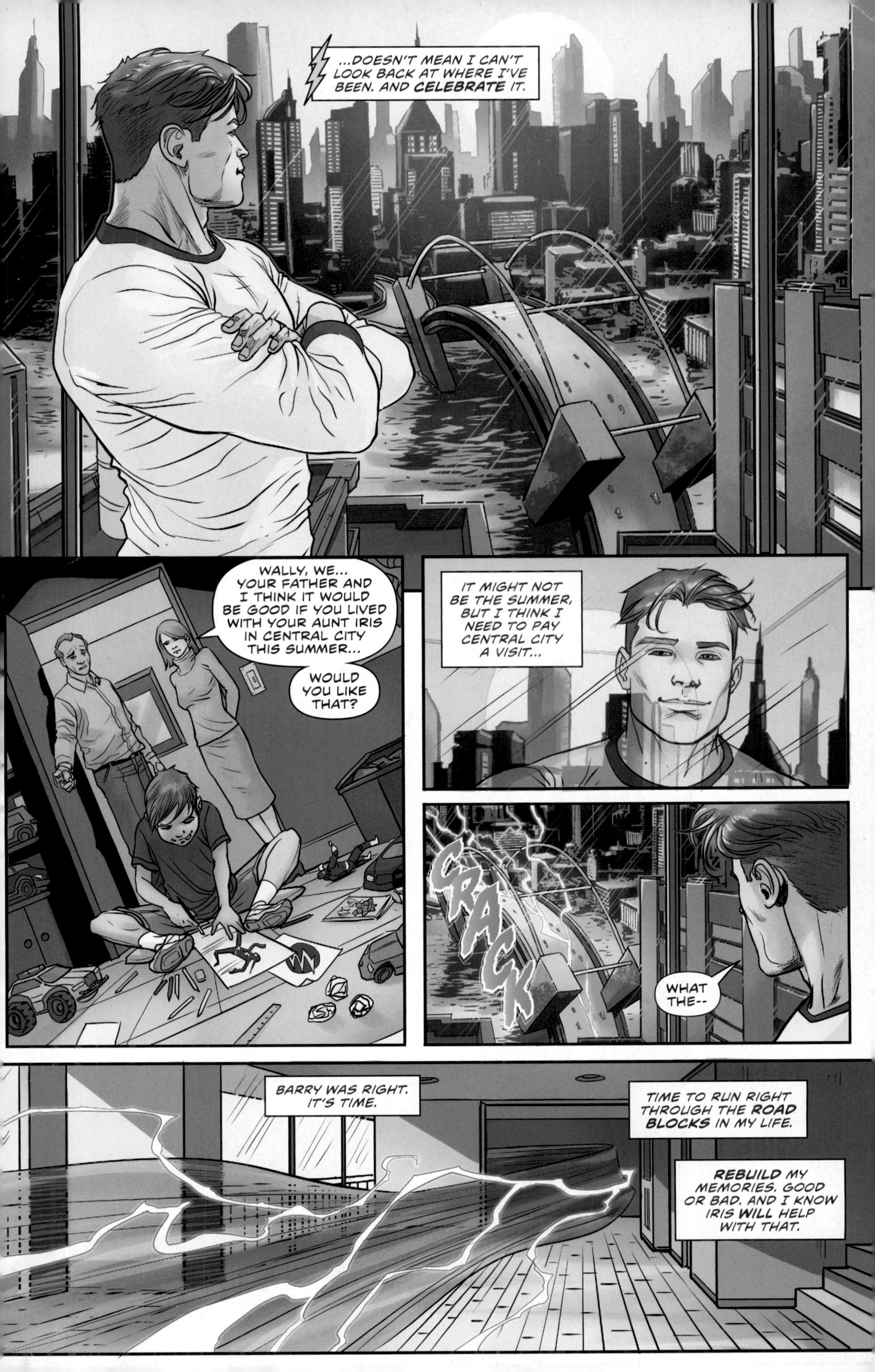
...DOESN'T MEAN I CAN'T LOOK BACK AT WHERE I'VE BEEN. AND **CELEBRATE** IT.
WALLY, WE... YOUR FATHER AND I THINK IT WOULD BE GOOD IF YOU LIVED WITH YOUR AUNT IRIS IN CENTRAL CITY THIS SUMMER...
WOULD YOU LIKE THAT?
IT MIGHT NOT BE THE SUMMER, BUT I THINK I NEED TO PAY CENTRAL CITY A VISIT...
CRACK
WHAT THE--
BARRY WAS RIGHT. IT'S TIME.
TIME TO RUN RIGHT THROUGH THE **ROAD BLOCKS** IN MY LIFE.
REBUILD MY MEMORIES. GOOD OR BAD. AND I KNOW IRIS **WILL** HELP WITH THAT.

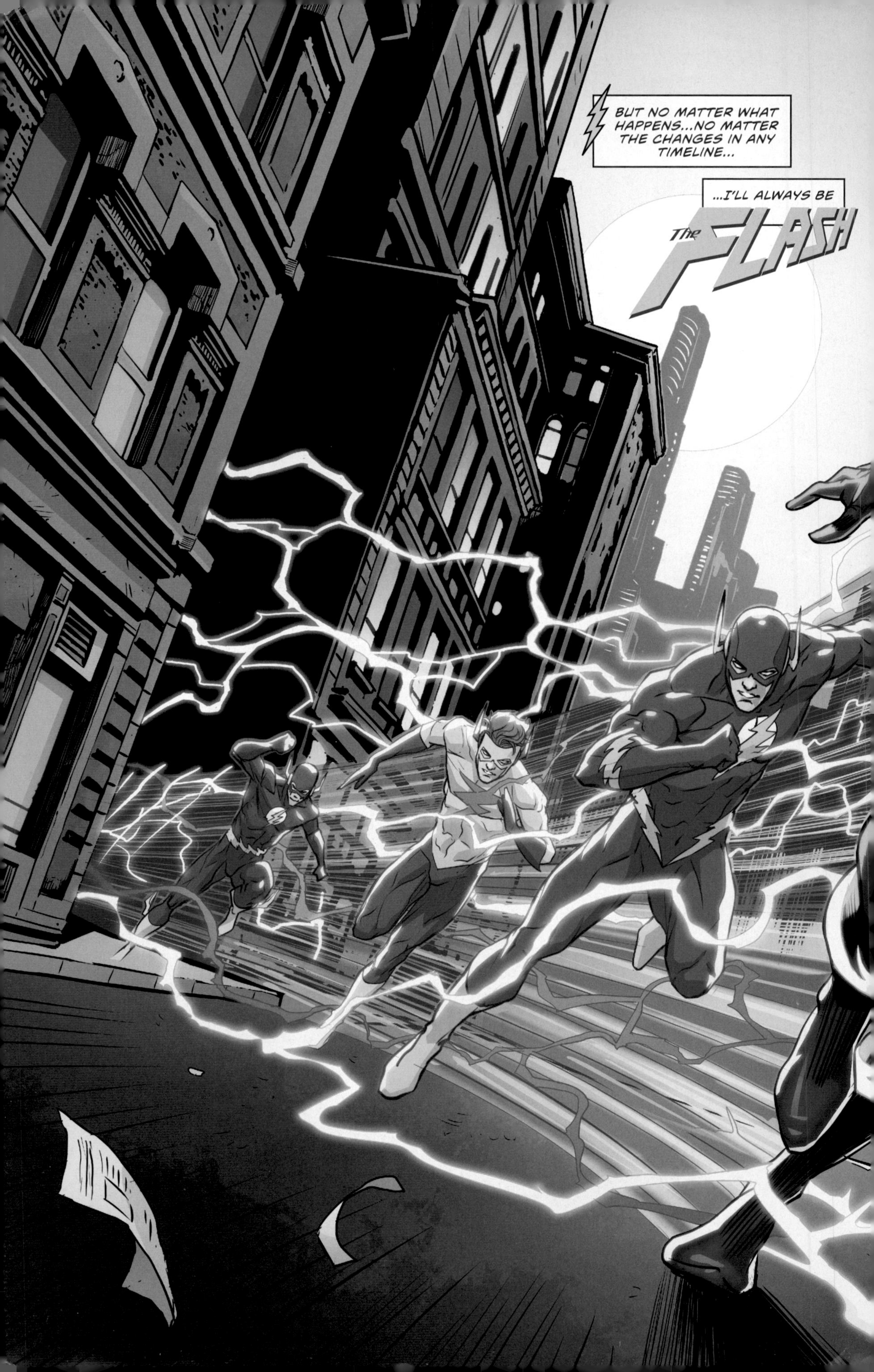
BUT NO MATTER WHAT HAPPENS...NO MATTER THE CHANGES IN ANY TIMELINE...
...I'LL ALWAYS BE
The FLASH

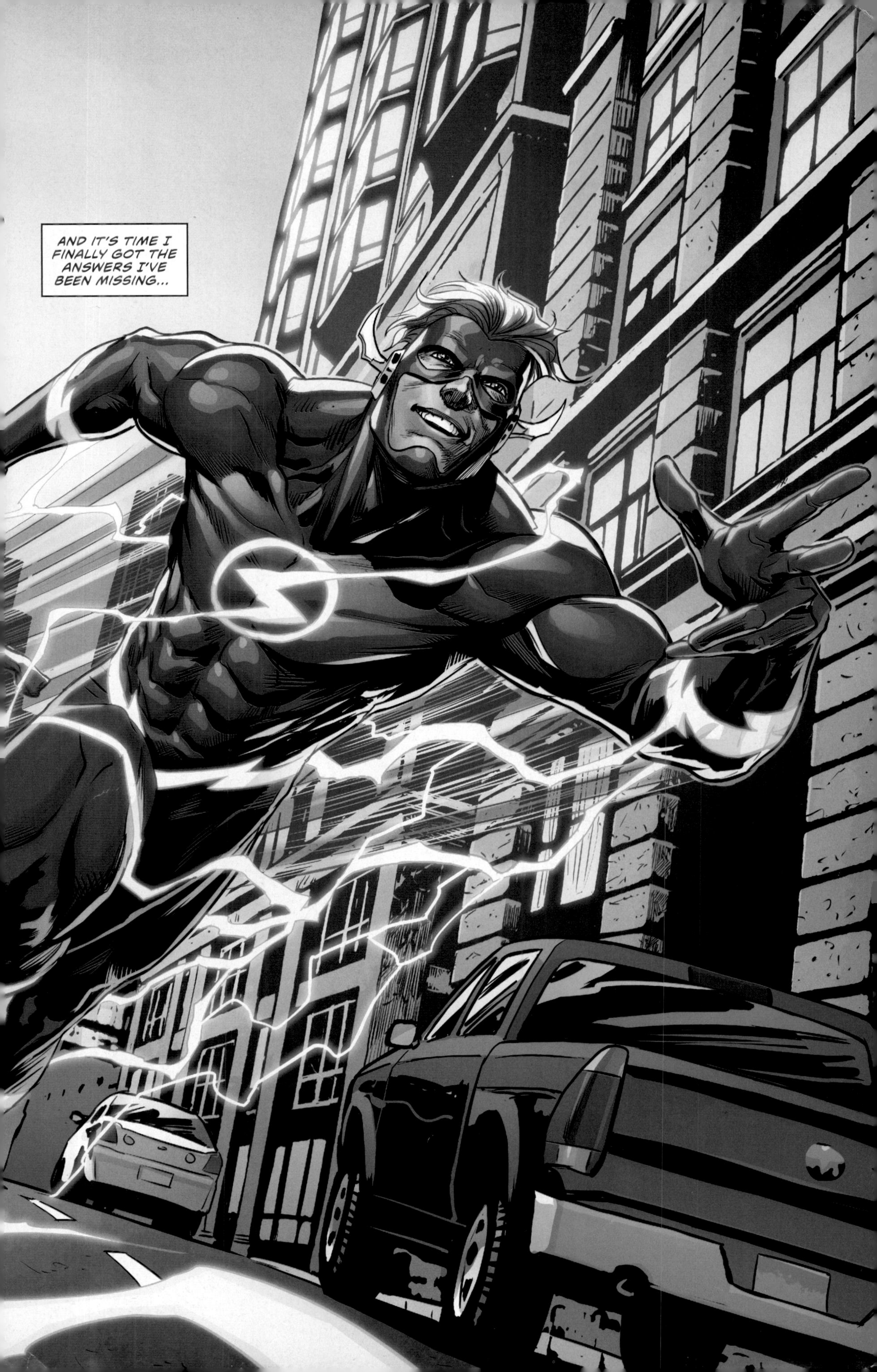
AND IT'S TIME I FINALLY GOT THE ANSWERS I'VE BEEN MISSING...

The FLASH
VARIANT COVER GALLERY

THE FLASH #34 variant cover by
MIKE McKONE and ROMULO FAJARDO JR.

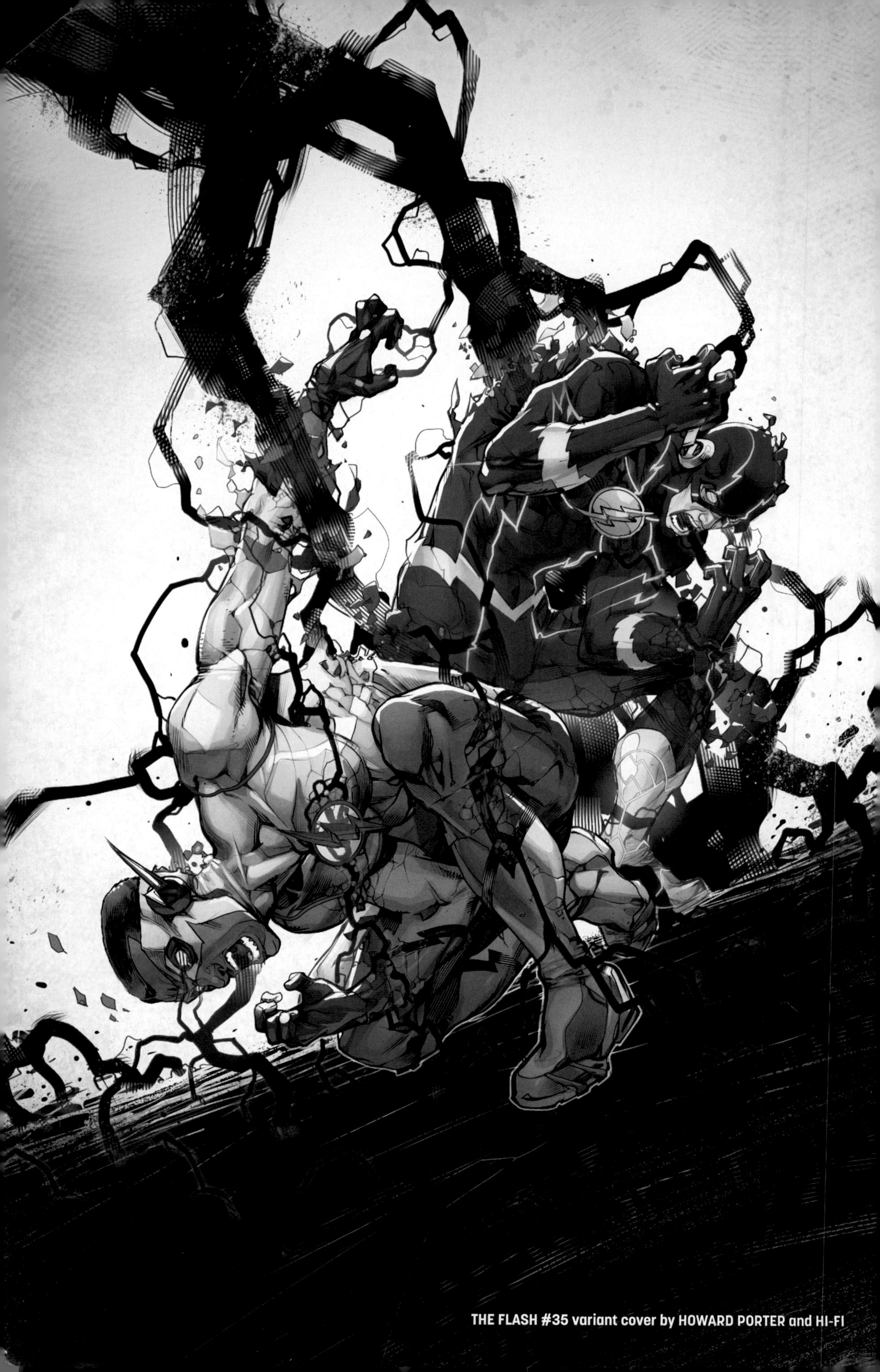

THE FLASH #35 variant cover by HOWARD PORTER and HI-FI

THE FLASH #36 variant cover by HOWARD PORTER and HI-FI

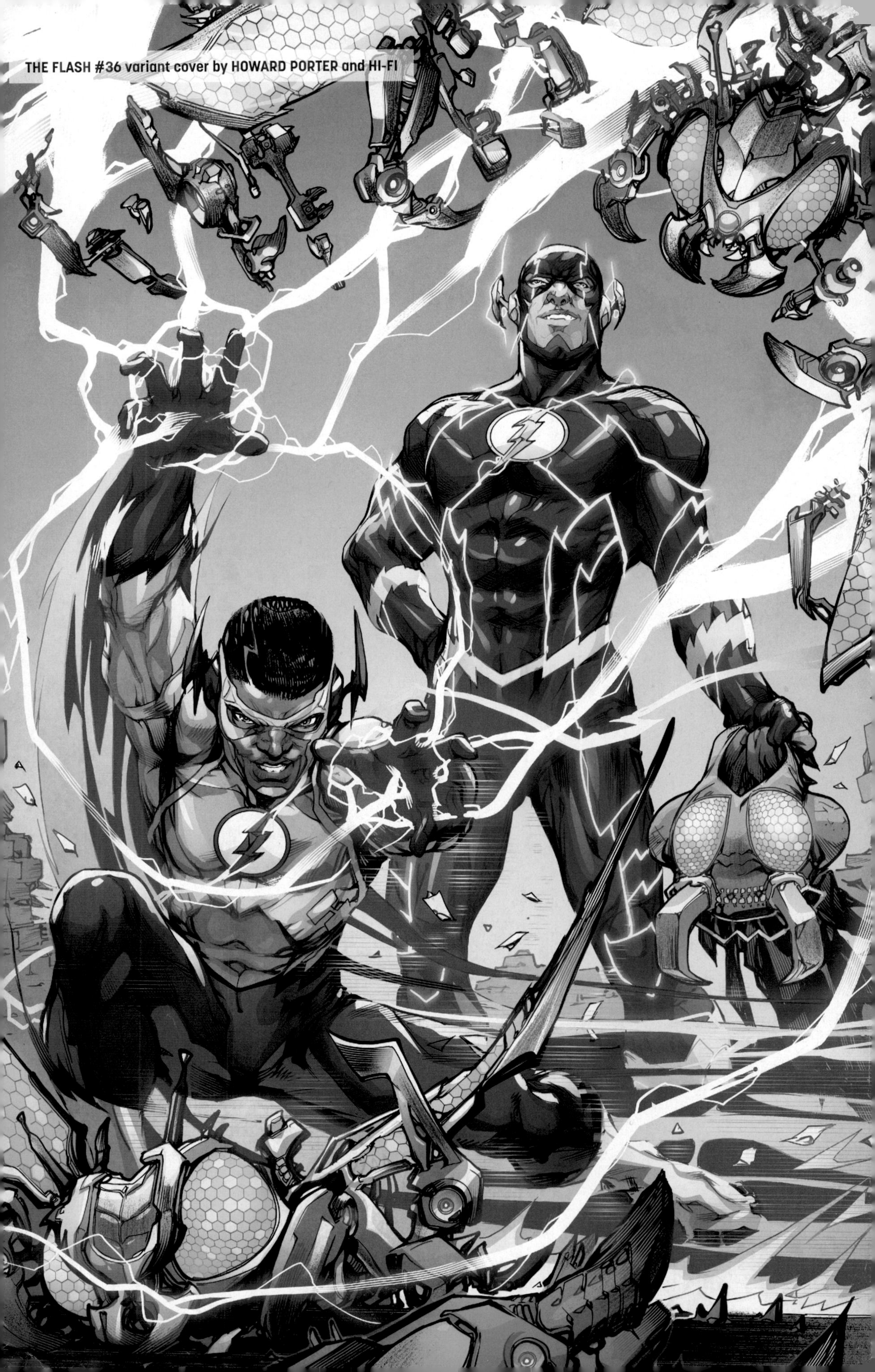

THE FLASH #37 variant cover by HOWARD PORTER and HI-FI

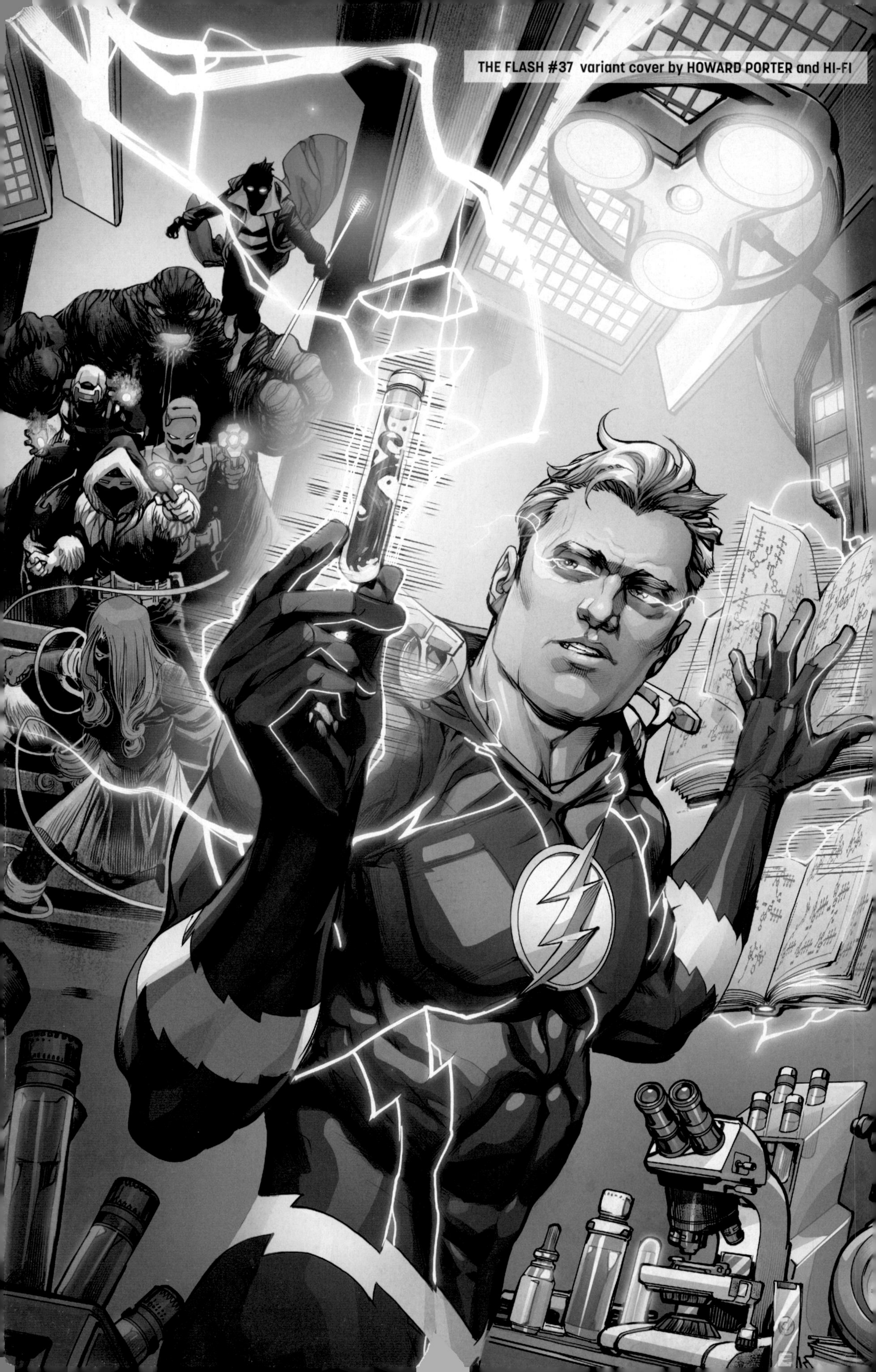

THE FLASH #38 variant cover by FRANCESCO MATTINA

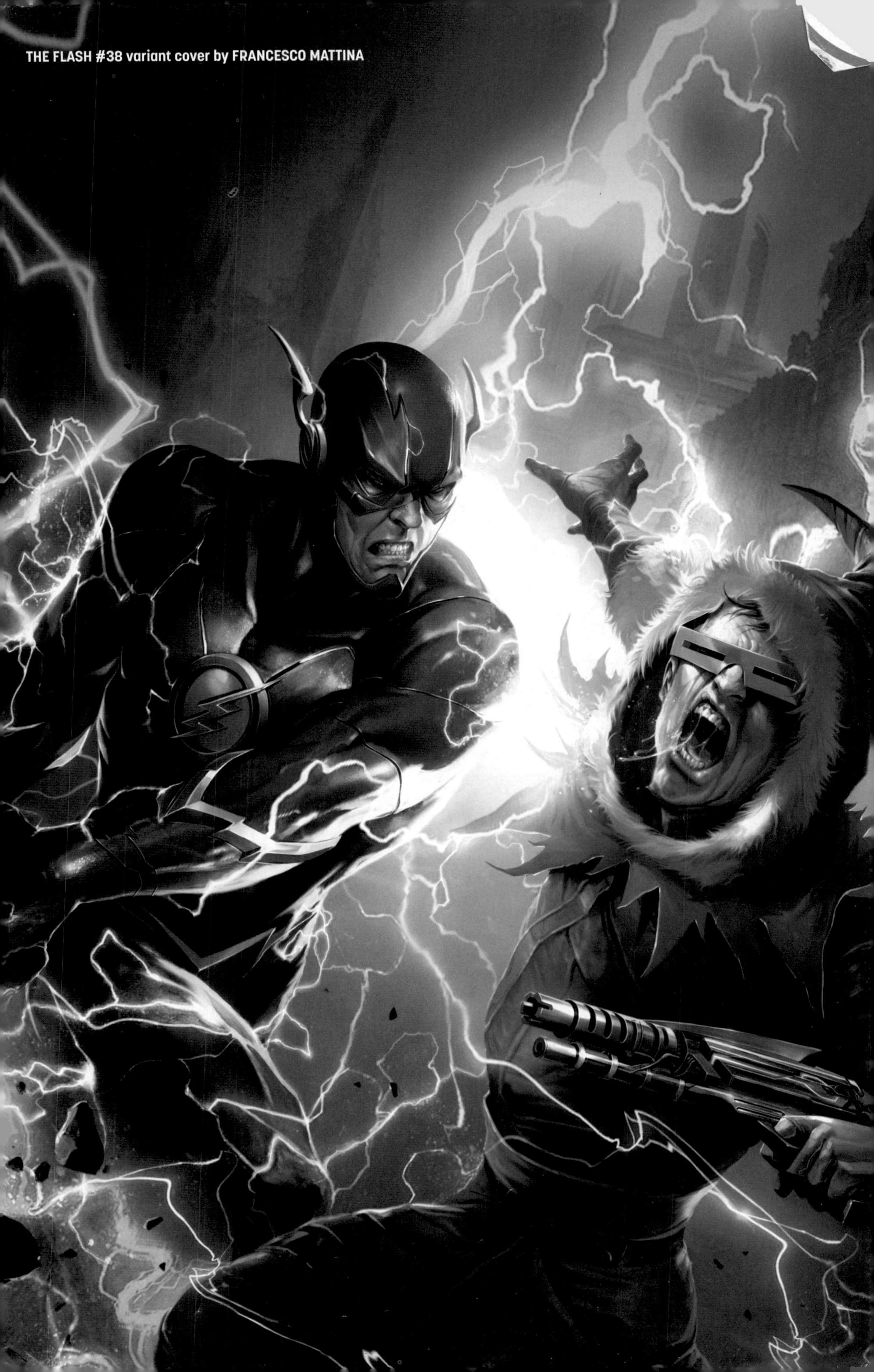

DC UNIVERSE REBIRTH

THE FLASH

VOL. 1: LIGHTNING STRIKES TWICE

JOSHUA WILLIAMSON
with CARMINE DI GIANDOMENICO
and IVAN PLASCENCIA

**JUSTICE LEAGUE VOL. 1:
THE EXTINCTION MACHINES**

**TITANS VOL. 1:
THE RETURN OF WALLY WEST**

**HAL JORDAN AND
THE GREEN LANTERN CORPS VOL. 1:
SINESTRO'S LAW**

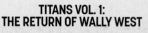

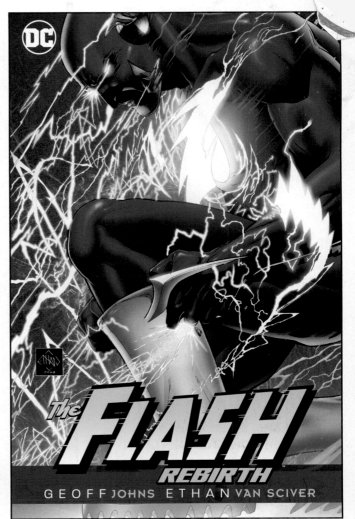
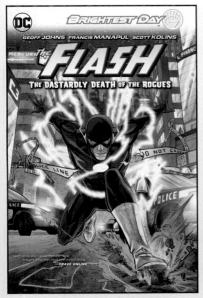

"THE NEW YORK TIMES BEST-SELLING SERIES."
THE NEW 52!
The FLASH
VOLUME 1
MOVE FORWARD
FRANCIS MANAPUL BRIAN BUCCELLATO

"Flash fans should breathe a sigh of relief that the character is 100% in the right hands." **– MTV**

START AT THE BEGINNING!

THE FLASH

VOL. 1: MOVE FORWARD

FRANCIS MANAPUL
with BRIAN BUCCELLATO

THE NEW YORK TIMES BEST-SELLING SERIES
THE NEW 52!
"THE FLASH IS ONE OF DC'S BEST LOOKING AND MOST FUN BOOKS." —IGN
The FLASH
VOLUME 2
ROGUES REVOLUTION
FRANCIS MANAPUL BRIAN BUCCELLATO

**THE FLASH VOL. 2
ROGUES REVOLUTION**

THE #1 NEW YORK TIMES BESTSELLER
THE NEW 52!
"THIS IS WHY COMIC BOOKS ARE AWESOME." — CRAVEONLINE
The FLASH
VOLUME 3
GORILLA WARFARE
FRANCIS MANAPUL BRIAN BUCCELLATO

**THE FLASH VOL. 3
GORILLA WARFARE**

READ THE ENTIRE EPIC!

THE FLASH VOL. 4: REVERSE

THE FLASH VOL. 5: HISTORY LESSONS

THE FLASH VOL. 6: OUT OF TIME

THE FLASH VOL. 7: SAVAGE WORLD

THE FLASH VOL. 8: ZOOM

THE FLASH VOL. 9: FULL STOP

Get more DC graphic novels wherever comics and books are sold!